WP 34S OWNER'S MANUAL

This manual documents *WP 34S*, a free software replacing the original firmware of an *HP-20b* or *HP-30b* business calculator. You can redistribute *WP 34S* and/or modify it under the terms of the GNU General Public License as published by the Free Software Foundation, either version 3 of the License, or (at your option) any later version.

WP 34S is distributed in the hope that it will be useful, but <u>without any warranty</u>; without even the implied warranty of <u>merchantability</u> or <u>fitness for a particular purpose</u>. For the GNU General Public License and more details, see *http://www.gnu.org/licenses/* .

This manual documents build 3901,
though *WP 34S* might change without notice if we – the developers – modify it. We reserve our right to do so at any time. The project *WP 34S* is officially closed, however, and entered maintenance stage. Stay up-to-date by watching the updated files at
http://sourceforge.net/p/wp34s/code/HEAD/tree/

HP is a registered trade mark of Hewlett-Packard. Excel and WordPad are applications of Microsoft.

The pictures on pp. 89f, 92f, 96, 119, and 120f were taken from vintage HP calculator manuals (and sometimes modified a bit); those on p. 393 as well as the historic advertisements on pp. 155, 394 (bottom), and 395 were kindly supplied by Hewlett-Packard. The ones on pp. 293 (top) and 365 (top) are based on photographs published by Eric Rechlin. The picture on p. 287 was contributed by Harald Pott, the two on pp. 370 (bottom) by Barry Mead. Some pictures were taken from the internet where they were put by thereminworld.com (p. 51), Marcus von Cube (pp. 69, 369, and 370 top), Chris Osburn (p. 70), Steve Hodgson (p. 286), Gerson Barbosa (p. 293 bottom), Alexander Oestert (p. 293), Michael Kathke (p. 297), Mark Harris (pp. 295 and 360), Geoff Quickfall (pp. 365 bottom and 371), and NASA (p. 399); those on pp. 13, 133, 164, 291, 394 (top), and 406 are from anonymous internet sources. The diagrams on p. 101 and in Appendix I are based on material found in Wikipedia. The other photographs, pictures, diagrams, and graphics were created by the author.

Internet addresses are specified as found and verified at 15.5.2015. Please note such addresses may change without notice at any time though. Also the references to other applications (like Excel) may change with future versions of these applications.

This manual is published in English since it became the lingua franca of our time – using it we can reach the maximum number of people without further translations. I apologize to the people of other mother tongues and inserted some 'translator's notes' where applicable.

Printed in the USA

ISBN-13: 978-1-5336-6238-5
ISBN-10: 1-5336-6238-X

WP 34S would not live without our love for *Classics*, *Woodstocks*, *Stings*, *Spices*, *Nuts*, *Voyagers*, and *Pioneers*. Thus we want to quote what was printed in *Hewlett-Packard* pocket calculator manuals until 1980, so it will not fade:

"The success and prosperity of our company will be assured only if we offer our customers superior products that fill real needs and provide lasting value, and that are supported by a wide variety of useful services, both before and after sales."

Statement of Corporate Objectives.
Hewlett-Packard

Just in Case You Do Not Have Your Own *WP 34S* Calculator yet …

WP 34S runs on an *HP-30b Business Professional*, a financial pocket calculator available for less than 40 US$ today. It also runs on an *HP-20b* but we recommend the *HP-30b* for its better keyboard. So get hold of one of them – they are out of production meanwhile. Then turn to *App. A* (starting on p. 285) of this manual for instructions how to convert it into a full-fledged *WP 34S* yourself – it may be a rewarding experience.

On the other hand, you can purchase a *WP 34S* readily on the internet; see e.g.

- *http://commerce.hpcalc.org/34s.php* (shipping from the USA) or
- *http://www.thecalculatorstore.com/epages/eb9376.sf/en_GB/?ObjectPath=/Shops/ eb9376/Products/%22WP34s%20Pack%22* (shipping from Spain).

The first way (converting it yourself) will cost you little money plus some time, the second will cost you significantly more money and less time. If you choose buying your *WP 34S* at one of those two sites, we (the developers) will get a very modest fraction of the price to support our otherwise unpaid efforts on the *WP 34S* project. Either way will work – it is your choice.

> The basic *WP 34S* may be expanded via <u>optional</u> hardware modifications requiring some fine soldering, cutting, gluing, and drilling a little hole in the plastic case of your business calculator. It is no sorcery for a young electronics engineer with a slow hand and good eyesight, but might come close to it for others (including me). So check *App. H* (pp. 359ff) and decide if you want to do that yourself. Else look for somebody else who is able to do it for you if you want it.

The *WP 34S* software package includes a full size emulator (see *App. D* on pp. 315ff), so you may check it out on your computer before buying any hardware. And later on, you may test your programs there as well before sending them to your *WP 34S* calculator. The function sets are identical on both platforms.

For the following, we assume the conversion is done and you hold your own *WP 34S* in your hands – or have access to its emulator at least.

TABLE OF CONTENTS

WELCOME!

Dear user, now you have got your very own *WP 34S*. Congratulations! It uses the mechanics and hardware of an *HP-20b Business Consultant* or an *HP-30b Business Professional*, respectively, so you benefit from their excellent processor speed. With an *HP-30b* you also get the famous rotate-and-click keys, giving you the tactile feedback appreciated in vintage *Hewlett-Packard* pocket calculators since 1972.

On the other hand, the firmware and user interface of your *WP 34S* were thoroughly thought through and discussed by us, newly designed and written from scratch, loaded with functions, pressed into the little memory available, and tested over and over again to give you **a fast and compact <u>scientific</u> calculator like you have never had before** – fully keystroke programmable, comfortably fitting into your shirt pocket, and *RPN.* [1]

The function set of your *WP 34S* is based on the famous *HP-42S RPN Scientific* of 1988, the most powerful programmable *RPN* calculator industrially built so far. [2] *WP 34S* is the fastest *RPN* programmable calculator ever built – up to 348 times faster than the *HP-42S* ! [3] And we expanded its commands, incorporating the functions of the renowned computer scientist's *HP-16C*, the fraction mode of the *HP-32SII*, and probability distributions of the *HP-21S*. We also **included numerous additional useful functions for mathematics, statistics, physics, engineering, programming, I/O, etc.**, such as

+ *Euler's Beta* and *Riemann's Zeta* functions, *Bernoulli* and *Fibonacci* numbers, *Lambert's W*, the *error function*, and the *Chebyshev*, *Hermite*, *Laguerre*, and *Legendre* orthogonal polynomials (no more need to carry heavy printed tables),

+ many statistical distributions and their inverses: *Poisson, binomial, geometric, Cauchy-Lorentz, exponential, logistic, Weibull, log-normal*, and *Gaussian*, in addition to standard *normal, F, t*, and *chi-square*,

---

[1] *RPN* stands for *reverse Polish notation*, a very effective and coherent method of calculating. See below.

[2] The menu system of the *HP-42S* cannot be supported by your *WP 34S* for hardware reasons, as well as its data types. Hence, the Solver and Integrator look more like they did on the *HP-15C*. And for calculating with vectors and matrices, your *WP 34S* features a set of basic matrix commands and several library routines instead.

[3] See *http://www.hpmuseum.org/cgi-sys/cgiwrap/hpmuseum/articles.cgi?read=700* – this comprehensive survey is updated continuously since 2007.

+ functions for finding and checking primes,

+ programmable sums and products, first and second derivatives, solving of quadratic equations for real and complex roots, on top of the numerical integrator and solver as known before,

+ integer computing in fifteen bases from binary to hexadecimal,

+ extended date and time operations and a stopwatch[4] based on a real-time clock,

+ basic financial operations such as mean rate of return and margin calculations,

+ 88 conversions, mainly from old *Imperial* to universal *SI* units and vice versa,

+ 50 fundamental physical constants as accurate as used today by national standards institutes such as *NIST* or *PTB*, plus a selection of important constants from mathematics, astronomy, and surveying,

+ Greek and extended Latin letters covering the languages of almost half of the world's population (upper and lower case in two fonts), plus mathematical symbols,

+ battery-fail-safe on-board backup memory,

+ bidirectional serial communication with your computer, as well as immediate printing on an *HP 82240A/B*.[5]

In 2011, *WP 34S* was the first *RPN* calculator overcoming the limits of a 4-level *stack*.[6] It features a choice of two *stack* sizes expanded by a complex LAST*x* register: traditional four *stack* levels for *HP* compatibility, eight levels for advanced real calculus, convenient calculations in complex domain, vector algebra in 4D, or whatever application you have in mind. You will find a full set of commands for *stack* management in either *stack* size.

---

[4] The stopwatch requires adding a quartz crystal and two capacitors to the electronic hardware of your calculator.

[5] *IR* Printing requires an *IR* diode and a resistor added to the stopwatch hardware setup. Even a *USB* board is available to be installed in your *WP 34S*.

[6] Yes, we know there are *RPL* calculators featuring an almost <u>infinite</u> stack (*RPL* is an calculator operating system developed from *RPN* in the 1980's). Classical *RPN* features a <u>finite</u> stack with top level repetition, however. See below for more.

Furthermore, your *WP 34S* features up to 107 global general purpose registers, 112 global user flags, up to 928 program steps in *RAM*, up to 6014 program steps in flash memory, a 30 *byte* alpha register for message generation, 16 local flags as well as up to 144 local registers allowing for recursive programming, and 4 user-programmable *hotkeys* for your personal favorite functions. Most of the memory layout is conveniently user-settable.

WP 34S is the result of a collaboration of two individuals, an Australian and a German, that started in 2008. We developed *WP 34S* in our free time – so you may call it our hobby (although some people close to us found other names for it). From its very beginning, we have discussed our project in the forum of the online *Museum of HP Calculators* (at http://www.hpmuseum.org/forum/). We would like to thank all its international members who taught us a lot, contributed their ideas, and lent their support throughout several stages of our project. Special thanks go to *Marcus von Cube* (Germany) who joined us in 2011 bringing *WP 34S* to life by designing an emulator for v1.14, allowing for widespread use and convenient testing. With v1.17, the software began running on *HP-20b* calculator hardware. A very useful assembler/disassembler has been provided by *Neil Hamilton* (Canada) since v1.18 – incl. a symbolic preprocessor since v2.1. *Eric Rechlin* (USA) printed (and prints) excellent adhesive keyboard overlays. For v3.0, *Pascal Méheut* (France) contributed a versatile flashing tool for various operating systems. With v3.1, printing on an *HP82240A/B* printer became possible thanks to the gracious support by *Christoph Gießelink* (Germany); a set of micro *USB* boards was developed by *Harald Pott* (Germany); *Ciaran Brady* (UK) wrote a *Beginner's Guide* for our *WP 34S* in 2012. A forum member called *Bit* meticulously checked many features of *WP 34S* since 2014; he discovered quite some bugs unseen before and contributed many respective fixes. We greatly appreciate all your support!

We baptized our baby in honor of the *HP-34C* of 1979, one of the most powerful LED pocket calculators. *WP 34S* is our humble approach – within the constraints of *HP's* hardware – to a future *43S* succeeding the *HP-42S* at one point. May our project help to convince those that have access to more resources than we do: Catering to the market for serious scientific instruments is well worthwhile!

This edition documents v3.3 of the firmware. While updating it from the edition covering v3.2 (featuring a larger footprint), I introduced a smaller format and spiral binding for easier handling, and revised several parts of the text. After two batches of spiral bound manuals, I had to reformat again to meet the specifications of the new printer since spiral binding is not available in individual print-on-demand.

Edition 3.3a has one section and three more chapters added, underwent several refinements, and takes care of recent developments – please see the *Release Notes* on pp. 400ff.

We carefully checked all aspects of the new firmware again to the best of our ability. By five years' experience in the field, *WP 34S* is free of severe bugs – this cannot be guaranteed, however. While the project is closed, we promise to continue maintaining *WP 34S* whenever necessary. If you discover anything strange, please report it to us; if it turns out being caused by internal errors of *WP 34S*,[7] we will provide you with a firmware update as soon as we have built it for ourselves. Just as before, we will continue striving to maintain short response times.

Enjoy!

Walter Bonin

Such a package may become the beginning of a long lasting friendship – even better if you detest the finance 'industry': here you learn how to convert one of its gadgets to something really useful.

---

[7] Since *WP 34S* is open source, variants of it may be found in the field (e.g. the so-called Complex Lock mode). There may be also corresponding builds published on the project website *http://sourceforge.net/projects/wp34s/* . We, the developers of *WP 34S*, may have little to no information about the innards of those variants, however. Hence we cannot support those to an extent we care for the official firmware as described in this manual.

Print Conventions and Common Abbreviations

- Throughout this manual, standard font is Arial. Emphasis is added by underlining or **bold** printing. *Specific terms, titles, trademarks, names* or *abbreviations* are printed in italics, <u>*internet addresses*</u> are referenced in blue underlined italics, plain blue text is quoted literally.

- Calculator COMMANDS and <u>CATALOGS</u> are generally called by their names, printed in capitals in running text.

- Bold italic Arial letters such as *n* are used for variables; bold normal letters for constant **sample** values (e.g. labels, numbers, or characters).

- This KEY font is taken for explicit references to calculator keys. Alphanumeric or numeric output (such as **Hello!** or **1234**) are quoted using the respective calculator fonts.

- Courier is employed for `file names` and for describing numeric formats.

- Times New Roman bold capitals are used for register **ADDRESSES**, lower case bold italics for register *contents*. For example, the value *y* lives in register **Y** and *r45* in **R45**, and *alpha* in the alpha register. Overall *stack* contents are generally quoted in the order $[x, y, z, ...]$.

- Lower case normal Times New Roman italics are for *units*.

- We will use decimal points in most parts of this manual (but you may set your *WP 34S* to commas as well, of course). Although that point is less visible than a comma, 'comma people' seem to be more tolerant against points used as radix marks than vice versa (based on the number of complaints read).

All this holds unless stated otherwise locally.

The following abbreviations are used throughout this manual (if a page is given it points to the first occurrence or explanation of the respective term):

CDF	=	*cumulated distribution function* (see p. 99).
DP	=	*double precision* (see p. 351).
FM	=	*flash memory* (a special kind of *RAM*, see p. 168).
HP	=	*Hewlett-Packard*.

IR	=	infrared.
IOP	=	*Index of Operations* (starting on p. 171).
LCD	=	*liquid crystal display.*
OH	=	*Owner's Handbook.*
OHPG	=	*Owner's Handbook and Programming Guide.*
PDF	=	*probability density function* (see p. 99). Do not confuse with the file format *pdf.*
PMF	=	*probability mass function* (see p. 99).
QF	=	*quantile function* (see p. 102).
RAM	=	*random access memory,* allowing for read and write operations.
ROM	=	*read-only memory.*
RPN	=	*reverse Polish notation* (see p. 36).
SI	=	*système international d'unités.*[8]
SP	=	*single precision* (see p. 80).
SRS	=	*subroutine return stack* (see p. 301).
USB	=	*universal serial bus,* a specific interface.
XROM	=	extended *ROM* (see p. 168).

Some more abbreviations may be used (and explained) locally.

Finally:

WARNING indicates the risk of severe errors. There are only six warnings printed in this manual although it is distributed in the USA, too. Resetting your calculator will help in most cases – but it will erase all your data in *RAM.*

Two warnings cover conditions which may turn your calculator permanently unusable – they are headed by <u>**WARNING**</u>. See the corresponding texts below for further instructions.

---

[8] *SI* is a coherent system of units of measurement agreed on internationally and adopted by almost all countries on this planet – only Liberia, Myanmar, and the USA are missing still. We do not know what they are afraid of, and they seem not being aware of what they miss.

SECTION 1: GETTING STARTED

At its heart, your *WP 34S* is an extremely powerful problem-solving tool. It allows you to solve problems in two different ways:

Manual problem solving: Using the *RPN* logic system, you can manually work through complex problems while seeing intermediate answers every step of the way. The advantages of *RPN* become particularly apparent when working with exploratory type problems where intermediate answers are an important part of the solving process.

Programmed problem solving: Your *WP 34S* can remember a sequence of keystrokes you entered and run them as often as needed. This simple example of programmability is particularly useful in providing answers to repetitive problems that require different data inputs. Advanced programs may also be written to solve more complex problems, e.g. iterative computations containing tests and automated decisions.

If you know how to deal with a good old *HP RPN* scientific calculator, you can start using your *WP 34S* right away. Browse this manual to get information on some basic design concepts that put your *WP 34S* ahead of previous scientific pocket calculators. A good start is the *Key Response Table* on p. 25. Continue using this manual for reference, in particular the alphabetic *Index of Operations* starting on p. 171.

On the other hand, if this is your first *RPN* calculator (or the first one you use after many years), we recommend you also read sections 1 to 2 of this manual entirely.

WP 34S stands in the tradition of a long line of vintage *HP* calculators from 1968 on. *HP* launched the world's first scientific pocket calculator in 1972, and they were famous for their quality calculators as long as they made them. You find almost complete information about those devices (including all their renown user's and programmer's manuals printed until 1990) on media distributed by the online *Museum of HP Calculators*[9] at low cost (see *http://www.hpmuseum.org/cd/cddesc.htm*).

---

[9] Said museum is in no way affiliated with *HP*. In fact it is driven by hobbyists. We recommend it since you can find an astounding amount of calculator-related information there, and you may ask questions on its forum. Though be aware that the majority of its members must be regarded as math or electronics nerds, are focused

Most traditional commands on your *WP 34S* will work as they did on the *HP-42S*. Knowing vintage calculators of that kind eases understanding your *WP 34S*. Nevertheless, this manual provides the necessary information about all the features of your *WP 34S*, including some equations and technical explanations.

> This manual is not intended, however, to replace textbooks on mathematics, statistics, physics, nor engineering. Also this is no hypothetical *'Beginner's Guide to RPN Calculating'*. Neither can it be an *'HP-20b/30b Hardware Modification Manual'* nor anything like *'An Easy Guide to Writing Calculator Firmware from Scratch'*. All these topics have to be learned elsewhere.

The following text starts with presenting the keyboard of your *WP 34S*, so you learn where you will find what you are looking for. It continues demonstrating basic calculation methods, the memory of your *WP 34S* and addressing objects therein, the display and its indicators giving you feedback about what is going on. Then a major part is taken by an index of all available operations (more than 700), what they do, and how to call them. This manual closes with appendices covering special topics, e.g. the error messages your *WP 34S* will return if abnormal conditions prevent it from executing your command as expected. There you will also find instructions for keeping your *WP 34S* up-to-date when new firmware revisions will be released.

Before diving into it, however, here is something we ask you to remember:

> **Your *WP 34S* is designed to help you solving problems. But it is just a tool** – it cannot think for you nor can it check the sensibility of a problem you apply it to. Do not blame us nor your *WP 34S* for errors you may make. Gather information, think before and while keying in and calculating, and check your results: these tasks will remain your responsibilities always.

---

on calculator technology, take their hobby very seriously, and live in a very self-referred country (everything done there is great and right per definition – don't try telling them other people(s) may dissent about it for good reason). You will find brilliant minds and very supportive people there – just remember only a small fraction of all registered members is actively posting on said forum. Understanding dry wit, for example, requires a certain above-average level of intelligence – an active poster may welcome such messages but another member might denunciate since feeling disturbed by something going over its head. And that forum does not have a constitution protecting also its minorities but is ruled autocratically up to 2016, and everyone may denunciate. Thus, handle with extreme care!

Problem Solving, Part 1: First Steps

Start exploring your *WP 34S* by turning it on: Press its bottom left key – notice that **ON** is printed below that key. Doing this the very first time, you will get a display like this:

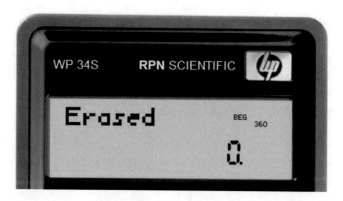

To turn it off, press the green key **h** (notice a little **h** showing up top left in display), then **EXIT** (which has **OFF** printed on its lower part). Since your *WP 34S* features *Continuous Memory*, turning it off does not affect the information it contains. To conserve battery power, your *WP 34S* will shut down automatically about five minutes after you stop using it – turn it on again and you can resume your work right where you left off.

To adjust display contrast, hold down the key **ON** and press **+** or **–** repeatedly until it suits your needs. That works as on preceding *HP* pocket calculators (like an *HP-42S*).

Your new *WP 34S*, however, *looks* significantly more colorful than an *HP-42S*: You get <u>five</u> functions per key on average. White print on key top is for the *primary* function of the key. Additionally, green labels are put on the slanted lower faces of 34 keys, golden and blue labels are printed be-low them on the *key plate*, grey

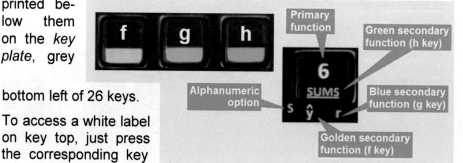

bottom left of 26 keys.

To access a white label on key top, just press the corresponding key

letters are

(thus it is called its *primary* function). For a golden, blue, or green label (a *secondary* function), first press the *prefix* , , or , respectively, then the corresponding key.

Take the key ⑤, for example:[10]

- Pressing just ⑤ will enter the digit **5** in the display.

- Pressing ▪ + ⑤ will call x̄ to calculate the *arithmetic mean* values of the data accumulated in the statistic registers.

- Pressing ▪ + ⑤ will call s to compute the *standard deviations* of the same data.

- Pressing ▪ + ⑤ will open a *catalog* [11] of further statistical functions via STAT.

- The grey letter R will become relevant in *alpha mode* for text input.

---

[10] For better readability on paper, we refer to keyboard labels using dark print on white from here on, like e.g. ⑤ or x̄, omitting the *prefix* ▪ for the latter since the printed color makes it redundant.

[11] All labels printed underlined on the keyboard point to such sorted set of items, e.g. functions

Time for a little problem solving example:

Let us assume you want to fence a small rectangular patch of land, 40 *yards* long and 30 *yards* wide.[12] You have already set the first corner post (A), and also the second (B) in a distance of 40 *yards* from A. Where do you set the third and fourth posts (C and D) to be sure that the fence will form a proper rectangle? Simply switch your *WP 34S* on again and key in

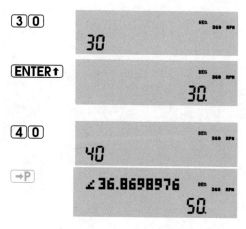

This [ENTER↑] separates the two numbers in input here.[13]

Note →P is reached by pressing g + → top right on the keyboard.[14]

Now all you need is a friend and 80 *yards* of rope. Ask your friend to hold both ends of the rope for you, take the loose loop and walk away as far as you can – when the loop is stretched, mark that position on the rope and return to your friend. Ask him or her to hold this point of the rope as well, fetch the two loose loops and walk again as far as possible – when the loops are stretched, mark both positions on the rope. Return again; hand over the two new points and walk once more, now with four loose loops. After marking as before, your rope has got marks every 10 *yards* now.

Nail its one end on post A now and its other end on B, fetch the loose loop and walk 3 marks away. When both sections of the rope are tightly stretched, stop and place post C there. You may set post D the same way.

---

[12] Most of you are fond of *SI*. Despite this fact, we use (*British*) *Imperial* units here so our US-American readers can follow. But the example will work with *meters* as well.

[13] Note the number 30 was adjusted to the right and a radix mark is added. This indicates input being closed for this number. Further effects of [ENTER↑] will be discussed below.

[14] The characters displayed in the top row here are not relevant for solving this problem; they will be explained later.

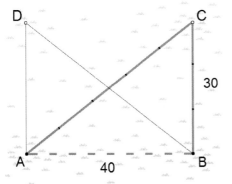

This method works for arbitrary rectangles, whatever other distances may apply (you may need a tapeline in general case in the field). As soon as you press →P, your *WP 34S* does the necessary calculation of the length of the diagonal automatically for you. You just provide the land, posts, rope, hammer and nails. And it will be up to you to set the posts!

You have found →P on the keyboard next to two other labels showing arrows as well. This is typical for your *WP 34S* – its labels are generally grouped according to their purposes. – There are nine basic functional groups. Four of them are shown here:

Hotkeys (see below)

Numeric input keys (see p. 23)

Basic arithmetic operations (see p. 36)

General navigation keys (see p. 52)

The *hotkeys* Ⓐ, Ⓑ, Ⓒ, and Ⓓ allow you making your four favorite functions directly accessible via a single keystroke each. Find more about those keys and all the other ones featured on your *WP 34S* in the Key Response Table on pp. 25ff.

The remaining five groups are:

'Common' mathe-
matical functions
typically working
with *real numbers*
(see p. 33)

Stack and register
operations (see
pp. 40 and 55)

Integer and logic
operations (see p.
123)

Functions for
probability and
statistics (see p. 99)

Programming
operations
(see p. 156)

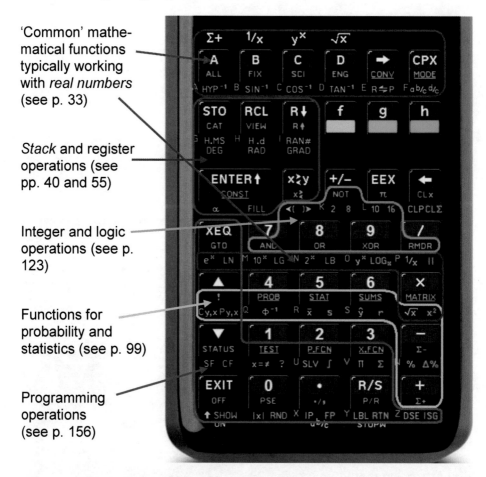

Getting used to these groups, you will very soon locate operations on your *WP 34S* easily. Functions and their inverses – if existent – are placed next to each other. If a function is called using ▩, its inverse is called using ▩ usually.

Find each and every command out of more than 700 provided on your *WP 34S*, the keystrokes calling it, and the necessary individual explanation for your reference in the *Index of Operations* (*IOP*, on pp. 171ff) and in the subsequent section about *catalogs* and *browsers*.

Before proceeding to the next chapter, let us return to our little introductory land fencing problem solving example with four remarks:

1. We presume you have graduated from an US High School at minimum, passed Abitur, Matura, or an equivalent graduation. So we will not explain basic mathematical rules and concepts in this manual.

2. In four decades of scientific pocket computing, a wealth of funny to sophisticated sample applications has been created and described by different authors – more and better than we can ever invent ourselves. We copied a few of them. In addition, we recommend the media mentioned above once again: they contain nearly all the user guides, handbooks, and manuals published for vintage *Hewlett-Packard* calculators in two decades beginning with their very first, the *HP-9100A* of 1968. Be assured that every calculation described there for any scientific calculator can be done significantly faster on your *WP 34S* – and most of them even in a more elegant way.

3. There is absolutely no need to enter any units in your calculations. Just stay with a consistent set of units during your calculations and you will get meaningful results within this set.[15] If, however, you need to convert special input values into units being part of such a set or you want results converted into special or local units, [CONV] will help (see pp. 270ff).

4. Although we entered integer numbers only for both sides of our little patch of land, your *WP 34S* calculated the diagonal using real (floating point) numbers. It lets you enter decimal *yards* as well. Alternatively you may enter fractions such as e.g. 6 ¼ if you need them. We will introduce fraction mode and other modes further below.

Now, let us show you more general actions: how to enter the numbers and select the commands you want to use on your *WP 34S*, and how to deal with these objects in typical calculations straightforward.

How to Enter Numbers

It is as easy as typing: e.g. for entering 12.34 simply press [1][2][.][3][4]. You may put in up to 12 digits and a radix mark for the mantissa, optionally multiplied by a three-digit power of ten (the latter is

---

[15] The big advantage of *SI* is that it is the largest consistent set of units available.

generally called the *exponent* here). Any digit mistyped may be deleted immediately by ⌫ and entered correctly thereafter.

For negative numbers such as –5.6 , enter ⑤ ⁺⁄₋ ⦾ ⑥ or ⑤ ⦾ ⁺⁄₋ ⑥ or ⑤ ⦾ ⑥ ⁺⁄₋ – pressing ⁺⁄₋ changes the sign of the number being entered.

For a really big figure such as the age of the universe in years as we know it, enter ① ③ ⦾ ⑧ ② EEX ⑨ [16] which is echoed

When you complete input by pressing ENTER↑ [17] you will see the equivalent:

in the startup default display format.

Really tiny numbers such as the typical diameter of an atom (i.e. 0.000 000 000 1 *m* – with ten zeroes leading the 1) are entered by full analogy: EEX ⁺⁄₋ ① ⓪ [18] is echoed

and will be displayed like

as it should be after completing input.

It may be also shown more compact as

with other settings.

---

[16] EEX stands for 'enter exponent'.

[17] Before completing input, it is just echoed in the numeric line. Input is closed and released for interpretation by a command – e.g. by ENTER↑ here.

[18] Note you do not have to enter ① EEX ⁺⁄₋ ① ⓪ here: if there is no open numeric input heading EEX, 1 is assumed for the mantissa. – And a ⁺⁄₋ entered after EEX will always change the sign of the exponent – if you want to change the sign of the mantissa instead, do it before pressing EEX or after closing input.

How to Execute Commands

Just enter the sequence of keystrokes required to access the command you wish to execute. Pending input will be echoed top left of the screen until the command is completed. The active *prefix* is displayed top left on the screen by **f**, **g**, or **h** for visual feedback, if applicable.

For many commands, that will be the only echo you will see during input since the next keystroke will terminate command entry, execute the command, and show the result (as with ⟦→P⟧ above).

Some commands (like STO and RCL), however, require one or more trailing parameters and will thus stay displayed for longer. Examples will be shown at the end of this section.

Key Response Table

In the following, you find the meanings of all direct keystroke inputs, top left to bottom right on the keyboard. For each key on your *WP 34S*, its unshifted function is mentioned first, then its shifted functions in the order ⟦h⟧, ⟦f⟧, and ⟦g⟧, if applicable (strictly top down). See the pages mentioned explicitly in this table and/or the *IOP* on pp. 171ff for details of these functions.

Most keys will switch their functionality in *alpha mode* – this is explained in detail on pp. 148ff. Some keys may have special meanings if called in a browser or an application – see pp. 248ff.

Row	Keystrokes	Meaning
1	⟦A⟧	Calls and executes the routine labeled **A**. If label **A** is <u>not</u> defined in the *current program* (see p. 156), ⟦A⟧ defaults to ⟦Σ+⟧ adding a data point (x, y) to the summation registers – note the white print above ⟦A⟧.
	⟦ALL⟧	Displays all digits of the number x as long as they fit the display. See p. 79 for more.
	⟦HYP⟧	Prefix for ... hyperbolic functions, to be trailed by ⟦SIN⟧, ⟦COS⟧, or ⟦TAN⟧. No
	⟦HYP⁻¹⟧	Prefix for inverse need for pressing ⟦f⟧ again.

Row	Keystrokes	Meaning
1	**B**	Calls and executes the routine labeled **B**. If label **B** is not defined in the *current program* (see p. 156), **B** defaults to $\boxed{1/x}$ inverting x.
	FIX	Displays the number x with the specified fixed number of decimals as long as it fits the display. See p. 79 for more.
	SIN	Computes the sine ··· of x (in the angular mode
	SIN⁻¹	Returns the arcsine selected).
	f **B**	If pressed in CONV, inverts the current conversion (p. 270).
1	**C**	Calls and executes the routine labeled **C**. If label **C** is not defined in the *current program*, **C** defaults to $\boxed{y^x}$ raising y to the power x.
	SCI	Displays the number x in scientific notation with the number of decimals specified. See p. 79 for more.
	COS	Computes the cosine ··· of x (in the angular mode
	COS⁻¹	Returns the arccosine selected).
1	**D**	Calls and executes the routine labeled **D**. If label **D** is not defined in the *current program*, **D** defaults to $\boxed{\sqrt{x}}$ returning the square root of x.
	ENG	Displays the number x in engineering notation with the number of decimals specified. See p. 79 for more.
	TAN	Computes the tangent ··· of x (in the angular mode
	TAN⁻¹	Returns the arctangent selected).
1	→	Prefix for a) converting angular units (p. 82) or b) showing integers in different bases (p. 246). Also employed for indirect addressing (p. 64).
	CONV	Calls a *catalog* of unit conversions (see p. 270 for its contents).
	R←	Interprets x and y as polar coordinates r and ϑ in 2D and converts them to Cartesian coordinates x and y.
	→P	Interprets x and y as Cartesian coordinates in 2D and converts them to polar coordinates r and ϑ.

Row	Keystrokes	Meaning
1	**CPX**	Prefix for complex operations (p. 123).
	MODE	Calls a *catalog* of operations to set the mode your *WP 34S* shall work in (see p. 255 for its contents).
	a b/c	Converts *x* into a proper fraction.
	d/c	Converts *x* into an improper fraction.
2	**STO**	Stores *x* into the address specified (see pp. 64 and 134 for more).
	CAT	Calls a global label browser (p. 249).
	H.MS	Assumes **X** contains <u>decimal</u> *hours* or *degrees*, and displays them converted into hhhh°mm′ss.dd″ until the next keystroke (see p. 85 for an example).
	DEG	Sets angular mode to *degrees*.
2	**RCL**	Recalls the contents of the address specified into **X** (see pp. 64 and 134 for more).
	VIEW	Displays the contents of the address specified until the next keystroke.
	H.d	Sets DECM.
	RAD	Sets angular mode to *radians*.
2	**R↓**	Rolls the *stack* one level down or up, respectively (p. 40).
	R↑	
	RAN#	Returns a random number between 0 and 1. You can set a start value for random number generation using SEED (p. 215). – In integer mode, returns a random bit pattern in the word size set.
	GRAD	Sets angular mode to *gradians* (a.k.a. *gon*).
2	f	
2	g	*Prefixes* as described on p. 18.
2	h	

Row	Keystrokes	Meaning
3	**ENTER↑**	Closes input in **X** and copies x into **Y** (see pp. 37 and 40 for more). Also used in parameter input (p. 64). Furthermore, it closes alpha mode. If pressed in an open catalog, it selects an entry. See p. 243 for its complete functionality.
	CONST	Calls a *catalog* of constants (see p. 261 for its contents).
	α	Switches to alpha mode for input of characters (p. 148).
	FILL	Copies x into all stack levels allocated.
3	**x⇄y**	Swaps x and y (p. 40).
	x⇄	Swaps x and the contents of the address specified.
	◄ **►**	If x is integer and needs more than 12 digits, ◄ / ► will shift the display window to the left / right to show further digits. See p. 140 for an example.
		If x is real (*SP*), both keys display its full mantissa and full exponent until the next keystroke (see p. 80).
		If x is real (*DP*), ◄ shows its most significant 16 digits and full exponent while ► shows its least significant 16 digits, both until the next keystroke (see p. 354).
3	**+/−**	Swaps the sign of x (see p. 23 for more).
	NOT	Negates x.
	2	Sets your *WP 34S* to binary integer mode.
	8	Sets your *WP 34S* to octal integer mode.
3	**EEX**	Enters a power of 10 for convenient input of very large or very small numbers (see p. 23 for more).
	π	Recalls the constant π.
	10	Sets your *WP 34S* to decimal integer mode.
	16	Sets your *WP 34S* to hexadecimal integer mode.

Row	Keystrokes	Meaning
3	←	Deletes the last digit, radix mark, or character entered. See p. 246 for its complete functionality.
	CLx	Clears x.
	CLP	Deletes the current program.
	CLΣ	Clears all summation registers.
4	XEQ	Executes the routine beginning with the label specified. See p. 245 for more.
	GTO	Goes to the label specified. See p. 196 for more.
	e^x	Raises Euler's **e** to the power x.
	LN	Returns the natural logarithm of x.
4	7	Enters the digit **7**.
	AND	Returns Boole's AND of x and y.
	10^x	Raises **10** to the power x.
	LG	Returns the decadic logarithm of x.
4	8	Answers the question **Sure?** with **N** for 'no'. Else enters the digit **8**.
	OR	Returns Boole's OR of x and y.
	2^x	Raises **2** to the power x.
	LB	Returns the binary logarithm of x.
4	9	Enters the digit **9**.
	XOR	Returns Boole's exclusive OR of x and y.
	y^x	Raises y to the power x.
	LOG_x	Returns the logarithm of y to the base x.

Row	Keystrokes	Meaning
4	$/$	Divides y by x.
	RMDR	Returns the remainder of the integer division of y by x.
	$1/x$	Inverts x.
	$\parallel$	Returns $\left(1/x + 1/y\right)^{-1}$, i.e. the resulting resistance of two resistors x and y connected in parallel, for example.
5	▲	Navigates through *catalogs*, alphanumeric strings, and programs. See p. 247 for its complete functionality.
	$!$	Returns the factorial of x.
	C y,x	Returns the number of possible <u>subsets</u> (or combinations) of x items taken out of a set of y items. See p. 187 for more.
	P y,x	Returns the number of possible <u>arrangements</u> (or permutations) of x items taken out of a set of y items. See p. 207 for more.
5	4	Enters the digit **4**.
	PROB	Calls a *catalog* of probability distributions and more (see p. 255 for its contents).
	Φ	Returns the *standard normal CDF* (p. 383).
	Φ^{-1}	Returns the *standard normal quantile function*.
5	5	Enters the digit **5**.
	STAT	Calls a *catalog* of statistical functions (see p. 256 for its contents).
	$\bar{x}$	Returns the arithmetic means ... of the x and y data accumulated in the summation registers
	s	Returns the sample standard deviations

Row	Keystrokes	Meaning
5	**6**	Enters the digit **6**.
	[SUMS]	Calls a *catalog* of all sums accumulated (see p. 256 for its contents).
	[ŷ]	Returns a forecast $\hat{y} = f(x)$ ... based on the fit model selected for the x and y
	[r]	Returns the coefficient of correlation data accumulated in the summation registers.
5	**x**	Multiplies y times x.
	[MATRIX]	Calls a *catalog* of matrix and vector operations (see p. 255 for its contents).
	[√x]	Returns the square root of x.
	[x²]	Returns x squared.
6	**▼**	Navigates through *catalogs*, alphanumeric strings, and programs. See p. 247 for its complete functionality.
	[STATUS]	Calls the status browser (see p. 251).
	[SF]	Sets the flag specified.
	[CF]	Clears the flag specified.
6	**1**	Enters the digit **1**.
	[TEST]	Calls a *catalog* of binary tests especially useful in programs (see p. 257 for its contents).
	[x= ?] [x= ?]	Tests if x is equal (or not equal) to the number or register content specified (see pp. 64 and 134 for more).
6	**2**	Enters the digit **2**.
	[P.FCN]	Calls a *catalog* of functions for programming (see p. 256 for its contents).
	[SLV]	Calls the numeric solver (p. 217).
	[∫]	Calls the numeric integrator (p. 236).

Row	Keystrokes	Meaning
6	3	Enters the digit 3.
	X.FCN	Calls a *catalog* of additional (extra), mainly mathematical functions (see pp. 257f for its contents).
	π Σ	Calculates a product (or a sum) under program control (p. 230).
6	−	Subtracts x from y.
	Σ−	Subtracts a data point (x, y) from the summation registers.
	%	Returns $\dfrac{x \cdot y}{100}$, leaving y unchanged.
	Δ%	Returns $100 \cdot \dfrac{x - y}{y}$ leaving y unchanged.
7	ON	If your *WP 34S* is off, turns it on. Else may be used in ON-key combinations (see the appendices; most important is ON + + or ON + − for adjusting display contrast).
	EXIT	Exits *catalogs* and pending inputs. See p. 244 for more.
	OFF	Turns your *WP 34S* off. In programming, inserts a step to turn your *WP 34S* off under program control.
	↑	Prints x. In alpha mode, toggles upper and lower case. See p. 247 for more.
	SHOW	Calls the register browser (p. 251).
7	0	Enters the digit 0.
	PSE	In programming, inserts a pause to halt program execution for the number of ticks specified (see p. 209).
	|x|	Returns the absolute (i.e. unsigned) value of x.
	RND	In fraction mode, rounds x using the current denominator. Else rounds x to the current display format.

WP 34S v3.3d

Row	Keystrokes	Meaning
7	⚬	Enters a decimal radix mark. If two marks are entered in one input, it will be read as a fraction (see p. 123 for more).
	./.	Toggles decimal radix marks (comma and point).
	IP	Returns the integer part of x.
	FP	Returns the fractional part of x.
7	R/S	Answers the question Sure? with Y for 'yes'. Else resumes execution of a stopped program or stops a running program. See p. 245 for its complete functionality.
	P/R	Toggles programming mode.
	LBL	In programming, inserts a step with the label specified.
	RTN	In programming, inserts a step returning to the caller. Else positions the program pointer to step 000.
7	+	Adds x to y.
	Σ+	Adds a data point (x, y) to the summation registers.
	DSE ISG	Loop control operations in programming (see p. 161 for a picture).

Resetting your *WP 34S*

For your reference, the *startup default* settings of your *WP 34S* are:

24h, 2COMPL, ALL **0**, DBLOFF, DEG, DENANY, DENMAX **0**, D.MY, JG1752, LinF, LocR **0**, LZOFF, PROFRC, RDX., REGS **100**, RM **0**, SCIOVR, SEPON, SSIZE4, TSON, WSIZE **64**, YDOFF, and finally DECM.

Please find the descriptions of all these commands in the *IOP* on p. 179ff.

After a while, the settings of your *WP 34S* may differ significantly from the *startup default* state. To return to that state again, you may reset your *WP 34S* (if, instead, you want to return just some settings to their original values, change these settings one by one).

There are two ways of resetting – note the *RAM* of your *WP 34S* will be completely erased by both, i.e. the contents of all registers and all programs in *RAM* will be deleted as well (but you can save your current *RAM* contents in *FM* calling SAVE before resetting – see the *IOP*).

1. Press [P.FCN] [R] [F] [▲]

[XEQ]. This will call the command RESET, asking you for confirmation:

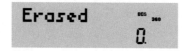

Enter [Y] and your *WP 34S* will display:

2. Open the battery door on the back of your *WP 34S*. Use a suitable tool (e.g. a pencil) for actuating the contact behind the little hole labeled RESET:

It will turn your *WP 34S* off. Turn it on again and it will display:

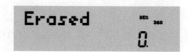

Problem Solving, Part 2: Elementary *Stack* Mechanics

Most of the commands of your *WP 34S* are mathematical operations or functions taking and returning real numbers such as 1 or -2.34 or 3.141 592 653 59 or 5.6×10^{-7}. Note that integer numbers like 3, 10, or −1 are just a subset of real numbers.

One-number (*monadic*) functions: Many real number functions provided operate on <u>one</u> such number only.

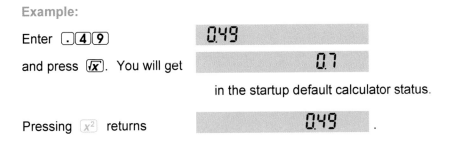

Example:

Enter ⌐.⌐4⌐9   `0.49`

and press ⌐√x⌐. You will get   `0.7`

in the startup default calculator status.

Pressing ⌐x²⌐ returns   `0.49` .

There are many more *monadic* functions directly provided on the keyboard of your *WP 34S*:

- ⌐LN⌐ and ⌐eˣ⌐, ⌐LG⌐ and ⌐10ˣ⌐, ⌐LB⌐ and ⌐2ˣ⌐,

- the reciprocal ⌐1/x⌐,

- trigonometric functions (⌐SIN⌐, ⌐COS⌐, and ⌐TAN⌐) and their inverses (⌐SIN⁻¹⌐, ⌐COS⁻¹⌐, and ⌐TAN⁻¹⌐),

- hyperbolic functions (⌐HYP⌐⌐SIN⌐, ⌐HYP⌐⌐COS⌐, and ⌐HYP⌐⌐TAN⌐) and their inverses (⌐HYP⁻¹⌐⌐SIN⌐, ⌐HYP⁻¹⌐⌐COS⌐, and ⌐HYP⁻¹⌐⌐TAN⌐),

- the factorial ⌐!⌐, Boole's ⌐NOT⌐, some conversions, etc.

You will find calculated examples for said functions further below (see e.g. pp. 82ff).

Generally speaking, *monadic* functions replace the value displayed in the numeric line (it is called x) by the numeric function result **f(x)** (e.g. **f(x)** = x^2 in the last example). The vast majority of electronic calculators works this way, so this is no real surprise.

Two-number (*dyadic*) functions: Some of the most popular mathematical functions, however, operate on <u>two</u> numbers. Think of + and − , for instance.

Example:

Assume having an account of 1,234 US$ and taking 56.7 US$ away from it. What will remain? One easy way to solve such a task works as follows:

On a sheet of paper		On your *WP 34S*		
Write down the first number:	*1234*	Key in the first number:	①②③④	*1234*
Start a new line.		Close 1st input:	(ENTER↑)	
Write down the 2nd number; draw a line below:	*56.7*	Key in the 2nd number:	⑤⑥.⑦	*56.7*
Subtract:	*1177.3*	Subtract:	(−)	*1177.3*

This is the essence of *RPN*:

**Provide the necessary operands,
then execute the requested function
by pressing the corresponding function key.** [19]

And a major advantage of *RPN* compared to other calculator operating systems is that it sticks to this basic logic − always.[20]

HP itself explained the *RPN* method using the following very compact picture in 1974:

---

[19] This way of writing calculations is called *postfix* notation since the operator is entered <u>after</u> the operands. It suits electronic calculating very well.

[20] Some people claim this being true for *RPL* only (see footnote 6 on p. 10). Maybe they are even right. In my opinion, however, *RPL* strains the underlying *postfix* principle beyond the pain barrier, exceeding the limit where it becomes annoying for human brains. Not for everybody, of course, but also for many scientists and engineers. Thus we stick to classical *RP<u>N</u>* on the *WP 34S*.

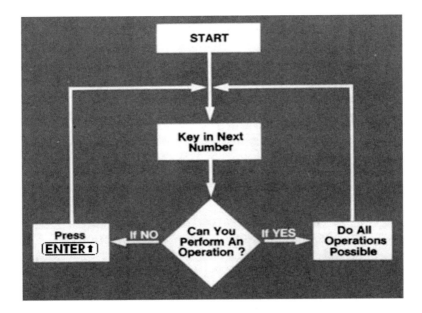

As the paper holds your operands before you start calculating manually, a place holding your operands on your *WP 34S* is required, too. The *stack* does that.

Stack register content

Think of the *stack* like a pile of registers.[21] They are traditionally named **X**, **Y**, **Z**, and **T**, optionally followed by **A**, **B**, **C**, and **D** on your *WP 34S*.

New input is always entered in the bottom register **X** and is displayed in the bottom line. Also y may be shown on the screen on demand.

[ENTER↑] separates two input numbers following each other immediately. It does so by closing the first number x and copying it into **Y**, so **X** can take the

Stack register	content
D	d
C	c
B	b
A	a
T	t
Z	z
Y	y
Display X	x

second number then without losing information (compare p. 20).[22]

---

[21] Learn more about all the registers your *WP 34S* provides in next chapter.

[22] This is the classical way [ENTER↑] also worked from the *HP-35* of 1972 until the *HP-42S* ceased in 1995. It is often said [ENTER↑] 'pushes x on the *stack*' (although it pushes x <u>under</u> the *stack* in our picture). The higher *stack* contents are lifted out of the way before: in a 4-level *stack*, z is put into **T** and y into **Z** before x is stored in **Y**. See next chapter for details and pictures.

After having keyed in the second number (the new x) in the account example above, pressing ⊟ subtracts this x from the first number (now in Y) and puts the result $f(x, y) = y - x$ in X.

This procedure applies to most *dyadic* functions featured:

> **Put both operands on the *stack***
> **then execute the operation f(x, y)**
> **and the result will be displayed in X.**

This completely eliminates the need for ⊟ on the keyboard.

A large part of mathematics is covered by *dyadic* functions and combinations of them. Let us look at a chain calculation:

Example:

$$\frac{(12.3-45.6)(78.9+1.2)}{(3.4-5.6)^7} .$$

This formula is as a combination of six *dyadic* functions: two subtractions, an addition, a multiplication, an exponentiation, and a division.

And this is how that problem is solved on your *WP 34S* – starting top left – and what happens on the *stack* during the solution (each column in the following tables shows the *stack* at each stage of the calculation):[23]

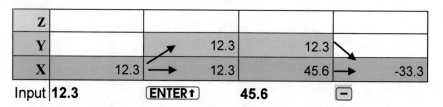

Z				
Y		12.3	12.3	
X	12.3	12.3	45.6	-33.3
Input 12.3	ENTER↑	45.6	⊟	

You will have recognized that the first parenthesis was solved exactly as demonstrated in our little account example on p. 36. Now proceed to the second parenthesis:

---

[23] Following this example, it may be helpful to see both x and y displayed simultaneously on your *WP 34S*. If you want it, enter (MODE) (Y) (▼) (XEQ) at the beginning, calling YDON.

Starting this calculation, some data may be present in the higher *stack* levels, too. They are from previous operations and are not relevant for this calculation, so we leave them aside here.

We will generally use plain bold text for numeric input from here on for space reasons.

T					
Z		-33.3	-33.3		
Y	A -33.3	78.9	78.9	-33.3	
X	78.9	78.9	1.2	80.1	-2667.33
	78.9	ENTER↑	1.2	+	×

This second parenthesis is solved like the first. Note in step 1 of this row, however, the prior result (of first parenthesis) is lifted automatically (A) to **Y** to avoid overwriting it with the next number keyed in. This move is called *automatic stack lift*[24] and is standard in *RPN* calculators. Thus we do not need parentheses (gaining the keyboard space else required for ❪ and ❫).

And after having evaluated the second parenthesis by executing ❪+❫, we had the results of both upper parentheses on the *stack* – so everything was well prepared for the multiplication to complete the numerator. So we simply pressed ❪×❫.

Now we will start calculating the denominator – once again the intermediate result is lifted automatically in the first step:

	-2667.33	-2667.33		-2667.33	
-2667.33	3.4	3.4	-2667.33	-2.2	-2667.33
3.4	3.4	5.6	-2.2	7	-249.43..	10.693...
3.4	ENTER↑	5.6	−	7	yˣ	/

Note the *automatic stack lift* in step 5 affects <u>two</u> of our intermediate results now. Thus, everything is prepared for the exponentiation in step 6 and the final division of numerator (in **Y**) by denominator (in **X**) in step 7. Voilà! [25]

---

[24] For the traditional 4-level *stack*, the complete procedure is: Move z to **T**, then y to **Z**, and finally x to **Y**. So *automatic stack lift* works like an automatic ENTER: it affects all *stack* levels, and the previous contents of the <u>top</u> level get lost. *Automatic stack lift* will not be indicated from here on. In fact it is worth mentioning when *automatic stack lift* is <u>disabled</u> instead – only four commands do this, and ENTER is one of them.

[25] We followed this chain calculation using *stack* tables for explanation. They are, however, neither necessary for calculating with *RPN* nor does *RPN* require mental gymnastics to "keep track of the *stack*". The latter is just a legend often told by older members of the order who are proud they can still do it – let them keep their pride. In the vast majority of cases, however, all what is really required in real world calculations is done by your *WP 34S* automatically. Please read the next chapter and you will see this proven by some more advanced examples.

Following this example, you have seen the five most popular *dyadic* functions: ⊞, ⊟, ⊠, ⊘, and ⊡. Your *WP 34S* provides many more *dyadic* functions – you find them all in the *IOP* (on pp. 171ff).

As you have observed several times now, the contents of the *stack* registers drop whenever a *dyadic* function is executed. Like the *automatic stack lift* mentioned above, this *stack drop* affects all levels: x and y are combined giving the result $f(x, y)$ loaded into $\mathbf{X}$; then z drops to $\mathbf{Y}$, and t to $\mathbf{Z}$; since there is nothing available above for dropping, the <u>top</u> *stack* content will be repeated (see p. 50 for special benefits of this *top level repetition*).

There are also a few **three-number (*triadic*) real functions** featured by your *WP 34S* (e.g. →DATE and %MRR) replacing x by the result $f(x, y, z)$. Then t drops into $\mathbf{Y}$ and so on, and the content of the top *stack* level is repeated twice.

Some real functions (e.g. DECOMP, cf. p. 52) operate on one number but return two. Other operations (such as RCL or SUM) do not consume any *stack* input at all but just return one or two numbers. Then these extra numbers will be pushed on the *stack*, taking one level each (see p. 42).

Problem Solving, Part 3: Advanced *Stack* Mechanics

To understand the genius of *RPN*, we will look a bit closer at the functions operating on the *stack*. In addition to one-, two-, and three-number functions explained above, there are some dedicated *stack* commands: The traditional *stack* and register control operations ENTER↑, x⇄y, R↓ [26], STO, RCL, LASTx, R↑, and x⇄ have been known for decades and are mostly found within the small area of the

---

As a footnote to the footnote, we admit there are some special cases where "keeping track of the *stack*" allows for really nice tricks. But that is nothing more than the cream topping on an already very delicious piece of cake. Those tricks were most impressive at the times when *RPN* calculators were confined to the traditional 4-level *stack* and (even more important) the competing calculators had just a few levels of parentheses – and a major part of user programming was done on such calculators, in particular at universities. In fact, those tricks served as major arguments in the so-called "calculator wars" in the Seventies of last century. Some people may remember.

[26] This traditional command label stands for <u>r</u>olling the stack one level down. See the next page to find out why it carries that name.

keyboard shown here. Beyond these, 13 commands were added to your *WP 34S*: FILL, DROP, RCLS, STOS, SSIZE4, SSIZE8, SSIZE?, YDOFF and YDON, Y⇆, Z⇆, T⇆, and ⇆.

Your *WP 34S* was the first calculator model worldwide offering you a choice of four or eight *stack* levels in 2011 (see SSIZE4 and SSIZE8). Now its little brother, the *WP 31S*, offers the same choice as well.

See below what (ENTER↑), FILL, DROP, (x⇄y), (R↓), and (R↑), recalling, *monadic*, and *dyadic* functions do in detail on *stacks* of either size (startup default display format is assumed for these examples). See the *IOP* on pp. 171ff for detailed information about the other commands mentioned above.

	Stack level	Assumed stack contents at start:	Stack contents _after_ executing …					
			ENTER↑	FILL	DROP	x⇄y	R↓	R↑
With 4 stack levels	T	$t = 4.$	3.	1.1	4.	4.	1.1	3.
	Z	$z = 3.$	2.	1.1	4.	3.	4.	2.
	Y	$y = 2.$	1.1	1.1	3.	1.1	3.	1.1
	X	$x = \mathbf{1.1}$	**1.1**	1.1	2.	2.	2.	**4.**
With 8 stack levels	D	$d = 8.$	7.	1.1	8.	8.	1.1	7.
	C	$c = 7.$	6.	1.1	8.	7.	8.	6.
	B	$b = 6.$	5.	1.1	7.	6.	7.	5.
	A	$a = 5.$	4.	1.1	6.	5.	6.	4.
	T	$t = 4.$	3.	1.1	5.	4.	5.	3.
	Z	$z = 3.$	2.	1.1	4.	3.	4.	2.
	Y	$y = 2.$	1.1	1.1	3.	1.1	3.	1.1
	X	$x = \mathbf{1.1}$	**1.1**	1.1	2.	2.	2.	8.

Stack level	Assumed stack contents at start:		Stack contents after executing ...			
			RCL L	s [27]	x^2 [28]	$+$ [29]
T	$t = 4.$		3.	2.	4.	4.
Z	$z = 3.$		2.	1.1	3.	4.
Y	$y = 2.$		1.1	s_y	2.	3.
X	$x = 1.1$		*last x*	s_x	1.21	3.1

D	$d = 8.$		7.	6.	8.	8.
C	$c = 7.$		6.	5.	7.	8.
B	$b = 6.$		5.	4.	6.	7.
A	$a = 5.$		4.	3.	5.	6.
T	$t = 4.$		3.	2.	4.	5.
Z	$z = 3.$		2.	1.1	3.	4.
Y	$y = 2.$		1.1	s_y	2.	3.
X	$x = 1.1$		*last x*	s_x	1.21	3.1

Now you know why [ENTER↑] and [R↑] contain an arrow pointing up while [R↓] contains an arrow down. DROP, in a way, does the opposite of [ENTER↑].[30] We expect you may often find that x and y should be swapped before a [−], [/], or [y^x] operation – then use [x⇄y] for that.

[RCL][L] represents the vintage command LASTx (see pp. 47f for more).[31] Note the top *stack* level is lost in this recall operation.

---

[27] This stands for an arbitrary function returning two values. The top two levels are lost.

[28] This represents an arbitrary monadic function.

[29] This represents an arbitrary dyadic function. Note what happened to the top level.

[30] There were two keys [↑] and [↓] on *HP*'s first calculator, the 9100A. See *App. J*.

[31] Note the grey L printed bottom left of the key [EEX]. We will quote these keystrokes as [RCL][L] instead of [RCL][EEX] for reasons becoming clear in the chapter about addressing below.

At the bottom line, the fate of *stack* contents depends on the particular operation executed as well as on the *stack* size chosen. Operations in the 4-level *stack* work as known from vintage *HP RPN* calculators for decades. In the optional larger *stack* of your *WP 34S* everything works by full analogy – just with twice the levels available for intermediate results. So, eight levels are for worry-free calculations of even the most complex real world formulas.

Using the *stack* as explained above, *RPN* completely eliminates the need for any parenthesis keys! See the following slightly more complicated formula than the chain calculation above, and the keystrokes used for solving it step by step (the colors represent the *stack* levels involved).

Example:

$$\sqrt{\frac{1 + \left|\left(\frac{30}{7} - 7.6 \times 0.8\right)^4 - \left(\sqrt{5.1} - \frac{6}{5}\right)^2\right|^{0.3}}{\left\{sin\left[\pi\left(\frac{7}{4} - \frac{5}{6}\right)\right] + 1.7(6.5 + 5.9)^{3/7}\right\}^2 - 3.5}}$$

RAD 7 ENTER↑ 4 /	
5 ENTER↑ 6 / − π × SIN	$sin\left[\pi\left(\frac{7}{4} - \frac{5}{6}\right)\right]$
6.5 ENTER↑ 5.9 +	
3 ENTER↑ 7 / y^x 1.7 ×	$1.7 \times (6.5 + 5.9)^{3/7}$
+ x^2 3.5 −	complete denominator
7.6 +/− ENTER↑ .8 ×	
30 ENTER↑ 7 / + 4 y^x	$(30/7 - 7.6 \times 0.8)^4$
6 ENTER↑ 5 / 5.1 $\sqrt{x}$ − x^2	$\left(\sqrt{5.1} - 6/5\right)^2$
− |x| .3 y^x 1 +	complete numerator
x⇄y / $\sqrt{x}$	complete result (0.35)

Even solving this formula requires only four *stack* levels. Note there are <u>no</u> *pending operations* – each operation is executed individually, one at a time, allowing **perfect control of each and every intermediate result.** This is another characteristic advantage of *RPN*.

In many real life applications, intermediate results carry their own value, so further calculations may depend on the numbers you see while calculating – this is called 'exploratory math' and may well occur more frequently in your professional work than evaluating textbook formulas (see p. 48f).

Solving a formula like the one above from inside out is always a wise strategy.

Example (continued):

If you had, instead, started with its numerator straight ahead, stubbornly calculating from left to right, you would have needed six levels for the complete solution:

1 [ENTER↑] 30 [ENTER↑] 7 [/]
7.6 [ENTER↑] .8 [×] [−] 4 [yˣ]
5.1 [√x̄] 6 [ENTER↑] 5 [/] [−] [x²] [−] [x²] [√x̄] .3 [yˣ] [+] [RAD]
[π] [ENTER↑] 7 [ENTER↑] 4 [/] 5 [ENTER↑] 6 [/] [−] [×] [SIN]
1.7 [ENTER↑] 6.5 [ENTER↑] 5.9 [+] 3 [ENTER↑] 7 [/] [yˣ] [×]
[+] [x²] 3.5 [−] [/] [√x̄]

With eight levels as provided on your *WP 34S*, you will be on the safe side even with the most advanced equations you will meet in your life as scientist or engineer.[32]

Example:

For decades, solving the following formula for the *Mach* number as a function of aircraft speed in *knots*[33] (here: 350) and altitude in *feet*[34] (here: 25 500) was used for demonstrating the simplicity and coherence of *RPN*:

---

[32] Of course, it is trivial to construct examples leading to *stack* overflow even for eight levels. But first of all these will be exactly that: constructed examples – no real world formulas. And last not least, there will be still an intelligent person operating the calculator, solving from inside out as recommended above. You will never encounter an 8-level *stack* overflow with real world formulas following this strategy.

[33] For readers beyond aviation business: The *knot* is an ancient *Imperial* unit surviving in said niche:

$$1 \ knot = 1 \ {nautical \ mile}/{hour} = {463}/{900} \ {m}/{s} \approx 0.5144 \ {m}/{s} \ .$$

[34] The *foot* is another traditional *Imperial* unit made obsolete by *SI* (see <u>CONV</u> below). We quote this old Mach number formula on next page without checking it.

$$\sqrt{5\left(\left[\left\{\left(1+0.2\left[\frac{350}{661.5}\right]^2\right)^{3.5}-1\right\}\{1-6.875\times10^{-6}\times25500\}^{-5.2656}+1\right]^{0.286}-1\right)}$$

Start with the innermost parenthesis and solve the total expression like this:

350 [ENTER↑] 661.5 [/] [x²] .2 [×] 1 [+] 3.5 [y^x] 1 [−]
6.875 [EEX] [+/-] 6 [ENTER↑] 25500 [×] [+/-] 1 [+] 5.2656 [+/-] [y^x]
[×] 1 [+] .286 [y^x] 1 [−] 5 [×] [√x] ,

resulting in approximately 0.84, i.e. 84% of the speed of sound. Note only three *stack* levels were required for this solution.

At the bottom line, we recommend:

**Choose SSIZE8 and
let your *WP 34S* care for the arithmetic
while you care for the mathematics!**

Error Recovery

Nobody is perfect – errors will happen. With your *WP 34S*, however, error recovery is easy even in long calculations: your *WP 34S* loads x into the special register **L** (for **L**ast x) automatically just before a function is executed.[35] How does this help in real life?

1. If you got an **error message** in response to your function call, press ← to erase that message and return to the state before that error happened. Now do it right!

2. If you have erroneously called a wrong *monadic* **function** (or [%] or [Δ%]), just press ← [RCL][L] to undo it. These two steps restore the *stack* exactly as it was before the error happened. Then resume calculating where you were interrupted. Try it out!

---

[35] There are only a few commands changing x but not loading **L**. Those are mentioned explicitly in the *IOP*.

In vintage *HP* calculators starting with the *HP-45* of 1973, LASTx was a standard keyboard label. The *WP 34S* allows for recalling the last x via [RCL][L] , so we can drop the dedicated label LASTx here.

3. Recovering from erroneous **dyadic function** calls requires three steps as demonstrated in the following.

Example:

Assume – while you were diverted by watching an attractive fellow student or collaborator – you pressed ⓧ inadvertently instead of ⦸ in the second last step of the example on p. 43. Murphy's law! Do you have to start the calculation all over now? No, that error is easily undone as follows:

L	7	-249.43...	-249.43...	-249.43...	-249.43...	-249.43...
...						
Z						
Y	-2667.33		665312 ...		-2667.33	
X	-249.43...	665312 ...	-249.43...	-2667.33	-249.43...	10.693...
Input	⟨yˣ⟩	⟨x⟩	(RCL)(L)	⟨/⟩	(RCL)(L)	⟨/⟩
	Fine so far	Oops! 1		2	3	Resume

In step 1, (RCL)(L) recalls the complete denominator, the last x before the error.

Step 2 undoes the erroneous operation by executing its inverse.

Finally, step 3 regains the *stack* exactly as it was before the mistake. This is all you need to simply resume your calculation where it was interrupted. You will get the correct complete result.

An erroneous ⟨yˣ⟩ may be undone following the same method:

L	unknown	*den*	*den*	*den*	*den*
...					
Z					
Y	*num*		*num* ^{den}		*num*
X	*den*	*num* ^{den}	*den*	*num*	*den*
Input		⟨yˣ⟩	(RCL)(L)	⟨x↔y⟩ [36]	(RCL)(L)
		Oops! 1		2	3

---

[36] Both ⟨x↔y⟩ and DROP are not printed on the keyboard. You will find them in *catalogs* (see below).

Generally, this kind of recovery procedure requires that the inverse of the erroneous operation is provided. If this condition is fulfilled, it goes without saying that the procedure demonstrated here works for both *stack* sizes.

4. Inadvertent **pushes on the *stack*** can be undone by executing DROP [36]

  - once (for (ENTER↑), (RCL), Ⓨ, Ⓡ, and alike) or
  - twice (e.g. for Ⓧ or Ⓢ).

You will lose the contents of the top (two) *stack* level(s) by this mistake, however, so set your *stack* to eight levels to minimize the effects.

Special Tricks: LASTx

Beyond error recovery as explained on p. 45f, you can benefit from the special register **L** in other ways as well:

Example:

Assume a calculation like e.g. $\dfrac{1.234 + 5.67809}{5.67809}$.

It is most easily solved this way (shown here starting with a cleared *stack* and YDON – the latter is reached via (MODE)(Y)(▼) (XEQ)):

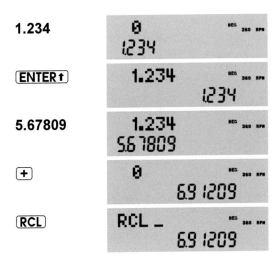

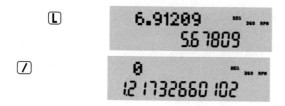

So, recalling the last x via [RCL][L] saves you from having to key in a lengthy second number more than once. It also allows for reusing intermediate results without the need for storing them explicitly.

Enter YDOFF via [MODE][▲][XEQ] now since you will not need the permanent y display in the next steps.

A Little Real Life Example

Beyond the examples printed above, the following one[37] shows how *RPN* is useful and fast in solving step-by-step problems where there is no formula, and where the next calculation depends on the result of the previous one.

> **Example:**
>
> You need to fix a tile that has fallen off your roof. The roof is 28 feet up, and you have a stepladder that is 29 feet long. You could also borrow your neighbor's 38 foot ladder. Is either ladder good for the job? You could try leaning each one in turn against the roof and seeing which is better, but it's raining, so why not work it out first on your *WP 34S* by seeing what angle each ladder will make with the vertical when you lean it against the roof?
>
> **Solution:**
>
> We do not need more than two decimals for the following calculation, so enter [FIX][2].
>
> First try it for your own ladder. Enter its length:
>
> [2][9] [ENTER↑].
>
> Then enter the height and divide so you can get the angle,
>
> [2][8] [/].

---

[37] This example is courtesy of *Gene Wright*.

WP 34S v3.3d

You get 1.04. That cannot be right; *sines* and *cosines* should be smaller than 1. Use

[RCL][L] [×] [RCL][L]

to get the numbers back, then

[x≷y]

to swap them. Now press

[/]

to divide them again, in the right order, and see 0.97. (Actually, simply pressing [¹/ₓ] would get the same result, making the correction more quickly.) Anyway, this is the *sine* of the angle between the ladder and the vertical. Or is it the *cosine*? Press

[SIN⁻¹]

and see the answer, 74.91 *degrees*. No, that is not right, it must be the *arc cosine* that you need. Press

[RCL][L]

to undo the *arc sine*, then

[COS⁻¹]   returning

Your ladder would be only 15 *degrees* away from the vertical. That is uncomfortably steep (and it may even tip over as you stand on it). So try the same calculation for your neighbor's 38 foot ladder.

Type

[2][8] [ENTER↑]   [3][8] [/]   [COS⁻¹].

This time the answer is 42.54 *degrees*. The ladder would be at a rather shallow angle and might slip away as you stand on it.

Neither ladder is really suitable. Maybe you should ask some other neighbors if they would lend you a ladder with a better length. What would be a good length? 30 *degrees* would probably still be too much; about 20 *degrees* would be about right. So type the height again and divide by the *cosine* of 20 *degrees*.

Type

[2][8] [ENTER↑]   [2][0] [COS]   [/].

That gives 29.80. A 30 foot long ladder would be almost ideal if a neighbor has one.

Special Tricks: Top *Stack* Level Repetition

Whenever dyadic or *triadic* functions are executed, the *stack* will drop and its top level will be repeated as mentioned above. You may employ this top level repetition for some nice tricks. See the following biological calculation as found in the *HP-21 OH* of 1975:

Example:

Bacteriologist *Martin Arrowsmith* tests a certain strain whose population increases by 15% each day under ideal conditions. If he starts a sample culture of 1000, what will be the bacteria population at the end of each day for six consecutive days?[38]

Solution:

FIX 2 will do. It causes the output being shown rounded to two decimals (internally, numbers are kept with far higher precision).

T		1.15	1.15 →	1.15 →	1.15	1.15	1.15
Z		1.15	1.15	1.15 ↘	1.15 ↘	1.15	1.15
Y		1.15	1.15	1.15	1.15	1.15	1.15
X	1.15	1.15 1000	1150.00	1322.50	1749.01	2313.06

1 . 0 1 5   FILL   1 0 0 0 ⌧   ⌧   ⌧ ⌧   ⌧ ⌧

after 1 day   after 2 days   after 4 days   after 6 days

Each multiplication consumes x and y for the new product put in **X**, followed by z dropping to **Y**, and t copied to **Z**. Due to top *stack* level repetition the growth factor is automatically kept as a constant on the *stack*, so the accumulated population computation becomes a simple series of ⌧ strokes.

This method works on an 8-level stack exactly the same way.[39]

Debt calculations are significantly more complicated – so avoid debts whenever possible! In the long run, it is better for you and the economy. Nevertheless, you can cope with such calculations using your *WP 34S* as well (see further below).

---

[38] This is the most persistent example in *HP's* manuals: it appeared for the first time in the *HP-55 OH* of February 1975 and was reprinted for each and every scientific calculator all the way through thirteen years until the *HP-15C OHPG* of June 1987 – just the names of the bacteriologists changed every once in a while.

[39] It will not work, however, with an infinite stack as featured by *HP's RPL* calculators.

The picture below
shows the great-
grandfather of
your *WP 34S* –
the *HP-34C* – with his favorite great-grandson.   Both calculators
feature *hotkeys*, both have three prefixes.   Note for the *HP-34C*,
however, all its functions had to be visible on its keyboard
since *catalogs* could not be supported based on its
seven-segment LED display. Your *WP 34S*,
on the other hand, features more
functions and operations
than can be printed
on four of its
own key-
boards.

Reaching Commands Not Printed on the Keyboard

Your *WP 34S* features more than 700 different commands. 168 labels are printed on the keyboard. So how do you learn about the other commands? Where are they and how can you call them?

The answer to the first question is easy: <u>read</u>! The *IOP* contains everything on pp. 171ff. The answer to the second question is less obvious, but easy as well: the 'hidden commands' are stored in *catalogs*. Remember each underlined label on the keyboard points to such a collection of commands or other items. You will find them on the slanted fronts of ten keys. For example, 🄷 + ③ points to <u>X.FCN</u>, the largest *catalog* provided.

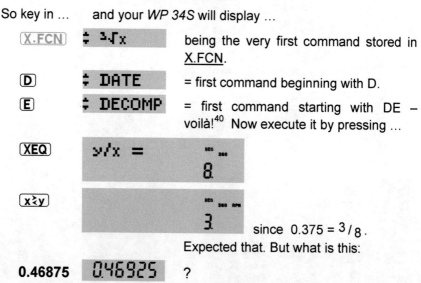

Example:

Assume you want to learn about DECOMP – this command was mentioned on p. 40 but is not seen on the surface of your *WP 34S*. So you return to the *Table of Contents*, look for the *Index of Operations*, jump directly to the letter **D** therein, and look up DECOMP to get the necessary information where it lives and what it does. OK, enter **0.375** on your *WP 34S* and check it – calling it is even easier than looking it up:

You have read DECOMP lives in <u>X.FCN</u>.

So key in ... and your *WP 34S* will display ...

(X.FCN)	‡ ³√x	being the very first command stored in X.FCN.
Ⓓ	‡ DATE	= first command beginning with D.
Ⓔ	‡ DECOMP	= first command starting with DE – voilà![40] Now execute it by pressing ...
(XEQ)	y/x = 8.	
(x⇄y)	3.	since 0.375 = 3/8. Expected that. But what is this:
0.46875	0.46925	?

---

[40] You shall press Ⓓ Ⓔ within 3 seconds – else the catalog browser will jump to the first command starting with E.

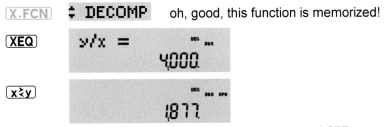

meaning $0.46925 = 1\,877\,/\,4\,000$.

As ▼ browses forwards through X.FCN, ▲ will browse backwards. And EXIT will leave the *catalog* without executing anything. See p. 280 for details about searching in *catalogs*.

Answering the two questions arisen on p. 46:

⬚ is stored in X.FCN as well; just key in X.FCN Y ▲ and you will get ↕ ˣ√y ;

and the command DROP is found in P.FCN.

We had also learned earlier about the commands YDON and YDOFF stored in MODE – see p. 47 for the way they were called.

That's all you need to know about calling commands and real calculations on the *stack*. There are, however, far more places in your *WP 34S* where you can store and save your data, and there are also more objects than just real numbers your *WP 34S* can handle for you. Let us show them to you.

Problem Solving, Part 4: Registers

Data storage space in your *WP 34S* is divided in registers. Each register can hold one real number. You have used registers above already – the *stack* consists of 4 or 8 registers (depending on your choice) managed by the operating system, and also the register $\mathbf{L}$ is maintained automatically (cf. p. 45).[41]

As mentioned above, an 8-register *stack* shall be sufficient for all your straight calculations. Additional registers are beneficial for storing e.g.

- special numbers you need more than once,
- sets of numbers (like vectors or matrices).

All these additional registers are controlled by you. You set the total amount of global numbered general purpose registers by REGS:

Example:

MODE R E $\div$ **REGS**

XEQ 5 6   allocates 56 such registers, i.e. **R00** through **R55**.

(Within programs, you may also allocate some local general purpose registers, using the command LOCR. See pp. 168f for more.)

Address and access a typical such register by specifying its two-digit number.

Example R1:

A beekeeper carefully counted his colony of bees contains 45 327 bees. And a shepherd has got 132 sheep in her herd. Neither one wants to count again. Thus, they request you to store these numbers in the *Continuous Memory* of your *WP 34S*.

Solution:

4 5 3 2 7 STO 2 3   stores the number of bees in **R23**.

1 3 2 STO 1 9   stores the number of sheep in **R19**.

---

[41] This also applies for register $\mathbf{I}$ sometimes, see below.

The content of such a register will stay constant unless you manipulate it explicitly using an applicable command. The contents will even survive run-down batteries if you backup your data using SAVE (P.FCN S XEQ stores a backup of all your *RAM* data in battery-fail-safe *flash memory*; you can recall the saved register contents using LOADR at any time thereafter).

Example R1 (continued):

Three months later, a little lambkin is born. Update the total number of sheep.

Solution:

INC 1 9   increments the current number of sheep. Note there is no need for you to remember the size of the herd. If you have forgotten it, view the updated value:

VIEW 1 9

> BEG   360 RPM
> 133.

or recall it via RCL 1 9

> BEG   360 RPM
> 133.

What is the difference?

VIEW 1 9 just displays the contents of **R19** (i.e. *r19*) until the next keystroke returns the previous content of **X**. On the other hand, RCL 1 9 recalls *r19* into **X** for further calculations.

Registers can also be beneficial storing temporary results for repeated use. Assume the following expression:

Example:

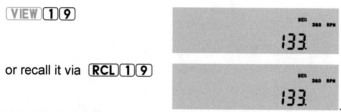

$$\sqrt{3 + \left(\frac{1.09}{1.78}\right)^2} \times \frac{\ln\left[3 + \left(\frac{1.09}{1.78}\right)^2\right]}{4 \times \cos\left[3 + \left(\frac{1.09}{1.78}\right)^2\right]}$$

Solution:

First calculate the repeating term $3 + \left(\frac{1.09}{1.78}\right)^2$ and store it:

1 . 0 9 ENTER↑ 1 . 7 8 /

x^2 3 + STO 0 3

Solve the entire expression then:

$\boxed{\sqrt{x}}$	solves the first factor of the expression,
$\boxed{\text{RCL}}\boxed{0}\boxed{3}$ $\boxed{\text{LN}}$	solves the numerator,
$\boxed{\times}$	multiplies,
$\boxed{\text{RCL}}\boxed{0}\boxed{3}$ $\boxed{\text{COS}}$	solves the second part of the denominator,
$\boxed{/}$	divides by it,
$\boxed{4}$ $\boxed{/}$	divides by four finally.

That's it – solving this expression has become really easy this way.

In addition to STOring and ReCalLing, you can also swap x and the contents of an arbitrary register you specify.

Example:

$\boxed{x \gtrless}\boxed{1}\boxed{1}$ exchanges x and the content of **R11**.

For clearing an individual register, simply store **0** in it. For clearing all registers, use CLREGS (contained in P.FCN).

Register Arithmetic

Arithmetic can be performed upon the contents of registers or variables by pressing $\boxed{\text{STO}}$ followed by the function key followed in turn by the address or name of the storage space.

Example R1 (continued):

Ten days later, another three lambkins are born. Update the total number of sheep.

Solution:

$\boxed{3}$ $\boxed{\text{STO}}\boxed{+}\boxed{1}\boxed{9}$ adds **3** to $r19$. The sum is kept in **R19**. The stack and the "Last x" register **L** remain unchanged.

The same result could be achieved without using this special store operation by the sequence

③ [RCL][1][9]

[x≷y] [+]

[STO][1][9]

[P.FCN] [D] [▼]   ≑ DROP

          [XEQ]

[RCL][L]   but that is far clumsier, costs one *stack* level, and overwrites the previous contents of **L**.

Similar operations may be performed employing [RCL] as well.

Example R1 (continued):

Now the herd became too big. It shall be divided in two. You shall continue keeping the records.

Solution:

② [RCL][/][1][9]   recalls *r19* and divides it by **2**. This operation is performed in **X** alone. The rest of the *stack* as well as the contents of **R19** remain unchanged in this step.   Your *WP 34S* displays

[STO][1][9] and [STO][2][0] store the headcount of both new herds.

Again, the same result could be achieved without using this special recall arithmetic operation by the sequence

② [RCL][1][9]

[x≷y] [/]

[STO][1][9] and [STO][2][0] but that needs two steps more and would also cost one *stack* level again.

Note this so-called *store and recall arithmetic* may operate on any register, also on the *stack* and even on **L**. There are a few true adepts on this planet who have learned some very nice tricks making use of these particular arithmetic operations, especially in programs. Therein, store and recall arithmetic saves steps, which makes programs faster, shorter, and easier to read. Although these techniques have been more important in times when program memory was very limited, they may be still of use today.

Computing with Pointers: Indirect Register Addressing

What is 'indirect addressing'? In the preceding chapters, we addressed registers on your WP 34S <u>directly</u>: we directly specified the address of the register whereto we want to write or wherefrom we want to read.

Example:

Assume the number **34.5678** is stored in **R18** and **18.0123** is stored in **R34**, then

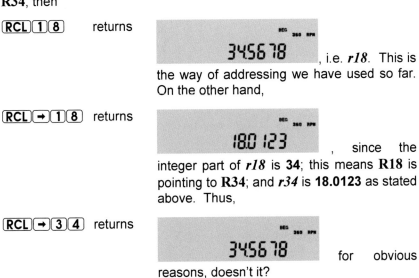

(RCL)(1)(8)   returns

`345678` , i.e. *r18*. This is the way of addressing we have used so far. On the other hand,

(RCL)(→)(1)(8) returns

`180123` , since the integer part of *r18* is **34**; this means **R18** is pointing to **R34**; and *r34* is **18.0123** as stated above. Thus,

(RCL)(→)(3)(4) returns

`345678` for obvious reasons, doesn't it?

Since the content of the register specified is used as a pointer to the register wherefrom we want to read (or whereto we want to write), this method is called <u>indirect</u> addressing. Note the arrow key used! Each and every register of your WP 34S can be used for indirect addressing. And this method carries benefits, in particular in programs (see pp. 161ff).

Addressing Objects in *RAM*

The picture below and the one overleaf show the complete address space of your *WP 34S*. Depending on the way you configure its memory, a subset of all these addresses will be accessible for you at a time.

Special registers and *stack*

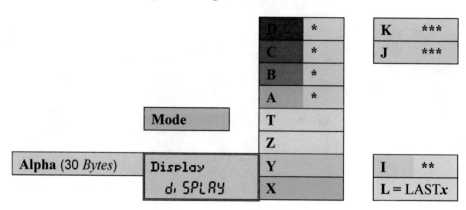

As mentioned above, the content of **X** will be displayed almost always. The content of **Y** may be displayed in addition.

Depending on *stack* size chosen, either **T** or **D** will be the top *stack* level. **A** – **D** will be allocated for the *stack* if required. **I** will be loaded in addition to **L** in complex calculations (see pp. 123ff). Registers **J** and **K** may carry parameters of statistical distributions. Unless required for the purposes just mentioned, **A, B, C, D, I, J,** and **K** are available as additional general purpose registers (see overleaf).

For numeric addressing of registers and flags, see the tables on pp. 64f and 134f. Addresses ≥112 are used for *local* registers and flags (see pp. 168f).

General purpose registers[42]	Program steps	User flags
	000	**127** = .15
R255	**001**	...
R254	**002**	
R253	...	...
...		**113** = .1
	...	**112** = .0
...	**925**	**111** = K
R128	**926**	**110** = J
R127 = R.15	**927**	**109** = I
...		**108** = L
		107 = Danger
...	K = R111	**106** = Carry
R113 = R.01	J = R110	**105** = Big, Overflow
R112 = R.00	I = R109	**104** = A : =
	L = R108	**103** = Tracing
	D = R107	**102** = Z
	C = R106	**101** = Y
	B = R105	**100** = X
R99	A = R104	**99**
...	T = R103	...
	Z = R102	
...	Y = R101	...
R02	X = R100	**02**
R01		**01**
R00		**00**

---

[42] Your *WP 34S* features **14** more registers, dedicated to statistical sums. They are allocated and accessed differently as explained in the *IOP* and *App. B*.

Note you will <u>not</u> get 928 program steps, 270 registers, and 128 flags all together <u>at the same time</u> – see *App. B* for memory management.

Some user flags have special use or effects:

- Flag **A** lights the big '**=**' symbol in display.
- The system sets flags **B** ('big') and **C** in integer modes (see p. 137) like the overflow and carry flags of the *HP-16C* – some integer operations also read flag **C**.
- Flag **D** allows for special (i.e. infinite or non-numeric) results without getting an error, flag **T** sets the print line to 'tracing mode' – both flags are only read by the system.

During input processing in memory addressing, e.g. while entering parameters for storing, recalling, swapping, copying, clearing, or comparing, you will not need all the labels presented on the keyboard. Just 34 keyboard labels will do instead:

The calculator mode supporting exactly these labels (and no more) is called *transient alpha mode* (α_T). As shown in examples on the next pages, it may be automatically set in addressing.

Entering α_T, the operational keyboard is temporarily reassigned as pictured here. This kind of picture is called a *virtual keyboard* since it deviates from the physical (or real) keyboard of your *WP 34S*. In such a picture, dark red background is used to highlight changed key functionality.

White print denotes *primary* functions also on virtual keyboards (e.g. the top left key accessing register (or *stack* level) A in α_T directly). On the other hand, what is printed white on your <u>physical</u> *WP 34S* is called a *default primary function*.

☞ All keys are primary in α_T – no shift keys are needed. This allows for fast and easy input of a limited character set. So you can reach all register addresses available with a minimum of keystrokes (special rules may apply for **T**, **X**, and **Z** here – see pp. 64f).

Mode α_T will be terminated or left (automatically returning to the mode set before) as soon as sufficient characters are entered for the respective operation. You may delete pending input character by character using ⬅ – or just abort the pending command by (EXIT) ; the latter will leave α_T immediately.

ATTENTION: You have unlimited access to all global registers and flags allocated. There is nothing like *"memory protection"* on your *WP 34S*. You are the sole and undisputed master of the memory! Thus it is also your responsibility to take care of it – keep suitable records to avoid overwriting or inadvertently deleting your precious data.

Further below, however, you will learn about a method preventing your programs from overwriting data of other applications.

Now, how does addressing real numbers really work if these data are placed at an arbitrary location in memory?

Addressing Real Numbers

<table>
<tr>
<td rowspan="2">1</td>
<td>User input</td>
<td colspan="4">$x = ?$, $x \neq ?$, x∢ ?, x≰ ?, x≂ ?, x≳ ?, or x≳ ?</td>
</tr>
<tr>
<td>Echo</td>
<td colspan="4">OP _ ? (with α$_T$ set),
e.g.
x≳_?</td>
</tr>
<tr>
<td rowspan="2">2</td>
<td>Input</td>
<td>0 or 1</td>
<td>Stack level or lettered register A, ..., D, I, ..., L, T, Y, Z</td>
<td>ENTER↑ [43]
leaves α$_T$</td>
<td>→
opens indirect addressing</td>
</tr>
<tr>
<td>Echo</td>
<td>OP n ?
e.g.
x≰0?</td>
<td>OP? x
e.g.
x≳? Y</td>
<td>OP? _</td>
<td>OP? → _</td>
</tr>
<tr>
<td></td>
<td></td>
<td>Compares x with the number 0.</td>
<td>Compares x with the number on stack level Y.</td>
<td>Register number
00 ... 99
and .00
... .15 [44]

OP? _
e.g.
x≠? 23</td>
<td>See overleaf for more about indirect addressing.</td>
</tr>
</table>

Compares x with the number stored in R23.

---

[43] You may skip this keystroke for register addresses >19 or local registers. The latter start their addresses with a . – see the chapter about *Programming Your WP 34S* and *App. B* below.

[44] ... if the respective register is allocated.
Note you can also enter A, ..., D, I, ..., L, T, Y, or Z here though the green way is shorter. Even comparisons with x are possible entering .. (for X) although they are of very limited use.

1	User input	$\boxed{RCL}$, $\boxed{STO}$, RCLS, STOS, $\boxed{\alpha RCL}$, $\boxed{\alpha STO}$, $\boxed{VIEW}$, $\boxed{VW\alpha+}$, $\boxed{x\gtrless}$, $y\rightleftharpoons$, $z\rightleftharpoons$, $t\rightleftharpoons$, $\boxed{DSE}$, $\boxed{ISG}$, DSL, DSZ, ISE, ISZ, $\boxed{ALL}$, $\boxed{FIX}$, $\boxed{SCI}$, $\boxed{ENG}$, DISP, BASE, bit or flag commands, etc.		
	Echo	OP _ (with α_T set), e.g. RCL _ [45]		
2	Input	*Stack level or lettered register* [46] $\boxed{A}$, ..., $\boxed{D}$, $\boxed{I}$, ..., $\boxed{L}$, $\boxed{T}$, $\boxed{X}$[47], $\boxed{Y}$, $\boxed{Z}$	*Register or flag **number** or base or number of bit(s) or decimals* [48]	$\boxed{\rightarrow}$ opens indirect addressing
	Echo	OP x e.g. SF K	OP nn e.g. SCI 10	OP $\rightarrow$ _
3	Input	Sets flag 111.	*Register number as specified overleaf*	*Stack level or lettered register* $\boxed{A}$, ..., $\boxed{D}$, $\boxed{I}$, ..., $\boxed{L}$, $\boxed{T}$, $\boxed{X}$[47], $\boxed{Y}$, $\boxed{Z}$
	Echo		OP $\rightarrow$ nn e.g. STO$\rightarrow$45	OP $\rightarrow$ x e.g. VIEW$\rightarrow$L

---

[45] For $\boxed{RCL}$ and $\boxed{STO}$, any of the operations $\boxed{+}$, $\boxed{-}$, $\boxed{\times}$, $\boxed{/}$, $\boxed{\blacktriangle}$, or $\boxed{\blacktriangledown}$ may precede step 2, except in $\boxed{RCL}$ $\boxed{MODE}$ (calling RCLM) and $\boxed{STO}$ $\boxed{MODE}$ (calling STOM). Entering such an operator twice will remove it, so e.g. $\boxed{RCL}$ $\boxed{/}$ $\boxed{/}$ equals $\boxed{RCL}$. – Note this so-called store and recall arithmetic may operate on any register, also on the *stack* and even on L. There are a few true adepts on this planet who have learned some very nice tricks making use of these particular arithmetic operations.

[46] Exceptions: $\boxed{ALL}$, $\boxed{FIX}$, $\boxed{SCI}$, $\boxed{ENG}$, DISP, and BASE accept lettered registers in indirect addressing only. And RCL T, STO T, RCL× T, STO× T, RCL Z, STO Z, RCL+ Z and STO+ Z require an $\boxed{ENTER\uparrow}$ heading the letter, e.g. $\boxed{STO}$ $\boxed{+}$ $\boxed{ENTER\uparrow}$ $\boxed{Z}$ for the latter. Pressing $\boxed{ENTER\uparrow}$ generally at the beginning of step 2 will give you a more consistent access to lettered registers but requires an extra keystroke in most cases.

[47] Press $\boxed{.}\boxed{.}$ (for $\boxed{X}$) to access X.

[48] See valid number ranges listed overleaf.

`STO→45` stores x in the register where the *r45* is pointing to. Note **R45** may contain any positive number less than 256 if the respective register is allocated at execution time.

`VIEW→L` shows the content of the register where the content of **L** is pointing to.

See pp. 59 and 161ff for further examples of use and benefits of indirect addressing.

The following table shows the valid ranges for the numeric parameters of the commands listed above:

Kind	Valid number range[49]
Registers	0 ... 99 for direct addressing of global numbered registers .0 ... .15 for direct addressing of local registers 0 ... 255 for indirect addressing (≤111 without local registers) — upper limits depend on allocation
Flags	0 ... 99 for direct addressing of global numbered flags .0 ... .15 for direct addressing of local flags if at least one local register is allocated 0 ... 127 for indirect addressing (≤111 without local flags)
Decimals	0 ... 11
Integer bases	2 ... 16
Bits	0 ... 63
Word size	1 ... 64 *bits*

---

[49] Some registers and flags also carry letters. For numbers less than ten, you may key in e.g. [STO] [5] [ENTER↑] instead of [STO] [0] [5]. The summation registers used for statistical calculations are accessed differently (see below).

Addressing Real Matrices and Vectors

So far, we dealt with one or two or (seldom) three numbers at once. Your *WP 34S* can do more for you. E.g. four, six, eight, nine, or more numbers arranged in table-like grids are called *matrices* by mathematicians. If you do 'not know of matrices yet, feel free to set them aside; you can use your *WP 34S* perfectly without them.

If you know of matrices, however, note your *WP 34S* features a set of operations for adding, multiplying, inverting and transposing matrices, as well as for manipulating rows in such matrices. In general, the respective commands are building blocks designed to provide the low level support routines for creating more useful matrix functions in the form of keystroke programs. I.e. they represent the basic *linear algebra* subroutines of the *WP 34S* matrix support. On the other hand, your *WP 34S* also provides functions for computing *determinants* or for solving *systems of linear equations*.

A matrix on your *WP 34S* is represented by its *descriptor*[50], formatted `bb.rrcc` with

r being the number of rows and

c the number of columns it features.

Thus this matrix has $r \times c$ elements. They are stored in consecutive registers starting at base address |**bb**| .

Example:

A *descriptor* **7.0203** represents a 2×3 matrix – let us call it (*M*). Its six elements are arranged in 2 rows and 3 columns, and they are numbered like this:

$$(M) = \begin{pmatrix} m_{11} & m_{12} & m_{13} \\ m_{21} & m_{22} & m_{23} \end{pmatrix}$$

The matrix *descriptor* **7.0203** also tells you where these matrix elements are stored:

$$(M) = \begin{pmatrix} r07 & r08 & r09 \\ r10 & r11 & r12 \end{pmatrix}$$

---

[50] The *HP-42S* supported a special data type for matrices. This is not viable using the hardware of the *HP-20b* or *HP-30b*, however. Thus, vector and matrix calculations are less straightforward here. See *App. F* for the reasons.

Depending on the current numeric contents of the registers **R07** through **R12**, the actual matrix may look like this:

$$(M) = \begin{pmatrix} -2.3 & 0 & 7.1 \\ 0.4 & 8.5 & -6.9 \end{pmatrix} \text{, for example.}$$

Typically, however, this work is done vice versa in real life: You know a particular matrix with a certain number of rows and columns; you allocate a free area in memory of required size and store the matrix elements there; then you enter the corresponding *descriptor* and call the matrix command of your choice.

Example:

We want to invert a 2×2 matrix $(A) = \begin{pmatrix} 1 & 2 \\ 3 & 4 \end{pmatrix}$.

Assume the memory is free above the first thirty registers, let us put the matrix up there:

1 (STO) **30**   **2** (STO) **31**   **3** (STO) **32**   **4** (STO) **33**

30.0202 (MATRIX) **M-1**   does the inversion (without changing x).

(RCL) **30**	returns	-2.
(RCL) **31**	returns	1
(RCL) **32**	returns	1.5
(RCL) **33**	returns	-0.5

Thus, the inverted matrix reads $(A)^{-1} = \begin{pmatrix} -2 & 1 \\ 1.5 & -0,5 \end{pmatrix}$.

If **c** is omitted in a *descriptor* it defaults to **r** so a square matrix is assumed. For example, a *descriptor* 13.04 belongs to a 4×4 matrix with its elements stored in **R13** through **R28**. The maximum number of matrix elements is 100 using *global* general purpose registers. With *local* registers, up to 144 are possible (see pp. 55f and 168f). So, LINEQS can solve systems of linear equations up to 9 or 11 unknowns.

See <u>MATRIX</u> (on p. 255) and the *IOP* (on pp. 171ff) for all commands featured. Beyond, there is a Matrix Editor contributed by *Marcus von Cube* for the program library – look for the label MED in CAT and see http://sourceforge.net/p/wp34s/code/HEAD/tree/library/matrixedit.wp34s . [51]

---

[51] You may find R-COPY useful for copying matrices. – And there are two articles about handling complex matrices contributed by *Thomas Klemm* (see the addresses

A *vector* may be regarded as a special case of a matrix featuring either one row or one column only. Thus, a vector *descriptor* looks like `bb.01cc` or `bb.rr01`. Library routines are readily provided for 3D vector calculus (e.g. for cross products).

If you just want to do vector operations in 2D, there are simple alternatives (known for long from earlier calculators) to full-fledged *descriptor* controlled computations: enter the Cartesian components of each vector in X and Y (e.g. by converting its polar components into Cartesian ones by →R, if necessary) and choose one of the following alternative opportunities:

1. use Σ+ for additions or Σ− for subtractions (see pp. 119ff) and recall the result via SUM, or

2. calculate in *complex domain* (see pp. 126ff). Therein, vector multiplication is possible, too, using the commands ^{C}DOT or ^{C}CROSS.

Turn to a good textbook covering *linear algebra* for more information about matrices and vectors and calculating with them.

← A glimpse of our European development laboratory in 2011.

The picture overleaf shows three generations of *RPN* calculators leading to yours: an *HP-34C*, *HP-41CX*, and *HP-42S* together with a *WP 34S*. We deny any responsibility for the first three – we just learned from them. →

http://www.hpmuseum.org/forum/thread-1347.html and http://www.hpmuseum.org/forum/thread-1357.html).

Please note your *WP 34S* cannot know where a particular real number is a matrix *descriptor* or a plain number. And it has no idea whether a particular register content belongs to a set of matrix elements or stands alone. It is your responsibility to take care of both.

SECTION 2: PROBLEM SOLVING IN VARIOUS OPERATING MODES

The *LCD* is your window to your *WP 34S* – there you see what is going on and what the results are. This display sports a total of 400 elements in three sections: numeric, dot matrix and fixed symbols.

The numeric section features a minus sign and 12 digits for the mantissa, as well as a minus sign and 3 digits for the exponent. The dot matrix is 6 dots high and 43 dots wide, allowing for some 7 to 12 characters, depending on their widths. The fixed symbols on the top right side are called *annunciators*.

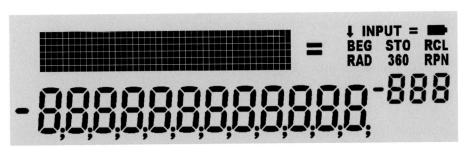

The ten annunciators are for indicating modes.

The numeric section in the lower part of the *LCD* is used for displaying numbers in different formats, status data, or message parts. See the examples below for more.

The dot matrix section above is used for passing additional information to the user.

Example:

During command input, the dot matrix displays the command chosen until input is completed, i.e. until all required trailing parameters are entered. The prefixes 🄵, 🄶, 🄷, CPX and → are shown until they are resolved (→ goes with 🄶 by default). If you pressed such a prefix erroneously, recovery is as easy as follows:

- 🄵 🄵 = 🄶 🄶 = 🄷 🄷
  = CPX CPX = → → = NOP

- CPX ⬅ = CPX → = CPX EXIT = NOP

- → ⬅ = → CPX = → 🄷 = NOP

- **g f** = **h f** = **f**
  f g = **h g** = **g**
  f h = **g h** = **h**

In addressing, progress is recorded as explained in the tables above (on pp. 64ff and 134f) in detail. You may edit a pending operation by **◄** or cancel it entirely by **EXIT** (see pp. 243ff).

If two or more requests compete for display space, priorities are:

1. echoing command entry,
2. error messages as listed in *App. C* on pp. 311ff,
3. other *temporary messages* as explained below,
4. integer mode or complex result information,
5. displaying *y* if YDON is set, and
6. date mode information.

Recognizing Calculator Modes

The **annunciators** or specific characters either in the dot matrix or in the exponent section indicate most modes and system states:

Indicator	Set by	Cleared by	Explanation, remarks
↓	⬆	⬆	Lower case letters will be entered in alpha mode (see pp. 148ff).
INPUT	α, αON	**ENTER↑**, αOFF, **EXIT**	Alpha mode (see pp. 148ff).
=	look at right	look at right	**Steady** if debug mode is turned on (see pp. 294 and 349f) or while serial I/O is in progress (see pp. 317ff). **Flashing** if the timer is running (except in STOPW, see pp. 282ff). Else clear.

Indicator	Set by	Cleared by	Explanation, remarks
▬▶	battery low	battery voltage > 2.5 V	Low battery will reduce processor speed (see SLOW on p. 217). Your *WP 34S* will shut off when voltage drops below 2.1V. It will recall what is stored in backup (then displaying 𝗋𝖾𝗌𝗍𝗈𝗋𝖾𝖽) as soon as it is turned on again with proper voltage supplied (see BATT on p. 184 and *App. A* on p. 297).[52]
=	SF A	CF A	
BEG	program pointer at step 000 or 001	otherwise	
STO	P/R	P/R, EXIT	Programming mode
RCL	flashes while a routine is running	program execution stopped	
RAD	RAD	DEG, GRAD	Angular mode (see p. 82)
360	DEG	GRAD, RAD	
RPN	almost every command	a *temporary message*	See p. 76 for handling of *temporary messages* in general.

The indicators following below are important in integer mode and are all lit in the exponent section exclusively:

---

[52] While the processor is running a heart beat interrupt is active which performs, among other things like the keyboard scan, the voltage measurement. The value is derived continuously from a circuit that compares the actual supply voltage to a given threshold. To determine the voltage the threshold is modified until a change in the comparator status bit is detected. BATT only reports the internal value so it does not consume any additional power for doing the measurement.

Indicator	Set by	Cleared by	Explanation, remarks
b__	2		Binary integer mode
3__ ... 7__	BASE 3 ... BASE 7	any other BASE setting. a b/c, d/c, and FRACT will set fraction mode (see p. 123). ALL, FIX, SCI, ENG, H.d, H.MS, →H.MS, and TIME will set default floating point decimal mode (i.e. DECM, see pp. 77ff).	Respective integer mode (see p. 137 for all these modes)
o__	8		Octal integer mode
9__	BASE 9		Integer mode of base 9
d__	10		Decimal integer mode
-1__ ... -5__	BASE 11 ... BASE 15		Respective integer mode
h__	16		Hexadecimal integer mode
_C_	carry set, SF C	CF C, carry clear	Indicate the respective bits set in integer modes (see p. 137).
__o	overflow, SF B	CF B	

The indicators following below are all lit in the dot matrix exclusively:

Indicator	Set by	Cleared by	Explanation, remarks
c	CPX	see pp. 123ff	Transient signal of prefix pending. **RAD** will be lit with ᶜ.
D	DBLON	DBLOFF	*Double precision* mode, see p. 351.
f	f	see pp. 71f	Transient signal of prefix pending.
g	g		
G	GRAD	DEG, RAD	Angular mode (see p. 82).
g →	→	see pp. 71f	Transient signal of pending prefix.
h	h		

Indicator	Set by	Cleared by	Explanation, remarks
i	complex result	else	See pp. 123ff.
m.dy	M.DY, SETUS	any other date or region setting	See pp. 82ff for more about date modes. Note default D.MY is not indicated. Date mode setting is not indicated as long as YDON is set.
y.md	Y.MD, SETJPN, SETCHN		
↕	entering a *catalog*	leaving it	See pp. 248ff for more about *catalogs*.
A number in the dot matrix	YDON	YDOFF	Permanent display of *y* may help keeping track of the stack. Note numbers will appear up there temporarily after →POL and →REC as well as after complex calculations in any case.

Default DECM is not indicated. Radix marks and separators are seen in the numeric display immediately, time modes (12h / 24h) in a time string. The numeric format of fraction mode is unambiguous as well; check the examples shown on pp. 123ff.

Some mode and display settings may be stored collectively by STOM and recalled by RCLM. These are *stack* height, display contrast, complete decimal display settings, trig mode, choices for date and time display, parameters of integer and fraction mode, curve fit model, rounding mode, and precision selected. STOM puts this information in the register you specify. RCLM recalls the register content and sets your *WP 34S* modes accordingly.

> **WARNING:** Be sure you actually recall mode data – else your *WP 34S* may be driven into very strange settings and it may cost you considerable effort to recover from that unless you find your previous modes stored elsewhere – else you have to use the command RESET or even the **RESET** button under the hood of your *WP 34S*. Both will erase all your data except those you saved in *FM*. See pp. 347f.

All keyboard input will be interpreted when the input is completed, according to the modes set at that time.

Common Commands Returning Specific Displays

Some common commands use the *LCD* for presenting *temporary messages* as defined here:

> Whenever anything different from the actual contents of **X** in current mode is displayed or any additional information is shown in the dot matrix, this extra information is considered being a *temporary message*. This is further indicated by the annunciator **RPN** turned off as mentioned on p. 73.

> If such extra information is displayed outside of a *catalog* or *browser*, it will vanish with the next keystroke. Pressing (EXIT) or ⬅ will just clear the *temporary message* and return to the normal display, any other key will be executed in addition.

Now here are the common commands delivering special information:

1. (STATUS) returns very useful information about current memory allocation and the free space available. It continues showing the status of the user flags. See pp. 251f for a detailed description of this *browser*.

2. (SHOW) allows for displaying the contents of all registers and (CAT) shows all the programs available. Both are *browsers* as well and are described on pp. 249ff.

3. Browsing an arbitrary *catalog* will display the commands contained therein as *temporary messages* (see pp. 248ff for more).

4. ERR and MSG display the corresponding error message as a *temporary message*. See the *IOP* on pp. 192 and 202ff and *App. C* on pp. 311ff for more.

5. A few far-reaching commands (e.g. CLALL) will ask you for confirmation before executing. Answer (Y) (by pressing (R/S)) or (N) (pressing (8)). Also (EXIT) or ⬅ will be read as (N), all other input will be ignored.

6. VERS generates a *temporary message* showing you version and build of the firmware running on your *WP 34S*.

- If the basic firmware is installed, the build number (e.g. 3316) will follow the version number (e.g. 3.1) immediately.

  `34S 3.1 3316`
  `PAULI, WALTEr`

- If the timer firmware is installed, a 'T' will trail the version number.

  `34S 3.1T 3316`
  `PAULI, WALTEr`

- If the firmware for printing is installed, a printer character will trail the version number instead. Compare also the picture on p. 1.

  `34S 3.1▴ 3316`
  `PAULI, WALTEr`

See *App. A* on pp. 285ff about how to install these different packages.

Further commands returning special displays and *temporary messages* are specific to particular modes of your *WP 34S* and are thus covered in the chapters following.

Real Stuff – 1: Introduction, Localisation, and Displaying Decimals

Floating point modes cover the 'usual' numbers you calculate with: decimal real (or complex) numbers, fractions, measured values, times and dates. DECM is the startup default mode of your *WP 34S*. Many commands apply exclusively to DECM and its sub-modes.

You can conveniently set display preferences according to your region's practices and customs using one of the dedicated commands following below:

Command	Radix mark[53]	Time	Date[54]	JG[55]	TS	Remarks
SETCHN	RDX.	24h	Y.MD	1949	TSOFF	Would require separators every four digits.
SETEUR	RDX,	24h	D.MY	1582	TSON	Applies to Latin America as well (and to Russia, Vietnam, Indonesia, and South Africa, but with deviating JG's).
SETIND	RDX.	24h	D.MY	1752	TSOFF	Would require separators every two digits over 10^3. Applies also to Pakistan, Bangladesh, and Sri Lanka.
SETJPN	RDX.	24h	Y.MD	1873	TSON	
SETUK	RDX.	12h	D.MY	1752	TSON	Applies also to Australia and New Zealand. 24h is taking over in the UK.
SETUSA	RDX.	12h	M.DY	1752	TSON	
RESET	RDX.	24h	D.MY	1752	TSON	Startup default – do not use this command unless you really want to since it has many more effects beyond these settings.

---

[53] See *http://upload.wikimedia.org/wikipedia/commons/a/a8/DecimalSeparator.svg* for a world map of radix mark use. Looks like an even score in this matter. Thus, the international standard ISO 31-0 allows either a decimal point or a comma as radix mark, and requires a narrow blank as separator of digit groups to avoid misunderstandings. The display hardware of *HP-20b* or *HP-30b*, however, does not allow for narrow blanks in the numeric section.

[54] See *http://upload.wikimedia.org/wikipedia/commons/0/05/Date_format_by_country.svg* for a world map of date formats used. The international standard ISO 8601 states 24h for times, Y.MD for dates. This combination is commonly used in East Asia (see SETCHN and SETJPN).

[55] This column states the year the Gregorian calendar was introduced in the particular region, typically replacing the Julian calendar (in East Asia, national calendars were replaced in the respective years). Your *WP 34S* supports both 1582 and 1752. See the *IOP* for JG1582 and JG1752.

For **floating point decimal numbers**, startup default displays all digits as long as they fit the display width; it will switch to SCIentific (i.e. mantissa plus exponent) notation to avoid flowing over the display limits. This format is ALL 0. Besides ALL and SCI, there are two more numeric display formats, FIX and ENG. Their effects can be most easily demonstrated and distinguished using an example:

Format Input	ALL 00	FIX 4	SCI 3	ENG 3
107.123456	107.123456	107.1235	$1.071\ ^{2}$	$107.1\ ^{0}$
$[1/x]\ 2\ [×]$	$18.670047389\ 1\ ^{-2}$	0.0187	$1.867\ ^{-2}$	$18.67\ ^{-3}$

Within FIX, the radix mark will always stay at the FIXed position defined. The radix mark floats in the other notations, where e.g. $1.071\ ^{2}$ represents $1.0712 \cdot 10^{2}$, while $1.867\ ^{-3}\ V$ means $18.67 \cdot 10^{-3}\ V = 18.67\ mV$. Within ENG, the exponent will always be a multiple of three corresponding to the unit prefixes in *SI* – thus, it is called the ENGineer's notation.

As soon as a numeric entry is completed, the mantissa will be displayed adjusted to the right, the exponent to the left. Within the mantissa, either points or commas may be selected as radix marks (use $[./.]$ to make your choice), and additional marks may be chosen to separate thousands.

Example:

Assume the format is set to FIX 4 again. Key in 12345678 $[.]$ 901 $[ENTER↑]$, and you will get

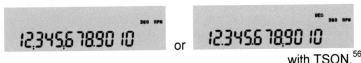

or with TSON.[56]

Without these separators (i.e. with TSOFF), the same number will look like this

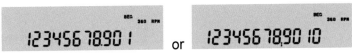

or

---

[56] These separators may also be beneficial in fraction mode described below.

With ENG 3 and after ⊕, you will see

$$- 12.35^{6}$$ or $$- 12.35^{6}$$.

With SCI 4 , the same number will look like this

$$- 12346^{7}$$ or $$- 12346^{7}$$.

See also DISP in the *IOP* (on pp. 188ff).

Floating point numbers within $10^{-383} \leq |x| < 10^{+385}$ may easily be entered directly in default DECM. Within this range, your *WP 34S* calculates with 16 digits and will display up to twelve usually (see the next point for an exception). Values $< 10^{-398}$ are set to zero (see pp. 305ff for the reasons). For results $|x| \geq 10^{+385}$, error 4 or 5 will appear unless flag **D** is set (see pp. 311ff).

◄ and ► display the <u>full</u> real number stored in **X**, i.e. usually all 16 digits present internally in the mantissa of standard floating point (i.e. single precision) numbers and all digits of the exponent almost like in scientific display format. All this is shown in one *temporary message*, working almost like the old SHOW command featured by the *Pioneers*.

Example:

π 3 y^x ◄   returns

$$3.100,627$$
$$.668,029,981 \quad 001$$

reading 3.100 627 668 029 981 · 10^1, i.e. 31.006 276 680 299 81 – note the digit group separators are displayed always here for easier recording regardless of TSON / TSOFF setting.

Exception: If a **D** is displayed top left in the display, ◄ and ► will be interpreted differently (see p. 354).

For **fitting** measured and accumulated data points with a regression curve, four mathematical models are provided as in the *HP-42S*. See the commands EXPF, LINF, LOGF, and POWERF in the *IOP* on pp. 192ff. As shown in this example

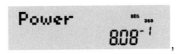

,

the fit model applied is displayed *temporarily* after each command related to fitting (i.e. after CORR, COV, L.R., s_{XY}, $\hat{x}$, $\hat{y}$).

The command BESTF will set your *WP 34S* to select the model resulting in the greatest absolute *correlation coefficient* (see CORR). Like with all other auto-functionality, you should know what you are doing here.

Results of **complex operations** will be displayed like this (with ALL 0 set):

$$i\,1.3799732 \quad \text{BEG} \,_{360} \,^{RPN}$$
$$4.3479\,1053534$$

with the real part in the numeric section of the LCD and the imaginary part in the dot matrix, headed by an **i**. Both parts obey the format selected as explained in previous point. Note the top number, however, is just (1) a *temporary message* and (2) a rounded view of the imaginary part stored in **Y**, with the number of decimals limited by the fixed width of the dot matrix section – press ⌊x⇄y⌋ to see the imaginary part completely; then press ⌊x⇄y⌋ again to return to the complex number as it was for continuing complex calculations (explained in detail on pp. 123ff).

⌊→R⌋ and ⌊→P⌋ both operate on and return two numbers in the display (see p. 88ff for more examples).

(see p. 88ff for more examples).

Example:

Assume $x = 1.2$ and $y = 3.4$, then pressing

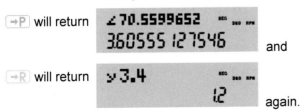

⌊→P⌋ will return ∠70.5599652 and

⌊→R⌋ will return ⅄3.4 again.

Note both are *temporary messages* – the additional information in the upper line will vanish with the next keystroke.

Real Stuff – 2: Displaying Angles, Times, and Dates, and Calculating with Them

There are two different ways of measuring time: *decimal hours* and *sexagesimal hours, minutes, seconds*. Watches and clocks indicate time in its traditional sexagesimal form – decimal times ease calculations. Use →[f][H.MS] [57] to convert from *decimal hours* to *hours, minutes,* and *seconds*. Take →[f][H.d] for converting vice versa.

And there are three different ways of expressing angular measurements: *decimal degrees, gradians* (also known as *gon*),[58] and *radians*, corresponding to the three **angular modes** featured: DEG, RAD, and GRAD.[59] And *degrees* may be displayed in decimal numbers as well as in *degrees, minutes, seconds* and hundredth of *seconds* (H.MS). More than just the usual angular conversions are provided:

From	degrees H.MS	decimal degrees	radians	gon (grad)	current angular mode
… to degrees H.MS	—	→[f][H.MS]	—	—	—
… to decimal degrees	→[f][H.d]	—	[h][CONV] rad→°	[h][CONV] G→°	→[DEG]
… to radians	—	[h][CONV] °→rad	—	[h][CONV] G→rad	→[RAD]
… to gon (grad)	—	[h][CONV] °→G	[h][CONV] rad→G	—	→[GRAD]
… to current angular mode	—	[h][X.FCN] DEG→	[h][X.FCN] RAD→	[h][X.FCN] GRAD→	—

---

[57] Within this chapter, we explicitly write all *prefixes* where they are required. You will note you will not need pressing [g] in some cases – in fact, you must not press it then.

[58] Nowadays, *gradians/gon* are used by surveyors almost exclusively.

[59] Translator's note: This traditional calculator notation is misleading in German at least: DEGrees mean "*Grad*", while GRADs are called "*Gon*".

Example:

Set the display to FIX 4 and press [g] [RAD] to choose *radians* as current angular mode. Then enter the following:

[h] [π] **300** [/]	`0.0105`	So π/300
[→] [DEG] [60]	`0.6000`	are exactly 0.6°
[→] [f] [H.MS]	`0.3600`	or 0°36'0".

Generally, you should watch the annunciators of angular modes.

Note that for any conversion to *degrees* (or *hours*), *minutes*, and *seconds*, your *WP 34S* always assumes the input being measured in *decimal degrees* (or *decimal hours*), regardless of the angular mode set. And for any conversion to *decimal degrees* (or *decimal hours*), [→] [f] [H.d] assumes the input being measured in sexagesimal *degrees* (or *hours*), *minutes*, and *seconds*.

The conversions [→] [DEG], [→] [RAD], and [→] [GRAD], however, as well as the trigonometric functions [f] [SIN], [f] [COS], and [f] [TAN] assume their input given in the current angular mode as indicated by the annunciator lit.

You have learned about the functions *sine*, *cosine*, and *tangent* as well as their inverses *arcsine, arccosine,* and *arctangent* in school. Thus, we demonstrate their use just with one example we found in the *HP-25C OH* of 1975: [61]

Example:

Lovesick sailor *Oscar Odysseus* dwells on the island of *Tristan da Cunha* (37°03'S, 12°18'W), and his sweetheart, *Penelope*, lives on the nearest island. Unfortunately for the course of true love, however, *Tristan da Cunha* is the most isolated inhabited spot in the world. If *Penelope* lives on the island of *St. Helena* (15°55'S, 5°43'W), use the following formula to calculate the great circle distance that *Odysseus* must sail in order to court her.

---

[60] Note that the key [→] also calls the prefix [g], so you don't have to press [g] explicitly here.

[61] This example was reprinted in every manual of an *HP* scientific pocket calculator until the *HP-41C/41CV OHPG* of 1980.

Solution:

The formula for the great circle distance **d** in *nautical miles* [62] is:

$$d = 60 \times arccos[sin(B_s)sin(B_d) + cos(B_s)cos(B_d)cos(L_d - L_s)]$$

with B_s and L_s being the latitude[63] and longitude of the start (*Tristan da Cunha*) and B_d and L_d being the latitude and longitude of the destination (*St. Helena*). Hence, with the numbers inserted, this formula reads:

$$d = 60 \times arccos[sin(37°03'S)sin(15°55'S)$$
$$+ cos(37°03'S)cos(15°55'S)$$
$$\times cos(5°43'W - 12°18'W)]$$

Remember the trigonometric functions assume their input being in the current angular mode as indicated by the annunciator lit. Start-up default mode is *degrees*. Set the appropriate number of decimals and calculate from inside out:

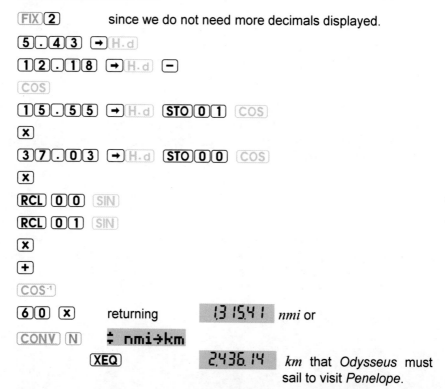

FIX 2   since we do not need more decimals displayed.

5 . 4 3   → H.d

1 2 . 1 8   → H.d   −

COS

1 5 . 5 5   → H.d   STO 0 1   COS

×

3 7 . 0 3   → H.d   STO 0 0   COS

×

RCL 0 0   SIN

RCL 0 1   SIN

×

+

COS⁻¹

6 0   ×   returning   `13 15.41`   *nmi* or

CONV N   `≑ nmi→km`

          XEQ   `2,436.14`   *km* that *Odysseus* must sail to visit *Penelope*.

---

[62] See the *catalog* CONV for this non-*SI* unit.

[63] Translator's note: *Latitude* means "*Geographische Breite*" in German. Hence **B** is used in the formula above.

In **H.MS display mode**, entered via  H.MS, decimal numbers are converted and displayed as a *temporary message* formatted `hhhh°mm'ss.dd"`. This may look like

246°54' 32.10 "   or   246°54' 32,10 "   for RDX. or RDX, , respectively.

You can calculate with times and angles as long as they are <u>decimal</u> values. This means you can multiply or divide them by real numbers, and you can sum them up or calculate differences. For adding (or subtracting) <u>sexagesimal</u> times, you can use H.MS+ (or H.MS−); these are both stored in <u>X.FCN</u>.

Example:

To meet your date at 5:25 p.m. at Stanford, you need 15' from your office to get your car out of the parking garage, 1.5 *hours* for the ride, and 12' for walking from the parking lot to lecture hall. Being careful, you count in another 15' for a possible traffic jam on the expressway. When do you have to leave your office?

Solution 1:

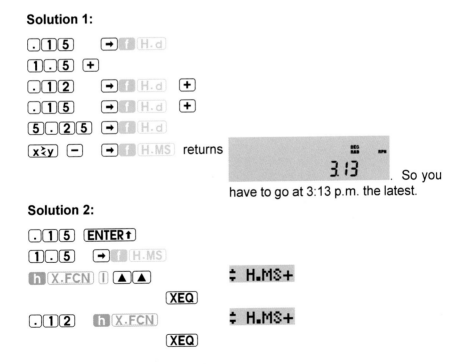

. So you have to go at 3:13 p.m. the latest.

Solution 2:

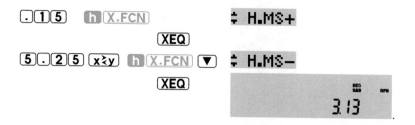

Choose the solving method you like best. If you plan using H.MS+ and H.MS- frequently, you may assign these functions to two hotkeys (see pp. 25f for more information about them).

Those of you being used to a.m. and p.m., please note that time calculations operate with and result in plain decimal times (except H.MS+ and H.MS- which operate with and result in plain sexagesimal times). Calculations will never return a.m. or p.m. but what is called 'military time' in India.

For decimal times less than $5ms$ or sexagesimal angles less than 0.005 *angular seconds* but greater than zero, a ∪ for underflow will be lit in the exponent section in H.MS display mode. Internally, however, the decimal value is kept at full precision, so do not bother – just continue your calculations.

Example:

EEX +/- 7 → f H.d f H.MS displays

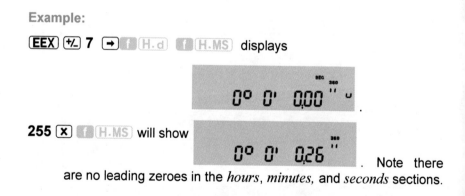

255 x f H.MS will show

. Note there are no leading zeroes in the *hours*, *minutes*, and *seconds* sections.

The number of *hours* or *degrees* is limited to 9 000 in this mode. For times or angles exceeding 9 000, an ☐ is shown in the exponent section signaling an overflow, and the value is displayed modulo 9 000.

For example,

will become after 🔳 H.MS

.

With the next key pressed, it will return to

WDAY returns a display looking like the following for an input of 13.01201 in default D.MY mode (equivalent to inputs of 2010.0113 in Y.MD or 1.13201 in M.DY):

DAYS+ works alike: Put in **8.082018** ENTER↑ **27** and call DAYS+ (which is stored in X.FCN) and you will get in startup default modes:[64]

Dates will be displayed numerically according to the date mode chosen – and this mode (except startup default D.MY) will be indicated in the dot matrix as shown on p. 75 according to the display priorities stated on p. 72.

---

[64] Calculation of weekdays for the past depends on the calendars used at that time – there may be different true results for different countries depending on the date the particular country introduced the Gregorian calendar. Officially, that calendar became effective in October 1582 in the catholic world. Large parts of the world took their time and switched later (see pp. 81f). Note, however, there are still also other calendars in use on this planet, e.g. in the Muslim world or in Israel.

Dates before the year 8 A.D. may be indicated differently than they were at the time due to the inconsistent application of the leap year rule before. We count on your understanding and hope this shortcoming will not affect too many calculations.

By the way, note that 8 A.D. should be better written A.D. 8 or even A.D. VIII correctly – quite some false Latin is found in the English language. Nobody, however, counted years this way at that time – around the Mediterranean Sea, it was the year DCCLXI A.V.C. then. Also note the Julian calendar was introduced and became valid not earlier than DCCVIII A.V.C. – before, months were organized differently. Julius Caesar was murdered in DCCIX A.V.C.; calendars seem a sensitive topic.

Real Stuff – 3: Coordinate Conversion and Vectors in 2D

Two functions are provided for converting polar / rectangular coordinates in two dimensions. Input and output data are in the stack levels **X** and **Y** here.

→P converts 2D Cartesian coordinates *x* and *y* to polar magnitude or radius *r* in **X** and angle *ϑ* in **Y**.

> **Example:**
>
> Convert (*x*, *y*) = (**6**, **4.5**) to polar.
>
> **Solution:**
>
> 4 . 5 ENTER↑ 6 →P returns   ∡36.8698976   360 RPH
>   7.5
>
> ,
> i.e. a vector of magnitude 7.5 pointing up right from the origin with an angle of some 37° to the positive *x*-axis.

→R converts 2D polar coordinates radius *r* in **X** and angle *ϑ* in **Y** to Cartesian coordinates *x* and *y*.

Both functions honour the angular mode settings as described in previous paragraph.

> **Example** (continued):
>
> Convert the returned angle of the conversion executed above to *radians*, and then convert the resulting coordinates (*r*, *ϑ*) to rectangular.
>
> **Solution:**
>
> x⇄y →RAD
> x⇄y RAD →R returns   y4.5   RAD RPH
>   6.
>   as expected.

Note angular input can range from −∞ to +∞; angular output, however, is confined to −180° to +180° or its equivalents in *radians* (−π to +π) or *gon* (−200^g to +200^g).

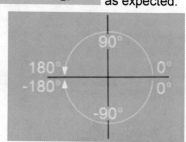

Example:

In an electronic circuit designed for alternating current, an overall impedance of 82.4 Ω is measured, and voltage lags current by 28°. Replacing said circuit by an equivalent containing just one resistor and one capacitor in series, what would be the resistance R and the capacitive reactance X_C therein?

Solution:

The values measured correspond to an impedance vector of magnitude 82.4 pointing down right at an angle of -28° to the positive x-axis. R is its component parallel to

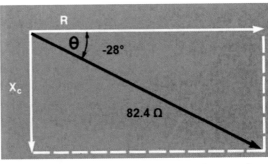

the x-axis, and X_C is its perpendicular component parallel to the y-axis.

DEG FIX 0 1

2 8 +/- ENTER↑ 8 2 . 4 →R   returns

$$\mathcal{y}-38.7$$

$$72.8$$

, i.e. a resistance

of 72.8 Ω and a reactance of 38.7 Ω.

By the way, you can use →R and →P also to convert 3D cylinder coordinates to Cartesian and vice versa, since z is kept unchanged.

Real Stuff – 4:   Hyperbolic Functions

Your *WP 34S* features three hyperbolic functions and their inverses:

HYP SIN	*Hyperbolic sine (sinh)* of x given in *radians*.
HYP COS	*Hyperbolic cosine (cosh)* of x given in *radians*.
HYP TAN	*Hyperbolic tangent (tanh)* of x given in *radians*.
HYP⁻¹ SIN	Inverse *hyperbolic sine (arsinh)* returning *radians*.
HYP⁻¹ COS	Inverse *hyperbolic cosine (arcosh)* returning *radians*.
HYP⁻¹ TAN	Inverse *hyperbolic tangent (artanh)* returning *radians*.

We found the following application example in the *HP-32 OH* though we modified it a bit. The *HP-32* of 1978 was *HP*'s first pocket calculator providing hyperbolic function keys whereas the *SR50* of *Texas Instruments* (*HP*'s arch rival in those years) featured these functions four years earlier already.

Example:

In *Upper Lagunia*, a tram carries tourists between two peaks in the *Baruvian Alps* that are the same height and 437 *meters* apart. How long does it take the tram to travel from one peak to the other if it moves along its cable at 135 *meters per minute*? Before the tram latches onto the cable, the angle from the horizontal to the cable at its point of attachment is found to be **33°**.

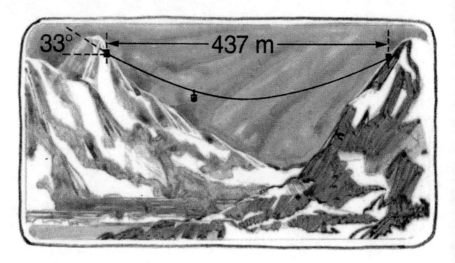

Solution:

The travel time is given by the formula $t = \dfrac{d}{v} \times \dfrac{\tan\alpha}{arsinh(\tan\alpha)}$.

Let us start with

FIX 2	since we do not need more decimals displayed.
3 3 TAN	
ENTER↑	duplicates that value on the *stack* since we need it twice, in numerator and denominator.
HYP⁻¹ SIN	
/	
4 3 7 ×	
1 3 5 /	returning 3.44 , i.e. almost 3 ½ *minutes*.

Real Stuff – 5: Logarithms and Powers

Your *WP 34S* features four logarithmic functions on its keyboard:

LN   calculates the *natural logarithm* of the value in **X**, i.e. the logarithm of x to the base **e** (being Euler's constant, see **e̊E** in CONST). Thus, LN inverts the command e^x.

LG   returns the (*common*) *decadic logarithm*, i.e. the logarithm of x to the base **10**. LG inverts the command 10^x.

LB   calculates the *binary logarithm*, i.e. the logarithm of x to the base **2**. LB inverts the command 2^x.

LOG$_x$ is the most general of these four functions: it returns the logarithm of y to the base x. LOG$_x$ can be used to invert the power command y^x.

You may be used to the calculator label LOG for the common logarithm; though this is mathematically ambiguous, so we avoided it.

In the operating manual of the world's very first pocket calculator featuring transcendental functions, the *HP-35* of 1972, is printed just one single example concerning this then new class of calculator functions:

Example:

Suppose you wish to use an ordinary barometer as an altimeter. After measuring the sea level pressure (30 inches of mercury) you climb until the barometer indicates 9.4 inches of mercury. How high are you? Although the exact relationship of pressure and altitude is a function of many factors, a **reasonable** approximation is given by:

$$\frac{altitude}{[feet]} = 25\,000 \times ln\left(\frac{30}{pressure\Big/[inches\ of\ Hg]}\right)$$

Solution:

3 0 ENTER↑ 9 . 4 /

LN

2 5 EEX 3 ✕   returns

```
                                    360 RPN
29,0 12.1923097
```

[We suspect that you may be on Mt. Everest (29 028 *feet*)]

Note the concise and factual style of this text. The *HP-35* was a calculator made by engineers for engineers, and the manual was alike. Said example was reprinted in the *HP-45 OH* of 1973. It underwent slight modifications before reappearing two years later again:

> **Example** (in the *HP-21 OH* of 1975):
>
> Having lost most of his equipment in a blinding snowstorm, ace explorer *Buford Eugobanks* is using an ordinary barometer as an altimeter. After measuring the sea level pressure (30 inches of mercury) he climbs until the barometer indicates 9.4 inches of mercury. Although the exact relationship of pressure and altitude is a function of many factors, *Eugobanks* knows that an **approximation** is given by the formula …

This example stayed in the next calculator manuals though the explorer changed for unknown reason and not every snowstorm was worth mentioning anymore:

> **Example** (in the *HP-25 OH* – later in 1975 – and the *HP-27 OH* of '76):
>
> Ace explorer *Jason Quarmorte* is using an ordinary barometer as an altimeter. After measuring the sea level pressure …

> **Example** (from the *HP-91 OH* of 1976, the *HP-67 OHPG* – when it went along with a picture for the first time – the *HP-19C / HP-29C OHPG* of '77, to the *HP-97 OHPG* of '78):
>
> Having lost most of his equipment in a blinding snowstorm, ace explorer *Jason Quarmorte* is using an ordinary barometer as an altimeter. After measuring the sea level pressure …

Then, however, a change of units reached even our explorers in the *Himalayas* – and also the weather and the methods changed:

Example (in *Solving Problems with Your Hewlett-Packard Calculator* of 1978):

With most of his equipment lost in an avalanche, mountaineer Wallace Quagmire must use an ordinary barometer as an altimeter. Knowing the pressure at sea level is 760 mm of mercury, Quagmire continues his ascent until the barometer indicates 238 mm of mercury. Although the exact relationship of pressure and altitude is a function of many factors, Quagmire knows that an approximation is given by the formula:

$$\frac{altitude}{[m]} = 7\,620 \times ln\left(\frac{760}{pressure \Big/ [mm\ of\ Hg]}\right)$$

Where is Wallace Quagmire?

Solution:

⑦⑥⓪ (ENTER↑) ②③⑧ (/)

(LN)

⑦⑥②⓪ (×)   returns

$$8{,}847.18392822$$

Quagmire appears to be near the summit of Mount Everest (8 848 *m*).

And it seems neither he nor his barometer did return from this trip since that example did not show up in the *HP-41C OHPG* of 1980 anymore. Maybe there was something wrong with his recalibrated instrument? Note it is said *Quagmire* "knew" the pressure at sea level, he did not measure it with his barometer like his precursors *Quarmorte* and *Eugobanks*.

By the way, the altitude approximation formula for standard *SI* units reads:

$$\frac{altitude}{[m]} = 7\,620 \times ln\left(\frac{1\,013}{pressure \Big/ [mbar]}\right)$$

Beyond the barometric scale mentioned above, there are more logarithmic scales used in science and engineering, e.g.

- in astronomy for assessing the brightness of stars or
- in chemistry for the power of acids (*pH*); most popular may be
- the *decibel* (*dB*) in acoustics (see <u>CONV</u> below) or
- the so-called *Richter* scale[65] for assessing the magnitude of earth-quakes.

Example:

One of the strongest earthquakes observed recently was the one causing a devastating tsunami in the Indian Ocean in December 2004. It had a magnitude of 9.1. Another earthquake in March 2011 – with a magnitude of 9.0 – led to the Fukushima nuclear accident. Compare with the San Francisco earthquake of 1906, having had a magnitude of 7.9.

Solution:

The formula for comparing the energies released in two different earthquakes (with their magnitudes known) reads

$$\frac{E_2}{E_1} = 10^{1.5(M_2 - M_1)}$$

We will not need more than one decimal in our results here. Thus,

FIX 0 1

9 . 1 ENTER↑ 7 . 9 −
1 . 5 ×
10ˣ   returns

So the energy released in said Japanese earthquake was 45 times greater than the "*great San Francisco earthquake*". And said earthquake in the Indian Ocean was even 63 times more intense.

---

[65] This name is still popular in the news although not quite true anymore. The actual moment magnitude scale for earthquakes differs but is still logarithmic.

Taking into account that published magnitudes of earthquakes never show more than one decimal, we would not have lost anything real setting the *WP 34S* to FIX **0** here so it would have done the display rounding for us immediately.

Even small numeric differences will gain significance when raised to powers. Human brains are not well equipped for such operations, so we recommend taking care.

Example:

What difference in magnitude will double destruction?

Solution:

Rewriting the formula above results in $\quad \Delta M = \frac{2}{3} lg \left(\frac{E_2}{E_1}\right).$

Thus, for double destruction we need a magnitude difference of

2 LG 2 × 3 / equalling only $\boxed{0.2}$.

But there are also friendlier applications of logarithms:

Example:

How many bits are required if the number 3.7×10^9 shall be the maximum to be handled by a processor?

Solution:

3 . 7 EEX 9 LB returns $\boxed{3\ 1.8}$, so 32 bits shall suffice.

If we had a tri-state logic,

RCL L 3 LOG$_x$ returns $\boxed{20.1}$, so 21 cells would be sufficient then.

Providing y^x, your *WP 34S* also allows for raising any positive real number to an arbitrary real power, as well as any negative real number to an arbitrary integer power. Working with powers frequently, you will benefit from label **C** being undefined on your *WP 34S* – so you can use the shortcut y^x in top row.

Examples:

Calculate 3^{21}, π^e, $(-2)^{15}$, and $((-e)^7)^{-11}$.

Solutions:

ENG 2 .

3 ENTER↑ 2 1 y^x returns $105.\ ^9$, confirming the result of previous example.

π 1 e^x y^x returns $22.5\ ^0$ (note we got Euler's constant by calculating e^1).

2 +/− ENTER↑ 1 5 y^x returns $-32.8\ ^3$.

1 e^x +/− $-2.72\ ^0$

7 y^x $-110\ ^3$

1 1 +/− y^x returns $-363.\ ^{-36}$.

See also the *Mach number* formula shown on p. 44. − Another example, noticed in a calculator manual of 1976:

Example:

Finding himself floating dangerously close to the jagged peaks of the Canadian Rockies, intrepid balloonist *Chauncy Donn* frantically cranks open the helium valve on his spherical balloon. Gas from the helium tank increases the balloon's radius from 7.5 meters to 8.25 meters. *Donn* clears the mountain tops safely. How much did the volume of the balloon increase?

Solution:

Since the volume of a sphere is $V = \frac{4}{3}\pi \times r^3$, the difference of two such volumes is $\Delta V = \frac{4}{3}\pi \times (r_2^3 - r_1^3)$. One decimal should do here.

FIX 0 1

8 . 2 5 ENTER↑ 3 y^x 561.5 ,

7 . 5 ENTER↑ 3 y^x 421.9 ,

− 139.6 ,

$\boxed{\pi}$ $\boxed{\times}$		$\boxed{438.7}$,
$\boxed{4}$ $\boxed{\times}$		$\boxed{1754.8}$,
$\boxed{3}$ $\boxed{/}$	returns	$\boxed{584.9}$ m^3.

Example (continued):

That is a volume increase of how many percent?

Solution:

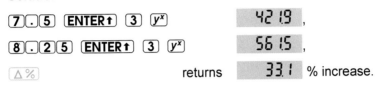

$\boxed{7}\boxed{.}\boxed{5}$ $\boxed{\text{ENTER↑}}$ $\boxed{3}$ $\boxed{y^x}$		$\boxed{42.19}$,
$\boxed{8}\boxed{.}\boxed{2}\boxed{5}$ $\boxed{\text{ENTER↑}}$ $\boxed{3}$ $\boxed{y^x}$		$\boxed{56.15}$,
$\boxed{\Delta\%}$	returns	$\boxed{33.1}$ % increase.

In conjunction with $\boxed{1/x}$, $\boxed{y^x}$ also provides a simple way to extract roots:

Example:

What is the fifth root of **17**?

Solution:

This is equivalent to $17^{1/5}$, so

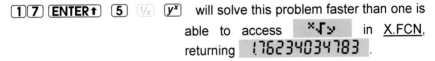

$\boxed{1}\boxed{7}$ $\boxed{\text{ENTER↑}}$ $\boxed{5}$ $\boxed{1/x}$ $\boxed{y^x}$ will solve this problem faster than one is able to access $\boxed{^x\!\sqrt{y}}$ in X.FCN, returning $\boxed{1.76234034783}$.

Again, it may pay if you leave also label **B** undefined to allow for using the shortcut $\boxed{1/x}$ top left.

Let us return to Fukushima for a final and more down-to-earth application of powers and logs:

Example:

Locations in a distance of 30 km to the nuclear plant being devastated by the tsunami in March 2011 showed radioactivity in the soil of some 1...3 MBq / m^2 corresponding to an annual radiation dose of 4 mSv in 2013. Assume this is mainly caused by ^{137}Cs; this radioactive isotope has a half-life of 30.2 years. To the best of our knowledge today, an unborn child shall not receive more than 1 mSv before birth. So when will it be reasonably safe to allow the evacuated inhabitants of the villages in that area returning to their homes finally?

Solution:

Assuming there will be no further nuclear accidents in that area and no special measures will be taken, the isotopes set free will stubbornly decay following the inescapable laws of physics. So the (radio-) activity **a** at an arbitrary time **t** will be

$$a = a_0 \times 2^{-(t/T_{1/2})} .$$

$$\text{Hence,} \quad t = T_{1/2} \times lb\left(\frac{a_0}{a}\right).$$

1 mSv in nine months corresponds to an annual dose of $4/3$ mSv. Since 4 divided by $4/3$ equals 3, and

[FIX] [0] [0]

[3] [LB]

[3] [0] [.] [2] [x]   returns   48. *years,*

you can estimate reproductive people shall rather not live in that area earlier than 2061. Elderly inhabitants may return far sooner.

> Note there are different limits considered "reasonably safe" for the public by different national authorities. If an <u>annual</u> dose of 1 mSv would be the limit, people shall be kept out of that area for two half-lifes of the dominant isotope, i.e. 60 *years,* instead.

There are further risks linked to agriculture in that area – they are beyond the scope of this simple example though.

Please note this is a worst case scenario. Actually, radioactivity will be washed to deeper layers of earth with time, reducing the activity seen at the surface. And there are mitigation efforts in the area (many km^2): the contamination shall be washed off houses and trees, and the top layers of soil shall be removed, storing them in bags 'elsewhere'. Success of these efforts will reduce the waiting time calculated above; failure will not extend it at least. Today (2016) it is too early to assess.

None of these efforts and effects, however, can ever reduce the physical half-life of the radioactive isotopes set free in this nuclear accident. Note quite similar considerations are necessary in the matter of nuclear waste – at the bottom line, there are greater amounts of radioactive material decaying with half-lifes exceeding thousand years; and this means you have to 'put it away' safely for really long times – a task that was kept under wraps for decades but was not solved by waiting.

Real Stuff – 6: Functions for Probability and Statistics

Besides the basic functions % and Δ% , you will find many statistical commands in your *WP 34S*, going far beyond the *Gaussian distribution*. They are all concentrated in the light green frame shown in the picture.

Many preprogrammed operations were implemented in your *WP 34S* for the first time ever in an *RPN* calculator – we packed-in everything we always had missed.

The labels to the right of the broken line cover sample statistics. The six labels left of it deal with general probability.

! , Cy,x , and Py,x stand for *x!*, COMB, and PERM as introduced above. – Two thirds of the following example are taken from the *HP-32E OH* of 1978:

Example:

Willie's Widget Works wants to take photographs of its product line for advertising. How many different ways can the photographer arrange their eight widget models?

Solution:

The total number of possible arrangements is given by the *factorial* $8 \times 7 \times 6 \times 5 \times 4 \times 3 \times 2 \times 1 = 8!$

FIX 0 0

8 !   returns   **40,320.**   for the total number of arrangements possible.

Example (continued):

The photographer looks through his viewfinder and decides that he can show only five widgets if his camera is to capture the intricate details of the widgets ... How many different sets of five widgets can he select from the eight?

Solution:

The number of sets equals the number of possible *combinations*.

⑧ **ENTER↑** ⑤ C y.x   returns   **56.**   for the number of sets.

Example (continued):

Again, there are different arrangements feasible. How many pictures of different widget arrangements are possible within these limits?

Solution:

The number of arrangements is $5 \times 4 \times 3 \times 2 \times 1 = 5!$ according to what was stated above. Thus,

⑤ ⌷   returns   **120.**   and

⊠   returns   **6,720.**   for the number of significantly different pictures.

This is the number of possible *permutations* of 5 items out of 8. It can be obtained in one step by keying in ⑧ **ENTER↑** ⑤ P y.x.

The shifted functions of ④ cover statistical distributions: *standard normal* Φ and its inverse Φ⁻¹, as well as PROB containing nine more continuous distributions and three discrete ones. All these functions have a few features in common:

- Discrete statistical distributions (*Poisson, binomial,* and *geometric*) are confined to integers. Whenever your *WP 34S* sums up a *probability mass function* (*PMF* [66]) $p(n)$ to get a *cumulated distribution function* (CDF) $F(m)$ it starts at $n = 0$. Thus,

---

[66] In a nutshell, discrete statistical distributions deal with "events" governed by a known mathematical model. Such events may be persons entering a store, radioactive nuclei decaying, faulty parts showing up, etc. The *PMF* then tells the probability to observe a certain number of such events, e.g. 7. And the *CDF* gives the probability to observe up to 7 such events, but not more.

For doing statistics with continuous statistical variables – e.g. the heights of three-year-old toddlers – similar rules apply: Assume we know the applicable mathematical model. Then the respective *CDF* gives the probability for their heights being less than an arbitrary limit value, for example less than $1m$. And the corresponding *PDF* tells how these heights are distributed in a sample of e.g. 1000 children of this age.

  BEWARE: This is a very rudimentary sketch of this topic only – turn to a good textbook about statistics to learn dealing with it properly.

Translator's note: The terms *PMF* and *PDF* translate to German „Dichtefunktion bzw. Wahrscheinlichkeitsdichte", *CDF* to „Verteilungsfunktion bzw. Wahrscheinlichkeitsverteilung".

$$F(m) = \sum_{n=0}^{m} p(n) = P(m) .$$

- Integrating a <u>continuous</u> *probability density function* (PDF) $f(x)$ to get a *CDF* $F(x)$ typically works as

$$F(x) = \int_{-\infty}^{x} f(\xi) d\xi = P(x) .$$

- Many frequently used continuous *PDF*s look more or less like the ones drawn here. The corresponding *CDF*s are shown overleaf, using the same scale and colors. Typically, any *CDF* starts with a slope of almost zero, becomes steeper then, and runs out with its slope returning to zero.

This holds even if the respective *PDF* does not

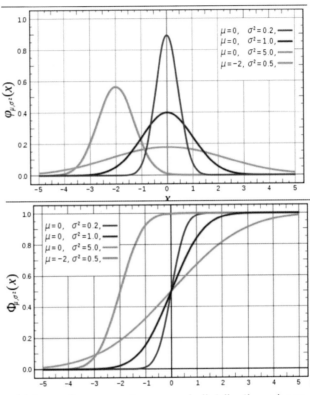

look as nicely symmetric as the sample *normal distributions* here. Obviously, you will get the most precise results on the left side of the *CDF* using P. On its right side, however, where P approaches 1, the *error probability* Q is more precise. Thus, also Q is computed in your *WP 34S* for each distribution, independent of P. The definitions are:

- for discrete distributions (see p. 99): $Q(m) = \sum_{n=m}^{\infty} p(n)$,

- for continuous distributions: $Q(x) = \int_{x}^{\infty} f(\xi) d\xi$.

- On your *WP 34S*, with an arbitrary *CDF* named **XY(x)** you will find the name

  XY$_u$ (x) for its *error probability* Q (also known as upper tail probability for obvious reasons), if applicable,

  XY^{-1}(p) for the inverse of the *CDF* (the so-called *quantile function* or *QF*),[67] and

  XY$_p$ (x) for its *PDF* or *PMF*.

For long names, the parameter *x* or *p* must be omitted since command names must not exceed six characters. This naming convention holds for **binom**ial, **Cauch**y (a.k.a. *Lorentz* or *Breit-Wigner*), **expon**ential, *Fisher's* **F**, **geom**etric, **log-norm**al, **logis**tic, **norm**al, **Poiss**on, *Student's* **t**, and **Weibull** distributions. For reasons of tradition, *standard normal* (*Gaussian*) and *Chi-square* distributions are named differently. See the *catalog* <u>PROB</u> (on p. 255) and the respective entries in the *IOP* (on pp. 183ff). Some mathematical background is found in *App. I* on pp. 375ff.

There are also plenty of commands for sample statistics featured on your *WP 34S*, applicable in one or two dimensions. All these are located to the right of key ④ on the keyboard:

- For accumulating sample data – typically counted or measured values – use ⟨Σ+⟩ (after clearing the summation registers by ⟨CLΣ⟩) as on previous scientific calculators; weighted data require the weight in Y, pairs of data or coordinates of data points must be provided in X and Y as usual. ⟨Σ-⟩ is provided for easy data correction.[68]

- Regarding the analysis functions provided, you will find the *arithmetic mean* ⟨x̄⟩ and *standard deviation* ⟨s⟩ handy on the keyboard, as well as a forecasting function ⟨ŷ⟩ and the *correlation coefficient* ⟨r⟩ (see CORR) for four different regression models

---

[67] The *HP-21S* returns Q instead of P for its four statistical distributions. Thus, also the inverse works differently there. Be aware of that when comparing results of the *F*, *t*, *Gaussian*, and χ^2 distributions.

[68] Note that ⟨Σ+⟩ and ⟨Σ-⟩ operate on a set of fourteen summation registers – they suffice for calculating all the statistical functions provided and more (although the individual data points are not available anymore after pressing ⟨Σ+⟩ or ⟨Σ-⟩).

And you may use ⟨A⟩ (also labeled ⟨Σ+⟩) instead of ⟨Σ+⟩ as long as label A is not used in the current program (see below).

(linear, exponential, logarithmic, and power – see the commands LINF, EXPF, LOGF, and POWERF). Many more functions (such as *standard errors*, *covariances*, means and standard deviations for weighted data, standard deviations for *populations*, curve fit parameters, *geometric means* and *scattering factors*) are in <u>STAT</u>, and all the accumulated data are in <u>SUMS</u> – just look them up in these *catalogs* (see p. 255) and then check the respective entries in the *IOP* on pp. 171ff.

Example:

Since many of our customers live in a country where long range weapons play a greater role than in most civilized societies, let us use the following explanatory example: *Archibald* is champion of the *Golden Bow*, his archers club. In his standard exercise, aiming at a black target disk of 1.5*m* diameter at a distance of 50*m*, his arrows scatter symmetrically around the center of the target with quite a small variance. Actually, *Archibald's* statistics show his arrows having a standard deviation (SD) of 1 *foot* at that distance. Assume his shots are distributed normally around the center, how often must he walk further than 50*m* to collect an arrow?

Solution:

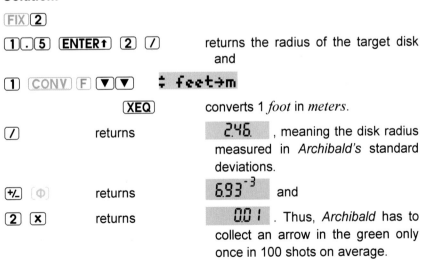

FIX 2

1 . 5 ENTER↑ 2 ÷   returns the radius of the target disk and

1 CONV F ▼ ▼   ÷ feet→m

          XEQ   converts 1 *foot* in *meters*.

÷   returns   2.46   , meaning the disk radius measured in *Archibald's* standard deviations.

+/– Φ   returns 6.93^{-3} and

2 ×   returns   0.01. Thus, *Archibald* has to collect an arrow in the green only once in 100 shots on average.

Example (continued):

One of his competitors, *Bill*, also sends his arrows into the target with his hits scattering symmetrically around the center. He, however, has to pick up about one out of fifteen arrows in the green on average. What is his SD in the target plane?

Solution:

[FIX] [3]

[1] [5] [1/x]   returns

| 0.067 | , i.e. about 7% of Bill's arrows miss the target disk.

[2] [/]

| 0.033 | , ~3% on either side.

[Φ⁻¹]

| - 1.834 | , the corresponding lower limit of the standardized normal distribution.

[+/-] [.] [7] [5] [x≷y] [/]

| 0.409 | m. Just store it since we will need that again soon:

[STO] [0] [0]

And note that the SD of Archibald's arrows is just ...

[1] [CONV] [XEQ]

(converts 1 *foot* in *meters* again)

[Δ%]

| -25.47 | % better than Bill's, but his number of misses is more than ten times lower than Bill's.

There are applications of this methodology in industry as well, where the scattering or variation of a process (e.g. in production) is compared with its tolerance limits. Resulting from such comparisons, so-called *capability indices* can be calculated directly linked to the amount of scrap to be expected in said process. Please consult applicable literature and standards – look for *process capability*.

On the other hand, we may continue our example as is, leading you over the border of advanced statistics.

Example (continued):

Bill quietly practiced in a *Zen* cloister during his summer vacation. Returning, he went to the *Golden Bow* immediately on next weekend, and sent 50 arrows to his club's standard disk. Only two missed with one of them scratching the very edge of the disk. Cheers! Though, is this just a lucky chance success or probably a consequence of his extra training efforts?

Solution:

Calculate *Bill's* new SD:

⬭1⬭⬭.⬭⬭5⬭ ⬭ENTER↑⬭ ⬭5⬭⬭0⬭ ⬭/⬭

⬭2⬭ ⬭/⬭　　　　　returns　　　　　 0.015 , i.e. 1.5% misses on either side.

⬭Φ⁻¹⬭　　　　　returns　　　　　 -2.170 , the corresponding lower limit of the standardized normal distribution.

⬭+/-⬭ ⬭.⬭⬭7⬭⬭5⬭ ⬭xᶻy⬭ ⬭/⬭　 0.346 *m*. Now, is this *significantly* better than his previous SD?

It is better (based on a *confidence level* of 95%) if it is lower than the 95% *confidence limit* of the old SD. We assume the old SD was calculated based on 60 shots. Then the formula for its single-sided lower 95% confidence limit reads:

$$\sigma_L = s_o \times \sqrt{\frac{59}{\left(\chi^2_{59,0.95}\right)^{-1}}}$$

The expression in the denominator is the *inverse chi-square* for a probability of 95% and a *degree of freedom* of 59. Calculate inside out as usual:

⬭5⬭⬭9⬭ ⬭STO⬭⬭J⬭　　　　Store the degrees of freedom.

⬭.⬭⬭9⬭⬭5⬭ ⬭PROB⬭⬭g⬭⬭H⬭⬭▼⬭ ⬌ x^2INV

　　　　　⬭XEQ⬭　　　 calls the inverse chi-square as required, returning 77.931 .

⬭1/x⬭ ⬭5⬭⬭9⬭ ⬭×⬭　returns　　 0.757 .

⬭√x⬭　　　　　　　　　 0.870 .

⬭RCL⬭⬭0⬭⬭0⬭ ⬭×⬭　returns　　 0.356 *m*.

Bill's training really made a difference! Well … with 95% confidence. If we had required 99% confidence instead, the lower confidence limit had been 0.337 *m* – then *Bill's* weekend result would have been insufficient for a *significant* improvement.[69]

---

[69] Statistics may mean you might have more doubts than without – but such is life: doubts increase with knowledge.

Real Stuff – 7: More Problem Solving Using Statistics

To get an idea of the possibilities provided by your *WP 34S* and of some constraints inherent to statistics, see the sample applications shown here. All of them are demonstrated employing the traditional 4-level *stack* but will work with the 8-level stack as well.

Appl. 1a: Acquiring and analyzing sample data

Dealing with multiple measurements or counts, you can accumulate these data for drawing some conclusions later. Use ⟨Σ+⟩ for adding data to the statistical registers. Actually, easing accumulations and statistical evaluations was one of the big benefits electronic calculators carried with them when introduced.

When you press ⟨Σ+⟩, your *WP 34S* will use the data being present in x and y to update the 14 statistical registers. Without going into details, this update will be done in a way allowing later evaluation of the various sums in order to calculate means, standard deviations, correlations, regression curves, etc. One of those registers is just incremented by one: it holds the number of data points you have entered so far. ⟨Σ+⟩ returns this number in X leaving all other *stack* levels unchanged. L is loaded with previous x.

The next numeric input will overwrite x.

Before starting accumulations, do not forget to reset the statistical registers using ⟨CLΣ⟩. And you will benefit from label **A** being undefined on your *WP 34S* – so you can use the shortcut ⟨Σ+⟩ top left.

If any data entry error is recognized after pressing ⟨Σ+⟩ or ⟨Σ+⟩, you can remove said false values entered via ⟨Σ−⟩ and enter the correct ones instead.

The following example was first published in the *HP-55 OH* of 1975 – you might become nostalgic looking at the numbers.

> **Example:**
>
> In a recent survey to determine the age and net worth (in millions of dollars) of six of the 50 wealthiest persons in the United States, the following data were obtained (sampled). Calculate the average age and net worth of the sample, and calculate the standard deviations for these two sets of data.

Age	62	58	62	73	84	68	59	47	60	71
Net Worth	1200	1500	1450	1950	1000	1750	1350	1250	1300	1100

Solution:

First, we have to accumulate these data:

CLΣ

6 2	ENTER↑	1 2 0 0	Σ+	returns	1.
5 8	ENTER↑	1 5 0 0	Σ+	returns	2.
6 2	ENTER↑	1 4 5 0	Σ+	returns	3.
7 3	ENTER↑	1 9 5 0	Σ+	returns	4.
8 4	ENTER↑	2 0 0 0	Σ+	returns	5.
6 8	ENTER↑	1 7 5 0	Σ+	returns	6.

Oh, that senior was not <u>that</u> rich!

8 4	ENTER↑	2 0 0 0	Σ−	returns	5.
8 4	ENTER↑	1 0 0 0	Σ+	returns	6.
5 9	ENTER↑	1 3 5 0	Σ+	returns	7.
4 7	ENTER↑	1 2 5 0	Σ+	returns	8.
6 0	ENTER↑	1 3 0 0	Σ+	returns	9.
7 1	ENTER↑	1 1 0 0	Σ+	returns	10.

We will continue with this dataset below.

For the arithmetic mean or average of the data you accumulated, simply press x̄. It will return both the mean of your *x*-data in **X** and the mean of your *y*-data in **Y** at once. And the sample standard deviation (a measure for the spread or scattering of your data) is returned via s – again just one keystroke for both *x*- and *y*-data accumulated.

Solution (continued):

One decimal shall do for this evaluation:

FIX 0 1

x̄	returns	1385.0	for the mean net worth and
x⇄y		64.4	for the average age in this sample.

[s]	returns	`290.6`	for the sample standard deviation of net worth and
[x⇄y]		`10.1`	for the sample standard deviation of age.

If the ten persons used in the sample were actually the *ten wealthiest persons*, the data would have to be considered statistically as a population rather than as a sample. Then the *population standard deviation σ* had to be used instead of the *sample standard deviation s*.

Solution (continued):

[STAT] [g] [S]   ÷ σ

[XEQ]	returns	`275.7`	for the population standard deviation of net worth and
[x⇄y]	returns	`9.6`	for the population standard deviation of age.

Actually, you can draw further conclusions from these calculated average and standard deviation values, using the laws of statistics. We recommend reading a good textbook to learn about it.

Appl. 1b: Correlations, Regressions, Extrapolations, and Interpolations

You might be interested whether particular *x*- and *y*-data correlate. Your *WP 34S* supports ways to check this. *Regression* is a statistical method for finding a curve that best fits a set of data points, thus showing a relationship between two variables (see *Appendix J* for the mathematical formulas). Once your pairs of *x*- and *y*-data are accumulated in the statistical registers, you can check this data set:

Example (continued):

Do age and net worth correlate in the sample of Appl. 1a?

Solution:

Calculate the parameters of the curve best fitting the sample data using the least squares method:

[MODE] [B]   ÷ BestF

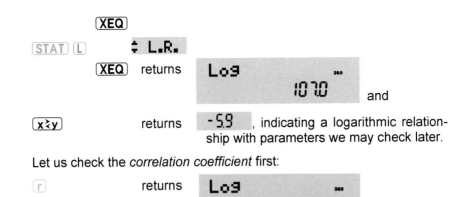

STAT L ÷ **L.R.**

XEQ returns **Log** and

x⤸y returns **-5.9** , indicating a logarithmic relationship with parameters we may check later.

Let us check the *correlation coefficient* first:

r returns **Log** **-0.1** .

Its square is called the *coefficient of determination*:

x² returns **1.4⁻²** , meaning that for these ten
persons, only about 1.4% of the variation
of net worth is determined by age. Forget
further searching for correlation here!

We found another linear regression example in calculator owner's
handbooks of 1976 through 1978. It reads typical for the thinking at
that time (looks like it was also a time before CEOs and large staffs
became fashionable):

Example:

Big *Lyle Hephaestus*,[70] owner-operator of the *Hephaestus Oil Company*,
wishes to know the slope and y-intercept of a least squares line for the
consumption of motor fuel in the United States against time since 1945.
He knows the data given in the table.

Motor fuel demand (millions of *barrels*)	696	994	1330	1512	1750	2162	2243	2382	2484
Year	1945	1950	1955	1960	1965	1970	1971	1972	1973

Solution:

Hephaestus could draw a plot of motor fuel demand against time.
However, with his *WP 34S*, *Hephaestus* has only to key the data into the
calculator using the Σ+ key, then press STAT L XEQ .

---

[70] Maybe his ancestors emigrated from Greece, since *Hephaistos* is the ancient Greek
god of fire.

CLΣ

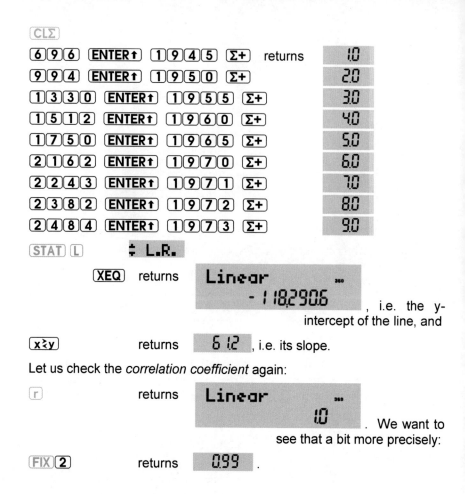

696 ENTER↑ 194.5 Σ+   returns   *1.0*

994 ENTER↑ 1950 Σ+   *2.0*

1330 ENTER↑ 1955 Σ+   *3.0*

1512 ENTER↑ 1960 Σ+   *4.0*

1750 ENTER↑ 1965 Σ+   *5.0*

2162 ENTER↑ 1970 Σ+   *6.0*

2243 ENTER↑ 1971 Σ+   *7.0*

2382 ENTER↑ 1972 Σ+   *8.0*

2484 ENTER↑ 1973 Σ+   *9.0*

STAT L   ⇵ **L.R.**

      XEQ   returns   **Linear**   *-118,290.6* , i.e. the y-intercept of the line, and

x⇄y   returns   *6.12* , i.e. its slope.

Let us check the *correlation coefficient* again:

r   returns   **Linear**   *1.0* . We want to see that a bit more precisely:

FIX 2   returns   *0.99* .

With these data in the statistical registers and such a good correlation, extrapolations may make sense.

Example (continued):

If *Hephaestus* wishes to predict the demand for motor fuel for the years 1980 and 2000, he keys in the new *x* values and presses ŷ. Similarly, to determine the year that the demand for motor fuel is expected to pass 3 500 million *barrels*, *Hephaestus* keys in **3 500** (the new value for *y*) and presses STAT X ▼ ▼ XEQ (calling 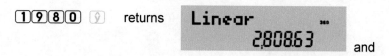).

1980 ŷ   returns   **Linear**   *2,808.63*   and

2️⃣0️⃣0️⃣0️⃣ ⓨ returns **Linear** ▪▪▪ **4,03 185** . These are the predicted (extrapolated) demands for 1980 and 2000.

3️⃣5️⃣0️⃣0️⃣ (STAT) (X) (▼)(▼) ⁑ x̂

(XEQ) returns **1,99 130** – the demand was expected to pass 3.5 billion *barrels* during 1992.

By the way, *Hephaestus* was a busy man – he could have saved more than twenty keystrokes in solving this problem by omitting the leading '19' in the year's data.

Note that some sets of data points consist of a series of *x*-values (or *y*-values) that differ from each other by a comparatively small amount. You can maximize the precision of any statistical calculation involving such data by keying in only the differences between each value and a number close to the average of the values. This number must be added to the result of calculating x̄, x̂, ŷ, or the y-intercept of **L.R.** then. For example, if your *x*-values consist of 665 999, 666 000, and 666 001, you should enter the data as -1, 0, and 1. If afterwards you calculate x̄, add 666 000 to the answer. In some cases your *WP 34S* cannot compute s, r, **L.R.**, ŷ, or x̂ with data values that are too close to each other; and if you attempt to do so, your *WP 34S* will throw an error. This will not happen, however, if you normalize the data as described above.

The predicting or extrapolating functions ŷ and x̂ can be used for linear interpolations as well, e.g. if you have two values in a table and need a third one in between.

Six years after *Hephaestus'* first appearance (and after at least two name changes of said exemplary oil company and its owner-operator), the linear regression example was modified. We read in the *HP-10C Owner's Handbook*:

Example:

Electrical energy researcher *Helen I. Voltz* suspects a possible relationship between the rise in worldwide coal production in the years 1972 through 1976 and a similar rise in worldwide electricity output for the same period. To assist in a study of the data, *Voltz* will use her *WP 34S* to accumulate the coal production (*y*) and electrical output (*x*) statistics.

Year	1972	1973	1974	1975	1976
Coal production (*Gt*)	1.761	1.775	1.792	1.884	1.946
Electricity output (*TWh*)	5.552	5.963	6.136	6.313	6.713

And in 1987, the respective example in the *HP-15C Owner's Handbook* reads:

Example:

Agronomist *Silas Farmer* has developed a new variety of high-yield rice, and has measured the plant's yield rate as a function of fertilization. Use the $\boxed{\Sigma+}$ function to accumulate the data below ... for nitrogen fertilizer application (*x*) versus grain yield (*y*).

Nitrogen applied (*kg/ha*)	0	20	40	60	80
Grain yield (*t/ha*)	4.63	5.78	6.61	7.21	7.78

Solutions:

Solving these two problems follows the same methodology as explained in the previous example. We leave it to you though we provide *Helen's* and *Silas'* results for comparison with yours:

Helen: y-intercept = 0.78, slope = 0.17, correlation coefficient = 0.92.

Silas: y-intercept = 4.86, slope = 0.04, correlation coefficient = 0.99.

Appl. 2: Scrap rate, confidence limits

Assume you own a little tool shop and want to know the quality of the parts you produce. You drew a *representative sample* of nominally equal parts and precisely measured their real sizes.

Example:

10 pins drawn from a production batch, diameters measured: 12.356, 12.362, 12.360, 12.364, 12.340, 12.345, 12.342, 12.344, 12.355, and 12.353. From earlier large scale investigations, it is known that diameters from this production process follow a *Gaussian distribution*.

How can you know your batch will be ok? That is easy, based upon analysis of that sample.

First, you shall know your objective: Do you want to know what pin diameters you will get? Statistics cannot tell you about all of them here but it will tell you where to find almost all (e.g. 99%) of them.

Example (continued):

Clear the summation registers, set the display to show three decimals, and accumulate the ten values measured (it pays to use the shortcut Ⓐ = (Σ+) as long as possible, cf. the *IOP* on p. 232):

(CLΣ)

(FIX) **3**

12.356 (Σ+)	*1.000*
12.362 (Σ+)	*2.000*
12.360 (Σ+)	*3.000*
12.364 (Σ+)	*4.000*
12.340 (Σ+)	*5.000*
12.345 (Σ+)	*6.000*
12.342 (Σ+)	*7.000*
12.344 (Σ+)	*8.000*
12.355 (Σ+)	*9.000*
12.353 (Σ+)	*10.000*

By knowing these pin diameters are from a *Gaussian* process, you get the best estimates for the mean and standard deviation of your batch by pressing

$\overline{x}$ (STO)(J)   *12.352*   and

s (STO)(K)   *0.009* .

Note we have already stored these two values where they belong for the next step.

So, based on the ten pins analyzed, you can expect only 0.5% of all pins showing diameters smaller than

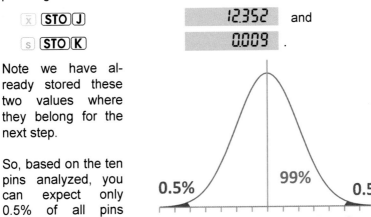

0.005 PROB O▲ ≑ Norml⁻¹

XEQ   *12.330*

and another 0.5% showing diameters greater than

0.995 PROB   ≑ Norml⁻¹

XEQ   *12.375* .

If you observe *significantly*[71] more or less than these percentages then your production (or measuring) process has changed.

Are you interested in the mean pin diameter of your batch? Do you want to know both upper and lower limits confining the mean pin diameter of that batch with a probability of e.g. 95%?[72] Then determine the applicable sample mean value and its variation. Use them to find said limits.

Example (continued):

Since it is a *Gaussian* process, the <u>arithmetic</u> mean is applicable, the standard error tells its variation, and *Student's t* is needed. For that we need its *degrees of freedom*. Press …

SUMS   ≑ nΣ

            XEQ   *10.000*

1 ⊟ STO J   *9.000*

STAT S ▼   ≑ SERR

            XEQ   *0.003*

Having 95% inside means having 2.5% outside at either end of the bell curve. Thus generally one must take 0.025 and 0.975 as arguments in two subsequent calculations using the *QF* to get both limits below and above the sample result:

0.025 PROB U▲ ≑ t⁻¹(ₚ)

            XEQ   *-2.262*

⊠   *-0.006*

x̄   *12.352*

---

[71] Note the term '*significant*' is well defined in statistics – this definition may deviate from common language, however.

[72] This value of 95% is called the *confidence level* of this calculation. Here, we calculate the 95% *confidence limits* for the mean value. 99% are frequently applied as well.

$\boxed{x \geq y}$ $\boxed{R\downarrow}$ [73] $\boxed{x \geq y}$	-0.006
$\boxed{+}$	12.346 = lower limit.
$\boxed{RCL}\boxed{L}$	-0.006 = last x
$2 \boxed{x} \boxed{-}$	12.358 = upper limit.[74]

Now you know you can expect the mean diameter of such a batch between the *confidence limits* 12.346 and 12.358 – with a confidence of 95%. I.e. there will be a chance of 2.5% that the mean will be smaller than 12.346 and an equal chance that it will be greater than 12.358.

These chances are an inevitable consequence of the fact that you know something about a *sample* only (being a limited, usually small number of specimens drawn from a population), but want or have to tell something about said total population.[75] If you cannot live with these chances or the widths of the confidence limits, do not blame statistics but collect more (or more precise) data instead.

Appl. 3: Quick measuring system analysis

Your colleagues in R&D have specified that a particle accelerator beam pipe shall have a magnetic susceptibility less than 0.01. How can you verify whether or not the measuring instrument available in your shop is sufficiently precise to do the control job for those tubes?

1. Collect 30 samples of material covering the susceptibility range you are interested in[76] (e.g. here from 0 to about 0.015). Mark them unambiguously (e.g. by numbers).

2. Use the instrument under investigation to measure all samples carefully under controlled conditions. Record as many decimals as possible. Write each measured value in a table next to the respective sample number.

---

[73] $\boxed{\bar{x}}$ returns two numbers: $\bar{x}$ and $\bar{y}$. Only $\bar{x}$ is interesting in this example. Pressing $\boxed{x \geq y}$ $\boxed{R\downarrow}$ moves $\bar{y}$ quickly out of the way here.

[74] The upper limit can be calculated this easy way since $t^{-1}(p)$ is symmetric.

[75] Statisticians call these chances '*probabilities of a type I error*' or '*probabilities of an error of the first kind*'.

[76] Note there is no need to know the <u>exact</u> parameters of these samples beforehand – they shall just fall in said range and must be robust enough to stay constant in repeated measurements. Actually, this method works best with random samples you collect without knowing their exact parameters yet.

3. Measure a second time, but following another sample sequence. Don't look at the values measured in step 2!! Write each second measured value behind the first one of the respective sample.

4. Clear the summation registers by [CLΣ]. Then enter all 30 pairs of data using [Σ+]. The first measurement value shall be y, the second x for each sample.

5. It is recommended to plot those 30 points (even manual plotting on quadrille paper will do). Usually, the diagram should look like an ant trail around the center line $y = x$. [77] Find the most distant point (x, y) from said line. Remove it from the data set using [Σ−].

6. Let your *WP 34S* fit a straight line through the remaining 29 points. Then compute $c_0 = \dfrac{T}{30 s_x s_y} \sqrt{\dfrac{s_x^2 + r^2 s_y^2}{1 - r^2}}$ with T being the width of the tolerance zone:

[MODE] [L]	‡ LinF	select the linear fit model.
[XEQ]		
[r] [x²] [STO] 00		get the *coefficient of correlation* and store its square.
[s] [x²]		get s_x^2.
[R↓]		shift it out of the way.
[x²] [×] [R↑] [+]		calculate the numerator.

The last three steps may have looked a bit obscure. Thus we show what has happened on the *stack* there:

T			s_x^2	s_x^2	s_x^2	s_x^2	s_x^2
Z	r^2	r^2			s_x^2		s_x^2
Y	s_y	s_y	r^2	r^2		$r^2 s_y^2$	
X	s_x	s_x^2	s_y	s_y^2	$r^2 s_y^2$	s_x^2	$s_x^2 + r^2 s_y^2$
	[s]	[x²]	[R↓]	[x²]	[×]	[R↑]	[+]

Although we demonstrated it for a traditional 4-level *stack* here, it will work for an 8-level *stack* as well.

Now let us calculate the denominator:

---

[77] Go to an expert if the diagram deviates significantly from this picture.

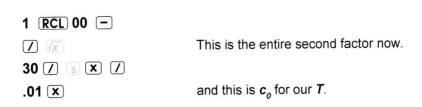

1 [RCL] **00** [−]

[/] [√x̄]   This is the entire second factor now.

30 [/] [s] [×] [/]

.01 [×]   and this is c_0 for our **T**.

For $c_0 \geq 1$ this instrument may be used for controlling this tolerance zone under those conditions – else strive for a more precise instrument, better measuring conditions, or a wider tolerance zone.

Appl. 4: Significant changes

Assume you are dealing with an industrial process producing particular products in series. You have taken a representative sample of several specimens out of that process at day 1 for proof what is going on there. Then you have changed the process parameters, waited for stabilization, and have taken another sample of same size at day 2. Being serious, you have thoroughly measured and recorded the critical value (e.g. a characteristic dimension) for each specimen investigated at both days. Now the question: do the results of both samples show any *significant difference*?

The following simple three-step test is well established. It may easily save yourself some unwanted embarrassments in your next presentation or after your next publication: [78]

1. Let your *WP 34S* compute $\bar{x}$ and the *standard error* s_E for both

   samples, then their *normalized distance* $d = \dfrac{\left|\bar{x}_1 - \bar{x}_2\right|}{\sqrt{s_{E1}^2 + s_{E2}^2}}$. Working

   with <u>four</u> *stack* levels, this calculation could look like the following:

   [STAT] [S]   ↕ **SERR**

            [XEQ]   returns both standard errors in **X** and **Y**.

   [x²] [x⇄y] [x²] [+] [√x̄]   This is the complete denominator now.

---

[78] This test goes back to *DGQ* (*Deutsche Gesellschaft für Qualität*). It assumes your data are drawn from a Gaussian process, which is frequently the case in real life (but needs to be checked). Note the term '*significant*' is well defined in statistics – this definition may deviate from common language. – Generally, standard confidence limits and levels, also those defined for indicating *significant differences*, may depend on the country or industry you are working in. Be sure to check the applicable valid standards before simply copying the example calculations shown here.

$\boxed{\bar{x}}$ $\boxed{-}$ $\boxed{|x|}$ This is the absolute value of the difference of both mean values (remember $\boxed{\bar{x}}$ recalls them both). Thus, this is the numerator required.

$\boxed{x \gtrless y}$ $\boxed{/}$ $\boxed{\text{STO}}$ $\boxed{D}$ And this is d.

Also provide the *degrees of freedom* for the next two steps:

$\boxed{\text{SUMS}}$ **≑ n∑**

         $\boxed{\text{XEQ}}$ recalls the number of specimens measured.

1 $\boxed{-}$ $\boxed{\text{STO}}$ $\boxed{J}$ calculates the *degrees of freedom* and stores them for the next step.

2. Let your *WP 34S* calculate the critical limit t_{cr} of *Student's t* for f *degrees of freedom* and a probability of 97.5% now:

.975

     $\boxed{\text{PROB}}$ $\boxed{U}\boxed{\blacktriangle}$ **≑ t⁻¹(p)**   As mentioned above, the requested *QF* lives in <u>PROB</u>.

         $\boxed{\text{XEQ}}$ executes this function, taking the *degrees of freedom* stored in **J** to get t_{cr}.

If $d < t_{cr}$ then the test indicates the difference between both samples being due to random deviations only. Congratulations – you have got a robust process regarding the parameters you changed.

3. Let your *WP 34S* compute the new critical limit t_{cs} for f and 99.5% now:

     .995 $\boxed{\text{PROB}}$ **≑ t⁻¹(p)** Note this function showing up immediately when opening <u>PROB</u> again.

         $\boxed{\text{XEQ}}$ get t_{cs}.

If $d \geq t_{cs}$ then the test indicates a *significant difference* between both samples. Congratulations – your parameter change caused an effect.

For $t_{cr} \leq d < t_{cs}$, however, you simply cannot decide based on the information provided – your samples may contain too little data or your measurements were not precise enough or the process is scattering too far – so do not let your audience lead you into temptation: you better stay silent or mumble something like "investigation in progress" at the utmost.

We strongly recommend you turn to a good statistics textbook for more information about statistical methods in general, the terminology used, and the mathematical models provided.

Real Stuff – 8: Flight Directions, Courses over Ground, and more Vectors in 2D

Having learned about →P and →R as well as about Σ+ and Σ–, we can profit from combining these functions. Here is an example, taken from the *HP-21 Owner's Handbook* of 1975:

Example:

The instruments in fearless bush pilot *Apeneck Sweeney's* converted P-41 indicate an air speed of 125 *knots* and a heading of 225°. However the aircraft is also being buffeted by a steady 25-*knot* wind that is blowing from north to south. What is the actual course and speed of the aircraft?

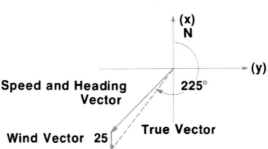

Solution:

Combine the vector indicated on the aircraft instruments with the wind vector to yield the actual course and speed. Convert the vectors to rectangular, then combine the *x*- and *y*-coordinates in the statistical summation registers. Finally, recall the summed *x*- and *y*-coordinates and convert them to polar coordinates giving the actual vector of the aircraft. (North becomes the *x*-coordinate in order that the problem corresponds with navigational convention.)

CLΣ   clears the summation registers.

FIX 2

2 2 5 ENTER↑ 1 2 5   indicated air speed and heading.

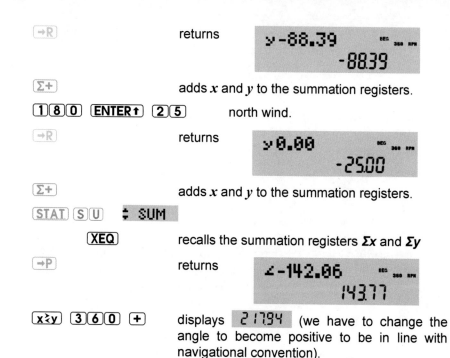

| ⇥R | returns | y-88.39 BEG 360 RPM -88.39 |

| Σ+ | adds x and y to the summation registers. |

1 8 0 ENTER↑ 2 5   north wind.

| ⇥R | returns | y0.00 BEG 360 RPM -25.00 |

| Σ+ | adds x and y to the summation registers. |

STAT S U   ‡ SUM

XEQ   recalls the summation registers Σx and Σy

| ⇥P | returns | ∠-142.06 BEG 360 RPM 143.77 |

x⇄y 3 6 0 +   displays 217.94 (we have to change the angle to become positive to be in line with navigational convention).

So, Mr. *Sweeney* is actually flying at 143.77 *knots* on a course of 217.94° over ground.[79]

This example appeared modified in the *HP-55 Owner's Handbook* of 1975 and was copied then for some years in this form. We quote the respective drawing from the *HP-19C/HP-29C OHPG* of 1977 and the corresponding text from the *HP-33E Owner's Handbook* of 1978:

Example:

On his way to search for an albino caribou, grizzled bush pilot *Apeneck Sweeney's* converted *Swordfish* aircraft has a true air speed of 150 *knots* and an estimated heading of 45°. The *Swordfish* is also being buffeted by a headwind of 40 *knots* from a bearing of 25°. What is the actual ground speed and course of the *Swordfish*?

Start of solution:

Method 1: The course and ground speed are equal to the <u>difference</u> of the two vectors.

---

[79] See p. 133 for another method to calculate this kind of 2D vector problems.

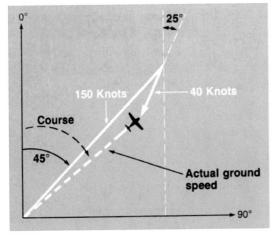

Method 2: Taking into account that a bearing of 25° equals a heading of 25° + 180° = 205°, the corresponding headwind vector may be added (cf. the *HP-97 OHPG* of 1978).

We leave it to you to solve this problem using $\boxed{\Sigma+}$ and $\boxed{\Sigma-}$ (results for crosschecking: 51.94° and 113.24 *knots*).

Additionally, here is an advanced problem from a universe far, far away (and quoted from the *HP-32E Owner's Handbook* of 1978 (sic!)):

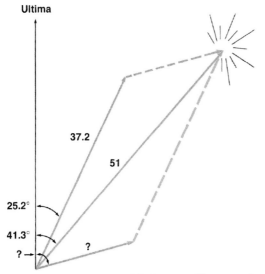

Example:

Federation starship *Felicity* has emerged victorious from a furious battle with the starship Θανατος[80] from the renegade planet *Maldek*. However, its automatic pilot is kaput,[81] and its main thrust engine is locked on at 37.2 *meganewtons* (*MN*) directed along an angle of 25.2° from the star *Ultima*.[82] Consulting the ship's star map, the navigator reports a hyperspace entrance vector of 51 *MN* at an angle of 41.3° from *Ultima*. To what thrust and angle should the auxiliary engine be set, for *Felicity* to achieve alignment with the hyperspace entrance vector?

---

[80] Translator's note: this is the ancient Greek word for 'death', pronounced like 'Tunnatoss' in English but like 'Thanatos' in Spanish, German, Italian, and Finnish, for example. Actually, they printed *Thanatos* in the English handbook.

[81] Yes, I know this is spelled 'kaputt' originally, but they printed this German word with only one 't' in said manual. Oh, why can't the English learn to spell?

[82] Latin for 'the last' (female). – By the way, the plane of action in 3D space seems to be defined sufficiently by *Felicity*, *Ultima*, and said entrance (hopefully, its center) here – this problem was reprinted unmodified in the *HP-34C OH* one year after.

Solution:

The required thrust vector of the auxiliary engine is equal to the hyper-space entrance vector minus the thrust vector of the main engine. The vectors are converted to rectangular coordinates using the [→R] key, and their difference is calculated using the [Σ+] and [Σ−] keys. This difference is recalled to the X- and Y-registers using [STAT] [S][U] [XEQ]. Then, these rectangular coordinates of the auxiliary engine thrust vector are converted to polar coordinates using [→P].

[MODE] [Y] [▼] ‡ YDON	
[XEQ]	sets permanent display of y
[CLΣ]	clears the summation registers
41.3 [ENTER↑] **51**	hyperspace entrance vector
[→R]	returns ⟩33.66 380 RPM 383 1
[Σ+]	adds x and y of the hyperspace entrance vector to the summation registers
25.2 [ENTER↑] **37.2**	main engine thrust vector
[→R]	returns ⟩15.84 380 RPM 3366
[Σ−]	subtracts x and y of the main engine thrust vector from the summation registers
[STAT] [S][U] ‡ SUM	
[XEQ]	recalls the summation registers Σx and Σy : 17.82 380 RPM 465
[→P]	returns ∠75.36 380 RPM 18.42
	meaning the auxiliary engine shall be set at 18.42 *MN* and an angle of 75.36° from *Ultima*.[83]

Real adepts of vector algebra may prefer subtracting the main engine thrust vector first and adding the hyperspace entrance vector second. This will work as well although the count of 'data points' will become negative once – simply don't bother.

---

[83] See previous footnote – a proper error calculation would be appreciated.

Almost Real Stuff: Calculating with Fractions

Fractions are handled like in previous *RPN* calculators (i.e. in *HP-32SII*, *HP-33S*, and *HP-35S*).   In particular, DENMAX sets the maximum allowable denominator (see the *IOP* on pp. 188ff).   Fraction mode is entered via a b/c , d/c , or by entering a second radix mark in numeric input.   It is left towards floating point decimal mode via ALL , FIX , SCI , ENG , H.d , or H.MS .   Fraction mode will be temporarily suspended when CPX is pressed; it will stay so as long as complex operations are executed but will return with the first keystroke thereafter.

The display will look like the examples below – fractions are adjusted to the left.   If the fraction is exactly equal, slightly less, or greater than the floating point number converted, ⹀, ⌊ᵗ, or ⌈ᵗ is indicated in the exponent, respectively.   On your *WP 34S*, fraction mode can handle numbers with absolute values less than 100,000 and greater than 0.0001.   The maximum denominator is 9 999 (greater denominators may be entered but will be reduced as soon as input is closed).   Underflows and overflows will be displayed in the format set before fraction mode was entered.

The following examples show some displays you may encounter using your *WP 34S* in fraction mode:

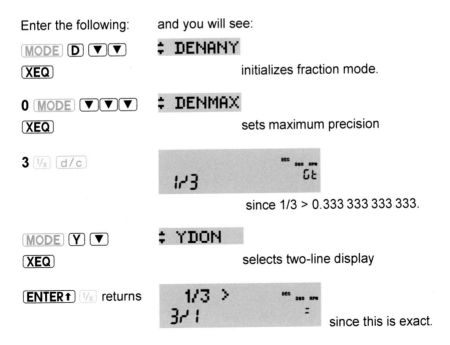

Enter the following:	and you will see:	
MODE D ▼▼ XEQ	‡ DENANY	initializes fraction mode.
0 MODE ▼▼▼ XEQ	‡ DENMAX	sets maximum precision
3 ¹/ₓ d/c	1⸍3 Gᵗ	since 1/3 > 0.333 333 333 333.
MODE Y ▼ XEQ	‡ YDON	selects two-line display
ENTER↑ ¹/ₓ returns	1⸍3 > 3⸍1 ⹀	since this is exact.

50 ⌷ 40625

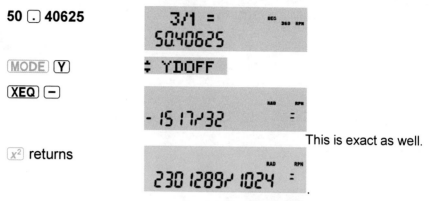

3/1 =
5040625   BEG   360 RPN

MODE Y   ‡ YDOFF

XEQ ─

- 15 17/32   RAD RPN
                                   =

This is exact as well.

x² returns

230 1289/ 1024   RAD RPN
                                   =

Now, enter a b/c for converting this into a *proper* fraction.[84] You get

ᴸ47 36 1/ 1024   RAD RPN
                                   =

with a little hook left of the first digit shown. This indicates the leading integer number is displayed incompletely – there are at least two digits preceding 47 here but no more display space. Press ◀ to unveil the integer part of this proper fraction as 2247.

Numeric input in fraction mode is straightforward and logically coherent. If you enter two radix points, the first is interpreted as a space, the second as a fraction mark. Assuming proper fraction mode is chosen, see these **examples:**

Key in:	and get:	
① ② ⌷ ③ ⌷ ④ ENTER↑	12 3/4	
① ⌷ ② ENTER↑	1 1/5	(decimal input)
⌷ ① ⌷ ② ENTER↑	1/2	
⌷ ① ② ENTER↑	3/25	(decimal input)
① ⌷ ⌷ ② ENTER↑	1 0/1	(= 1 ⁰/₂) [85]

---

[84] Translator's note: *Proper fractions* cover both "echte Brüche" (like ¾) and "gemischte Brüche" (like 2 ½) in German.

[85] This display of a pure integer number tells you unambiguously your *WP 34S* is in proper fraction mode. For comparison, note the *HP-32SII* reads ① ⌷ ⌷ ② as ½ –

Input of very long fractions may be echoed like shown above on this page.

By the way, please note that DECOMP indicates the precision of its results in quite a similar way as explained one page above:

Enter the following: and you will see:

0.33333 H.d

X.FCN DE   ‡ DECOMP

XEQ

y/x >   BEG 360

                 3.

x⇄y   BEG 360 RPN

                 ↳   since $1/3 > 0.33333$.

If you are focussed on real numbers and fractions and are looking for a simpler user interface than the one of the *WP 34S*, please check the *WP 31S*. It features only one prefix key, hence shows a significantly cleaner keyboard, is optimized for manual problem solving (a.k.a. real number crunching), and is based on the same hardware and software platform as your *WP 34S*.

---

though this is not consistent with its other input interpretations in fraction mode (and does not even save keystrokes but adds confusion only).

Complex Stuff – 1:   Complex Calculations

So far, we dealt with real (or even integer) numbers only. Your *WP 34S* can do more for you. Mathematicians know of more complicated items than real numbers. There are also *complex numbers*. If you do not know of them, leave them aside; you can use your *WP 34S* perfectly without them.

If you know of complex numbers, however, note your *WP 34S* supports many operations in complex domain as well. The key (CPX) is employed as prefix for calling complex functions.[86] E.g. (CPX) ▐ [COS] calls the complex cosine – it is displayed as ⁣`COS` and listed as ᶜCOS (the elevated C is the signature for complex functions in your *WP 34S*).

☞ **All functions operating on complex numbers require complex input in <u>Cartesian coordinates exclusively</u> on your WP 34S. Each such number takes two adjacent registers: the lower one for its real part and the higher one for its imaginary part.**

Thus the complex number lowest on *stack* is $x + i \cdot y = x_c$. Pure real numbers feature a zero imaginary part – pure imaginary numbers a zero real part.

You may use ⟶P to convert $x_c = x + i \cdot y$ to its polar equivalent $x_c = r \cdot e^{i\varphi}$ any time you like – just remember reverting this by (R←) before starting a complex calculation.

☞ **All complex functions work with <u>radians exclusively</u> where an angular input is required, and return radians where they output angular data.**

As a reminder, **RAD** is lit when (CPX) is pressed. The user is responsible for providing suitable input values; there will be <u>no</u> automatic conversion of angular data if the angular mode is switched.

Generally, if an arbitrary <u>real</u> function **f** operates on …

- … one real number x only, then its <u>complex</u> sibling ᶜ**f** will operate on the complex number $x_c = x + i \cdot y$. Note x_c will consume two

---

[86] The *HP-42S* supported a special data type for complex numbers. This is not viable using the hardware of the *HP-20b* or *HP-30b*, however. Thus, complex calculations have to be a bit more complex here. See *App. F* for the reasons.

stack registers but represents just one complex number. [87]

- ... one register, e.g. **R12**, then ^{C}**f** will operate on two registers, e.g. **R12** and **R13**.

- ... *x* and *y*, then ^{C}**f** will operate on *x, y, z* and *t* .

Whenever a complex operation is executed, the imaginary part of its result is shown in the top row of the LCD headed by an i, regardless of YDON / YDOFF (see the examples following below and compare pp. 72ff).

Where **monadic** *real* functions replace *x* by the result **f(x)**, *monadic* *complex* functions replace *x* by the real part and *y* by the imaginary part of the complex result ^{C}**f(x_c)**. Higher *stack* levels remain unchanged.

Monadic complex functions are e.g. $^C1/x$, ^CABS, ^CFP, ^CIP, ^CROUND, $^Cx!$, $^Cx^2$, $^C\sqrt{x}$, $^C+/-$, $^C\Gamma$, the logarithmic and exponential functions with bases 10, 2, and e, as well as hyperbolic and trigonometric functions and their inverses.

Example:

$\sqrt{-1}$ is calculated as follows:

0 (ENTER↑) **1** (+/−) enters −1 as a complex number.

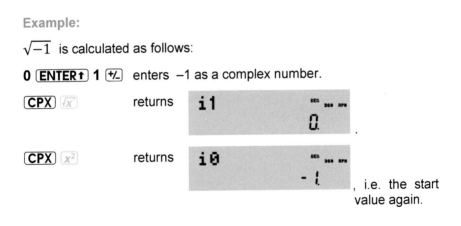

(CPX) (√x)   returns   i1   0.

(CPX) (x²)   returns   i0   -1. , i.e. the start value again.

Dyadic *real* functions replace *x* by the result **f(x, y)** as was shown on pp 25ff. By full analogy, *dyadic complex* functions replace *x* by the real part and *y* by the imaginary part of the complex result ^{C}**f(x_c, y_c)**. The next *stack* levels are filled with the complex contents of higher levels,

---

[87] Also note that $x + i \cdot y$ is entered like a 2D data point (x, y), i.e. *y* (ENTER↑) *x* . You have got an *RPN* calculator. (If you prefer entering a complex number as you speak instead, that requires one more keystroke: *x* (ENTER↑) *y* (x⇄y). But take care for not mixing real and imaginary parts.)

and the complex number contained in the top two *stack* levels is repeated as shown overleaf. Such complex functions are the basic arithmetic operations in complex domain as well as ^{C}IDIV, ^{C}LOG$_x$, ^{C}y^x, $^{Cx}\sqrt{y}$, $^C\beta$, and $^C||$. Turn to the *stack* diagrams overleaf for further details.

Press $\boxed{\text{ENTER}\uparrow}$ for separating input numbers like you did in real domain.

Example:

$(1 + i \cdot 2) \cdot (3 + i \cdot 4)$ is entered like this:

2 $\boxed{\text{ENTER}\uparrow}$ 1 $\boxed{\text{ENTER}\uparrow}$ 4 $\boxed{\text{ENTER}\uparrow}$ 3 $\boxed{\text{CPX}}\boxed{\text{x}}$,

returning

	BEG
i 1𝟬	𝟯𝟲𝟬 RPM
	-5.

You will reach the same result also by keying in the sequence

2 $\boxed{\text{ENTER}\uparrow}$ 1 $\boxed{\text{CPX}}\boxed{\text{ENTER}\uparrow}$ 4 $\boxed{\text{ENTER}\uparrow}$ 3 $\boxed{\text{CPX}}\boxed{\text{x}}$

which may be even more logical although requiring one keystroke more.

Where a complex operation (such as ^{C}RCL) does not consume any *stack* input at all but just returns a complex number, this number will be pushed on the *stack* taking two levels.

Summing up, complex number calculations use two registers or *stack* levels for each such number as explained above and shown in more detail on the next two pages:

Stack contents after executing the complex stack register operation

	Level	Assumed stack contents at the beginning:	^{C}ENTER	^{C}FILL	^{C}x⇄y	^{C}R↓	^{C}R↑
With 4 stack levels	T	Im(y_c)	Im(x_c)		Im(x_c)		
	Z	Re(y_c)	Re(x_c)		Re(x_c)		
	Y	Im(x_c)	Im(x_c)		Im(y_c)		
	X	Re(x_c)	Re(x_c)		Re(y_c)		
With 8 stack levels	D	Im(t_c)	z_c	x_c	t_c	x_c	z_c
	C	Re(t_c)	z_c	x_c	t_c	x_c	z_c
	B	Im(z_c)	y_c	x_c	z_c	t_c	y_c
	A	Re(z_c)	y_c	x_c	z_c	t_c	y_c
	T	Im(y_c)	x_c	x_c	x_c	z_c	x_c
	Z	Re(y_c)	x_c	x_c	x_c	z_c	x_c
	Y	Im(x_c)	x_c	x_c	y_c	y_c	t_c
	X	Re(x_c)	x_c	x_c	y_c	y_c	t_c

The dyadic operation $^Cy^x$ is called via (CPX) y^x or (CPX)(y^x) directly and executes $y_c{}^\wedge x_c$ as it should. The same holds for $^{Cx}\sqrt{y}$ in full analogy. Please note, however, that although the operation $^Cx⇄y$ is called via (CPX)(x⇄y) and executes $x_c⇄y_c$ (as expected) it is actually listed as $^Cx⇄$ Z for addressing reasons (see pp. 134f). We apologize for this inconsistency in naming but could not agree on a way around.

Stack contents after executing the complex …

Level	Assumed *stack* contents at the beginning:	… *stack register operation* °DROP	… °LASTx	… *monadic function* °x^2	… *dyadic function* °/
T	y_c	$y_c = t_c$	x_c	$y_c = t_c$	$y_c = t_c$
Z					
Y	x_c	y_c	*last* x_c	$(x_c)^2$	y_c/x_c
X					

Level	Assumed *stack* contents at the beginning:	°DROP	°LASTx	°x^2	°/
D	t_c	t_c	z_c	t_c	t_c
C					
B	z_c	t_c	y_c	z_c	t_c
A					
T	y_c	z_c	x_c	y_c	z_c
Z					
Y	x_c	y_c	*last* x_c	$(x_c)^2$	y_c/x_c
X					

Looking at these tables, it is obvious why we strongly recommend to set the *WP 34S* to SSIZE8 for complex calculations.

After pressing CPX, your *WP 34S* allows for the complex operations shown on this *virtual keyboard* (except STOPW representing an application in real domain, see pp. 282ff for more about it). Note that a second press of CPX, a ◄, or EXIT directly after CPX will just cancel the prefix CPX, so you return to the calculator state as it was before.

Constants in complex domain and such calculations occupy two registers like all other complex numbers. Complex constants are simply entered as

> *imaginary_part* ENTER↑ *real_part* .

Pure <u>real</u> constants – identified by a zero imaginary part – are easily entered for complex calculations as follows:

> 0 ENTER↑ *real_constant* , or alternatively

> CPX *n* for integers $0 < n \leq 9$ only.

In programming, CPX CONST # *n* with $0 \leq n \leq 256$ will save steps.

Example:

The real number π may be loaded for complex calculations via
0 ENTER↑ π or CPX π – both will result in $y = 0$ and $x = \pi$, but only the latter will return

```
i0                    BEG  360 RPN
3.14159265359
```
.

Pure <u>imaginary</u> constants, on the other hand, having a zero real part, are entered thus:

imaginary_constant (ENTER↑) **0** .

Example (continued):

The complex unit i may be loaded via **1** (ENTER↑) **0** or (CPX) (.) – both will result in $y = 1$ and $x = 0$, but only the latter will return

```
i1                      BEG  360  RPN
                   0.
```
.

Press (CPX)(×) now to multiply i with the real number π stored in Z and T, and you will get

```
i 3.14159265            BEG  360  RPN
                   0.
```
,

and **1** (ENTER↑) (CPX)(×) will then return

```
i 3.14159265            BEG  360  RPN
         -3.14159265359
```
.

Note complex calculations work with either display – just the contents of X and Y, Z and T are important after all.   Compare the *stack* mechanics demonstrated on p. 129.

☞ Except immediately after a complex operation, your *WP 34S* cannot know where and when a particular pair of real numbers is representing a complex number or something else (this applies as well when you turn your *WP 34S* on again). It is your responsibility to take care of that.

For this reason, actually, complex numbers and operations also come handy for some 2D vector calculations. We can, for **example**, compute Mr. *Sweeney's* ground course easier than shown on pp. 119f above:

(FIX) **2**

225 (ENTER↑) **125**   indicated air speed and heading

(→R)   returns
```
y -88.39                BEG  360  RPN
            -88.39
```

180 (ENTER↑) **25**   north wind

→R	returns	y 0.00 BEG 360 RPN -25.00
CPX +	returns	i -88.39 BEG 360 RPN -113.39
→P	returns	∠ -142.06 BEG 360 RPN 143.77

x⮂y 360 +   displays **217.94** (according to navigational convention, the angle must be positive).

Compare with the approach demonstrated above. We needed four steps less here and got the same results. Feel free to transfer the second or third example printed above as well.

Complex Stuff – 2: Addressing Complex Numbers

1	User input	CPX x=? or CPX x≠?			
	Echo	OP _ (with α_T set) e.g. $^r x = \_?$			

2	User input	0 or 1	*Stack level or lettered register* A, C, J, L, or Z	ENTER↑ [88] leaves α_T	→ opens indirect addressing.
	Echo	OP n ? e.g. $^r x = 0?$	OP? x e.g. $^r x ≠ ?$ Z	OP? _	OP? → _

3	User input	Compares $x_c = x + i\,y$ with the real number 0.	Compares $x_c = x + i\,y$ with $y_c = z + i\,t$ [89].	*Register number* [90]	See next page for more about indirect addressing.
	Echo			OP? nn e.g. $^r x ≠ ?$ 26	

Compares
$x_c = x + i\,y$ with
$r26 + i\,r27$.

 A complex operation will always affect a pair of registers: the one specified and the subsequent one. To avoid ambiguity, we strongly recommend storing complex numbers with their real parts at <u>even</u> register addresses always. This is guaranteed if you specify an even register number in direct addressing.

---

[88] You may skip this keystroke for register numbers >19 or local registers. The latter start with a ⟨.⟩ – see *Programming Your WP 34S* and *App. B* below.

[89] We apologize for this inconsistency in command naming but found no way around.

[90] Recommended values are 0 0 … 9 8 and . 0 0 … . 1 4 if the respective register is allocated. Odd (global or local) general purpose register addresses are also legal but not recommended.

1	User input	[CPX][RCL], [CPX][STO], [CPX] VIEW, or [CPX] x⤓		
	Echo	OP _ (with α_T set) e.g. ᶠRCL _ [91]		
2	User input	*Stack level or lettered register* [A], [C], [J], [L], or [Z] [92]	*Register number* as specified on previous page.	[→] opens indirect addressing, generally working as in real domain (compare pp. 64f).
	Echo	OP *x* e.g. ᶠRCL L	OP *nn* e.g. ᶠVIEW 18	OP→_
3	User input	This is ᶜLASTx – the real part is recalled from register **L** to **X**, the imaginary part from **I** to **Y**.	*Stack level or lettered register* [A], ..., [D], [I], ..., [L], [T], [Y], [Z]	*Register number* [93]
	Echo		OP→ *x* e.g. ᶠx⇆→Z	OP→ *nn* e.g. ᶠSTO→45

ᶠx⇆→Z swaps *x* and the content of the register where *z* is pointing to, and *y* with the content of the subsequent one.

Assume e.g. *x* = 4, *y* = 3, *z* = 20, *r20* = 5, and *r21* = 6, then
you will find *x* = 5, *y* = 6,   *r20* = 4, and *r21* = 3 after ᶜx⇆→Z.

ᶠSTO→45 Stores $x_c = x + i\,y$ into two consecutive registers, starting with the register where *r45* is pointing to.

---

[91] For [CPX][RCL] and [CPX][STO], any of [+], [−], [×], or [/] may precede step 2. See the IOP.

[92] Exceptions: ᶜRCL Z, ᶜRCL+ Z, ᶜSTO Z, and ᶜSTO+ Z require an [ENTER↑] preceding the letter [Z], e.g. [CPX][STO][+] [ENTER↑] [Z] for the latter.

[93] [0][0] ... [9][9] and [.][0][0] ... [.][1][5] if the respective register is allocated.

Integers – 1:   Introduction and Virtual Keyboard

Integer modes are designed to deal exclusively with integers – in input, output, and calculations. This is useful e.g. for computer logic and system programming – typical applications of an *HP-16C*. Your *WP 34S* contains all the functions of the *HP-16C* and more, and it allows for integer computing in fifteen bases from binary to hexadecimal – these integer bases are entered as described on p. 72.

Therein, functions such as SIN make no sense for obvious reasons. Thus, for integer bases up to 10, the virtual keyboard of your *WP 34S* will look as shown right (where labels headed by a red arrow will leave integer modes when called, typically returning to floating point decimal mode).

For base 16, on the other hand, primary functions of the top six keys will be reassigned automatically, becoming direct numeric hexadecimal input. So this row will then look virtually as shown below.

Wherever a default primary function is not primary anymore after automatic reassignment, prefix ⬜ will

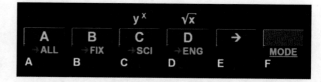

Calculating in bases 11 ... 15, those keys not ne
will work as shown in the first picture above.
attempts to enter an illegal digit from the keybo:
binary – will be blocked.

Integers – 2: Displaying Integers in Vari(

In integer modes, the mantissa section of num
integer in X. The exponent section is not neec
here but may transmit other information. Sigi
exponent indicate the base set:

Base	2	3	4	5	6	7	8	9	10	11
Exponent starts with	b	3	४	5	6	7	o	9	d	- ı

Carry and overflow – if set – show up as a c
in the third digit of the exponent, respectivel
exponent section may well look like -2co ⋅
missing, you would be in binary mode

Generally, carry and overflow behave as th
They are flags – if you want to set, clear, or c
use the flag commands of your *WP 34S*.

Word size and complement setting are indicated
a format xx . ww, with xx being 1c or 2c for ʹ
respectively, un for unsigned, or sm for sig
Startup default is 2c. These modes control th
numbers. They are understood most easily with

---

[94] In such cases, operations printed golden on the key plate
    This means for the key D, for example, we cannot a(
    mode – no loss here, of course. Reassignments are gene
    Note ⬛ D may call a program if defined.

Set your *WP 34S* to WSIZE **12**, LZON.[95] This setting allows seeing all 12 bits in one *WP 34S* display easily. Enter **147**. Then turn to 1COMPL, and press ⬛2. You will see:

1c 12   'I   ᴍ
oooo *100 100 11* ᵇ   and – after ⬛⁺ᐟ⁻ –   1c 12   'I   ᴍ
                                              ı ı ı ₀ı ıₒı ı₀₀ ᵇ .

Forget the 'I top right for the moment – it will be explained later. Note the low *byte* of our number is displayed larger than its top four bits for easy reading.

Obviously ⬛⁺ᐟ⁻ in **1c** inverts every bit, equivalent to NOT here.

Return to the original number via ⬛⁺ᐟ⁻ now, choose 2COMPL and you will get:

2c 12   'I   ᴍ
oooo *100 100 11* ᵇ   and – after ⬛⁺ᐟ⁻ –   2c 12   'I   ᴍ
                                              ı ı ı ₀ı ıₒı ı₀ı ᵇ .

Note the negative number equals the inverse plus one in **2c**.

Now return to the original number via ⬛⁺ᐟ⁻ again, choose SIGNMT and you will see:

ꜱm 12   'I   ᴍ
oooo *100 100 11* ᵇ   and – after ⬛⁺ᐟ⁻ –   ꜱm 12   'I   ᴍ
                                              ıooo *100 100 11* ᵇ .

Negating a number will just flip the top bit in **ꜱm** (hence its name).

Finally, return to the original number via ⬛⁺ᐟ⁻, choose UNSIGN and you will get:

un 12   'I   ᴍ
oooo *100 100 11* ᵇ   and – after ⬛⁺ᐟ⁻ –   un 12   'I   ᴍ
                                              ı ı ı ₀ı ıₒı ı₀ı ᵇ ₒ .

Note the second number looks like in **2c**, but in addition an overflow is set here. [96]

---

[95] All the commands required for this example are either on the keyboard or in MODE.

[96] This needs an explanation, since in **un** the most significant *bit* adds magnitude, not sign, so the largest value represented by a 12-*bit* word is 4095 instead of 2047. Changing signs in unsigned mode has no meaning. Thus, ⬛⁺ᐟ⁻ should be illegal here or result in no operation at least. The blue print above is clearly stated also in the *HP-16C Computer Scientist Owner's Handbook* of April 1982 on page 30. Unfortunately, however, they did not stick to this – instead, they allowed and

Thus, pressing ⌊+/−⌋ will not suffice anymore for returning to the original number in UNSIGN; you must also clear the overflow flag by ⌊CF⌋ ⌊B⌋ explicitly (see pp. 55f).

As you have seen, positive numbers stay unchanged in all these four modes. Negative numbers, on the other hand, are represented in different ways. Therefore, taking a negative number in one mode and switching to another one will lead to different interpretations. The fixed bit pattern representing, for

Example:

- `- 147 d` in default **2c** will be displayed as

- `- 146 d` in **1c**,

- `- 1901 d` in **sm**, and

- `3949 d` in **un**.

Keeping the mode (e.g. **2c**) and changing the bases will produce different views of the constant bit pattern as well. You will notice that the displays for bases 4, 8, and 16 will look similar to those shown above, presenting all twelve bits to you, while in the other bases a signed mantissa will be displayed instead.

Example:

Compare the outputs of `- 147 d` in different integer bases:

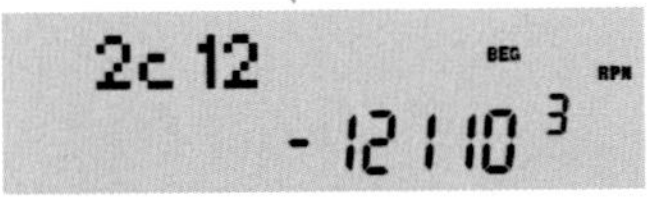

2c 12
    `- 12110 3` ,

2c 12
    `33 1231 4` , and

2c 12
    `- 1042 5` .

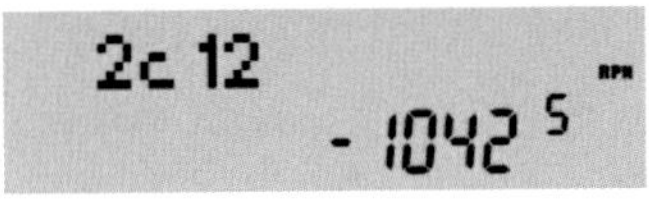

These display formats take into account that bases 2, 4, 8, and 16 are most convenient for bit and byte manipulations and further close-to-

---

implemented ⌊+/−⌋ in unsigned mode this very way in the *HP-16C*. So we follow that implementation – frowning – for sake of backward compatibility..

hardware applications. On the other hand, the bases in between will probably gain most interest in dealing with different number representations and calculating therein, where base 10 is the common reference standard.

Let us look to bigger words now:

Example:

Set UNSIGN, LZOFF, WSIZE **64**, BASE **16**, and enter **93A14B6**. Then your *WP 34S* will display:

un 64 93A 14b6 ʰ	un 64 93A 14b6 ʰ

with or without separators selected (see SEPON and SEPOFF).

In base 2, however, this number would need twenty-eight digits (1001.0011.1010.0001.0100.1011.0110). Obviously, your *WP 34S* cannot display this binary number at once (as far as we know, no pocket calculator can so far) – so what will it do? Return to SEPON and choose BASE 2; then you will see the 12 least significant digits of said number displayed initially:

un 64 "'|
0 100.101 1 101 1 10 ᵇ

They show up together with an indication "'| that there are four display windows required for this number in total with the rightmost shown. The least significant *byte* is emphasized as you know it from the example above. Press ◀ and you will get the more significant *bytes* (note the constant 4-*bit* overlap with the previous display here):

un 64 "|'
10 10.000 10 100 ᵇ

un 64 '|"
100 .00 1 1.10 10 ᵇ

un 64 |"'
100 1 ᵇ

The last display shows the four most significant bits of this binary number as the indication |"' confirms.

If leading zeroes were turned on (see LZON), there would be eight display windows (corresponding to eight *bytes*) here instead, with the four 'most significant' *bytes* containing only zeroes.

☞ Numeric <u>input</u> is limited to 12 digits in all bases.

Browsing large integers *byte*-wise is a specialty of base 2. In any other base the step size is the full display width, i.e. 12 digits without any overlap. So, integers of base 3 may take up to four windows, of base 4, 5, and 6 up to three, and the remaining ones up to two.

Example (continued):

Set BASE **3** and see the most and least significant parts of the same number in said base:

Integers – 3: Bitwise Operations

Your *WP 34S* carries all the bitwise operations you may know from vintage *HP-16C*, plus some more. Generally, bits are counted from right to left, starting with number 0 for the least significant bit. This is important for specifying bit numbers in the operations BC?, BS?, CB, FB, and SB.

The following examples deal with 8-*bit* words showing leading zeroes for easy reading. So set WSIZE **8**, LZON on your *WP 34S*. Then store `10 1 1.00 1 1` ^b as the common start-up number for the operations presented in the table below. For seven shift and rotate functions (all stored in <u>X.FCN</u>), you find schematic pictures here like printed on the backplane of the *HP-16C*. The 'C' in a box stands for the carry bit.

Op.	Schematic picture	Example	Output
Shift Left		SL 1	0110.0110 bc
		SL 2	1100.1100 b
Shift Right		SR 1	0101.1001 bc
		SR 2	0010.1100 bc
		SR 3	0001.0110 b
Arithmetic Shift Right	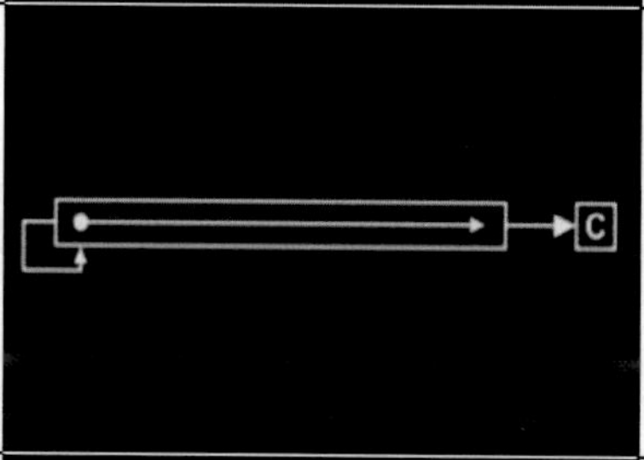	ASR 3	in 1COMP & 2COMP: 1111.0110 b in UNSIGN: 0001.0110 b in SIGNMT: 1000.0110 b
Rotate Left		RL 1	0110.0111 bc
		RL 2	1100.1110 b
Rotate Right		RR 1	1101.1001 bc
		RR 2	1110.1100 bc
		RR 3	0111.0110 b
Rotate Left through Carry		RLC 1	0110.0110 bc
		RLC 2	1100.1101 b
Rotate Right through Carry		RRC 1	0101.1001 bc
		RRC 2	1010.1100 bc
		RRC 3	1101.0110 b

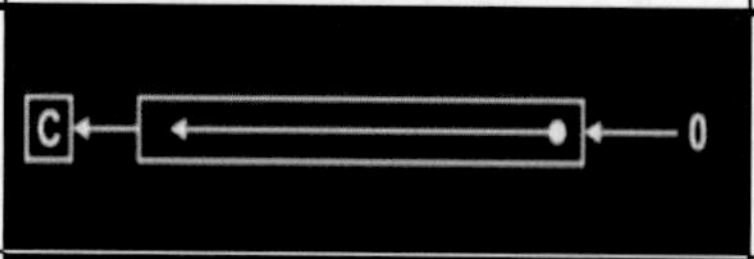

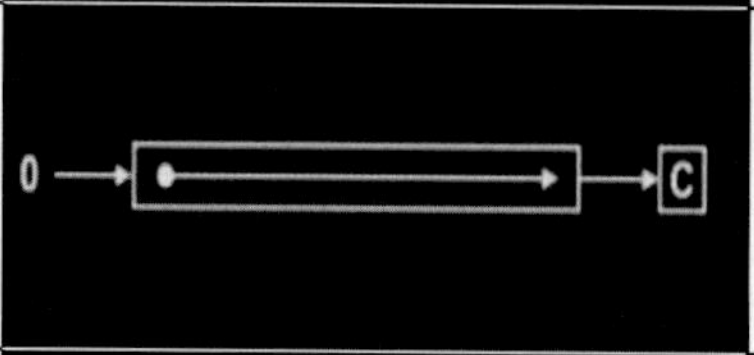

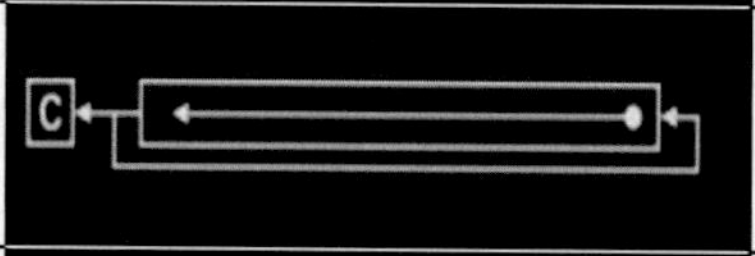

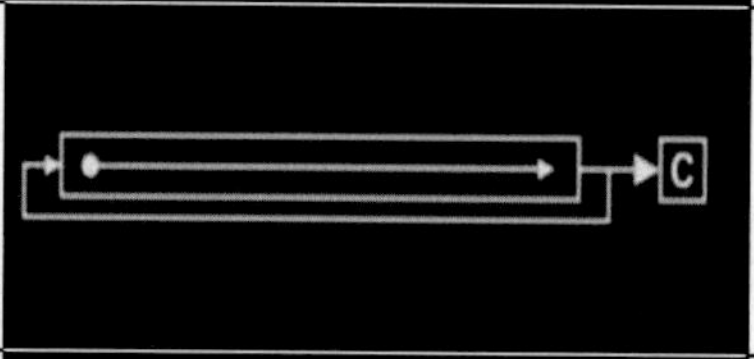

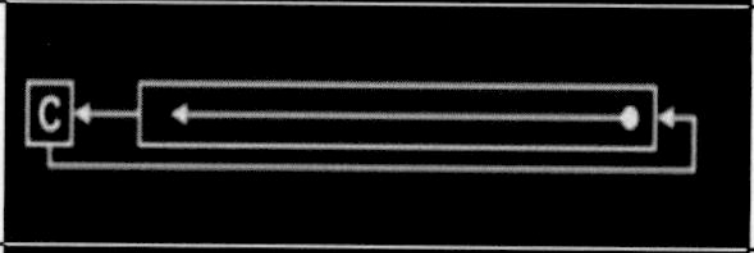

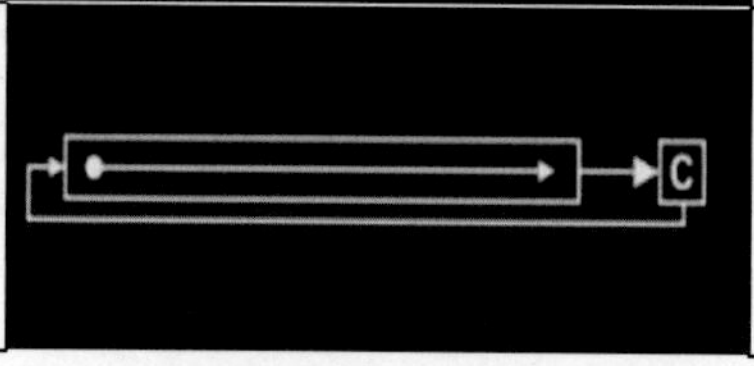

☞ The scheme for ASR correctly describes this operation for 1's and 2's complement modes only. In all modes of the *HP-16C*, however, ASR 3 equals a signed division by 2^3, hence the different results for the latter two modes shown above. The other bitwise operations are insensitive to complement mode setting. For further details about those operations, turn to the *IOP* at pp. 182ff.

Now let us show you the bitwise dyadic functions provided as well. Of these, Boole's operators AND, OR, and XOR are found in the light blue frame drawn here.

Again, we will use 8-*bit* words for the following examples:

Common input	Y	0110.1011 b
	X	1011.1001 b
Operation		**Output**
AND		0010.1001 b
NAND		1101.0110 b
OR		1111.1011 b
NOR		0000.0100 b
XOR		1101.0010 b
XNOR		0010.1101 b

See the *IOP* for these and further commands working on bit level in integer modes (NOT, LJ and RJ, MASKL and MASKR, MIRROR, RAN#, and nBITS). Unless on the keyboard, the commands mentioned so far are found in X.FCN in integer modes; and there are also BS? and BC? in TEST (see p. 255f).

Finally, note that no such operation will set an overflow. Carry is only settable by shift or rotate functions as demonstrated above. And ASR is the only bitwise operation being sensitive to complement mode settings – ASR is the link to integer arithmetic operations.

Integers – 4:   Integer Arithmetic Operations

Of the four basic arithmetic operations (+, -, ×, and /), the first three work in integer modes as they do in DECM, but with up to 64 digits precision in binary mode. Look at +/- like a multiplication times -1, and at y^x like a repeated multiplication. Depending on the input parameters and the mode settings, the overflow or carry flags will be set in such an operation (see the end of this chapter).

Divisions, however, must be handled differently in integer modes since the result cannot feature a fractional part here. Generally, the formula $\frac{a}{b} = (a \text{ div } b) + \frac{1}{b} \cdot \text{rmdr}(a; b)$ applies, with the horizontal fraction bar denoting <u>real</u> division, div representing <u>integer</u> division, and rmdr standing for the remainder of the latter. While remainders for positive parameters are simply found, remainders for negative dividends or divisors lead to confusion sometimes. The formula above, however, is easily employed for calculating such remainders (also for real numbers – see the first line of this example):

Examples:

$$\frac{25}{7} = 3 + \frac{1}{7} \cdot 4 \qquad\qquad \text{(and for reals: } \frac{25}{7,5} = 3 + \frac{1}{7,5} \cdot 2,5 \text{)}$$

$$\frac{-25}{7} = -3 + \frac{1}{7} \cdot (-4) \quad \Rightarrow \quad \text{rmdr}(-25; 7) = -4$$

$$\frac{25}{-7} = -3 + \frac{1}{-7} \cdot 4 \quad\;\; \Rightarrow \quad \text{rmdr}(25; -7) = 4$$

$$\frac{-25}{-7} = 3 + \frac{1}{-7} \cdot (-4) \quad \Rightarrow \quad \text{rmdr}(-25; -7) = -4$$

In general, $a - b \cdot (a \text{ div } b) =: \text{rmdr}(a; b)$.

Unfortunately, there is a second function doing <u>almost</u> the same: it is called mod. With the same pairs of numbers as above, it returns:

$$\text{mod}(25; 7) = 4 \ ,$$

$$\text{mod}(-25; 7) = 3 \ ,$$

$$\text{mod}(25; -7) = -3 \ ,$$

$$\text{mod}(-25; -7) = -4 \ .$$

So mod returns the same as rmdr if both parameters have equal signs but deviates else. The general formula for mod is a bit more sophisticated than the one above:

$$a - b \cdot \text{floor}\left(\frac{a}{b}\right) =: \text{mod}(a; b)$$

with e.g. $\text{floor}\left(\frac{25}{7}\right) = 3$ and $\text{floor}\left(-\frac{25}{7}\right) = -4$.

By the way, this formula applies to real numbers as well. So it may be used straightforwardly for calculating e.g. $\text{mod}(25.3; -7.5) = 25.3 - (-7.5) \cdot (-4) = -4.7$.

These four functions are called IDIV, RMDR, MOD and FLOOR in your *WP 34S* for obvious reasons.

Furthermore, the exponential and logarithmic operations, x^2 and $\sqrt{x}$, x^3 and $\sqrt[3]{x}$, Cy,x (i.e. COMB) and Py,x (i.e. PERM) work in integer modes, too. Beyond these and the operations mentioned further above, there are more in X.FCN (such as ×MOD and ^MOD). See the *IOP* on pp. 179ff for further information about them.

Finally, there are conditions where **overflow** or **carry** will be touched in integer arithmetic. Note there is a maximum and a minimum integer for each word size and complement setting – let us call them I_{max} and I_{min}.

For example,

- I_{max} = 15 and I_{min} = 0 for `un 04`, while
- I_{max} = 7 and I_{min} = -8 for `2c 04`,
- I_{max} = 7 and I_{min} = -7 for `1c 04` and `sm 04`.

Now let us start from 1 incrementing by 1 and see what will happen in these four modes:

un04		2c04		1c04		sm04	
0001 ᵇ	1 ᵈ	0001 ᵇ	1 ᵈ	0001 ᵇ	1 ᵈ	0001 ᵇ	1 ᵈ
0010 ᵇ	2 ᵈ	0010 ᵇ	2 ᵈ	0010 ᵇ	2 ᵈ	0010 ᵇ	2 ᵈ
...	...	...	...	...	...	...	...
0111 ᵇ	7 ᵈ	0111 ᵇ	7 ᵈ	0111 ᵇ	7 ᵈ	0111 ᵇ	7 ᵈ
1000 ᵇ	8 ᵈ	1000 ᵇᵒ	-8 ᵈᵒ	1000 ᵇᵒ	-7 ᵈᵒ	1000 ᵇᶜᵒ	-0 ᵈᶜᵒ
1001 ᵇ	9 ᵈ	1001 ᵇ	-7 ᵈ	1001 ᵇ	-6 ᵈ	0001 ᵇ	1 ᵈ
...	...	...	...	...	...		
1110 ᵇ	14 ᵈ	1110 ᵇ	-2 ᵈ	1110 ᵇ	-1 ᵈ		
1111 ᵇ	15 ᵈ	1111 ᵇ	-1 ᵈ	1111 ᵇ	-0 ᵈ		
0000 ᵇᶜᵒ	0 ᵈᶜᵒ	0000 ᵇᶜ	0 ᵈᶜ	0001 ᵇᶜ	1 ᵈᶜ		
0001 ᵇ	1 ᵈ	0001 ᵇ	1 ᵈ				

We start another turn from 1 but <u>decrementing</u> by 1 now:

un04		2c04		1c04		sm04	
0001 ᵇ	1 ᵈ	0001 ᵇ	1 ᵈ	0001 ᵇ	1 ᵈ	0001 ᵇ	1 ᵈ
0000 ᵇ	0 ᵈ	0000 ᵇ	0 ᵈ	0000 ᵇ	0 ᵈ	0000 ᵇ	0 ᵈ
1111 ᵇᶜᵒ	15 ᵈᶜᵒ	1111 ᵇᶜ	-1 ᵈᶜ	1110 ᵇᶜ	-1 ᵈᶜ	1001 ᵇᶜ	-1 ᵈᶜ
1110 ᵇ	14 ᵈ	1110 ᵇ	-2 ᵈ	1101 ᵇ	-2 ᵈ	1010 ᵇ	-2 ᵈ
...	...	...	...	...	...	...	...
...	...	...	...	...	...	...	...
0010 ᵇ	2 ᵈ	1001 ᵇ	-7 ᵈ	1001 ᵇ	-6 ᵈ	1110 ᵇ	-6 ᵈ
0001 ᵇ	1 ᵈ	1000 ᵇ	-8 ᵈ	1000 ᵇ	-7 ᵈ	1111 ᵇ	-7 ᵈ
		0111 ᵇᵒ	7 ᵈᵒ	0111 ᵇᵒ	7 ᵈᵒ	1000 ᵇᵒ	-0 ᵈᵒ
		0110 ᵇ	6 ᵈ	0110 ᵇ	6 ᵈ	1001 ᵇ	-1 ᵈ
		...	...	...	...		

☞ The most significant bit is #3 in **sm04** and #4 in all other modes here. And subtractions are actually additions in SIGNMT.

With these results, I_{max}, and I_{min}, the general rules for setting and clearing carry and overflow in integer modes are as follows:

Operation	Effect on carry	Effect on overflow
Shift and rotate	As shown on p. 141.	None.
+, RCL+, STO+, INC, etc.	Sets **c** if there is a carry <u>out of</u> the most significant bit, else clears **c**.	Sets **o** if the result exceeded $[I_{min}; I_{max}]$, else clears **o**.
×, RCL×, STO×, +/-, $(-1)^x$, x^2, x^3, LCM, $x!$, etc.	None.	Thus in UNSIGN, ⊞ always sets **o** and $(-1)^x$ does so for odd x.
-, RCL-, STO-, DEC, etc.	Sets **c** in a subtraction $m - s$ if • in 1COMP / 2COMP the binary subtraction causes a *borrow*[97] <u>into</u> the most significant bit, • in UNSIGN m is smaller than s, • in SIGNMT m is smaller than s <u>and</u> both have the same sign. Else clears **c**.	Sets **o** if the result exceeded $[I_{min}; I_{max}]$, else clears **o**.
y^x, 10^x	Sets **c** for $x < 0$ (as well as for 0^0), else clears **c**.	
2^x	Clears **c**. Sets **c** only if $x = -1$, or in UNSIGN if $x =$ **wsize** or in the other modes if $x =$ **wsize** - 1	
e^x	Sets **c** for $x \neq 0$, else clears **c**.	

---

[97] See e.g. the examples above.

Translator's note: Both *carry* and *borrow* translate to "Übertrag" in German; the *borrow* in subtraction is a specialty of the USA. See the subtle methodic differences in written subtraction demonstrated in detail in the article http://de.wikipedia.org/wiki/Subtraktion#Schriftliche_Subtraktion . The corresponding English article is far less instructive.

Operation	Effect on carry	Effect on overflow
DBL×	None.	Clears **o**.
ABS	None.	Clears **o** (but sets it for $x = I_{min}$ in 2COMP).
/, RCL /, STO /, DBL /, LB, LG, LN, LOG$_x$, $\sqrt{x}, \sqrt[3]{x}, \sqrt[x]{y}$	Sets **c** if the remainder is $\neq 0$, else clears **c**.	Clears **o** (but sets it for the division $I_{min}/(-1)$ in 2COMP).

Full Alpha Mode – 1:   Introduction and Virtual Keyboard

Alpha mode is designed for text entry, e.g. for entering prompts and answers. It is typically entered via ⓐ (see p. 72). In this mode, the contents of the alpha register are displayed in the upper part of the LCD. All direct input goes into that register, and the numeric line (kept from your last calculation) is accessible by commands only.

In alpha mode, most mathematical operations are neither necessary nor applicable. So the keyboard is reassigned automatically when you enter alpha mode – see the *virtual keyboard* printed overleaf.

All labels printed there on **red background** append corresponding characters to *alpha* directly or via alpha *catalogs*.

Within alpha mode, primary function of most keys becomes appending the letter printed bottom left of this key – grey on the key plate – to *alpha*. PSE appends a space. When *alpha* exceeds 30 characters, the leftmost character(s) are discarded. Alpha mode starts with capital letters, and ⬆ toggles upper and lower case. As in integer modes, f will access default primary functions wherever necessary.[98]

Note four new *catalogs* become active in this mode. See the keys ➡ and CPX, and the labels R↑ and ./. on your *WP 34S*.

The keys STO, RCL, as well as the labels VIEW and CLx change their functionality in other ways.

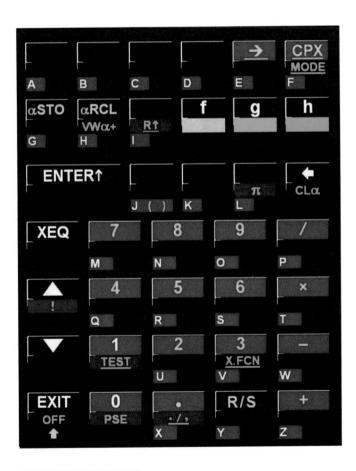

---

[98] The digits 0 and 1 may also be called using f 0 or f 1, respectively, for sake of consistency.

Looking at the standard labels on the keyboard, we can safely offer you direct access to even more characters in this mode. All the labels printed on `dark blue background` in the virtual alpha keyboard printed overleaf append characters to *alpha* as well. They are <u>related</u> to the labels printed on your *WP 34S* keyboard at these locations, but <u>deviate</u> from them.

Prefix g generally leads to homophonic <u>G</u>reek letters where applicable. [99] And h allows also accessing logic symbols via the Boolean operations.

---

[99] The corresponding letters are "homophonic" according to classical Greek pronunciation. Kudos to Thales, Pythagoras, Heraclitus, Leucippus, Democritus, Aristotle, Archimedes, Euclid (i.e. ὁ Θαλῆς ὁ Μιλήσιος, ὁ Πυθαγόρας ὁ Σάμιος, ὁ Ἡράκλειτος ὁ Ἐφέσιος, ὁ Λεύκιππος, ὁ Δημόκριτος, ὁ Ἀριστοτέλης, ὁ Ἀρχιμήδης ὁ Συρακούσιος καὶ ὁ Εὐκλείδης), and their colleagues for laying the foundations of logics, mathematics, and physics (i.e. ἡ λογικὴ καὶ ἡ μαθηματικὴ τέχνη καὶ ἡ φυσικὴ ἐπιστήμη) as we know them today.

The alpha *catalogs* called by ▢▢, ▢(CPX), (R↑), (./.), and (TEST) feature even more characters (see pp. 259f). Check the *IOP* on pp. 221f for VWα+ and look up more alpha commands on pp. 226ff.

For a clearer picture of this virtual keyboard – with the extra colors and redundancies removed – look here. All labels shown in this picture append characters to *alpha* directly except

- those under-lined in red (they call alpha *catalogs*),

- those under-lined in green (they call *catalogs* of functions), and

- labels shown between heavier white key contours (they call functions directly).

If you print this virtual keyboard in a smaller size, you can attach it to the back of your *WP 34S* for ready reference. This will serve you

And we assigned **Gamma** also to **C** due to the alphabet, and **Chi** to **H** since this letter comes next in pronunciation. Three Greek letters require special handling: **Psi** is accessed via ▢(0) (below (PSE)), **Theta** via ▢(1) (below (TEST) and following **T**), and **Eta** via ▢(ENTER↑) .

Where we printed Greek capitals with lower contrast, they look like the respective Latin letters in our fonts. **Omicron** is not featured because it looks exactly like the Latin letter **O** in either case. Professors of Greek, we count on your understanding in this matter.

well also for learning the Greek letters and their relation to their Latin homophonic siblings. See p. 408 for such a small print ready to be cut out.

Full Alpha Mode – 2:   Displaying Text

Your *WP 34S* features a large and a small alphanumeric font for display. Both are based on fonts by *Luiz Viera* (Brazil) as distributed in 2004. Some letters were added and some modified for better legibility, also given that the dot matrix of your display is only six pixels high.

See here all characters directly evocable through the virtual alpha keyboard above:

ABCDEFGHIJKLMNOPQRSTUVWXYZ
abcdefghijklmnopqrstuvwxyz
ΑΒΓΔΕΖΗΘΙΚΛΜΝΞΟΠΡΣΤΥΦΧΨΩ
αβγδεζηθικλμνξοπρστυφχψω
0123456789 ()+−×/±.!?≒¬\&|≠

As soon as a string exceeds the visible display using this large font, your *WP 34S* will take the following small font automatically to show as much as possible:

ABCDEFGHIJKLMNOPQRSTUVWXYZ
abcdefghijklmnopqrstuvwxyz
ΑΒΓΔΕΖΗΘΙΚΛΜΝΞΟΠΡΣΤΥΦΧΨΩ
αβγδεζηθικλμνξοπρστυφχψω
0123456789 ()+−×/±.!?≒¬\&|≠

Many more characters of both fonts live in the alpha *catalogs* (see pp. 259f).

As long as you stay in alpha mode, the contents of the alpha register (abbreviated by *alpha*) are displayed in the dot matrix, showing its right end (i.e. the last characters it is containing), while the numeric section keeps the result of the last numeric operation. The display may look like:

`ANSWER =`
`-4242⁻⁴²`

Note you may use the big '=' controlled by flag **A** in addition to the dot matrix (see pp. 55ff). Different information may be appended to *alpha*. Check the commands starting with 'α' in the *IOP* on pp. 226ff.

For example,

TIME αTIME allows printing timestamps on messages like `It's 11:54:32 PM` or `Um 23:54:32 Uhr` depending on time mode setting and the time at execution.

And DATE αDATE will append – depending on date format setting – either `2017-04-16` or `16.04.2017` or `04/16/2017` to *alpha* if called on the 16th of April in 2017.

Note *alpha* can take up to 30 characters. Your *WP 34S* features a rich set of special letters and further characters. So you may easily store an actual Greek message like this, for example:

`Οι μέρλοϑ-ο`   `Ϝατοι σΕ κα`   `LρΕτοῦν.`

▲ and ▼ will browse such long messages in steps of 6 characters. ▲ will stop with the very first characters shown, ▼ stops showing the right end completely, i.e.

`κκLρΕτοῦν.`   in this very special case.

Taking advantage of the character set provided, it is no problem spelling French or Spanish prompts correctly as well as text strings in at least thirty-five more languages using letters based on Greek and Latin alphabets. Your *WP 34S* supports you in climbing the first step of politeness and respect by allowing you to adapt the software you write to the language your customers speak – instead of hacking in everything in English or using merely the very limited English letter set.

Having left alpha mode, you can still display *alpha*: use VIEWα or VWα+ for this – it will show you the left end (i.e. the first characters the alpha register contains).

Nevertheless, do not forget that your *WP 34S* is mainly designed as a programmable calculator. Look overleaf to see what can be done with such a device.

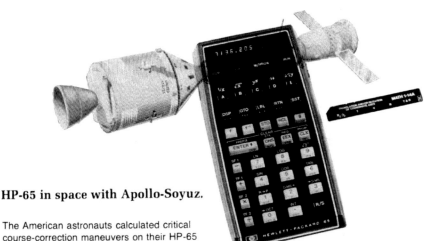

HP-65 in space with Apollo-Soyuz.

The American astronauts calculated critical course-correction maneuvers on their HP-65 programmable hand-held during the rendez-vous of the U.S. and Russian spacecraft.

Twenty-four minutes before the rendezvous in space, when the Apollo and Soyuz were 12 miles apart, the American astronauts corrected their course to place their spacecraft into the same orbit as the Russian craft. Twelve minutes later, they made a second positioning maneuver just prior to braking, and coasted in to linkup.

In both cases, the Apollo astronauts made the course-correction calculations on their HP-65. Had the on-board computer failed, the spacecraft not being in communication with ground stations at the time, the HP-65 would have been the only way to make all the critical calculations. Using complex programs of nearly 1000 steps written by NASA scientists and pre-recorded on magnetic program cards, the astronauts made the calculations automatically, quickly, and with ten-digit accuracy.

The HP-65 also served as a backup for Apollo's on-board computer for two earlier maneuvers. Its answers provided a confidence-boosting double-check on the coelliptic (85 mile) maneuver, and the terminal phase initiation (22 mile) maneuver, which placed Apollo on an intercept trajectory with the Russian craft.

Periodically throughout their joint mission, the Apollo astronauts also used the HP-65 to calculate

how to point a high-gain antenna precisely at an orbiting satellite to assure the best possible ground communications.

The first fully programmable hand-held calculator, the HP-65 automatically steps through lengthy or repetitive calculations. This advanced instrument relieves the user of the need to remember and exe-cute the correct sequence of keystrokes, using programs recorded 100 steps at a time on tiny magnetic cards. Each program consists of any combination of the calculator's 51 key-stroke func-tions with branching, logical comparison, and conditional skip instructions.

The HP-65 is priced at $795*. See it, and the rest of the HP family of professional hand-helds at quality department stores or campus bookstores. Call 800-538-7922 (in California, 800-662-9862) for the name of the retailer nearest you.

For more information on these products, write to us, Hewlett-Packard, 1504 Page Mill Road, Palo Alto, California 94304.

Mail to: Hewlett-Packard, 1504 Page Mill Road, Palo Alto, CA 94304.
Please send me further information on

( ) HP 1600A/1607A Logic State Analyzers
( ) HP-65 Hand-Held Programmable Calculator

Name _____
Company _____
Address _____
City _____ State _____ Zip _____

HEWLETT **hp** *PACKARD*

Sales and service from 172 offices in 65 countries

*Domestic USA prices only.

00548

An advertisement of 1975. Please note the "domestic USA price" of 795 US$ corresponds to an investment of 3 504 US$ in 2016. And the device was significantly more expensive outside of the USA. See also *App. J* on pp. 393ff.

SECTION 3: AUTOMATIC PROBLEM SOLVING

Your *WP 34S* is a *keystroke-programmable* calculator. If this statement makes you smile with delight, this section is for you. Else please turn to the *HP-42S Owner's Manual (Part 2)* first for an introduction into keystroke-programming – a very efficient method for solving repetitive tasks with your *WP 34S* using its program memory. Remember it provides space for some 6,000 program steps, more than 700 keystroke functions, and features 16-digit accuracy. That shall be sufficient for covering really huge challenges in comparison to the *HP-65* as advertised above.

Think of the first and the last step in program memory containing implicit END statements. [100] In between, *programs* are the basic building blocks.

Each **program** starts right after previous END and ends with the next END (i.e. its own). The **current program** is the one the program pointer is currently in; and the **current program step** is the one where the program pointer is pointing to.

Each *program* may contain *routines* and *subroutines*. Any **(sub-) routine** typically starts with a label (for calling it) and ends with RTN. In between, you may store a sequence of instructions (commands, operations, statements) for repeated use. Choose any operation featured – only a few commands are not programmable. The statements in your routine may use each and every global register provided – there are (almost) no limits. You are the sole and undisputed master of the memory!

This freedom, however, has a price: take care that the routines do not interfere with each other in their quest for data storage space. It is good practice to record the global registers a particular routine uses, and to document their purposes and contents for later reference.

In programming mode (i.e. while editing routines), the numeric display will indicate the *current program step* (000 – 927) in the mantissa and the number of free steps available in the exponent, while the dot matrix will show the command contained in the *current program step*, e.g.:

$$\text{'RCL/}\rightarrow\text{47} \qquad \substack{\text{STO} \\ \text{360}}$$
$$\text{StEP} \quad \text{017} \qquad \text{771}$$

---

[100] You cannot see that first END but the last one is visible.

There is no program-specific step counting like in the *HP-42S* or *HP-35S*.

The commands particularly required for programming are located within the violet frame on this picture. Here you find, starting top left, commands for executing (XEQ) or going to (GTO) a specific routine, keys for browsing routines (▲ and ▼), flag commands (SF, CF, and STATUS), catalogs of TESTs, programming and extra functions (P.FCN and X.FCN), commands for SoLVing, integrating,

calculating products and sums, keys for EXITing programming mode and for pausing program execution (PSE), some commands for extracting parts (|x|, IP, and FP), keys for Running / Stopping program execution (R/S) and switching between Programming and Run mode (P/R), commands for labeling a routine (LBL) or returning from a routine (RTN), and for loop control (DSE and ISG). See the contents of the *catalogs* on pp. 255ff and look up the *IOP* on pp. 185ff for more about all these commands.

Labels

Structuring program memory and jumping around in it is eased by labels you may tag to any program step – as known from previous programmable pocket calculators. Your WP 34S features a full set of alphanumeric program labels as described below.

Addressing labels works as demonstrated overleaf:

1	ⒶⒷⒸ, or Ⓓ	(XEQ), (GTO), (LBL), LBL?, (SLV), (∫y),			
		(π), (Σ), αGTO, or αXEQ			
	XEQ *label*	OP _			
	e.g.	e.g.			
	XEQ C	GTO _			

2	Calls the function labeled **C**.	ⒶⒷⒸ, or Ⓓ	(ENTER↑) sets alpha mode.	(→) [101] opens indirect addressing and sets α_T mode.	2-digit numeric (local) label ⓪⓪ ... ⑨⑨
		OP *label*			OP *nn*
		e.g.	OP '_	OP →_	e.g.
		Σ B			LBL 07

3	Sums up the function given in the routine labeled **B** within current program.		Alpha-numeric (global) label [102]	Stack level or lettered register Ⓧ, ... , Ⓚ	Register number [103]
			OP '*label*'	OP → x	OP → nn
			e.g.	e.g.	e.g.
			SLV'F1µ'	∫→T	XEQ→44

SLV'F1µ' solves the function given in the routine labeled **F1µ** (press (CPX) ① (f) (EXIT) (g) ⑦ to enter this label).

∫→T integrates the function whose label is on *stack* level **T**.

XEQ→44 executes the routine whose label is in **R44**.

---

[101] Works with all these operations except (LBL).

[102] A global label may consist of ≤ 3 characters (chars). Labels of 1 or 2 chars need a closing (ENTER↑) for closing alpha mode. Statements including alpha labels exceeding one char reduce the number of free program steps by two.

  ATTENTION: LBL A and LBL'A' are different animals! The latter is entered in alpha mode, the first via the *hotkey* directly. And the first is only a local label.

[103] This register number may be ⓪⓪ ... ⑨⑨, (.)⓪⓪ ... (.)①⑤, if the respective register is allocated. Some registers may be allocated to special applications. Check the memory table on p. 49.

Also look up GTO on p. 196 for special cases applying to this command exclusively.

Searching labels, however, works as follows:

When a command such as XEQ *lbl* is encountered with *lbl* representing a label of one, two or three characters (such as **A**, **BC**, **12**, **Tst**, **Pg3**, **x4π**, etc.), your *WP 34S* will look for this label using the following method:

1. If *lbl* is purely numeric or a *hotkey*, it will be searched forward from the *current program step*. When an END statement is reached without finding *lbl*, the quest will continue right after previous END (so the search will stay in the *current program*). This is the search procedure for **local labels**. It is as known from the *HP-41C*.

2. If, however, *lbl* is an alphanumeric label of up to three characters of arbitrary case (automatically enclosed in ' like 'Ab1'), searching will start at program step 000 and cover the entire memory in the order *RAM*, *FM*, and *XROM* (see p. 168 for the latter two), independent of the position of the program pointer. This is the search procedure for **global labels**.

> Example:
>
> Assume the program memory containing 153 program steps with a structure like the following for reasons unknown:

001	LBL B	routine B in first program
•••		routine B
012	RTN	routine B
013	LBL 'C'	routine 'C' in first program
•••		routine 'C'
034	LBL 01	routine 'C'
•••		routine 'C'
056	RTN	routine 'C'
057	LBL 02	routine 02 in first program
•••		routine 02
078	RTN	routine 02
079	END	end of first program
080	END	end of second program
081	LBL'ABC'	routine 'ABC' in third program
•••		routine 'ABC'
123	RTN	routine 'ABC'

124	LBL C	routine C in third program
...		routine C
135	RTN	routine C
136	LBL 02	routine 02 in third program
...		routine 02
152	RTN	routine 02
153	END	end of third program

With the program pointer being anywhere between step 001 and 079 (including both limits), **B** is defined and hence pressing Ⓑ will not call $1/x$ but the routine **B** starting at step 001. Ⓐ, Ⓒ, and Ⓓ will call their default functions.

With the program pointer on step 080, no *hotkey* is defined, so all shortcuts will work there.

Between step 081 and 136, **C** is defined and hence pressing Ⓒ will not call y^x but the routine **C** starting at step 124. Ⓐ, Ⓑ, and Ⓓ will call their default functions while the program pointer is in this interval. Note the local label **02** is used in the first and third program for different purposes.

GTO ⚬⚬ will move the program pointer from an arbitrary position to step 153 (i.e. the last END statement in program memory) where you can start entering a new routine. Furthermore, being outside of programming mode, RTN will move the pointer from an arbitrary location to step 001 and display **BEG**.

Note you cannot delete the last END statement in program memory. It is write-protected and may be entered automatically.

Tests

Like keystroke-programmable calculators before, your *WP 34S* features a set of tests. Their command names have a trailing '?'. Generally, tests will work as in the *HP-42S*: they will return **true** or **false** in the dot matrix if called from the keyboard; if called in a routine, they will execute the next program step only if the test is true, else skip that step. So the general rule reads 'skip if false' (exception: KEY? skips if true).

As mentioned above, routines typically end with RTN or END. In running programs, both statements work very similar and show only subtle differences: a RTN statement immediately after a test returning **false** will be skipped – an END will not. All binary tests are contained in <u>TEST</u> (see pp. 255ff); see the *IOP* on pp. 183ff for more information about the particular commands.

 There are also commands featuring a trailing '?' but returning numbers (e.g. BASE?) or codes (e.g. KTP?) instead of true or false only – you will find these commands in the *catalog* <u>P.FCN</u> (see pp. 255f).

Loops and Counters

The commands DSE, DSL, DSZ, ISE, ISG, and ISZ are all for controlling loops in routines. DSE and ISG are located bottom right on the keyboard, all the others are contained in <u>P.FCN</u>. Each of these commands decrements or increments a counter as specified (see p. 191, for example) and executes or skips the following program step depending on the result. See the picture for DSE and ISG here, copied from the back label of a Voyager. With a GTO statement placed in the skipped step pointing to a label upstream in the same routine you can create nice loops running until the specified condition is met.

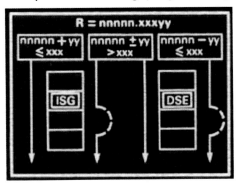

Example:[104]

Write a little routine to store random numbers in **R25** through **R39**.

Solution:

Initialize the loop counter via **25.039** (STO)(2)(4).

Reset the program pointer to the start of program memory by (RTN). Switch to programming via (P/R) and key in:

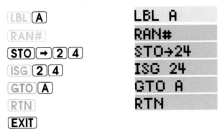

LBL (A)	LBL A
(RAN#)	RAN#
(STO)(→)(2)(4)	STO→24
(ISG)(2)(4)	ISG 24
(GTO)(A)	GTO A
(RTN)	RTN
(EXIT)	

---

[104] This example follows an idea of *Gene Wright*.

Start this program by pressing Ⓐ. It will stop with the last random number in display. Check the target registers using [SHOW].

Example (continued):

Now, write a routine to sort those fifteen stored numbers so the smallest moves to the register with the smallest address.

Solution:

We will use the so-called '*bubble sort*' algorithm. Re-initialize the loop counter via **25.039** [STO][2][4]   (*r24* was changed by program **A** above). Reset the program pointer to the start of program memory by [RTN]. Switch to programming via [P/R] and key in:

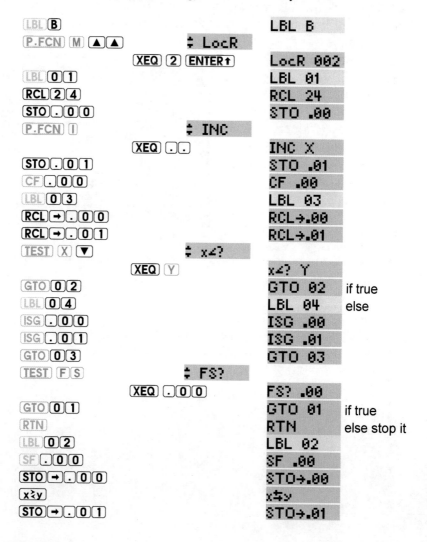

[LBL][B]		LBL B
[P.FCN][M][▲][▲]	÷ LocR	
[XEQ][2][ENTER↑]		LocR 002
[LBL][0][1]		LBL 01
[RCL][2][4]		RCL 24
[STO][.][0][0]		STO .00
[P.FCN][I]	÷ INC	
[XEQ][.][.]		INC X
[STO][.][0][1]		STO .01
[CF][.][0][0]		CF .00
[LBL][0][3]		LBL 03
[RCL][→][.][0][0]		RCL→.00
[RCL][→][.][0][1]		RCL→.01
[TEST][X][▼]	÷ x<?	
[XEQ][Y]		x<? Y
[GTO][0][2]		GTO 02 if true
[LBL][0][4]		LBL 04 else
[ISG][.][0][0]		ISG .00
[ISG][.][0][1]		ISG .01
[GTO][0][3]		GTO 03
[TEST][F][S]	÷ FS?	
[XEQ][.][0][0]		FS? .00
[GTO][0][1]		GTO 01 if true
[RTN]		RTN else stop it
[LBL][0][2]		LBL 02
[SF][.][0][0]		SF .00
[STO][→][.][0][0]		STO→.00
[x≷y]		x⇆y
[STO][→][.][0][1]		STO→.01

```
x≷y
GTO 04
EXIT
```

```
x⇆y
GTO 04
```

Start the program by pressing B. Then check the target registers using
SHOW. You will find the smallest value in **R25**, a greater one in **R26**,
etc., up to the greatest in **R39**.

By the way, note this program allocates two local registers for its
exclusive use (**R.00** and **R.01**). Furthermore, it uses one local flag and
four local labels.

The following alternative sorting program is even shorter (kudos to *Jean-
Marc Baillard* for this routine from the hpmusem.org software library):

```
LBL C
SIGN
LBL 01
RCL L
RCL L
RCL→L
LBL 02
RCL→Y
x≥? Y
GTO 03
x⇆y
RCL L
+
LBL 03
R↓
ISG Y
GTO 02
x⇆→L
STO→Z
ISG L
GTO 01
END
```

Just start it by keying in 2 5 . 0 3 9 C .

Programmed Input and Output, User Interaction and Dialogues

A number of commands may be employed for controlling the I/O of routines. A routine shall output some results at least, and it may also ask for user input. In the *IOP*, the behavior of those I/O commands is described if they are entered from the keyboard. Executed by a routine, however, they will behave differently.

When you start a routine by $\boxed{\text{XEQ}}$ or $\boxed{\text{R/S}}$, prior contents of the display are replaced by the Running ProGrAM message. The display will then be updated at certain events only – not after each operation. So where in manual mode each command may change the display immediately with its execution, in automatic mode only PROMPT, PSE, STOP, VIEW, VIEWα, or VWα+ will update the display, and this display will hold until the next such command is encountered or automatic mode is left.

For programmed I/O, see the following examples – parameters are omitted here:

- Take VIEW, VIEWα, or VWα+ for plain display updates. X is a valid parameter for VIEW and VWα+. VIEW works for complex numbers as well.

  ☞ Frequent updates will slow down program execution, since the anti-flicker logic waits for a complete display refresh cycle before allowing the next update.

- Use one of the following four code segments for displaying messages or other information for a defined minimum time interval, specified by PSE:

PSE	VIEW PSE	VIEWα PSE	VWα+ PSE
for plain numeric output	for more complex alphanumeric messages		

- Ask ('prompt') for <u>numeric</u> input employing one of these four:

STOP	VIEWα STOP	VWα+ STOP	PROMPT combines VWα+ X and STOP in one command

Whatever you key in will be in **X** when you continue the routine by pressing ⟨R/S⟩. If you want it elsewhere, take care of it.

- Prompt for <u>alphanumeric</u> input by the following three steps:

αON	sets alpha mode and prepares for showing the final part of *alpha*.
PROMPT	displays this part and waits for user input, terminated by ⟨R/S⟩.
αOFF	returns to the numeric mode previously set.

Whatever you key in will be appended to *alpha* here. The routine will continue when you press ⟨R/S⟩.

Once a programmed display as explained here has replaced that `Running Program` message mentioned above, ERR **00** or MSG **00** are the only ways to bring back `Running Program`. See the *IOP* on pp. 207ff for more information about PROMPT, PSE, STOP, VIEW, VIEWα, and VWα+ and their parameters.

If you press − instead of or after keying in numeric data − one of the *hotkeys* ⟨A⟩ to ⟨D⟩ in input, the program will call the next routine beginning with a label carrying this name (cf. p. 159).

The following example shows a typical structure of such a routine:

001	LBL'MYP'	
002	CLα	
003	α 'Hel'	Sets up a message ...
004	α 'lo!'	
005	LBL 00	
006	PROMPT	... and stops waiting for user input.
007	GTO 00	⟨R/S⟩ does nothing, it just returns to the prompt.

008	LBL A	Called if user input after step 6 was terminated by ⟨A⟩.
009	ENTRY?	Any new numeric data entered by the user?
010	GTO 03	Then go to step 12 where local label 03 lives.
011	XEQ 01	Else call subroutine 01 for computing a new number instead.

```
012   LBL 03
013   STO 21        Store the new number (input or computed).
014   RTN           Return to prompting via step 007.
015   LBL 01        Subroutine computing the new number for
...   ...                   missing numeric user input.

...   RTN

...   LBL B      Called if user input after step 6 was terminated by B.
...   ...

...   RTN

...   ...

...   END
```

This is the way the TVM application is implemented.

If there is more than one program using labels **A** to **D** in *RAM* or *FM* then you must move the program counter into the desired program and stop there (see p. 159 to learn which label will be found else).

Keyboard Codes and Direct Keyboard Access

Sometimes, the four *hotkeys* might not suffice. There is, however, an easy way to extend the number of directly callable subroutines: short-hand addressing of numeric labels using keyboard codes as defined here. Each key gets a code simply given by its row and column on the keyboard.

Whenever you are asked for the entry of a two-digit (i.e. local) label, any of the keys highlighted green in this picture may be used for direct input of two digits via a single keystroke. The row / column code of this key will be inserted as label then.

(Keys not available this way (since they have another fixed meaning in this context) may still be used for a short local label

A	B	C	D	→	CPX
11	12	13	14	15	16
STO	RCL	R↓	f	g	h
21	22	23	24	25	26
ENTER↑	x⇄y	+/−	EEX	←	
31	32	33	34	35	
XEQ	7	8	9	/	
41	42	43	44	45	
▲	4	5	6	x	
51	52	53	54	55	
▼	1	2	3	−	
61	62	63	64	65	
EXIT	0	.	R/S	+	
71	72	73	74	75	

input by pressing ⬜ before though the gain will be less. Only ⬜ itself cannot be used for shorthand addressing.)

If, for example, you want to link a routine to the key (STO), just put label **21** at the beginning of this routine; then it can be called via (XEQ) (STO) by the user conveniently.

The same keyboard codes are returned by the KEY? command, which allows 'real time' response to user input from the keyboard. KEY? takes a register argument (X is allowed but does not lift the *stack*) and stores the key most recently pressed during program execution in the register specified. R/S and EXIT cannot be queried; they stop program execution immediately. The keyboard is active during program execution – but it is desirable to display a message and suspend the routine by PSE while waiting for user input. Since PSE will be terminated by a key press, simply use PSE 99 in a loop to wait for input. Since KEY? acts as a test as well, a typical user input loop may well look like this example:

001	LBL'USR'	
002	CLα	
003	α 'KEY'	Sets up a message ...
004	α ?	
005	LBL 00	
006	VIEWα	... and displays it.
007	PSE 99	Waits 9.9*s* for user input unless a key is pressed.
008	KEY? 00	Test for user input and put the key code in **R00**.
009	GTO 00	If there was none then go back to step 5.
010	LBL?→00	If a label corresponding to the key code has been defined ...
011	XEQ→00	... then call it,
012	GTO 00	... else return to step 5.

Instead of the dumb waiting loop, the routine can do some computations and update the display before the next call to PSE and KEY? – think of e.g. a lunar landing game.

To be even more versatile, use KTP? to return the type of the key pressed if its row / column code is given (see the *IOP* on pp. 198f).

If you decide not to handle the key in your program you may feed it back to the main processing loop of the *WP 34S* with the command

PUTK **nn** . It will cause the program to halt, and the key will be handled as if pressed after the stop. This is especially useful if you want to allow numeric input while waiting for some special keys like the arrows. This command allows writing a vector or matrix editor in user code. After execution of the PUTK command you are responsible for letting the routine continue its work by pressing (R/S) or a *hotkey*.

Printer Graphics

There are a number of commands provided for setting up a string for printer graphics. Those commands may also be used in run mode but make more sense in routines. The basic ideas are as follow:

- A set of registers used to store pixels for printing graphics is called a *graphic block*. Such a block may contain **w** (up to 166) pixel columns and **h** pixel rows (defaults are **w** = 166 and **h** = 8).

- The first two *bytes* of said *graphic block* are reserved to take its parameters **w** and $\check{h} = floor\left(\frac{h+7}{8}\right)$.

- The number of registers required for such a block is $n = floor\left(\frac{w \cdot \check{h}+9}{8}\right)$ – see FLOOR. E.g. 21 registers are necessary for $166 \cdot 8$ pixels.

- GDIM initializes such a *graphic block*. The command can be exactly emulated in integer mode by storing $256 \cdot \check{h} + w$ in the first register and clearing the next $n - 1$ registers.

Note that all graphic commands provided on your *WP 34S* rely on that data structure. Your *WP 34S*, however, cannot know whether a particular register contains a (part of a) *graphic block* or not. It is your responsibility to track the *graphic blocks* you use.

Local Data

After some time with your *WP 34S* you will have a number of routines stored, so keeping track of their resource requirements may become a challenge. Most modern programming languages take care of this by declaring *local variables*, i.e. memory space allocated from general data memory and accessible for the current routine only – when the routine is finished, the respective memory is released. On your *WP 34S*, registers are for data storage – so we offer you *local registers* allocated to your routines exclusively.

Example:

Let us assume you write a routine labeled **P1** and need five registers for your computations therein. Then all you have to do is just enter the command LOCR **5** in **P1** specifying you want five *local registers*. Thereafter, you can access these registers by using local register numbers .00 … .04 throughout **P1**.

Now, if you call another routine **P2** from **P1**, also **P2** may contain a step LOCR requesting *local registers*. These will also carry local register numbers .00 etc., but the *local register* .00 of **P2** will be different from the *local register* .00 of **P1**, so no interference will occur. As soon as the return statement is executed, the *local registers* of the corresponding routine are released and the space they took is returned to free memory.

In addition, you get sixteen local flags as soon as you request at least one *local register*.

Local data holding allows for recursive routines, since every time such a routine is called again it will allocate a new set of *local registers* and flags being different from the ones it got before. See the commands LOCR, LOCR?, MEM?, and POPLR in the *IOP* on pp. 199ff and look up *App. B* on pp. 303f for more information, also about the limitations applying to local data.

Flash Memory (*FM*) and *XROM*

In addition to the *RAM* provided, your *WP 34S* allows you to access **FM** for voltage-fail safe storage of user programs and data. The first section of *FM* is a *2kB backup region*, holding the image of the entire *RAM* (i.e. user program memory, registers, and *WP 34S* states) as soon as you completed a SAVE. The remaining part of *FM* (up to some *12kB* depending on setup) is for programs only. Global labels in *FM* can be called using XEQ like in *RAM*. This allows creating program libraries in *FM*. Use CAT to see the global labels already defined – labels in *FM* are tagged with Ŀ b in CAT.

FM is ideal for backups or other relatively long-living data, but shall not be used for repeated transient storage like in programmed loops.[105] Conversely, registers and standard user program memory residing in *RAM* are designed for data changing frequently but will not hold data with the batteries removed. So both *RAM* and *FM* have their specific advantages and disadvantages you shall take into account for optimum benefit and longevity of your *WP 34S*. Find more about *FM* in *App. A* on pp. 296f.

Furthermore, there is a memory section called **XROM** (for 'extended *ROM*'). Therein live some 30% of all command routines (e.g. f'(x) and f"(x), SLV and SLVQ, $\int$, Π and Σ, all statistical distributions, orthogonal polynomials, the functions AGM, B_n, $B_n{}^*$, ERF, ERFC, FIB, g_d and its inverse, NEXTP, *Lambert's* W and its inverse, *Euler's* β, *Riemann's* ζ, and most functions operating in complex domain). These *XROM routines* are written in user code but can be called as commands. For you, it makes no difference neither in handling nor accuracy whether a preprogrammed *WP 34S* routine runs in *ROM* or *XROM*. While *ROM routines* (written in *C*) execute significantly faster; *XROM routines*, on the other hand,

- reduce the size of the binary image (`calc.bin` et al., see pp. 285ff), thus increasing the free space available for your programs in *FM*, and

- are easy to read and understand (and thus, to maintain) for all users knowing *HP* keystroke programming – see *http://sourceforge.net/p/wp34s/code/HEAD/tree/trunk/xrom/* for the *XROM routines* provided and pp. 355ff for additional information.

---

[105] *FM* may not survive more than some 10 000 flashes. Thus, we made commands writing to *FM* (SAVE or PSTO) non-programmable.

SECTION 4: ADVANCED PROBLEM SOLVING

There are some powerful commands provided in your *WP 34S* for computing programmable sums and products, for solving equations, for computing finite integrals as well as first and second derivatives. The commands Σ, Π, SLVQ, SLV, ∫, f'(x), and f"(x) are explained below in this order. All these commands may also be programmed. See below for details.

Programmable Sums

The command Σ is called with a loop control number in **X** and a label trailing the command. Said loop control number follows the format `cccccc.fffii` (as it does in DSE etc. mentioned on p. 161 above).

In its heart, Σ then works like this:

1. It sets the sum to **0** initially.

2. It fills all *stack* levels with `cccccc` and calls the routine specified by the label. That routine returns a summand in **X**.

3. It adds this summand to said sum.

4. It decrements `cccccc` by `ii`; if `cccccc ≥ fff` then Σ goes back to step 2, else it returns the final sum in **X**.

   If `ii = 0`, `cccccc` will be decremented by **1** in each loop.

Example:

Compute $\sum_{k=0}^{100} \sqrt{k}$.

Solution:

1. Write a little program for the internal calculation of the summands:

   ```
   LBL'SU'
   √
   RTN
   ```

2. Enter **100** Σ (ENTER↑) S U (ENTER↑)

   and get returned if FIX **4** is set.

Programmable Products

The command Π is called with a loop control number in **X** and a label trailing the command (like for the command Σ). In its heart, Π works almost as Σ described above:

1. It sets the product to **1** initially.

2. It fills all *stack* levels with cccccc and calls the routine specified by the label. That routine returns a factor in **X**.

3. It multiplies this factor with said product.

4. It decrements cccccc by ii; if cccccc ≥ fff then Π goes back to step 2, else it returns the final product in **X**.

    If ii = 0, cccccc will be decremented by **1** in each loop.

Example:

Compute $\Pi_{k=1}^{50} \frac{1}{\sqrt{k}}$.

Solution:

1. Write a little program for the internal calculation of the factors:

    ```
    LBL'Pro'
    √
    1/x
    RTN
    ```

2. Enter   **50.001** π (ENTER↑) P ↑ R O

    and get   5.734⁻³³   returned if SCI **3** is set.

Solving Quadratic Equations

The command SLVQ finds the real and complex roots of a quadratic equation $ax^2 + bx + c = 0$ with its parameters on the input *stack* [***c, b, a***, ...] :

*   If $r := b^2 - 4ac \geq 0$, SLVQ returns two real roots $-\dfrac{b \pm \sqrt{r}}{2a}$ in **Y** and **X**. If called in a routine, the step after SLVQ will be executed

then.

- Else, SLVQ returns the real part of the first complex root in X and its imaginary part in Y (the second root is the complex conjugate of the first – see CONJ). If run directly from the keyboard, the complex indicator **i** is lit then. If called in a routine, the step after SLVQ will be skipped.

In either case, SLVQ returns r in Z. Higher *stack* levels are kept unchanged. L will contain equation parameter c.

Example:

Find the roots of $4x^2 - 3x - 2 = 0$.

Solution:

4 (ENTER↑) 3 (+/–) (ENTER↑) 2 (+/–)

(X.FCN) (S)(L) (XEQ)   returns (if FIX **4** is set) $x = 1.1754$, $y = -0.4254$, $z = 41.0000$. Since z is positive, x and y are the two real roots of this equation here.

Check:

Store x in $R00$ and y in $R01$. Then enter

(RCL)(0)(0) (FILL) 4 (×) 3 (−) (×) 2 (−) returning $\boxed{- 1.0000^{-15}}$ and

(RCL)(0)(1) (FILL) 4 (×) 3 (−) (×) 2 (−) returning $\boxed{0.0000}$.

Remember your *WP 34S* calculates with 16 digit precision, so any result within $\pm 3 \cdot 10^{-15}$ is equal to zero in this matter.

The Solver

This command solves the equation $f(x) = 0$, with **f(x)** calculated by the routine specified.[106] Two initial estimates of the root must be supplied in X and Y when calling SLV.

Note that SLV fills all *stack* levels with x before calling the routine specified.

---

[106] As mentioned on p. 10 already, there are hardware reasons making the Solver on your *WP 43S* looking more like it did on the *HP-15C* than on the *HP-42S*.

SLV will return x_{root} in **X**, the second last x-value tested in **Y**, $f(x_{root})$ in **Z**, 0 in **T**, and x_{root} in all other *stack* levels. − If called in a routine, the step after SLV will be skipped if SLV fails to find a root.

Find the roots of $7x^3 + 5x^2 - 3x - 2 = 0$.

Solution:

1. Write a little program for the internal calculation of *f(x)*:

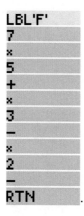

```
LBL'F'
7
×
5
+
×
3
−
×
2
−
RTN
```

2. Enter **0** (**ENTER↑**) **1** (SLV) (**ENTER↑**)(F) (**ENTER↑**) and you get ⎡ 6.43 ⎤⁻¹ returned if SCI **3** is set.

3. You can enter (FILL) (XEQ) (**ENTER↑**)(F) (**ENTER↑**) for checking and get ⎡ 0.000 ⎤⁰ confirming the result of the solver. Slightly greater x-values, e.g. **0.65**, return positive values for *f(x)*, slightly smaller values, e.g. **0.64**, return negative values for *f(x)*.

4. There may be one or two more roots:

   a. Enter **-2** (**ENTER↑**) **0** (SLV) (**ENTER↑**)(F) (**ENTER↑**) and you get ⎡ -8.064 ⎤⁻¹ ; checking returns 0 again. Slightly greater x-values, e.g. **-0.8**, return positive values for *f(x)*, slightly smaller values, e.g. **-0.81**, return negative values for *f(x)*. Thus, there must be one more root between the two found.

   b. Enter **-.7** (**ENTER↑**) **.5** (SLV) (**ENTER↑**)(F) (**ENTER↑**) and you get ⎡ -5.5 ⎤₁₀⁻¹ ; checking returns 0 again.

Note that even a polynomial of same grade deviating just a bit (e.g. $7x^3 + 4.5x^2 - 3x - 2 = 0$) may show one real root only. [107]

Numeric Integration

The command $\int$ lets your *WP 34S* compute definite integrals of the function *f(x)* given in the routine specified. Lower and upper integration limits must be supplied in Y and X, respectively – so $\int$ integrates *f(x)* from *y* to *x*.

Note that $\int$ fills all *stack* levels with *x* before calling the routine specified.

Example:

The *Bessel functions* belong to the most 'popular' advanced functions in physics. For integer *v*, $J_v(x) = \frac{1}{\pi} \int_0^\pi cos[v\, t - x\, sin(t)]\, dt$ is called the *Bessel function of the first kind of order v*.

Especially, $J_0(x) = \frac{1}{\pi} \int_0^\pi cos[x\, sin(t)]\, dt$ is the *Bessel function of the first kind of order 0*. Evaluate this function at *x* = 1.

Solution:

1. Write a little program for the internal calculation of the integrand $f(t) = cos[\, sin(t)]$:

```
LBL'J0'
SIN
COS
RTN
```

2. Enter

SCI 3

RAD

0 π ⏎ ENTER↑ J 0 ENTER↑

and your *WP 34S* returns

$\int$ ░░

2.404 0

$\boxed{\pi}$ $\boxed{/}$ finally displays $J_0(1) = $ `7.652⁻¹` .

The iteration exits and the result is displayed as soon as the last two approximations agree when <u>rounded to display precision</u> (the test command $\boxed{x\!\cong\!\,?}$ is used). Set the display to SCI n if you want to get $n+1$ <u>significant</u> digits. $\int$ returns the (approximated) integral in X, the penultimate approximation in Y, the upper integration limit in Z, the lower one in T, and fills also the remaining *stack* levels, if applicable.[108]

Derivatives

There are two commands provided returning the sizes of the first two derivatives of the function $f(x)$ at position x. This function $f(x)$ must be specified in a routine starting with the global label given as parameter of f'(x) or f"(x), respectively.

f'(x) returns the <u>first</u> derivative. For computing it, f'(x) will first look for a user routine labeled '**δx**' (or '**δX**', '**Δx**', or '**ΔX**', in this order), returning a fixed step size *dx* in X. If that routine is not defined, *dx* = 0.1 is set for default. Then, f'(x) fills all *stack* levels with x and calls $f(x)$. It will evaluate $f(x)$ at ten points equally spaced in the interval $x \pm 5\,dx$ (if you expect any irregularities within this interval, change *dx* to exclude them). On return, the first derivative will be in *stack* level X, while Y, Z, and T will be clear and the position x will be in L.

Example:

Take the function $f(x) = 7x^3 + 5x^2 - 3x - 2$ again (you used it above for solving). Instead of checking two function values left and right of the root you could check just the slope *f'(x)* at the root.

---

[108] Please refer to the *HP-34C Owner's Handbook and Programming Guide* (*Section 9* and *App. B*) or the *HP-15C Owner's Handbook* (*Section 14* and *App. E*) for more information about automatic integration and some caveats.

Your *WP 34S* uses a slightly different iterative algorithm than *HP's* vintage calculators: it employs the classical *Romberg* method (up to build 3889); each new iteration takes twice the time of the previous one until the exit-condition is met. Inspect the code at sourceforge.net – it is an XROM routine (cf. *App. H*) so you can read it almost as easily as a regular user program. – With build 3899, your *WP 34S* uses the *double exponential method* for integration (for background information, see *http://www.hpmuseum.org/forum/thread-8021.html?highlight=34s+integration*).

Solution:

You have **f(x)** in program memory already. For each of the three roots found, calculate the root first, then the first derivative of **f(x)** at that point:

1. **0** (ENTER↑) **1** SLV (ENTER↑) F (ENTER↑) returns 6.431^{-1} as above. Now, calling f'(x) via

   (P.FCN) F ▼ ▼ (XEQ) (ENTER↑) F (ENTER↑) returns 1.211^{-1}.

2. **0** (ENTER↑) **-1** SLV (ENTER↑) F (ENTER↑) returns $-5.5\,10^{-1}$.

   (P.FCN)(XEQ) (ENTER↑) F (ENTER↑) returns -2.134^{0}.

3. **-1** (ENTER↑) **-2** SLV (ENTER↑) F (ENTER↑) returns -8.064^{-1}.

   (P.FCN)(XEQ) (ENTER↑) F (ENTER↑) returns 2.591^{0}.

f"(x) works in full analogy, computing the <u>second</u> derivative of **f(x)**. This helps in checking for maxima or minima of **f(x)**.

Programming and Nesting Advanced Operations

You can use SLV, ∫, Σ, and Π in routines and nest them to any depth as far as memory allows and your patience lasts.

Example:

It is observed that light is diffracted when passing through circular holes. The effect is most obvious when using laser light. Its intensity behind the hole is

$$I(r) = I_0 \times \left(\frac{J_1(2\pi r)}{\pi r}\right)^2 \quad \text{with} \quad J_1(x) = \frac{1}{\pi}\int_0^\pi \cos[\,t - x\sin(t)]\,dt$$

being the *Bessel function of the first kind of order 1* (cf. p. 175).

Find the first three roots of the intensity (i.e. the radii where no light will be observed).

Solution:

1. Write a little program for the internal calculation of the integrand $f(t) = cos[\,t - x\,sin(t)]$:

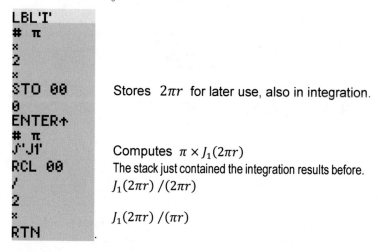

```
LBL'J1'
SIN          sin(t)
RCL 00       The entire stack is loaded with t, so x must be recalled.
×            x sin(t)
−            t − x sin(t)
COS          cos[ t − x sin(t)]
RTN
```

2. Write a little program for the internal calculation of the intensity $I(r)$. Note that just the parenthesis of the formula above must be evaluated since I_0 is a constant:

```
LBL'I'
#  π
×
2
×
STO 00       Stores 2πr for later use, also in integration.
0
ENTER↑
#  π
∫'J1'        Computes π × J_1(2πr)
RCL 00       The stack just contained the integration results before.
/            J_1(2πr) /(2πr)
2
×            J_1(2πr) /(πr)
RTN
```

3. Enter

   [SCI] **3**

   [RAD]

   0.1 [ENTER↑] **1** [SLV] [ENTER↑][I] [ENTER↑] and you will get
   6.098^{-1} after some time.[109]

4. Enter **1** [ENTER↑] **1.5** [SLV] [ENTER↑][I] [ENTER↑] and you get 1.117^{0} .

5. Enter **1.5** [ENTER↑] **2** [SLV] [ENTER↑][I] [ENTER↑] and you get 1.619^{0} .

---

[109] I.e. after some 25s using the *WP 34S* emulator (cf. *App. D*) on a PC running *Windows 7*. It will take some minutes on your calculator. Nesting advanced operations may require very large amounts of calculations to be performed! – Note the Solver was not started at **0** since that would cause an error when dividing by $2πr$.

SECTION 5: INDEX OF OPERATIONS (*IOP*)

All commands available (more than 700) are listed below with their *names* and the keystrokes necessary to call them – except the ones contained in CONV and CONST which are separately listed in *Section 6* (see pp. 261ff). Names printed in **bold** face in this table here belong to functions directly accessible on the keyboard; the other commands may be picked from *catalogs* (see pp. 52f and 248ff).[110] The names will show up identically in *catalogs* and program listings.

Sorting in this index, in CONV, CONST, and all other *catalogs* is case insensitive and works in the following order:

⌴ 0...9 A...Z α...ω ( ) + − × / ± , . ! ? : ;

' " ✳ @ _ ~ → ← ↑ ↓ ⇆ ∠ ≤ = ≈ ≠ ≥ ≫

× ± € £ ¥ √ ∫ ∞ & \ ^ | [ ] { } ⌂ #

Superscripts and subscripts are handled like normal characters in sorting.

Generally, functions and keystroke-programming will work as on the *HP-42S*, bit and integer functions as on the *HP-16C*, unless specified otherwise. There are also functions provided for printer graphics (as explained on p. 168). For functions inspired by other vintage calculators (mentioned in the index), their manuals may contain helpful additional information. A ^{c} heads the names of complex operations (see p. 123). CPX is a legal prefix for all functions whose *names are printed in italics* in this index.

Some 300 functions are featured in your *WP 34S* for the first time ever on an *RPN* calculator. They got their remarks printed on white background, the older ones on light grey. Operations carrying familiar names but deviating in their functionality from previous *RPN* calculators are marked light red.

For the vast majority of operations, remarks start with a number:

(0) represents functions without any effects on the *stack*, e.g. mode setting functions;

---

[110] For cataloged commands, we list the keys calling the respective *catalog* and print the command as shown therein. As mentioned above, there are various ways accessing such a command. We are confident you will find the ones suiting you best.

(1) is for *monadic* functions (cf. p. 35),

(2) for *dyadic* functions (cf. p. 36), and

(3) for three-number functions as defined on p. 40;

(-1) stands for functions pushing one real or complex number on the *stack* and

(-2) for functions pushing two real or complex numbers on the *stack*.

Operation or function **parameters** will be taken from the lowest *stack* level(s) unless mentioned explicitly in the second column of the index – then they have to trail the command. Some parameters of statistical distributions must be given in registers **J** and **K** as specified at the respective commands.

Three examples of the parameter notation used will be shown below. Assume **R12** contains 15.67 generally here, i.e. *r12* = 15.67.

- *n* represents an arbitrary integer number which must be keyed in directly, while

   <u>n</u> represents such a number which may be specified indirectly via a register as well (as shown in the tables on pp. 63f and 134f); and

   n stands for the respective number itself, regardless of the way it was specified;

   Example:

   RSD **12** rounds *x* to twelve significant digits, while RSD→**12** rounds *x* to fifteen significant digits.

- *s* represents an arbitrary register address which must be keyed in directly, while

   <u>s</u> represents such an address which may be specified indirectly as well; and

   s stands for the contents of the address specified – *s* may be used as an address again;

   Example:

   STO **12** stores *x* into **R12**, while STO→**12** stores *x* into **R15**.

- *label* represents an arbitrary label which must be keyed in directly, while

label represents such a label which may be specified indirectly as
well (as shown in the table following p. 157); and

label stands for the respective label itself, regardless of the way it
was specified.

Example:

GTO **12** goes to local label **12**, while GTO→**12** goes to local
label **15**.

The four commands CLx, ENTER, Σ+, and Σ- are the only ones
<u>disabling</u> *automatic stack lift* (compare p. 39).   Numeric input
immediately after such an operation will <u>overwrite</u> *x* instead of pushing
it on the *stack* as usual.

In the following, each function is listed stating the mode(s) it will work in
(unless it works in all modes): [d] stands for DECM, [n] for the integer
modes, [α] for alpha mode, and [**sto**] for programming (see pp. 72ff);
'&' stands for a Boolean AND, a comma for OR, and a leading ¬ for
NOT. So e.g. the function 10^x works in all modes but alpha, even in
complex domain. All operations may be entered in programming mode
as well unless stated otherwise (but many functions contained in <u>P.FCN</u>
make sense in routines only). Commands printed red require additional
hardware and the corresponding firmware installed (see *App. A* on pp.
285ff and *App. H* on pp. 359ff) – else those commands will not work.

Now, here the index of operations starts:

Name	Keystrokes	Remarks (see pp. 171ff for general information)
10^x	f 10^x	(1) [¬α] Returns 10^x.
12h	h MODE 12h	(0) Sets 12h time display mode: e.g. 1:23 will become 1:23 AM, and 23:45 will become 11:45 PM. This will make a difference in αTIME only.
1COMPL	h MODE 1COMPL	(0) Sets 1's complement mode (see p. 137).
1/x	f 1/x	(1) [d] Inverts the number in *x*. B may be used as shortcut as long as label B is not defined in the *current program*.

Name	Keystrokes	Remarks (see pp. 171ff for general information)
24h	h MODE **24h**	(0) Sets 24h time display mode. Compare 12h.
2COMPL	h MODE **2COMPL**	(0) Sets 2's complement mode (see p. 137).
2^x	f 2^x	(1) [¬α] Returns 2^x.
$\sqrt[3]{x}$	h X.FCN **$\sqrt[3]{x}$**	(1) [¬α] Returns the cube root of x.
ABS	f |x|	(1) [¬α] Returns the absolute (unsigned) value of x.
	CPX f |x|	(1) [d] Returns the absolute value of x_c, i.e. puts $r = \sqrt{x^2 + y^2}$ in **X** and clears **Y**.
ACOS	g COS⁻¹	(1) [d] Returns $arccos(x)$.[111]
ACOSH	g HYP⁻¹ COS	(1) [d] Returns $arcosh(x)$.[112]
AGM	h X.FCN **AGM**	(2) [d] Returns the *arithmetic-geometric mean* of x and y. Will throw an error for negative input. See p. 389 for more.
ALL	h ALL *n*	(0) [¬α] Sets the numeric display format to show all decimals whenever possible. ALL **0** works almost like ALL in the *HP-42S*. For $x \geq 10^{13}$, however, display will switch to SCI or ENG with the maximum number of digits necessary (see SCIOVR and ENGOVR, respectively). The same will happen if $x < 10^{-n}$ <u>and</u> more than 12 digits are required to show x completely. Example:

Example:

Input:	Display:
700	700
ALL **3**	700.
1/x	0.00142857143
10 /	142857142857⁻⁴

---

[111] Precisely, it returns the principal value of it, i.e. a real part $\in [0, \pi]$ in ∡ʳ, or $\in [0, 180]$ in ∡°, or $\in [0, 200]$ in ∡ᵍ. Compare ISO/IEC 9899.

[112] Note there is no need for pressing f here.

Name	Keystrokes	Remarks (see pp. 171ff for general information)
AND	h AND	(2) [d] Works like AND in the *HP-28S*, i.e. x and y are interpreted before executing this operation. Zero is 'false'; any other real number is 'true'.
		(2) [n] Works bitwise as in the *HP-16C*. See pp. 141ff.
ANGLE	h X.FCN **ANGLE**	(2) [d] Returns $arctan(^y/_x)$.
ASIN	g SIN⁻¹	(1) [d] Returns $arcsin(x)$.[113]
ASINH	g HYP⁻¹ SIN	(1) [d] Returns $arsinh(x)$.[112]
ASR	h X.FCN **ASR** *n*	(1) [n] Works in integer modes like n (≤ 63) consecutive ASRs in the *HP-16C*, corresponding to a division of x by 2^n. ASR **0** executes as NOP, but loads **L**. See pp. 141f for more.
ATAN	g TAN⁻¹	(1) [d] Returns $arctan(x)$.[113]
ATANH	g HYP⁻¹ TAN	(1) [d] Returns $artanh(x)$.[112]
BACK	h P.FCN **BACK** *n*	(0) [¬α] Jumps *n* steps backwards ($0 \leq n \leq 255$) in the *current routine*. E.g. BACK 1 goes to the previous program step. If BACK attempts to cross an END, an error is thrown. Reaching step 000 stops program execution and lights **BEG**. Compare SKIP. **ATTENTION:** If you edit a section of your routine crossed by one or more BACK, SKIP, or CASE jumps, this may well result in a need to **manually maintain all those statements individually.**

---

[113] Precisely, it returns the principal value of it, i.e. a real part $\in [-\pi/2, \pi/2]$ in ∡ʳ, or $\in [-90, 90]$ in ∡°, or $\in [-100, 100]$ in ∡ᵍ if flag D is set. <u>Else</u> the result interval for the arc tangent becomes e.g. $(-\pi/2, \pi/2)$. Compare ISO/IEC 9899.

Name	Keystrokes	Remarks (see pp. 171ff for general information)
BASE	**h** (MODE) **BASE** _n_	(0) Sets base _n_ for integer calculations ($2 \leq n \leq 16$, see pp. 72ff and 123ff).
BASE 10	**f** (10)	Furthermore, BASE **0** sets DECM, and BASE **1** calls FRACT (see there). The shortcuts will only work if *alpha mode* is not set.
BASE 16	**g** (16)	
BASE 2	**f** (2)	**ATTENTION:** *Stack* contents will change when switching between an integer mode and DECM, other register contents stay as they are (see pp. 305ff).
BASE 8	**g** (8)	BASE 10 is not DECM.
BASE?	**h** (P.FCN) **BASE?**	(-1) [¬α] Returns the integer base currently set (or in DECM the last base set before).
BATT	**h** (X.FCN) **BATT**	(-1) [¬α] Returns the actual battery voltage in the range between $1.9V$ and $3.4V$ (in units of $100mV$ if in an integer mode). Cf. also p. 73.
BC?	**h** (TEST) **BC?** _n_	(0) [n] Tests if the specified bit in x is clear.
BestF	**h** (MODE) **BestF**	(0) Selects the 'best' curve fit model for the current statistical data by picking the model with maximum *correlation* (like BEST in *HP-42S*). Relevant for L.R., CORR, and ŷ.
Binom		(1) [d] *Binomial distribution* with the number of successes *g* in **X**, the probability of a success p_0 in **J**, and the sample size *n* in **K**. See p. 376 for the formulas.
Binom$_p$	**h** (PROB) **Binom**	
Binom$_u$	etc.	Binom^{-1} returns the maximum number of successes *m* for a given probability *p* in **X**, p_0 in **J**
Binom^{-1}		and *n* in **K**.
B$_n$	**h** (X.FCN) **B**	(1) [d] B$_n$ returns the Bernoulli number for an integer *n* > 0 given in **X**. B$_n^*$ works with the old definition instead. See p. 374 for details.
B$_n^*$	**h** (X.FCN) **B***	
BS?	**h** (TEST) **BS?** _n_	(0) [n] Tests if the specified bit in x is set.

Name	Keystrokes	Remarks (see pp. 171ff for general information)

CASE	**h** `P.FCN`
	`CASE s`
		(0) [¬α] Works like SKIP below but *s* indicates the number of steps to skip.
		
		Example:
		Assume the following program section:
		
		``
		        •••
		100 CASE 12
		101 GTO 01
		102 GTO 02
		103 GTO 07
		104 GTO 05
		105 LBL 01
		        •••
		
		132 LBL 02
		        •••
		
		153 LBL 05
		        •••
		
		234 LBL 07
		        •••
		``
		
		In program execution, *r12* will be checked in step 100: for *r12* = 0 the program will proceed to step 101 and continue with a jump to step 105, for *r12* = 1 it will go to step 102, etc., resulting in a nice controlled dispatcher for $0 \leq r12 \leq 3$.
		
		ATTENTION: CASE will throw an 'out of range' error for *s* < 0. And CASE might surprise you for *r12* > 4 in the example above. Take care of the input you provide!
		
		If you edit a section of your routine crossed by one or more BACK, SKIP, or CASE jumps, this may well result in a need to **manually maintain all those statements individually.**

	h `CAT`	[¬α] Program *browser*. See p. 249.
Cauch Cauch$_p$ Cauch$_u$ Cauch $^{-1}$	**h** `PROB` `Cauch` etc.	(1) [d] *Cauchy-Lorentz distribution* (also known as *Lorentz* or *Breit-Wigner distribution*) with the location x_0 specified in **J** and the shape γ in **K**. See *App. I* on pp. 375ff for details. Cauch^{-1} returns *x* for a given probability *p* in **X**, with x_0 in **J** and γ in **K**.

Name	Keystrokes	Remarks (see pp. 171ff for general information)
CB	**h** X.FCN **CB** _n_	(1) [n] Clears the specified bit in x.
CEIL	**h** X.FCN **CEIL**	(1) [¬α] Returns the smallest integer $\geq x$.
CF	**g** CF _n_	(0) [¬α] Clears the flag specified.
CFALL	**h** P.FCN **CFALL**	(0) [¬α] Clears all global and local user flags.
CLALL	**h** P.FCN **CLALL**	(0) [¬α] Clears all registers in *RAM* if confirmed. Modes will stay as they are. Compare RESET.
CLP	**f** CLP	(0) Clears the *current program* (cf. p. 156) if confirmed, be it in *RAM* or *FM*.
CLPALL	**h** P.FCN **CLPALL**	(0) [¬α] Clears all programs in *RAM* if confirmed. Not programmable.
CLREGS	**h** P.FCN **CLREGS**	(0) [¬α] Clears all general purpose registers. The contents of the *stack* and **L** are kept.
CLSTK	**0** **g** FILL	[¬α] Clears all *stack* registers currently allocated (i.e. **X** … **T** or **X** … **D**, respectively). All other register contents are kept.
	h P.FCN **CLSTK**	
CLx	**h** CLx	(1) [¬α] Clears register **X**, disabling *automatic stack lift*.
CLα	**h** CLx	(0) [α] Clears the alpha register (like CLA in the *HP-42S*).
	h P.FCN **CLα**	(0) [¬α] Clears the alpha register.
CLΣ	**g** CLΣ	(0) [d] Clears the summation registers and releases the memory allocated for them (see p. 301).
CNST	**h** P.FCN **CNST** _n_	(-1) [¬α] Returns the constant stored at position _n_ in *catalog* CONST (see pp. 261ff). Allows for indirect addressing of these contents.

Name	Keystrokes	Remarks (see pp. 171ff for general information)
^{c}CNST	CPX h X.FCN ᶜCNST *n*	(-2) [¬α] Works like CNST but performs a complex recall as described for CONST on p. 253.
CNVG?	h TEST CNVG? *s*	(0) [d] Checks for convergence by comparing x and y as determined by the lowest five bits of s. a) The lowest two bits set the tolerance limit: $0 = 10^{-14}$, $1 = 10^{-24}$, $2 = 10^{-32}$, 3 = Choose the best for the mode set, resulting in taking 0 for *SP* and 2 for *DP* (see pp. 351ff in *App. H*). b) The next two bits determine the comparison mode using the tolerance limit set: 0 = compare the real numbers x and y relatively, 1 = compare them absolutely, 2 = check the absolute difference between the complex values $x + i y$ and $z + i t$, 3 = works as 0 so far. c) The top bit tells how special numbers are handled: 0 = NaN and infinities are considered converged, 1 = they are not considered converged. Now, $s = a + 4b + 16c$.
		(0) [n] Tests for $x = y$.
COMB	f Cy.x	(2) [¬α] Returns the number of possible subsets (or combinations) of x items taken out of a set of y items (i.e. choose x out of y). No item occurs more than once in a subset, and different orders of the same x items are not counted separately. Compare PERM on p. 207 and see p. 375 for the formulas.
^{c}CONJ	CPX h X.FCN ᶜCONJ	(1) [d] Flips the sign of y, returning the complex conjugate of x_c.

Name	Keystrokes	Remarks (see pp. 171ff for general information)
	h CONST	[¬α] *Catalog*, see pp. 261ff.
	h CONV	[d] *Catalog*, see pp. 270ff.
CORR	**g** **r**	(-1) [d] Returns the *coefficient of correlation* for the current statistical data and curve fit model. See *App. I* on pp. 383f for more.
COS	**f** COS	(1) [d] Returns the cosine of the angle x.
COSH	**f** HYP COS	(1) [d] Returns the hyperbolic cosine of x.
COV	**h** STAT **COV**	(-1) [d] Returns the population covariance for the two data sets entered via **Σ+**, depending on the curve fit model selected. See s_{XY} for the sample covariance and *App. I* on pp. 383ff for more.
^{c}CROSS	CPX **h** X.FCN **ᶜCROSS**	(2) [d] Interprets x and y as Cartesian components of a vector #1, and z and t as those of a vector #2, and returns the *cross product* of them $[x \cdot t - y \cdot z, 0, ...]$, dropping two *stack* levels.
DATE	**h** X.FCN **DATE**	(-1) [d] Recalls the date from the real time clock into the numeric section in the format selected. See D.MY, M.DY, and Y.MD. Set the display to FIX **6** or FIX **4** to see the full date information. In addition, DATE shows the day of week in the dot matrix. **ATTENTION:** The function DATE of the *HP-12C* corresponds to DAYS+ in your *WP 34S* (see below).
DATE→	**h** X.FCN **DATE→**	(-2) [d] Assumes x containing a date in the format selected and pushes its three components on the *stack*.
DAY	**h** X.FCN **DAY**	(1) [d] Assumes x containing a date in the format selected and extracts the day.

Name	Keystrokes	Remarks (see pp. 171ff for general information)
DAYS+	**h** X.FCN **DAYS+**	(2) [d] Adds x days on a date in **Y** in the format selected and displays the resulting date including the day of week in the same format as WDAY does. Works like DATE in the *HP-12C*.
DBLOFF	**h** MODE **DBLOFF**	(0) Toggles *DP* mode. Setting becomes effective in DECM only and is indicated by **D** in the dot matrix. See pp. 351ff.
DBLON	**h** MODE **DBLON**	
DBL?	**h** TEST **DBL?**	(0) [¬α] Checks if *DP* mode is set.
DBLR	**h** X.FCN **DBLR**	[n] Double word length commands for remainder, multiplication and division. DBLR and DBL/ accept a double size dividend in **Y** and **Z** (most significant bits in **Y**), the divisor in **X** as usual, and return the result in **X**. DBL× takes x and y as factors as usual but returns their product in **X** and **Y** (most significant bits in **X**). See the *HP-16C Owner's Handbook*, Section 4 (pp. 52ff).
DBL×	**h** X.FCN **DBL×**	
DBL /	**h** X.FCN **DBL/**	
DEC	**h** P.FCN **DEC** <u>s</u>	(0) [æ] Decrements s by 1. Does not load **L** even for target address **X**.
DECM	**f** H.d	(0) [¬α] Sets default decimal floating point mode.
DECOMP	**h** X.FCN **DECOMP**	(-1) [d] Decomposes x (after converting it into an improper fraction, if applicable), returning $y/x =$ in top row and a *stack* [*denominator(x), numerator(x),* …]. See pp. 52f and 125. Reversible by division. Example: If **X** contains 2.25 then DECOMP will return $x = 4$ and $y = 9$.
DEG	**g** DEG	(0) [d] Sets angular mode to *degrees*.
DEG→	**h** X.FCN **DEG→**	(1) [d] Takes x as *degrees* and converts them to the angular mode currently set.

Name	Keystrokes	Remarks (see pp. 171ff for general information)
DENANY	**h** (MODE) **DENANY**	(0) Sets default fraction format like in the *HP-35S* – any denominator up to the value set by DENMAX may appear. Example: If DENMAX = 5 then DENANY allows denominators 1, 2, 3, 4, and 5.
DENFAC	**h** (MODE) **DENFAC**	(0) Sets 'factors of the maximum denominator', i.e. all integer factors of DENMAX may appear in the denominator. Example: If DENMAX = 60 then DENFAC will allow denominators 1, 2, 3, 4, 5, 6, 10, 12, 15, 20, 30, and 60. Now you know why 60 was a holy number in ancient Babylon.
DENFIX	**h** (MODE) **DENFIX**	(0) Sets fixed denominator format, i.e. the one and only denominator allowed is the value set by DENMAX.
DENMAX	**h** (MODE) **DENMAX**	(0 or 1) [¬n] Works like /c on the *HP-35S*, but the maximum denominator settable is 9 999. For $x < 1$ or $x > 9\,999$, DENMAX will be set to 0 meaning 9 999. For $x = 1$, the current DENMAX setting is recalled, replacing x.
DET	**h** (MATRIX) **DET**	(1) [d] Takes a *descriptor* (see p. 67) of a square matrix in **X** and returns the determinant of the matrix. The matrix itself is not modified.
DISP	**h** (MODE) **DISP** *n*	(0) [d, α] Changes the number of decimals shown, keeping the basic display format (FIX, SCI, or ENG) as is. With ALL, DISP changes the switchover point (see ALL).
		(0) [n] Leaves integer mode and works like in DECM.

Name	Keystrokes	Remarks (see pp. 171ff for general information)
^{C}DOT	`CPX` `h` `X.FCN` `ᶜDOT`	(2) [d] Interprets x and y as Cartesian components of a vector #1, and z and t as those of a vector #2; returns their *dot product* $[x \cdot z + y \cdot t, \mathbf{0}, ...]$.
dRCL	`h` `P.FCN` `dRCL` $\underline{s}$	(-1) [¬α] Assumes the source contains *DP* data and recalls them as such. See pp. 351ff.
DROP	`h` `P.FCN` `DROP`	[¬α] Drops x. See pp. 40f for details.
	`h` `X.FCN` `DROP`	
	`CPX` `h` `X.FCN` `ᶜDROP`	[d] Drops x_c. See pp. 129f for details.
DSE	`f` `DSE` $\underline{s}$	(0) [¬α] Given `ccccc.fffii` in the source, DSE decrements s by `ii`, skipping next program step if then `ccccc ≤ fff` .
		If s features no fractional part then `fff` is 0.
		If `ii = 0`, `ccccc` will be decremented by 1.
		DSE does not load **L** even for target address **X**.
		Note that neither `fff` nor `ii` can be negative, and DSE makes only sense with `ccccc > 0` .
DSL	`h` `P.FCN` `DSL` $\underline{s}$	(0) [¬α] Works like DSE but skips if `ccccc < fff` .
DSZ	`h` `P.FCN` `DSZ` $\underline{s}$	(0) [¬α] Decrements s by 1 and skips the next step if $|s| < 1$ thereafter. Does not load **L** even for target address **X**. Known from the *HP-16C*.
D.MY	`h` `MODE` `D.MY`	(0) Sets the date format to `dd.mmyyyy`
D→J	`h` `X.FCN` `D→J`	(1) [d] Takes x as a date in the format set and converts it to a *Julian day number*[114] according to JG...

---

[114] Translator's note: *Julian day number* translates to "Julianisches Datum" in German. See the corresponding articles in *Wikipedia* for more.

Name	Keystrokes	Remarks (see pp. 171ff for general information)
D→R		(1) [d] See the *Catalog of Conversions (CONV)* on pp. 270ff for conversions from *degrees* to *radians*.
END	**h** **P.FCN** **END**	(0) [¬α] Last command in a program and terminal for searching local labels as described on p. 159. Works like RTN in all other aspects.
ENG	**h** **ENG** **n**	(0) [d] Sets engineer's display format (see pp. 79f).
		(0) [n] Turns to DECM and works like in DECM.
ENGOVR	**h** **ENG** **ENTER↑**	(0) [¬α] Defines that numbers exceeding the range displayable in ALL or FIX will be shown in engineer's format. Compare SCIOVR.
ENTER↑	**ENTER↑**	(-1) [¬α] Pushes *x* on the *stack*, disabling *automatic stack lift*. See pp. 40f for details. For ^{C}ENTER, see p. 129.
ENTRY?	**h** **TEST** **ENTRY?**	(0) [¬α] Checks the entry flag. This internal flag is set if: • any character is entered in alpha mode, or • any command is accepted for entry (be it via **ENTER↑**, a function key, or **R/S** with a partial command line). Useful in routines, e.g. after PSE.
erf	**h** **X.FCN** **erf**	(1) [d] Returns the error function or its complement. See p. 389 for more.
erfc	**h** **X.FCN** **erfc**	
ERR	**h** **P.FCN** **ERR** **n**	(0) [¬α] Raises the error specified. The consequences are the same as if the corresponding error really occurred, so e.g. program execution will be stopped. See *App. C* on pp. 311ff for the respective error codes. Compare MSG.
EVEN?	**h** **TEST** **EVEN?**	(0) [¬α] Checks if *x* is integer and even.

Name	Keystrokes	Remarks (see pp. 171ff for general information)
e^x	**f** e^x	(1) [¬α] Returns e^x.
	EXIT	See p. 244.
ExpF	**h** MODE **ExpF**	(0) Selects the exponential curve fit model $R(x) = a_0 e^{a_1 x}$. Relevant for CORR, COV, L.R., s_{XY}, $\hat{x}$, and $\hat{y}$.
Expon Expon$_p$ Expon$_u$ Expon^{-1}	**h** PROB **Expon** etc.	(1) [d] *Exponential distribution* with the rate λ in **J**. See *App. I* on pp. 375ff for more. Expon^{-1} returns the survival time t_s for a given probability *p* in **X**, with λ in **J**.
EXPT	**h** X.FCN **EXPT**	(1) [d] Returns the exponent *h* of the number displayed $x = m \cdot 10^h$. Compare MANT.
e^x -1	**h** X.FCN **e^x-1**	(1) [d] For $x \approx 0$, this returns a more accurate result for the fractional part than e^x does.
FAST	**h** MODE **FAST**	(0) Sets the processor speed to 'fast'. This is start-up default and is kept for fresh batteries. See p. 73 and compare SLOW on p. 217.
FB	**h** X.FCN **FB** *n*	(1) [n] Inverts ('flips') the specified bit in x
FC?	**h** TEST **FC?** *n*	(0) [¬α] Tests if the specified flag is clear.
FC?C FC?F FC?S	**h** TEST **FC?C** *n* etc.	(0) [¬α] Tests if the specified flag is clear. Clears, flips, or sets this flag after testing, respectively.
FF	**h** P.FCN **FF** *n*	(0) [¬α] Flips the flag specified.
FIB	**h** X.FCN **FIB**	(1) Returns the Fibonacci number for integer input, else the extended Fibonacci number. See p. 375 for more.

Name	Keystrokes	Remarks (see pp. 171ff for general information)
FILL	g FILL	[⍺] Copies x to all *stack* levels. For ^{C}FILL, see p. 129.
FIX	h FIX **n**	(0) [d] Sets fixed point display format (see pp. 79f).
		(0) [n] Turns to DECM and works like in DECM.
FLASH?	h P.FCN FLASH?	(-1) [¬⍺] Returns the number of free *words* in *FM* (1 *word* = 2 *bytes*).
FLOOR	h X.FCN FLOOR	(1) [¬⍺] Returns the largest integer $\leq x$.
FP	g FP	(1) [¬⍺] Returns the fractional part of x.
FP?	h TEST FP?	(0) [¬⍺] Tests x for having a nonzero fractional part.
$F_p(x)$ $F_u(x)$ $F(x)$ $F^{-1}(p)$	h PROB F▪(x) etc.	(1) [d] *Fisher's F distribution*. $F_u(x)$ equals Q(F) on the *HP-21S*. The *degrees of freedom* are specified in **J** and **K**. See *App. I* on pp. 375ff for more.
FRACT	h MODE FRACT	(0) Converts x into a *fraction* according to the format set by PROFRC or IMPFRC and the settings by DEN... See pp. 123ff.
FS?	h TEST FS? **n**	(0) [⍺] Tests if the specified flag is set.
FS?C FS?F FS?S	h TEST FS?C **n** etc.	(0) [¬⍺] Tests if the specified flag is set. Clears, flips, or sets this flag after testing, respectively.

Name	Keystrokes	Remarks (see pp. 171ff for general information)
f'(x)	**h** `P.FCN` **f'(x)** _label_	[d] Returns the first derivative of the function *f(x)* at position *x*. *f(x)* must be specified in a routine starting with LBL *label*. **ATTENTION:** f'(x) will look for a user routine labeled **δx** (or **δX**, **Δx**, or **ΔX**, in this order), returning a fixed step size **dx** in **X**. If that routine is not defined, **dx** = 0.1 is set for default (arbitrary, but it had to be specified). Then, f'(x) will fill all *stack* levels with *x* and will evaluate *f(x)* at ten points equally spaced in the interval *x* ± 5 **dx**. If you expect any irregularities within this interval, change **dx** to exclude them. On return, **Y**, **Z**, and **T** will be cleared, higher *stack* levels filled with *x - 5 dx*, if applicable, and the position *x* will be in **L**.
f"(x)	**h** `P.FCN` **f"(x)** _label_	[d] Works in full analogy to f'(x) but returns the second derivative.
GCD	**h** `X.FCN` **GCD**	(2) [¬α] Returns the *Greatest Common Divisor* of *x* and *y*. The result will always be positive.
gCLR	**h** `P.FCN` **gCLR** _s_	(0) [¬α] Clears the pixel at position *x*, *y* in the *graphic block* (see p. 168) starting at register address *s*. Valid inputs are $0 \le x \le w - 1$ and $0 \le y \le h - 1$. Pixel 0, 0 is top left. Inputs ≤ 0 will cause the maxima being set.
g_d	**h** `X.FCN` **gₔ**	(1) [d] Returns the Gudermann function or its inverse. See *App. I* on pp. 389f for details.
g_d^{-1}	**h** `X.FCN` **gₔ⁻¹**	
gDIM	**h** `P.FCN` **gDIM** _s_	(0) [¬α] Initializes a *graphic block* (see p. 168) starting at register address *s*, allowing for graphic data featuring *x* pixel columns and *y* pixel rows. Inputs ≤ 0 will cause the default sizes being set.
gDIM?	**h** `P.FCN` **gDIM?** _s_	(-2) [¬α] Assumes a graphic block starting at register address *s* and recalls *h* and *w* for it. See p. 168 for more.

Name	Keystrokes	Remarks (see pp. 171ff for general information)
Geom		(1) [d] *Geometric distribution*: The *CDF* returns the probability for a first success after $m = x$ Bernoulli experiments. The probability p_0 for a success in each such experiment must be specified in **J**. See *App. I* on pp. 375ff for more.
Geom$_P$	**h** PROB **Geom** etc.	
Geom$_u$		Geom^{-1} returns the number of failures f before 1st success for given probabilities p in **X** and p_0 in **J**.
Geom^{-1}		
gFLP	**h** P.FCN **gFLP** <u>s</u>	(0) [¬α] Flips the pixel at position x, y in the graphic block starting at register address s. See gCLR for valid ranges of x and y etc.
gPIX?	**h** P.FCN **gPIX?** <u>s</u>	(0) [¬α] Tests if the pixel at position x, y in the graphic block starting at register address s is set. See gCLR for valid ranges of x and y etc.
gPLOT	**h** P.FCN **gPLOT** <u>s</u>	(0) [¬α] Displays the top left sector of the graphic block (starting at register address s) in the dot matrix section of the *LCD*. See gCLR for more.
GRAD	**g** GRAD	(0) [d] Sets angular mode to *gon* (*grad*).
GRAD→	**h** X.FCN **GRAD→**	(1) [d] Takes x as given in *gon* and converts them to the angular mode currently set.
gSET	**h** P.FCN **gSET** <u>s</u>	(0) [¬α] Sets the pixel at position x, y in the graphic block starting at register address s. See gCLR for valid ranges of x and y etc.
GTO	**h** GTO <u>*label*</u>	(0) [**STO**] Inserts an unconditional branch to *label*.
		(0) [¬**STO**] Positions the program pointer to *label*.
	h GTO	See pp. 244f.
GTOα	**h** P.FCN **GTOα**	(0) [¬α] Takes the first three characters of *alpha* (or all if there are less than three) as a label and positions the program pointer to it.

Name	Keystrokes	Remarks (see pp. 171ff for general information)
H_n	**h** X.FCN **Hn**	(2) [d] *Hermite polynomials* for probability (H_n) and for physics (H_{np}). See p. 387 for details.
H_{np}	**h** X.FCN **Hnp**	
H.MS	**f** H.MS	(1) [d] Assumes **X** contains <u>decimal</u> *hours* or *degrees*, and displays them converted in the format hhhh°mm′ss.dd″ temporarily as shown on p. 85.
		(1) [n] Turns to DECM and works like in DECM.
H.MS+	**h** X.FCN **H.MS+**	(2) [d] Assumes **X** and **Y** contain *hours* or *degrees* in the hexadecimal format hhhh.mmssdd , and adds or subtracts them, respectively.
H.MS−	**h** X.FCN **H.MS−**	
IDIV	**h** X.FCN **IDIV** <u>*s*</u>	(2) [¬α] Integer division, working like ☐ IP in DECM and like ☐ in integer modes.
IMPFRC	**g** d/c	(1) [¬α] Sets fraction mode allowing *improper fractions* in the display (e.g. $^5/_3$ instead of $1\,^2/_3$). Converts *x* according to the settings by DEN... into an *improper fraction* if possible. See pp. 123ff. Compare PROFRC.
INC	**h** P.FCN **INC** <u>*s*</u>	(0) [¬α] Increments *s* by 1. Does not load **L** even for target address **X**.
INTM?	**h** TEST **INTM?**	(0) [¬α] Tests if your *WP 34S* is in an integer mode.
INT?	**h** TEST **INT?**	(0) [¬α] Tests *x* for being integer, i.e. having a fractional part equal to zero. Compare FP?.
IP	**f** IP	(1) [¬α] Returns the integer part of *x*.
iRCL	**h** X.FCN **IRCL** <u>*s*</u>	(-1) [¬α] Assumes the source contains integer data and recalls them as such. See pp. 305f.
ISE	**h** P.FCN **ISE** <u>*s*</u>	(0) [¬α] Works like ISG but skips if ccccccc ≥ fff .

Name	Keystrokes	Remarks (see pp. 171ff for general information)
ISG	g [ISG] s	(0) [¬α] Given cccccc.fffii in the source, ISG increments *s* by ii, skipping next program step if then cccccc > fff. If *s* has no fractional part then fff = 0. If ii = 0, cccccc will be incremented by 1. ISG does not load **L** even for target address **X**. Note that neither fff nor ii can be negative, but cccccc can.
ISZ	h [P.FCN] ISZ s	(0) [¬α] Increments *s* by 1, skipping next program step if then $\lvert s \rvert < 1$. Does not load **L** even for target address **X**. Known from the *HP-16C*.
I_x	h [X.FCN] Ix	(3) [d] Returns the *regularized beta function*. See *App. I* on pp. 389f for details.
JG1582	h [MODE] JG1582	(0) These commands reflect different dates the *Gregorian* calendar was introduced in different large areas of the world. DAYS+, WDAY, ΔDAYS, D→J, and J→D will be calculated accordingly. See pp. 77f.
JG1752	h [MODE] JG1752	
J→D	h [X.FCN] J→D	(1) [d] Takes *x* as a *Julian day number*[115] and converts it to a common date according to JG... and the format selected
KEY?	h [TEST] KEY? s	(0) [¬α] Tests if a key was pressed while a routine was running or paused. If <u>no</u> key was pressed in that interval, the next program step after KEY? will be executed, else it will be skipped and the code of said key will be stored in the address specified. Key codes reflect the rows and columns on the keyboard (see p. 166).

---

[115] Translator's note: *Julian day number* translates to "Julianisches Datum" in German. See the corresponding articles in *Wikipedia* for more.

Name	Keystrokes	Remarks (see pp. 171ff for general information)
KTP?	**h** [P.FCN] **KTP?** _s_	(-1) [¬α] Assumes a key code given in the address specified (see KEY?). Checks it and returns the key type: • 0 … 9 if it corresponds to a digit [0] … [9] , • 10 if it corresponds to [.], [EEX], or [+/-] , • 11 if it corresponds to **f**, **g**, or **h** , • 12 if it corresponds to any other key. May help in user interaction with routines (see pp. 166ff). An invalid code in the input register will throw an 'Invalid Range' error.
LASTx	[RCL] [L]	(-1) [¬α] See pp. 40ff and 129 for details. In fact, this command will be recorded as **RCL L** in routines.
LBL	**f** [LBL] *label*	(0) Identifies routines for execution and branching. Read more about specifying labels on pp. 157f.
LBL?	**h** [TEST] **LBL?** *label*	(0) [¬α] Tests for the existence of the label specified, anywhere in program memory. See LBL for more.
LCM	**h** [X.FCN] **LCM**	(2) [¬α] Returns the *Least Common Multiple* of x and y. The result will always be positive.
LEAP?	**h** [TEST] **LEAP?**	(0) [d] Takes x as a date in the format selected, extracts the year, and tests for a leap year. —— (0) [n] Takes x as a year and tests for a leap year.
LgNrm LgNrm$_p$ LgNrm$_u$ LgNrm^{-1}	**h** [PROB] **LgNrm** etc.	(1) [d] *Log-normal distribution* with $\mu = \ln \bar{x}_g$ specified in **J** and $\sigma = \ln \varepsilon$ in **K**. See x̄g and ε below and *App. I* on pp. 375ff for details. LgNrm^{-1} returns x for a given probability p in **X**, with μ in **J** and σ in **K**.

Name	Keystrokes	Remarks (see pp. 171ff for general information)
LINEQS	**h** (MATRIX) **LINEQS**	(3) [d] Solves a system of linear equations $(Z) \cdot \vec{x} = \vec{y}$. Takes • a base register number for $\vec{x}$ in **X**, • a vector *descriptor* (see p. 67) for $\vec{y}$ in **Y**, and • a *descriptor* of the square matrix (Z) in **Z**. Returns the filled in vector *descriptor* in **X**. Take care of proper dimensioning.
LinF	**h** (MODE) **LinF**	(0) Selects the linear curve fit model $R(x) = a_0 + a_1 x$. Relevant for L.R., CORR, COV, s_{XY}, $\hat{x}$, and $\hat{y}$.
LJ	**h** (X.FCN) **LJ**	(-1) [n] Left justifies a bit pattern within its word size as in the *HP-16C*: The *stack* will lift, placing the left-justified word in **Y** and the count (number of bit-shifts necessary to left justify the word) in **X**. Example for word size 8: $1\ 0110_2$ LJ results in $x = 3$ and $y = 1011\ 0000_2$.
LN	**g** (LN)	(1) [¬α] Returns the natural logarithm of x.
L_n	**h** (X.FCN) **Lₙ**	(2) [d] *Laguerre polynomials*. See *App. I* on p. 387f for more.
LN1+x	**h** (X.FCN) **LN1+x**	(1) [d] For $x \approx 0$, this returns a more accurate result for the fractional part than $\ln(x)$ does.
$L_n\alpha$	**h** (X.FCN) **Lₙα**	(3) [d] *Laguerre's generalized polynomials*. See *App. I* on p. 387f for more.
LN β	**h** (X.FCN) **LNβ**	(2) [d] Returns the natural logarithm of *Euler's* Beta function. See β.

Name	Keystrokes	Remarks (see pp. 171ff for general information)
LN Γ	**h** X.FCN **LNΓ**	(1) [d] Returns the natural logarithm of $\Gamma(x)$. Allows also for calculating really large factorials. Example: What is 5 432*!* ? Remember $\Gamma(x + 1) = x!$ Thus, keying in **5433 LNΓ 10** LN / will return 17 931.480 374 being the decadic logarithm of the result; then calling FP 10^x will return its mantissa 3.022 553 598 4. Thus, $5\,432! = 3.02 \cdot 10^{17\,931}$.
LOAD	**h** P.FCN **LOAD** ON + RCL + RCL	Restores the entire backup from *FM*, i.e. executes LOADP, LOADR, LOADSS, LOADΣ, and returns **Restored**. Not programmable. Compare SAVE. See the commands immediately below and pp. 296f for more.
LOADP	**h** P.FCN **LOADP**	(0) [¬α] Recovers the entire program memory from the backup (see SAVE) and appends it to the programs already in RAM. This will only work if there is enough space – else an error will be thrown. Not programmable.
LOADR	**h** P.FCN **LOADR**	(0) [¬α] Recovers numbered general purpose registers from the backup (see SAVE). Lettered registers will not be recalled. The amount of registers copied is the minimum of the registers held in the backup and allocated in RAM at execution time.
LOADSS	**h** P.FCN **LOADSS**	(0) [¬α] Recovers the system state from the backup (see SAVE). See pp. 299f for more.
LOADΣ	**h** P.FCN **LOADΣ**	(0) [¬α] Recovers the summation registers from the backup (see SAVE). Throws an error if there are none. See p. 301 for more.
LocR	**h** P.FCN **LocR** *n*	(0) [¬α] Allocates *n local registers* (≤ 144) and 16 local flags for the *current routine*. These new registers and flags are cleared. See p. 168.
LocR?	**h** P.FCN **LocR?**	(-1) [¬α] Returns the number of *local registers* currently allocated.
LOG₁₀	**g** LG	(1) [¬α] Returns the logarithm of x for base 10.

Name	Keystrokes	Remarks (see pp. 171ff for general information)
LOG₂ (LOG_2)	**g** **LB**	(1) [¬α] Returns the logarithm of x for base 2.
LogF	**h** **MODE** **Lo9F**	(0) Selects the logarithmic curve fit model $R(x) = a_0 + a_1 \ln(x)$. Relevant for CORR, L.R., and ŷ.
Logis		
Logis_P ($Logis_P$)	**h** **PROB** **Lo9is**	(1) [d] *Logistic distribution* with *μ* given in **J** and *s* in **K**. See *App. I* on pp. 375ff for details.
Logis_u ($Logis_u$)	etc.	
Logis⁻¹ ($Logis^{-1}$)		
LOG_x (LOG_x)	**g** **LOG_x**	(2) [¬α] Returns the logarithm of y for the base x.
	CPX **g** **LOG_x**	(2) [d] Returns the complex logarithm of $y_c = z + i\,t$ for the complex base $x_c = x + i\,y$.
LZOFF	**h** **MODE** **LZOFF**	(0) Toggles leading zeros like flag 3 does in the *HP-16C*. Relevant in integer bases 2, 4, 8, and 16 only.
LZON	**h** **MODE** **LZON**	
L.R.	**h** **STAT** **L.R.**	(-2) [d] Returns the parameters a_1 (in **Y**) and a_0 (in **X**) of the fit curve through the data points accumulated in the summation registers, according to the curve fit model selected (see LINF, EXPF, POWERF, and LOGF). For a straight line (LINF), a_0 is its y-intercept and a_1 its slope. See *App. I* on pp. 383ff for more.
MANT	**h** **X.FCN** **MANT**	(1) [d] Returns the mantissa *m* of the number displayed $x = m \cdot 10^h$. Compare EXPT.
MASKL	**h** **X.FCN** **MASKL** *n*	(-1) [n] Work like MASKL and MASKR on the *HP-16C*, but with the mask length (or its address) following the command instead of taken from **X**. Thus, the mask is pushed on the *stack*.
MASKR	**h** **X.FCN** **MASKR** *n*	Example: For WSIZE 8, MASKL 3 returns a mask word 1110 0000₂. Use it e.g. for extracting the 3 most significant bits from an arbitrary *byte* by AND.

Name	Keystrokes	Remarks (see pp. 171ff for general information)
	h (MATRIX)	[d] *Catalog*, see p. 255.
MAX	**h** (X.FCN) **MAX**	(2) [¬α] Returns the maximum of x and y.
MEM?	**h** (P.FCN) **MEM?**	(-1) [¬α] Returns the number of free *words* in program memory (1 *word* = 2 *bytes*), also taking into account the local registers allocated.
MIN	**h** (X.FCN) **MIN**	(2) [¬α] Returns the minimum of x and y.
MIRROR	**h** (X.FCN) **MIRROR**	(1) [n] Reflects the bit pattern in x (e.g. 00010111_2 would become 11101000_2 for word size 8).
MOD	**h** (X.FCN) **MOD**	(2) [¬α] Returns $y \bmod x$. Compare RMDR. See also pp. 144f. Examples: $\mod(25;7) = 4;$ $\mod(-25;7) = 3;$ $\mod(25;-7) = -3;$ $\mod(-25;-7) = -4$.
	h (MODE)	*Catalog*, see p. 255.
MONTH	**h** (X.FCN) **MONTH**	(1) [d] Assumes x containing a date in the format selected and extracts the month.
MROW+×	**h** (MATRIX) **MROW+×**	(0) [d] Takes a matrix *descriptor* x (see p. 67), a destination row number y, a source row number z, and a real number t. It multiplies each element m_{zi} of (X) by t and adds it to m_{yi}. The *stack* stays unchanged. MROW+× is similar to PPC[116] M3.
MROW×	**h** (MATRIX) **MROW×**	(0) [d] Takes a matrix *descriptor* x (see p. 67), a row number y, and a real number z. It multiplies each element m_{yi} of (X) by z. The *stack* stays unchanged. MROW× is similar to PPC M2.

---

[116] *PPC ROM* was one of the first user community created *ROMs*, a plug-in module built for the *HP-41C* in the 1980's. The routines stored therein were documented in a kind of telephone book (some 2 *cm* thick) at that time.

Name	Keystrokes	Remarks (see pp. 171ff for general information)
MROW⇆	**h** (MATRIX) MROW⇆	(0) [d] Takes a matrix *descriptor x* (see p. 67) and two row numbers *y* and *z*. It swaps the contents of rows *y* and *z* in (*X*). The *stack* stays unchanged. MROW⇆ is similar to *PPC M1*.
MSG	**h** (P.FCN) MSG *n*	(0) [¬α] Throws the error message specified. This will be a *temporary message*. See *App. C* on pp. 311ff for the respective error codes. Compare ERR.
M+×	**h** (MATRIX) M+×	(3) [d] Takes two matrix *descriptors x* and *y* (see p. 67), and a real number *z*. Returns $(X) + (Y) \cdot z = (X)$. Thus a scalar multiple of one matrix is added to another matrix. The multiply adds are done in internal high precision (39 digits) and results should be exactly rounded.
M^{-1}	**h** (MATRIX) M-1	(0) [d] Takes a *descriptor* (see p. 67) of a square matrix in **X** and inverts the matrix in-situ.
M-ALL	**h** (MATRIX) M-ALL	(1) [d] Takes a matrix *descriptor x* (see p. 67)[117] and returns a value suitable for ISG or DSL looping in that matrix. The loop shall process all elements in (*X*). The loop counter is for DSL if the *descriptor* was negative and for ISG otherwise.
M-COL	**h** (MATRIX) M-COL	(2) [d] Takes a matrix *descriptor x* (as for M-ALL) and a column number *y*. Returns a loop counter for processing all elements m_{iy} of that matrix column only.
M-DIAG	**h** (MATRIX) M-DIAG	(1) [d] Takes a matrix *descriptor x* (as for M-ALL) and returns a loop counter. The loop shall process all elements along the matrix diagonal, i.e. all elements m_{ii} in (*X*).
M-ROW	**h** (MATRIX) M-ROW	(2) [d] Takes a matrix *descr. x* (as for M-ALL) and a row number *y*. Returns a loop counter for processing all elements m_{yi} of that matrix row only.

---

[117] This *descriptor* will be saved in **L** as usual. This applies for the other matrix operations with a *descriptor* in **X** as well.

Name	Keystrokes	Remarks (see pp. 171ff for general information)
M×	**h** (MATRIX) **M×**	(3) [d] Takes two matrix *descriptors* y and z (see p. 67), and the integer part of x as the base address of the result. Returns $(Z) \cdot (Y) = (X)$. All calculations are done in internal high precision (39 digits). The fractional part of x is updated to match the resulting matrix – no overlap checking is performed.
M.COPY	**h** (MATRIX) **M.COPY**	(2) [d] Takes a matrix *descriptor* y (see p. 67) and a base register number x. Copies the matrix (Y) into registers starting at **R**x. Returns a properly formatted matrix *descriptor* in **X**.
M.DY	**h** (MODE) **M.DY**	(0) Sets the format for date display to mm.ddyyyy.
M.IJ	**h** (MATRIX) **M.IJ**	[d] Takes a matrix *descriptor* x (see p. 67) and a register number y. Returns the column that register represents in **Y** and the row in **X**. M.IJ is similar to *PPC M4*. Compare M.REG.
M.LU	**h** (MATRIX) **M.LU**	(1) [d] Takes a *descriptor* (see p. 67) of a square matrix in **X**. Transforms (X) into its LU decomposition in-situ. The value in **X** is replaced by a *descriptor* that defines the pivots that were required to calculate the decomposition. The most significant digit is the pivot for the first diagonal entry, the next most significant for the second and so forth.
M.REG	**h** (MATRIX) **M.REG**	(3) [d] Takes a matrix *descriptor* x (see p. 67), a row number y, and a column number z. M.REG returns the register number in **X**. It is similar to *PPC M5*. Compare M.IJ.
M.SQR?	**h** (TEST) **M.SQR?**	(0) [d] Tests a matrix *descriptor* x (see p. 67) and returns **true** if the matrix is square.
NAND	**h** (X.FCN) **NAND**	(2) [¬α] Works analogous to AND, cf. p. 183.
NaN?	**h** (TEST) **NaN?**	(0) [¬α] Tests if x is *not a number*.

Name	Keystrokes	Remarks (see pp. 171ff for general information)
nBITS	**h** X.FCN nBITS	(1) [n] Counts bits set in x (like #B on the HP-16C).
nCOL	**h** MATRIX nCOL	(1) [d] Takes a matrix *descriptor* x (see p. 67) and returns the number of columns of (X).
NEIGHB	**h** X.FCN NEIGHB	(2) [d] Returns the nearest machine-representable number to x in the direction towards y in the mode set. For ... • $x < y$, this is the machine successor of x ; • $x = y$, this is y ; • $x > y$, this is the machine predecessor of x . You may find NEIGHB useful investigating numeric stability (see NEIGHBOR in the *HP-71 Math Pac*). (2) [n] Returns ... • $x + 1$ for $x < y$; • y for $x = y$; • $x - 1$ for $x > y$.
NEXTP	**h** X.FCN NEXTP	(1) [∝] Returns the next prime number greater than x .
NOP	**h** P.FCN NOP	(0) [¬α] 'Empty' step, doing nothing. For backward compatibility.
NOR	**h** X.FCN NOR	(2) [¬α] Works analogous to AND, cf. p. 183.
Norml Norml$_p$ Norml$_u$ Norml^{-1}	**h** PROB Norml etc.	(1) [d] *Normal distribution* with an arbitrary mean μ given in **J** and a *standard deviation* σ in **K**. See *App. I* on pp. 375ff for details. Norml^{-1} returns x for a given probability p in **X**, with μ in **J** and σ in **K**.

Name	Keystrokes	Remarks (see pp. 171ff for general information)
NOT	**h** NOT	(1) [d] Returns 1 for $x = 0$, and 0 for $x \neq 0$.
		(1) [n] Inverts x bit-wise as on the *HP-16C*.
nROW	**h** MATRIX **nROW**	(1) [d] Takes a matrix *descriptor* x (see p. 67) and returns the number of rows of (X).
nΣ	**h** SUMS **nΣ**	(-1) [d] Recalls the number of accumulated data points.
ODD?	**h** TEST **ODD?**	(0) [œ] Checks if x is integer and odd.
OFF	**h** OFF	(0) [**STO**] Inserts a step to turn your *WP 34S* off under program control.
		(0) [¬**STO**] Turns your *WP 34S* off immediately.
OR	**h** OR	(2) [¬α] Works analogous to AND, cf. p. 183.
PERM	**g** Py.x	(2) [¬α] Returns the number of possible arrangements (or permutations) of x items taken out of a set of y items. No item occurs more than once in an arrangement, and different orders of the same x items are counted separately. Compare COMB on p. 187 and see p. 375 for the formulas.
P_n	**h** X.FCN **Pn**	(1) [d] *Legendre polynomials*. See *App. I* on p. 387f for more.
Poiss		(1) [d] *Poisson distribution* with the number of successes g in **X**, the gross error probability p_0 in **J**, and the sample size n in **K**. Note the parameters are the same as for BINOM. The Poisson parameter $\lambda = n\,p_0$ is calculated automatically.
Poiss$_p$	**h** PROB **Poiss**	
Poiss$_u$	etc.	
Poiss^{-1}		Poiss^{-1} returns the maximum number of successes m for a given probability p in **X**, p_0 in **J** and n in **K**.

Name	Keystrokes	Remarks (see pp. 171ff for general information)
Poisλ Poisλ $_p$ Poisλ $_u$ Poisλ $^{-1}$	**h** (PROB) **Poisλ** etc.	(1) [d] Poisλ works like POISS but just with λ in **J**. See *App. I* on pp. 375ff for more. Poisλ^{-1} returns *m* for a given probability *p* in **X** and λ in **J**.
PopLR	**h** (P.FCN) **PopLR**	(0) [¬α] Pops the *local registers* allocated to the *current routine* <u>without returning to the calling routine</u>. See LOCR and RTN.
PowerF	**h** (MODE) **PowerF**	(0) Selects the power curve fit model $R(x) = a_0 x^{a_1}$. Relevant for CORR, L.R., and ŷ.
PRCL	**h** (P.FCN) **PRCL** (or plain (RCL) if in CAT)	(0) [¬α] Copies the *current program* (from *FM* or *RAM*) and appends it to *RAM*, where it can then be edited (see pp. 156 and 168). PRCL allows for duplicating programs in *RAM*. It will only work with enough space at destination. By recalling a library program from *FM*, editing it, and re-storing it via PSTO you may modify this part of the *FM* library. See PSTO.
PRIME?	**h** (TEST) **PRIME?**	(0) [¬α] Checks if the absolute value of the integer part of x is a prime. The method is believed to work for integers up to $9 \cdot 10^{18}$.
	h (PROB)	[d] *Catalog*, see p. 255.
PROFRC	**f** (a b/c)	(1) [¬α] Sets *fraction* mode allowing only *proper fractions* or mixed numbers in display. Converts x according to the settings by DEN... into a *proper fraction*, if applicable, e.g. 1.25 or $^5/_4$ into $1\,^1/_4$. See pp. 123ff. Compare IMPFRC.
PROMPT	**h** (P.FCN) **PROMPT**	(0) [¬α] Displays *alpha* and stops program execution. See pp. 161f for more.

Name	Keystrokes	Remarks (see pp. 171ff for general information)
PSE	**h** (PSE) _**n**_	(0) [**RCL**] Refreshes the display and pauses program execution for _n_ ticks (see TICKS), with $0 \le n \le 99$. The pause will terminate early when you press a key.
		(0) [**STO**] Inserts a pause step as described above.
		(0) [¬**STO**, ¬**RCL**] Does nothing.
PSTO	**h** (P.FCN) PSTO	(0) [¬α] Copies the *current program* from *RAM* and appends it to the *FM* library. Not programmable. If a program with the same label already exists in the library it will be deleted first. Compare PRCL. Note alphanumeric labels contained in *FM* may be browsed by CAT (see p. 249) and called by XEQ.
PUTK	**h** (P.FCN) PUTK _s_	(0) [¬α] Assumes a key code in the address specified. Stops program execution, takes said code and puts it in the keyboard buffer resulting in immediate execution of the corresponding call. (R/S) is required to resume program execution. May help in user interaction with routines.
	h (P.FCN)	[¬α] *Catalog,* see pp. 255f.
RAD	**g** (RAD)	(0) [d] Sets current angular mode to *radians.*
RAD→	**h** (X.FCN) RAD→	(1) [d] Takes _x_ as *radians* and converts them to the angular mode currently set.
RAN#	**f** (RAN#)	(-1) [d] Returns a random number between 0 and 1 like RAN does in the *HP-42S.* See SEED on p. 215.
		(-1) [n] Returns a random bit pattern for the word size set.[118]

---

[118] RAN# produces a 64-bit random number using two sequential calls to a *Tausworthe Generator.* The *paper* by *Pierre L'Ecuyer* is enlightening and includes the derived generator on the second last page. The random number is then truncated and made unsigned according to the current mode (which will lose the sign bit and can change

Name	Keystrokes	Remarks (see pp. 171ff for general information)
RCL	RCL *s*	(-1) [¬α] Recalls a register content. See pp. 134f for ^{C}RCL.
RCLM	RCL MODE *s*	(0) [¬α] Recalls modes stored by STOM (see p. 75).[119]
RCLS	h P.FCN RCLS *s*	[¬α] Recalls 4 or 8 values from a set of registers starting at address *s*, and pushes them on the *stack*. This is the converse command of STOS.
RCL+	RCL + *s*	(1) [¬α] Recalls a register content, executes the specified operation and pushes the result on the *stack*.
RCL−	RCL − *s*	
RCL×	RCL × *s*	Example: RCL − 1 2 subtracts *r12* from *x* and displays the result (acting like RCL 1 2 −, but without losing a *stack* level).
RCL /	RCL / *s*	
RCL↑	RCL ▲ *s*	(1) [¬α] RCL↑ (↓) replaces *x* with the maximum (minimum) of *s* and *x*.
RCL↓	RCL ▼ *s*	
RDP	h X.FCN RDP *n*	(1) [d] Rounds *x* to *n* decimal places ($0 \le n \le 99$, think of FIX format), taking the RM setting into account. See RM and compare RSD. Example: 1.23456789E-95 RDP **99** will return 12346^{-95}.
RDX,	h MODE RDX,	(0) Selects a comma or a point as decimal radix mark. h ./. toggles the radix mark.
RDX.	h MODE RDX.	
REALM?	h TEST REALM?	(0) [¬α] Tests if your *WP 34S* is in real mode (DECM).

the bit pattern). Good properties and a period around 2^{88}. – In bases 2, 4, 8, or 16, the digits should be completely random (at least in unsigned mode and most likely in all other modes). In other bases, there will be some small bias. Additionally, a shorter word length will increase the bias typically.

[119] Note there is no need pressing h here.

Name	Keystrokes	Remarks (see pp. 171ff for general information)
RECV	**h** (P.FCN) **RECV**	(0) [¬α] Prepares your *WP 34S* for receiving data via serial I/O. See SEND... and pp. 317ff for more.
REGS	**h** (MODE) **REGS** _n_	(0) Specifies the number of global general purpose registers wanted. With REGS **100** you get the default state (**R00 – R99**), REGS **0** leaves not even a single such register for use.
REGS?	**h** (P.FCN) **REGS?**	(-1) [¬α] Returns the number of global general purpose registers allocated (0 ... 100).
RESET	**h** (P.FCN) **RESET**	[¬α] If confirmed, executes CLALL and resets all modes to start-up default, i.e. 24h, 2COMPL, ALL **0**, DBLOFF, DEG, DENANY, DENMAX **0**, D.MY, JG1752, LinF, LocR **0**, LZOFF, PROFRC, RDX., REGS **100**, RM **0**, SCIOVR, SEPON, SSIZE4, TSON, WSIZE **64**, YDOFF, and finally DECM. See these individual commands for more. RESET is not programmable.
RJ	**h** (X.FCN) **RJ**	(-1) [n] Right justifies, analogous to LJ on the *HP-16C*. **Example:** 101100_2 RJ results in $y = 1011_2$ and $x = 2$. See LJ.
RL	**h** (X.FCN) **RL** _n_	(1) [n] Works like *n* consecutive RLs / RLCs on the *HP-16C*, similar to RLn / RLCn there. For RL, $0 \le n \le 63$. For RLC, $0 \le n \le 64$. RL 0 and RLC 0 execute as NOP, but load **L**. See pp. 141f for more.
RLC	**h** (X.FCN) **RLC** _n_	

Name	Keystrokes	Remarks (see pp. 171ff for general information)
RM	**h** (MODE) **RM** *n*	(0) Sets floating point rounding mode. This is only used when converting from the high precision internal format (39 digits or more) to packed real numbers. It will <u>not</u> alter the display nor change the behavior of ROUND. The following modes are supported: 0: round half even: ½ = 0.5 rounds to next even number (default). 1: round half up: 0.5 rounds up *('businessman's rounding'* [120]). 2: round half down: 0.5 rounds down. 3: round up: rounds away from 0. 4: round down: rounds towards 0 (truncates). 5: ceiling: rounds towards $+\infty$. 6: floor: rounds towards $-\infty$.
RMDR	**h** (RMDR)	(2) [¬α] Returns the remainder of a division. Equals RMD on the *HP-16C* but works for real numbers as well. Compare MOD. See also pp. 144f. Examples: $\mathrm{rmdr}(25; 7) = 4;$ $\mathrm{rmdr}(-25; 7) = -4;$ $\mathrm{rmdr}(25; -7) = 4;$ $\mathrm{rmdr}(-25; -7) = -4 .$
RM?	**h** (X.FCN) **RM?**	(-1) [¬α] Returns the floating point rounding mode set. See RM for more.
ROUND	**g** (RND)	(1) [¬α] In fraction mode, rounds x using the current denominator like RND does in the *HP-35S* fraction mode. Else rounds x using the current display format like RND does in the *HP-42S*.
ROUNDI	**h** (X.FCN) **ROUNDI**	(1) [¬α] Rounds x to next integer. ½ rounds to 1.

---

[120] Translator's note: This corresponds to "kaufmännische Rundung" in German.

Name	Keystrokes	Remarks (see pp. 171ff for general information)
RR	**h** X.FCN **RR** _n_	(1) [n] Works like _n_ consecutive RRs / RRCs on the *HP-16C*, similar to RRn / RRCn there. For RR, $0 \le n \le 63$. For RRC, $0 \le n \le 64$. RR 0 and RRC 0 execute as NOP, but load **L**. See pp. 141f for more.
RRC	**h** X.FCN **RRC** _n_	
RSD	**h** X.FCN **RSD** _n_	(1) [d] Rounds x to n significant digits $(1 \le n \le 34)$, taking the RM setting into account. See RM, compare RDP.
RTN	**g** RTN	(0) [**STO**] Last executable command in a routine (see p. 156).
		(0) [**RCL**] Pops the local data (like PopLR) and returns control to the calling routine in program execution, i.e. moves the program pointer one step behind the XEQ instruction that called said routine. If there is none (i.e. this routine is top level), program execution halts, the program pointer is set to step 000, and **BEG** is lit.
		(0) [¬**RCL** & ¬**STO**] Puts the program pointer to the beginning of program memory in *RAM* and lights **BEG**.
RTN+1	**h** P.FCN **RTN+1**	(0) [¬α] Works like RTN, but moves the program pointer two steps behind the XEQ instruction that called said routine **in program execution**. Halts if there is none.
R-CLR	**h** P.FCN **R−CLR**	(0) [d] Interprets x in the form sss.nn . Clears **nn** registers starting with address **sss** .
		Example: For x = 34.567 , R-CLR will clear **R34** through **R89**.
		ATTENTION: For **nn = 0** , clearing will go to the maximum available.
		For $sss \in [0; 99]$, clearing will stop at the highest allocated global numbered register.
		For $sss \in [100; 111]$, it will stop at **K**.
		For $sss \ge 112$, it will stop at the highest allocated local register.

Name	Keystrokes	Remarks (see pp. 171ff for general information)
R-COPY	**h** (P.FCN) **R-COPY**	(0) [d] Interprets x in the form `sss.nnddd`. Takes **nn** registers starting with address **sss** and copies their contents to **ddd** etc. Also useful for matrix copying. For $x < 0$, R-COPY will take **nn** registers from *FM* instead, starting with register number |**sss**|. Destination will be in *RAM* always. **Example:** For $x = 7.03045678$, **r07, r08, r09** will be copied into **R45, R46, R47**, respectively. **ATTENTION:** The advice at R-CLR applies here, too, but with 'clearing' replaced by 'copying'.
R-SORT	**h** (P.FCN) **R-SORT**	(0) [d] Interprets x in the form `sss.nn`. Sorts the contents of **nn** registers starting with address **sss**. **Example:** Assume $x = 49.0369$, **r49** = 1.2, **r50** = −3.4, and **r51** = 0; then R-SORT will return **r49** = -3.4, **r50** = 0, and **r51** = 1.2. **ATTENTION:** The advice at R-CLR applies here, too, but with 'clearing' replaced by 'sorting'.
R-SWAP	**h** (P.FCN) **R-SWAP**	(0) [d] Works like R-COPY but <u>swaps</u> the contents of source and destination registers.
R→D		(1) [d] See the *Catalog of Conversions (CONV)* on pp. 270ff for conversions of *radians* to *degrees*.
R↑	**h** (R↑)	[¬α] Rolls the *stack* contents one level up or down, respectively. Will work unless browsing a *catalog*. See pp. 40f for details. For the complex commands, see p. 129.
R↓	(R↓)	
s	**g** (s)	(-2) [d] Takes the statistical sums accumulated, calculates the *sample standard deviations* s_y and s_x and pushes them on the *stack*. See *App. I* on pp. 383ff for the formula.

Name	Keystrokes	Remarks (see pp. 171ff for general information)
SAVE	**h** [P.FCN] **SAVE**	(0) Saves the system state, all register contents, and all programs from *RAM* into *FM*, and returns **Saved**. See pp. 296f for more.
	[ON] + [STO] + [STO]	Recall your entire backup using LOAD, specific parts of it via LOADP, LOADR, LOADSS, or LOADΣ (see there).
SB	**h** [X.FCN] **SB** _n_	(1) [n] Sets the specified bit in x.
SCI	**h** [SCI] _n_	(0) [d] Sets scientific display format (see pp. 79f).
		(0) [n] Turns to DECM and works like in DECM.
SCIOVR	**h** [SCI] [ENTER↑]	(0) [¬α] Defines that numbers exceeding the range displayable in ALL or FIX will be shown in scientific format. Compare ENGOVR, see RESET.
SDL	**h** [X.FCN] **SDL** _n_	(1) [d] Shifts digits left (right) by n decimal positions, equivalent to multiplying (dividing) x by 10^n. Compare SL and SR for integers.
SDR	etc.	
SEED	**h** [STAT] **SEED**	(0) [d] Stores a seed for random number generation.
SENDA	**h** [P.FCN] **SENDA** etc.	(0) [α] SENDA sends all *RAM* data, SENDP the program memory, SENDR the global general purpose registers, and SENDΣ the summation registers, respectively, to the device connected via serial I/O. See RECV and *App. A* on pp. 296f for more.
SENDP		
SENDR		
SENDΣ		
SEPOFF	**h** [MODE] **SEPOFF**	(0) Toggle the digit group separators for integers. Points or commas will be displayed every ... ... four digits in bases 2 and 4, ... two digits in base 16, and
SEPON	**h** [MODE] **SEPON**	... three digits in all other integer bases. You can use **h** [./.] in integer modes for this.

Name	Keystrokes	Remarks (see pp. 171ff for general information)
SERR	**h** (STAT) **SERR**	(-2) [d] Takes the statistical data accumulated, calculates and returns the *standard errors* (i.e. the *standard deviations* of $\bar{y}$ and $\bar{x}$).
SERR$_w$	**h** (STAT) **SERR$_w$**	(-1) [d] Returns the *standard error* for weighted data, i.e. the *standard deviation* of $\bar{x}_w$.
SETCHN	**h** (MODE) **SETCHN**	(0) Sets some regional preferences (see pp. 77f).
SETDAT	**h** (MODE) **SETDAT**	(0) Sets the date for the real time clock (the emulator takes it from the PC clock).
SETEUR SETIND SETJPN	**h** (MODE) **SETEUR** etc.	(0) Sets some regional preferences (see pp. 77f).
SETTIM	**h** (MODE) **SETTIM**	(0) Sets the time for the real time clock (the emulator takes it from the PC clock).
SETUK SETUSA	**h** (MODE) **SETUK** etc.	(0) Sets some regional preferences (see pp. 77f).
SF	**f** (SF) **_n_**	(0) [¬α] Sets the flag specified.
SHOW	**g** (SHOW)	[¬α] Register *browser*. See p. 251 for more.
^{c}*SIGN*	**h** (X.FCN) **SIGN**	(1) [¬α] Returns 1 for $x > 0$, −1 for $x < 0$, and 0 for $x = 0$ or non-numeric data. Corresponds to $\mathrm{signum}(x)$ for numeric input.
	(CPX) **h** (X.FCN) **SIGN**	(1) [d] Returns the unit vector of $x + i\,y$ in **X** and **Y**.
SIGNMT	**h** (MODE) **SIGNMT**	(0) Sets sign-and-mantissa mode (see pp. 137f).
SIN	**f** (SIN)	(1) [d] Returns the sine of the *angle x*.

Name	Keystrokes	Remarks (see pp. 171ff for general information)
SINC	**h** X.FCN **SINC**	(1) [d] Returns $\dfrac{\sin(x)}{x}$ for x in *radians* regardless of the angular mode chosen; returns 1 for $x = 0$.
SINH	**f** HYP SIN	(1) [d] Returns the hyperbolic sine of x.
SKIP	**h** P.FCN **SKIP** *n*	(0) [¬α] Skips *n* program steps forwards ($0 \le n \le 255$). So e.g. SKIP **2** skips the next two steps, going e.g. from step 123 to step 126. If SKIP attempts to cross an END, an error is thrown. **ATTENTION:** If you edit a section of your routine crossed by one or more BACK, SKIP, or CASE jumps, this may well result in a need to **manually maintain all those statements individually.**
SL	**h** X.FCN **SL** *n*	(1) [n] Works like *n* (≤ 63) consecutive SLs on the *HP-16C*. SL 0 executes as NOP, but loads **L**. See pp. 141f for more.
SLOW	**h** MODE **SLOW**	(0) Sets the processor speed to 'slow', about 50% of 'fast'. This is also automatically entered for low battery voltage (see p. 73). Compare FAST on p. 193.
SLV	**f** SLV *label*	[d] Solves the equation $f(x) = 0$, with $f(x)$ calculated by the routine specified. Two initial estimates of the root must be supplied in **X** and **Y** when calling SLV. It returns x_{root} in **X**, the second last x-value tested in **Y**, $f(x_{root})$ in **Z**, 0 in **T**, and x_{root} in all other *stack* levels. Additionally, SLV acts as a test, so the next program step will be skipped if SLV fails to find a root.[121] Note you can nest SLV, ∫, Σ, and Π in routines to any depth as far as memory allows. **ATTENTION:** SLV fills all *stack* levels with x before calling the routine specified.

---

[121] Please refer to the *HP-34C Owner's Handbook and Programming Guide* (*Section 8* and *App. A*) or the *HP-15C Owner's Handbook* (*Section 13* and *App. D*) for more information about automatic root finding and some caveats.

Name	Keystrokes	Remarks (see pp. 171ff for general information)
SLVQ	h X.FCN SLVQ	[d] Solves $ax^2 + bx + c = 0$ with its real parameters on the input *stack* [*c, b, a*, ...], and tests the result. • If $r := b^2 - 4ac \geq 0$, SLVQ returns $-\dfrac{b \pm \sqrt{r}}{2a}$ in Y and X. In a routine, the step after SLVQ will be executed. • Else, SLVQ returns the real part of the first complex root in X and its imaginary part in Y (the second root is the complex conjugate of the first – see CONJ). If run directly from the keyboard, the complex indicator **i** is lit then – in a routine, the step after SLVQ will be skipped. In either case, SLVQ returns *r* in Z. Higher *stack* levels are kept unchanged. L will contain equation parameter *c*.
SMODE?	h P.FCN SMODE?	(-1) [¬α] Returns the integer sign mode set, i.e. 2 (meaning 'true') for 2's complement, 1 ('true' again) for 1's complement, 0 (i.e. 'false') for unsigned, or -1 (i.e. 'true') for sign and mantissa mode.
SPEC?	h TEST SPEC?	(0) [¬α] True if x is 'special', i.e. infinite or non-numeric.
SR	h X.FCN SR _n_	(1) [n] Works like n (≤ 63) consecutive SRs on the *HP-16C*. SR 0 executes as NOP, but loads L. See pp. 141f for more.
sRCL	h X.FCN sRCL _s_	(-1) [¬α] Assumes the source contains *SP* data and recalls them as such. See pp. 305f and 351ff.
SSIZE4	h MODE SSIZE4	Set the *stack* size to 4 or 8 levels, respectively (see pp. 40ff). Note that the register contents will remain unchanged in this operation. The same will happen if *stack* size is modified by any other operation (e.g. by RCLM, see p. 75).
SSIZE8	h MODE SSIZE8	

Name	Keystrokes	Remarks (see pp. 171ff for general information)
SSIZE?	**h** (P.FCN) **SSIZE?**	(-1) [¬α] Returns the number of *stack* levels currently allocated.
	h (STAT)	[d] *Catalog*, see pp. 255f.
	h (STATUS)	[¬α] Flag *browser*. See pp. 251f.
STO	(STO) *s*	(0) [¬α] Stores *x* into destination. See pp. 134f for ^{c}STO.
STOM	(STO) (MODE) *s*	(0) [¬α] Stores mode settings for later use (see p. 75).[122] RCLM will recall such data.
STOP	(R/S)	(0) [**STO**] Stops program execution. May be used to wait for input, for example.
STOPW	**h** (X.FCN) **STOPW**	[d] Stopwatch application based on the real time clock and following the timer of the *HP-55*. See pp. 282ff for a detailed description. **ATTENTION**: This command is only part of the function set if the proper firmware is loaded. See *App. A* on pp. 285ff.
STOS	**h** (P.FCN) **STOS** *s*	(0) [¬α] Stores all current *stack* level contents in a set of 4 or 8 registers, starting at destination address *s*. See RCLS.
STO+	(STO) (+) *s*	(0) [¬α] Executes the specified operation on *s* and stores the result into said address.
STO–	(STO) (−) *s*	
STO×	(STO) (×) *s*	Example: (STO)(−)(0)(1) subtracts *x* from *r1* like the keystrokes (RCL)(0)(1) (x≷y) (−) (STO)(0)(1) would do, but the *stack* remains unchanged.
STO /	(STO) (/) *s*	
STO↑	(STO) (▲) *s*	(0) [¬α] STO↑ (↓) takes the maximum (minimum) of *s* and *x* and stores it at the address specified.
STO↓	(STO) (▼) *s*	

---

[122] Note there is no need for pressing **h** here.

Name	Keystrokes	Remarks (see pp. 171ff for general information)
SUM	**h** STAT SUM	(-2) [d] Recalls the linear sums Σy <u>and</u> Σx. Useful for elementary 2D vector algebra. See e.g. the *HP-25 Owner's Handbook* or (as well) the *HP-42S Owner's Manual*.
	h SUMS	[d] *Catalog*, see pp. 255f.
s_w	**h** STAT s_w	(-1) [d] Calculates the *standard deviation* for weighted data (where the weight y of each data point x was entered via $\Sigma+$). See *App. I* on pp. 383ff for the formula.
s_{XY}	**h** STAT s_{XY}	(-1) [d] Calculates the *sample covariance* for the two data sets entered via $\Sigma+$, depending on the curve fit model selected. See *App. I* for the formula and COV for the *population covariance*.
TAN	**f** TAN	(1) [d] Returns the tangent of the *angle x*.
TANH	**f** HYP TAN	(1) [d] Returns the hyperbolic tangent of *x*.
	h TEST	[d] *Catalog*, see pp. 255ff.
TICKS	**h** P.FCN TICKS	(-1) [¬α] Returns the number of ticks after power-up from the real time clock at execution time. With the quartz crystal built-in, 1 *tick* = 0.1 *s*. Without, it may be some 10% more or less. So the quartz crystal is inevitably required if the clock is to be useful in the long range. TICKS also works without the quartz, however. TICKS comes handy for measuring program execution times, for example.
TIME	**h** X.FCN TIME	(-1) [d] Recalls the time from the real time clock at execution, displaying it in the format hh.mmss in standard 24h-mode. Choose FIX **4** for best results.
T_n	**h** X.FCN T_n	(2) [d] *Chebychev polynomials of first kind*. See *App. I* on p. 387f for details.

Name	Keystrokes	Remarks (see pp. 171ff for general information)
TOP?	**h** **(TEST)** **TOP?**	(0) [¬α] Returns **false** if TOP? is called in a sub-routine, **true** if the program-running flag is set and the SRS pointer is clear.
$t_p(x)$		(1) [d] *Student's t distribution.* The *degrees of freedom* are stored in **J**. $t_u(x)$ equals Q(t) on the *HP-21S*. See p. 71 for an application example and *App. I* on pp. 375ff for details.
$t_u(x)$	**h** **(PROB)** **t₌(x)**	
$t(x)$	etc.	
$t^{-1}(p)$		
TRANSP	**h** **(MATRIX)** **TRANSP**	(1) [d] Takes a matrix *descriptor x* (see p. 67) and returns the *descriptor* of its transpose. The transpose is done in-situ and does not require any additional memory.
TSOFF	**h** **(MODE)** **TSOFF**	(0) Toggle the thousands separators for DECM (points or commas depending on radix setting).
TSON	**h** **(MODE)** **TSON**	
t⇆	**h** **(P.FCN)** **t⇆** **s**	[¬α] Swaps *t* and *s*, analogous to *x⇆* .
ULP	**h** **(X.FCN)** **ULP**	(1) [¬α] Returns 1 times the smallest power of ten which can be added to *x* or subtracted from *x* to actually change the value of *x* in your *WP 34S* in the mode set. Thus 1 is returned in integer mode.
U_n	**h** **(X.FCN)** **U.**	(2) [d] *Chebychev polynomials of second kind.* See *App. I* on p. 387f for details.
UNSIGN	**h** **(MODE)** **UNSIGN**	(0) Sets unsigned mode (see pp. 137f, compare UNSGN on the *HP-16C*).
VERS	**h** **(X.FCN)** **VERS**	(0) [¬α] Shows your firmware version and build number (see pp. 76f).
VIEW	**h** **(VIEW)** **s**	(0) [¬α] Shows *s* until the next key is pressed. See p. 81 for the complex output format and pp. 161f for applications.

Name	Keystrokes	Remarks (see pp. 171ff for general information)
VIEWα	**h** **P.FCN** `VIEWα`	(0) [¬α] Displays *alpha* in the top row and - - - in the bottom row until the next key is pressed (compare to AVIEW in the *HP-42S*). See pp. 161f for more.
	h **VIEW** **–**	(0) [α] Works as above.
VWα+	**h** **VIEW** **s**	(0) [α] Displays *alpha* in the top row and *s* in the bottom row until the next key is pressed. See pp. 161f for applications.
	h **P.FCN** `VWα+` **s**	(0) [¬α] Works as above.
WDAY	**h** **X.FCN** `WDAY`	(1) [d] Takes x as a date in the format selected, returns the name of the respective day in the dot matrix and a corresponding integer in the numeric line (Monday = 1, Sunday = 7).[123]
Weibl		(1) [d] *Weibull distribution* with its shape parameter b in **J** and its characteristic lifetime T in **K**. See *App. I* on pp. 375ff for details.
Weibl$_p$	**h** **PROB** `Weibl`	
Weibl$_u$	etc.	Weibl^{-1} returns the survival time t_s for a given probability p in **X**, with b in **J** and T in **K**.
Weibl^{-1}		
WHO	**h** **X.FCN** `WHO`	(0) [¬α] Displays credits to the brave men who made this project work.
W$_m$	**h** **X.FCN** `W.m`	(1) [d] W$_p$ returns the principal branch of *Lambert's* W for given $x \geq -1/e$. W$_m$ returns its negative branch. W^{-1} returns x for given W$_p$ ($\geq$ -1). See *App. I* on pp. 389ff for more.
W$_p$	**h** **X.FCN** `W.p`	
W^{-1}	**h** **X.FCN** `W-1`	

---

[123] Translator's note: These numbers correspond to Chinese weekdays 1 to 6 directly. For Portuguese weekdays ('segunda-feira' etc.), add 1 to days 1 to 5.

Name	Keystrokes	Remarks (see pp. 171ff for general information)
WSIZE	**h** MODE WSIZE *n*	(0) Works almost like on the *HP-16C*, but with the parameter $1 \le n \le 64$ trailing the command instead of taken from **X**. Reducing the word size truncates the values in the *stack* registers allocated and in **L**. All other memory content stays as is (see p. 347 for details). Increasing the word size will add empty bits to each *stack* level. WSIZE **0** sets the word size to maximum, i.e. 64 bits.
WSIZE?	**h** P.FCN WSIZE?	(-1) [¬α] Recalls the word size set.
x^2	**g** x^2	(1) [¬α] Returns the square of x.
x^3	**h** X.FCN x^3	(1) [¬α] Returns the cube of x.
XEQ	**XEQ** *label*	(0) [**STO**] Inserts a call to the subroutine with the label specified.
		(0) [¬**STO**] Executes the routine with the label specified.
	A, **B**, **C**, or **D**	(0) [**STO**] Inserts a call to the respective routine, so e.g. pressing **C** inserts XEQ C.
		(0) [¬**STO**] Executes the respective routine if defined in the *current program*. You may need **f** for reaching these *hotkeys* in integer bases >10.
XEQα	**h** P.FCN XEQα	(0) [¬α] Takes the first three characters of *alpha* (or all if there are fewer than three) as a label and calls or executes the corresponding routine.
XNOR	**h** X.FCN XNOR	(2) [¬α] Works analogous to AND, cf. p. 183.
XOR	**h** XOR	(2) [¬α] Works analogous to AND, cf. p. 183.
XTAL?	**h** TEST XTAL?	(0) [¬α] Tests if a quartz crystal is installed <u>and</u> activated (see p. 349). Said installation is necessary for a precise real time clock. For the command name, think of Xmas.

Name	Keystrokes	Remarks (see pp. 171ff for general information)
x̄	ⓕ x̄	(-2) [d] Returns the *arithmetic means* of the y- and x-data accumulated. See also s and SERR.
x̄g	ⓗ STAT x̄ɡ	(-2) [d] Returns the *geometric means* of the y- and x-data accumulated. See *App. I* on pp. 383ff for the formula. See also ε, ε_m, and ε_p.
x̄w	ⓗ STAT x̄w	(-1) [d] Returns the *arithmetic mean* for weighted data (where the weight y of each data point x was entered via Σ+). See *App. I* on pp. 383ff for the formula. See also s_w and $SERR_w$.
x̂	ⓗ STAT x̂	(1) [d] Returns a forecast x for a given y (in **X**) according to the curve fit model chosen. See L.R. for more.
	ⓗ X.FCN	*Catalog*, see pp. 255ff.
x!	ⓗ !	(1) [¬α] Returns $\Gamma(x + 1)$. For positive integers, returns the *factorial* $n!$.
x → α	ⓗ X.FCN x→α	(0) Interprets x as a character code. Appends the respective character to *alpha*, similar to XTOA in the *HP-42S*. Note that x→α uses the internal *WP 34S* character code, deviating from Unicode. Check using α→x. See also pp. 321ff.
x⇆	ⓗ x² **s**	[¬α] Swaps x and s, analogous to x⇆y . Will be listed like x⇆ J, x⇆.12, x⇆→12, etc. Note that capitals are listed but register contents are swapped. See pp. 134f for ^{c}x⇆ .
x⇆ Y	x⇆y	[¬α] Swaps the *stack* contents x and y, performing Re⇆Im if a complex operation was executed immediately before.
^{c}x⇆^{c}Y ^{c}x⇆Z	CPX x⇆y	[d] Swaps the *stack* contents x_c and y_c. See p. 129. Build 3815 uses the name ^{c}x⇆ Z, build 3810 uses ^{c}x⇆^{c}Y – choose what you prefer.

Name	Keystrokes	Remarks (see pp. 171ff for general information)
x < ?	[h] [TEST] x<_? s	(0) [¬α] Compare x with s. For example, [h] [TEST] x< ? [K] compares x with k, and will be listed as x<? K in a routine. See the examples on p. 63 for more.
x ≤ ?	[h] [TEST] x≤_? s	
x = ?	[f] x = ? s	
x = +0 ?	[h] [TEST] x=+0?	x ≈ ? will be true if the <u>rounded</u> values of x and s are equal (see ROUND).
x = −0 ?	[h] [TEST] x=−0?	The signed tests x = +0? and x = −0? are meant for integer modes 1COMPL and SIGNMT, and for DECM if flag **D** is set. In all these cases, e.g. 0 divided by −7 will display −0.
x ≈ ?	[h] [TEST] x≈_? s	
x ≠ ?	[g] x ≠ ? s	
x ≥ ?	[h] [TEST] x≥_? s	[CPX] [f] x = ? s / [CPX] [g] x ≠ ? s work as explained on p. 134.
x > ?	[h] [TEST] x>_? s	
$\sqrt[x]{y}$	[h] [X.FCN] ˣ√y	(2) [¬α] Returns the xth root of y.
YDOFF	[h] [MODE] YDOFF	Toggles the display of y in the dot matrix.
YDON	[h] [MODE] YDON	
YEAR	[h] [P.FCN] YEAR	(1) [d] Assumes x containing a date in the format selected and extracts the year.
y^x	[f] yˣ	(2) [¬α] Returns the xth power of y. [C] may be used as long as label **C** is not is not defined in *current program*.
$\hat{y}$	[f] ŷ	(1) [d] Returns a forecast **y** (in **X**) for a given **x** according to the curve fit model chosen. See L.R. for more.
Y.MD	[h] [MODE] Y.MD	(0) Sets the date format yyyy.mmdd.
y⇆	[h] [P.FCN] y⇆ s	[α] Swaps y and s, analogous to x⇆ .

Name	Keystrokes	Remarks (see pp. 171ff for general information)
$z\leftrightarrows$	**h** (P.FCN) **z⇄** **s**	[*æ*] Swaps z and s, analogous to $x\leftrightarrows$.
	(CPX) **h** (X.FCN) **ᶜz⇄** **s**	[*æ*] Swaps y_c and s, hence its name. Works analogous to $^Cx\leftrightarrows$. See there.
α	**f** (α)	(0) [¬**STO** & ¬α]: Enters alpha mode for appending characters to *alpha*. To start a new string, use CLα first.
		(0) [¬**STO** & α]: Leaves alpha mode.
		(0) [**STO** & ¬α]: Turns on alpha mode for keyboard entry of alpha constants. **INPUT** is set and the previous program step stays displayed until a character is entered. Each such character (e.g. '?') will be stored in one program step (such as α? here) and will be appended to *alpha* in program execution. To start a new string, use CLα first. (ENTER↑) leaves alpha mode.
		(0) [**STO** & α]: Turns on alpha group mode for direct entry of up to three characters in one program step taking two *words* (= 4 *bytes*). Your WP 34S will display α' in the top line and clears **STO**. Now enter the characters you want to append to *alpha*. To start a new string, use CLα before.
		Note alpha group mode is left automatically after three characters or (ENTER↑) is put in, returning to standard alpha mode as specified above; thus, **f** (α) must be entered again for another entry of a group of characters.

     Example: Entering

       (α) (T) (↑) (E) (S)
       (α) (T) (PSE) (1)

     will result in two program steps stored:

       α'Tes'
       α't 1'

     and Test 1 being appended to *alpha* in program execution.

Name	Keystrokes	Remarks (see pp. 171ff for general information)
		ATTENTION: Some particular characters must not be entered at third position (see pp. 321ff).
αDATE	**h** X.FCN αDATE	(0) [¬n] Takes *x* as a date and appends it to *alpha* in the format set. See DATE. To append a date stamp to *alpha*, call DATE αDATE. For a <u>short</u> European date stamp, set FIX 2, RDX. and call DATE αRC# X.
αDAY	**h** X.FCN αDAY	(0) [¬n] Takes *x* as a date, recalls the name of the corresponding day and appends its first three letters to *alpha*.
αGTO	**h** P.FCN αGTO <u>s</u>	(0) [¬n] Interprets *s* as character code. Takes the first 3 characters of the converted code (or all if there are less than 3) as an alpha label and positions the program pointer to it.
αIP	**h** X.FCN αIP <u>s</u>	(0) Appends the integer part of *s* to *alpha*, similar to AIP in the *HP-42S*. **ATTENTION:** The integer part will be pushed in *alpha* digit by digit, so the most significant digits may get lost e.g. for decimal numbers $>10^{30}$. No base indicator is appended.
αLENG	**h** X.FCN αLENG	(-1) Returns the number of characters found in *alpha*, like ALENG in the *HP-42S*.
αMONTH	**h** X.FCN αMONTH	(0) [¬n] Takes *x* as a date, recalls the name of the corresponding month and appends its first 3 letters to *alpha*.
αOFF	**h** P.FCN αOFF	(0) [¬α] Work like AOFF and AON in the *HP-42S*, turning alpha mode off and on.
αON	**h** P.FCN αON	
αRCL	**h** X.FCN αRCL <u>s</u>	(0) [¬α] Interprets *s* as characters and appends them to *alpha*. Compare αRC#.
	f RCL	(0) [α] Works as above.

Name	Keystrokes	Remarks (see pp. 171ff for general information)
αRC#	**h** X.FCN **αRC#** _s_	(0) Interprets _s_ as a number, converts it to a string in the format set, and appends this to **alpha**. [124] Compare αRCL. Example: If _s_ is 1234 and ENG 2 and RDX. are set, then 1.23e3 will be appended. See also αDATE for an application.
αRL αRR	**h** X.FCN **αRL** _n_ etc.	(0) αRL rotates **alpha** by _n_ characters like AROT in the *HP-42S*, but with $n \geq 0$ and the parameter trailing the command instead of taken from **X**. αRL **0** executes as NOP, but loads **L**. – αRR works like αRL but rotates to the right.
αSL αSR	**h** X.FCN **αSL** _n_ etc.	(0) αSL shifts the _n_ leftmost characters out of **alpha**, like ASHF in the *HP-42S*. αSL **0** equals NOP, but loads **L**. – αSR takes the _n_ rightmost characters instead.
αSTO	**h** X.FCN **αSTO** _s_	(0) [¬α] Stores the first (i.e. leftmost) 6 characters of **alpha** in the destination specified. Stores all if there are less than 6.
	f STO	(0) [α] Works as above.
αTIME	**h** X.FCN **αTIME**	(0) [¬n] Takes _x_ as a decimal time and appends it to **alpha** in the format hh:mm:ss according to the time mode selected. See 12h, 24h, and TIME. To append a time stamp to **alpha**, call TIME αTIME.
αXEQ	**h** P.FCN **αXEQ** _s_	(0) [¬α] Interprets _s_ as character code. Takes the first three characters (or all if there are fewer than three) of the converted code as an alpha label and calls or executes the respective routine.

---

[124] This command became necessary since the *WP 34S* cannot support data types like the HP-42S did.

Name	Keystrokes	Remarks (see pp. 171ff for general information)
$\alpha \to x$	**h** X.FCN α→x	(-1) Returns the <u>internal</u> *WP 34S* character code of the leftmost character in *alpha* and removes this character from *alpha*, like ATOX in the *HP-42S*. Compare $x\to\alpha$. See also pp. 321ff.
β	**h** X.FCN **β**	(2) [d] Returns *Euler's Beta function*. See *App. I* on pp. 389ff for details.
Γ	**h** X.FCN **Γ**	(1) [d] Returns $\Gamma(x)$. Additionally, **h** **!** calls $\Gamma(x+1)$. See also LNΓ.
Γ_p	**h** X.FCN **Γ⯀**	(2) [d] Returns the *regularized gamma function* (one of two kinds).
Γ_q	**h** X.FCN **Γ⯀**	
γ_{XY}	**h** X.FCN **γxy**	(2) [d] Returns the *lower* or *upper incomplete gamma function*, respectively.
Γ_{XY}	**h** X.FCN **Γxy**	
ΔDAYS	**h** X.FCN ΔDAYS	(2) [d] Assumes **X** and **Y** containing dates in the format chosen and calculates the number of days between them like in the *HP-12C*. If you want the difference incl. both limits, add **1** to the result.
Δ%	**g** Δ%	(1) [d] Returns $100 \cdot \dfrac{x-y}{y}$ leaving *y* unchanged, like %CH in the *HP-42S*.
ε	**h** STAT **ε**	(-2) [d] Returns the *scattering factors* ε_y and ε_x for *log-normally* distributed sample data. This ε_x works for the *geometric mean* $\bar{x}_g$ analogous to the *standard deviation* s for the *arithmetic mean* $\bar{x}$ but <u>multiplicative</u> instead of additive. See *App. I* on pp. 383ff for more.
ε_m	**h** STAT **εm**	(-2) [d] Works like ε but returns the *scattering factors* of the two *geometric means* (analogous to SERR for *arithmetic means*).
ε_P	**h** STAT **εp**	(-2) [d] Works like ε but returns the *scattering factors* of the two populations.

(Note in right margin spanning the Γ_p, Γ_q, γ_{XY}, Γ_{XY} rows: See *App. I* on pp. 389ff for details.)

Name	Keystrokes	Remarks (see pp. 171ff for general information)
ζ	**h** X.FCN **ζ**	(1) [d] Returns *Riemann's Zeta*. See *App. I* on pp. 389ff for more.
π	π	(-1) [d] Recalls **π**.
	CPX π	(-1) [d] Recalls **π** into **X** and clears **Y**. Compare the description of <u>CONST</u> on p. 253.
Π	**f** π *label*	(1) [d] Computes a product using the routine specified. Initially, **X** contains a loop control number in the format `cccccc.fffii`, and the product is set to 1. Each run through the routine specified by *label* computes a factor based on `cccccc`. At its end, this factor is multiplied with said product; the operation then decrements `cccccc` by `ii` and runs said routine again if then `cccccc ≥ fff`, else returns the resulting product in **X** and clears all other *stack* levels. If `ii = 0`, `cccccc` will be decremented by 1. See Σ for an application example and more. **ATTENTION:** Π fills all *stack* levels with *x* before calling the routine specified.
σ	**h** STAT **σ**	(-2) [d] Works like s but returns the *standard deviations* of the two *populations* instead. See *App. I* on pp. 383ff for the formula.
Σ	**g** Σ *label*	(1) [d] Computes a sum using the routine specified. Initially, **X** contains a loop control number in the format `cccccc.fffii`, and the sum is set to 0. Each run through the routine specified by *label* computes a summand based on `cccccc`. At its end, this summand is added to said sum; the operation then decrements `cccccc` by `ii` and runs said routine again if then `cccccc ≥ fff`, else returns the resulting sum in **X** and clears all other *stack* levels. If `ii = 0`, `cccccc` will be decremented by 1.

Name	Keystrokes	Remarks (see pp. 171ff for general information)
		Note you can nest SLV, ∫, Σ, and Π in routines to any depth as far as memory allows. But watch the *stack*!
		ATTENTION: Σ fills all *stack* levels with x before calling the routine specified.
$\Sigma\ln^2 x$ $\Sigma\ln^2 y$ $\Sigma\ln x$ $\Sigma\ln xy$ $\Sigma\ln y$	**h** (SUMS) **Σln²x** etc.	(-1) [d] Recall the corresponding statistical sums being necessary for curve fits beyond pure linear. See Σx for more. **ATTENTION:** Depending on input data, these sums may become non-numeric. If this happens no error will be thrown, however, regardless of flag **D**.
σ_w	**h** (STAT) **σw**	(-1) [d] Works like s_w but returns the *standard deviation* of the *population* instead. See *App. I* on pp. 383ff for the formula.
Σx Σx^2 $\Sigma x^2 y$ $\Sigma x\ln y$ Σxy Σy Σy^2 $\Sigma y\ln x$	**h** (SUMS) **Σx** etc.	(-1) [d] Recall the corresponding statistical sums. These sums are necessary for basic statistics and fits. Calling the sums by name significantly improves program readability. Note they are stored in special registers of your *WP 34S* (see p. 301). **ATTENTION:** Depending on input data, the sums containing logarithms may become non-numeric. If this happens no error will be thrown, however, regardless of flag **D**.
Σ+	**h** (Σ+) (or **A** as long as label **A** is not defined in *current program*)	[d] Adds a data point to the statistical sums.	Σ+ and Σ− return the new number of data points in **X** and disable *automatic stack lift*. Both may be also used for 2D vector adding and subtracting (see SUM).
Σ−	**h** (Σ−)	[d] Subtracts a data point from those sums.	

Name	Keystrokes	Remarks (see pp. 171ff for general information)
$\Phi_u(x)$	**h** (PROB) **Φ◻(x)**	(1) [d] *Standard normal error probability*, equaling Q in the *HP-32E* and Q(z) in the *HP-21S*.
$\varphi(x)$	**h** (PROB) **Φ(x)**	(1) [d] *Standard normal PDF.* See *App. I* on pp. 375ff for the formulas.
$\Phi(x)$	**f** (Φ)	(1) [d] *Standard normal CDF.*
$\Phi^{-1}(p)$	**g** (Φ⁻¹)	(1) [d] *Standard normal quantile function.*
χ^2		(1) [d] *Chi-square distribution* (with its *degrees of freedom* given in **J**). χ^2_u equals $Q(\chi^2)$ on the *HP-21S*. See *App. I* on pp. 375ff for more.
χ^2_P	**h** (PROB) **x²**	
χ^2_u	etc.	
χ^2INV		
$(-1)^x$	**h** (X.FCN) **(-1)ˣ**	(1) [α] If x is a non-integer number, returns $cos(\pi \cdot x)$.
+	⊞	(2) [¬α] Returns $y + x$.
	(CPX) ⊞	(2) [d] Returns $[\,x + z,\ \ y + t,\ \ \dots\,]$. May be used for adding 2D vectors as well.
−	⊟	(2) [¬α] Returns $y - x$.
	(CPX) ⊟	(2) [d] Returns $[\,x - z,\ \ y - t,\ \ \dots\,]$. May be used for subtracting 2D vectors as well.
×	⊠	(2) [¬α] Returns $y \cdot x$.
	(CPX) ⊠	(2) [d] Multiplies two complex numbers, returning $[\,x \cdot z - y \cdot t,\ \ x \cdot t + z \cdot y,\ \ \dots\,]$. Look at CROSS or DOT for multiplying 2D vectors instead.
×MOD	**h** (X.FCN) **×MOD**	(3) [n] Returns $(z \cdot y) \bmod x$ for $x > 1$, $y > 0$, $z > 0$.

Name	Keystrokes	Remarks (see pp. 171ff for general information)
/	$\boxed{/}$	(2) [d] Returns y / x.
		(2) [n] Returns y div x; compare IDIV.
	$\boxed{CPX}$ $\boxed{/}$	(2) [d] Returns $[\dfrac{x \cdot z + y \cdot t}{z^2 + t^2}, \dfrac{z \cdot y - x \cdot t}{z^2 + t^2}, \ ... \ ]$.
+/–	$\boxed{+/-}$	(1) [¬α] 'Unary minus', returns $x \cdot (-1)$.
	$\boxed{CPX}$ $\boxed{+/-}$	(1) [d] 'Unary minus', returns $x_c \cdot (-1)$.
→DATE	$\boxed{h}$ $\boxed{X.FCN}$ **→DATE**	(3) [d] Assumes the three components of a date (year, month, and day) supplied on the *stack* in proper order for the date format selected and converts them to a single date in x. Inverts DATE→.
→DEG	$\boxed{→}$ $\boxed{DEG}$	(1) [d] Takes x as an angle in the angular mode currently set and converts it to *degrees*. Prefix $\boxed{g}$ may be omitted.
→GRAD	$\boxed{→}$ $\boxed{GRAD}$	(1) [d] Works like →DEG, but converts to *gon* (*grad*).
→H	$\boxed{→}$ $\boxed{f}$ $\boxed{H.d}$	(1) [d] Takes x as *hours* or *degrees* in the format hhhh.mmssdd as in vintage *HP* calculators and converts it to a decimal time or angle, allowing for using standard arithmetic operations then.
→H.MS	$\boxed{→}$ $\boxed{f}$ $\boxed{H.MS}$	(1) [d] Takes x as decimal *hours* or *degrees* and converts it to the format hhhh.mmssdd as in vintage *HP* calculators. For further calculations, use H.MS+ or H.MS– then.
→POL	$\boxed{g}$ $\boxed{→P}$	[d] Assumes **X** and **Y** containing 2D Cartesian coordinates (x, y) of a point or components of a vector and converts them to the corresponding polar coordinates / components (r, ϑ) with a radius $r = \sqrt{x^2 + y^2}$. Compare →REC.
→RAD	$\boxed{→}$ $\boxed{RAD}$	(1) [d] Works like →DEG, but converts to *radians*.

Name	Keystrokes	Remarks (see pp. 171ff for general information)
→REC	f R←	[d] Assumes **X** and **Y** containing 2D polar coordinates (r, ϑ) of a point or components of a vector and converts them to the corresponding Cartesian coordinates or components (x, y).
⇅	h P.FCN ⇅____	[¬α] Shuffles the contents of the bottom four *stack* levels at execution time. **Examples:** ⇅XXYZ works like ENTER↑ (but does not disable *automatic stack lift!*), ⇅YXZT works like x⇆y, ⇅YZTX works like R↓, ⇅TXYZ works like R↑, ⇅ZTXY works like ^{C}x⇆y, but also ⇅ZZZX is possible. **ATTENTION:** Capital letters are written but the contents of the levels are shuffled! This is a very powerful command although it does not look it. Note it will only affect the lowest four levels regardless of *stack* size. There is no connection to level **A** and above. If you play with this command, you may easily lose some level contents and make a mess of the *stack*.
%	f %	(1) [d] Returns $\dfrac{x \cdot y}{100}$, leaving y unchanged.
%MG	h X.FCN %MG	(2) [d] Returns the margin $100 \cdot \dfrac{x - y}{x}$ in % for a price x and cost y, like %MU-Price in the *HP-17B*.

Name	Keystrokes	Remarks (see pp. 171ff for general information)
%MRR	**h** X.FCN %MRR	(3) [d] Returns the mean rate of return in percent per period, i.e. $100 \cdot \left[\sqrt[z]{\left(x \middle/ y \right)} - 1 \right]$ with $x =$ future value after z periods, $y =$ present value. For $z = 1$, $\Delta\%$ returns the same result easier.
%T	**h** X.FCN %T	(2) [d] Returns $100 \cdot x \middle/ y$, interpreted as % of total.
%Σ	**h** X.FCN %Σ **h** STAT %Σ	(1) [d] Returns $100 \cdot x \middle/ \sum x$.
%+MG	**h** X.FCN %+MG	(2) [d] Calculates a sales price by adding a margin of x % to the cost y, as %MU-Price does in the HP-17B. Formula: $p_{sale} = \dfrac{y}{1 - \left(x \middle/ 100 \right)}$ You may use %+MG for calculating net amounts as well – just enter a negative percentage in x. Example: Total billed = 221,82 €, VAT = 19%. What is the net? **221,82** ENTER **19** +/- X.FCN ▲ returns 186,40.
√	**f** √x	(1) [¬α] Returns the square root of x. **D** may be used as long as label **D** is not is not defined in current program.

Name	Keystrokes	Remarks (see pp. 171ff for general information)
∫	g 🔲 **_label_**	[d] Integrates the function given in the routine specified. Lower and upper integration limits must be supplied in **Y** and **X**, respectively. ∫ returns the (approximated) integral in **X**, the penultimate approximation in **Y**, the upper integration limit in **Z**, the lower one in **T**, and fills also the remaining *stack* levels, if applicable.[125] Note you can nest SLV, ∫, Σ, and Π in routines to any depth as far as memory allows. But watch the *stack*! **ATTENTION:** ∫ fills all *stack* levels with x before calling the routine specified. – The iteration exits and the result is displayed as soon as the last two approximations agree when <u>rounded to display precision</u> (x≈ ? is used). Set the display to SCI *n* if you want to get *n* + *1* <u>significant</u> digits.
∞?	h TEST ∞?	(0) [¬α] Tests x for infinity.
^MOD	h X.FCN ^MOD	(3) [n] Returns $(z^{y}) \bmod x$ for $x > 1$, $y > 0$, $z > 0$. Example 1: 10 73 ENTER↑ 55 ENTER↑ 31 X.FCN ▲ XEQ returns 26. Example 2: 10 2 ENTER↑ 1000 ENTER↑ 13 X.FCN ▲ XEQ returns 3.

---

[125] Please refer to the *HP-34C Owner's Handbook and Programming Guide* (*Section 9* and *App. B*) or the *HP-15C Owner's Handbook* (*Section 14* and *App. E*) for more information about automatic integration and some caveats.

Your *WP 34S* uses a slightly different iterative algorithm than *HP's* vintage calculators: it employs the classical *Romberg* method; each new iteration takes twice the time of the previous one until the exit-condition is met; inspect the code at sourceforge.net – it is an XROM routine (cf. *App. H*) so you can read it almost as easily as a regular user program.

Name	Keystrokes	Remarks (see pp. 171ff for general information)
‖	g ‖	(2) [d] Returns $\left(\dfrac{1}{x}+\dfrac{1}{y}\right)^{-1}$, being very useful in electrical engineering especially. Returns 0 for x or y being zero.
⌷ADV	h P.FCN ⌷ADV	(0) [¬α] Prints the current contents of the print buffer plus an *LF*.[126] **ATTENTION:** Any printing will only work with a hardware modification (see pp. 359ff) and the proper firmware installed (see pp. 285ff) or using the *WP 34S* emulator in combination with a printer emulator (see p. 320). Else print commands will be ignored.
⌷CHR	h P.FCN ⌷CHR *n*	(0) [¬α] Sends a single character (with the code specified) to the printer. Character codes $n > 127$ can only be specified indirectly. ⌷MODE setting will be honored. See ⌷ADV.
⌷$^c r_{XY}$	h P.FCN ⌷$^c r_{XY}$ *s*	(0) [¬α] Prints the contents of the register specified and the next one, i.e. prints an entire complex number. A semicolon will separate the real (first) and the imaginary component. Works like ⌷r otherwise. See ⌷ADV. Example: Assume ⌷MODE 1, SCI 1, $x = -1.2$ and $y = 0.34$. Then the output of ⌷$^c r_{XY}$ X would look like $\quad -1.2e0 \; ; \quad 3.4e-1$
⌷DLAY	h MODE ⌷DLAY *s*	(0) Sets a delay of s ticks (see TICKS) to be used with each *LF* on the printer. May be helpful in tailoring the print load.

---

[126] The printer will actually print only when an *LF* is sent to it.

Name	Keystrokes	Remarks (see pp. 171ff for general information)
⌷MODE	**h** (MODE) **⌷MODE** _n_	(0) Sets print mode. Legal print modes are: 0: Use the printer font and character set wherever possible (default). All characters feature the same width (5 columns + 2 columns spacing). 1: Use the variable pitch display font, resulting in some jitter on the printout but packing more characters in a line. 2: Use the small display font, which allows for packing even more info in a line. 3: Send the output to the serial channel. Works for plain ASCII only – no characters will be translated. Line setup is the same as for serial communication: 9600 *baud*, 8 *bits*, no parity.
⌷PLOT	**h** (P.FCN) **⌷PLOT** _s_	(0) [¬α] Sends the graphic block starting at register address *s* to the printer. If its width is 166, the data will be trailed by an *LF*. See ⌷ADV and gDIM.
⌷PROG	**h** (P.FCN) **⌷PROG**	(0) [¬α] Prints the listing of the *current program* (cf. p. 156), one line per step. See ⌷ADV.
⌷r	**h** (P.FCN) **⌷r** _s_	(0) [¬α] Prints *s*, right adjusted, <u>without</u> labeling the output. If you want a heading label, call ⌷α+ first or use ⌷REGS. See ⌷ADV.
⌷REGS	**h** (P.FCN) **⌷REGS**	(1) [¬α] Interprets *x* in the form sss.nn . Prints the contents of *nn* registers starting with number *sss* . Each register takes one line starting with a label. See also ⌷ADV. **ATTENTION for *nn* = 0 :** For *sss* ∈ [0; 99], printing will stop at the highest allocated global numbered register. For *sss* ∈ [100; 111], printing will stop at **K**. For *sss* ≥ 112 , printing will stop at the highest allocated local register.
⌷STK	**h** (P.FCN) **⌷STK**	(0) [¬α] Prints the *stack* contents. Each level prints in a separate line starting with a label. See ⌷ADV.

Name	Keystrokes	Remarks (see pp. 171ff for general information)
⏚TAB	h P.FCN ⏚TAB n	(0) [¬α] Positions the print head to print column **n** (0 to 165, where **n** > 127 can only be specified indirectly). Useful for formatting (in ⏚MODE 1 or 2 in particular). Allows also for printer plots. If **n** is less than current position, an *LF* will be entered to reach the new position. See ⏚ADV.
⏚WIDTH	h P.FCN ⏚WIDTH	(-1) [¬α] Returns the number of print columns that *alpha* would take in the print mode set. See ⏚ADV and ⏚MODE. Second use: in ⏚MODE 1 or 2, ⏚WIDTH returns the width of *alpha* in pixels (including the last column being always blank) in the specified font.
⏚α	h P.FCN ⏚α	(0) [¬α] Appends *alpha* to the print line, trailed by an *LF*. Compare ⏚α+ and ⏚+α . See ⏚ADV.
⏚α+	h P.FCN ⏚α+	(0) [¬α] Sends *alpha* to the printer without a trailing *LF*, allowing further information to be appended to this line. May be repeated. See also ⏚ADV, ⏚r and ⏚+α.
⏚Σ	h P.FCN ⏚Σ	(0) [¬α] Prints the summation registers. Each register prints in one line starting with a label. See ⏚ADV.
⏚+α	h P.FCN ⏚+α	(0) [¬α] Appends *alpha* to the print line, adjusted to the right and trailed by an *LF*. Compare ⏚α and ⏚α+. See ⏚ADV. Example: The program section CLα α'Lef' α t ⏚α+ CLα α'Rig' α'ht' ⏚+α will print, if ⏚MODE 1 is set: Left Right

Name	Keystrokes	Remarks (see pp. 171ff for general information)
⌂?	[h] [TEST] **⌂?**	(0) [¬α] Tests if a quartz crystal and the necessary firmware are installed for printing. I.e. **⌂?** will return **true** if XTAL? returns **true** and calc_ir.bin (or calc_ir_full.bin) is loaded. The *IR* diode must be checked visually.
⌂#	[h] [P.FCN] **⌂#** *n*	(0) [¬α] Sends a single *byte*, without translation, to the printer (e.g. a control code). *n* > 127 can only be specified indirectly. **⌂**MODE setting will not be honored. See **⌂**ADV.
#	[h] [CONST] **#** *n*	Inserts an integer $0 \le n \le 255$ in a single program step, thus saving up to two steps and an ENTER.
c#	[CPX] [h] [CONST] **#** *n* [CPX] *n*	Works like # but also clears *y*. The shortcut works for $1 \le n \le 9$ only.

Alphanumeric Input

Char.	Keystrokes	Remarks
⌴	[h] [PSE]	[α] Appends a blank space to *alpha*.
°	[.]	[d] Separates *degrees* or *hours* from *minutes*, *seconds*, and hundredths of *seconds*, so input format is hhhh.mmssdd. The user has to take care where an arbitrary real number represents such an *angle* or a *time*.
0 ... 9	[0] ... [9]	[¬α] Standard numeric input. For integer bases <10, input of illegal digits is blocked. Note you cannot enter more than 12 digits in the mantissa.
		Register input in addressing. See pp. 64ff for the valid number ranges.
0 ... 9	[0], [1], [f] [2], ...	[α] Appends the corresponding digit to *alpha*.

Char.	Keystrokes	Remarks
A ... F	[A] ... [F] (grey print)	[n] Numeric input for digits >10. See pp. 123ff for more.
Ḁ ... Ẕ	[A] ... [Z] (grey print)	Register input in addressing. See the *virtual keyboard* on p. 62 for the letters applicable. [α] Appends the corresponding Latin letter to *alpha*. Use ⬆ to toggle between cases.
Ḁ ... Ẕ	▮ [CPX] ...	[α] Appends the corresponding letter to *alpha*. Use ⬆ to toggle between cases. See p. 259 for more.
E	[EEX]	[d & ¬FRC] Works like the key [E] did in the *Pioneers*. See p. 23.
i	[CPX] [.]	[d & ¬FRC] Enters complex number *i* , i.e. enters $x = 0$ and $y = 1$ and returns i1 360 RPM 0, in ALL 0 format, for example.
Ḁ ... Ω	[g] [A], ..., [g] [O] (grey print)	[α] Appends the corresponding Greek letter to *alpha*. Use ⬆ to toggle between cases. See pp. 148ff for more.
[	▮ [◄(]	
]	[g] [)▶]	
+	▮ [+]	[α] Appends the corresponding character to *alpha*.
–	▮ [–]	
×	▮ [×]	

Char.	Keystrokes	Remarks
/	Second `.`	[d] A second `.` in input indicates a *fraction*, wherein the first `.` is interpreted as a space, second as a fraction mark. Note you cannot enter `EEX` after you entered `.` twice – but you may delete the second dot while editing the input line. In FRC, first `.` is interpreted as a space, second as a fraction mark.
*̸	`f` `/`	[α] Appends a slash to *alpha*.
+/–	`+/–`	[¬α] See p. 23.
±	`f` `+/–`	
،	`h` `./,` `XEQ`	[α] Appends the corresponding character to *alpha*.
▪	`f` `.`	
':' or ';'	`.`	[d] Inserts a radix mark as selected.
!	`h` `!`	
?	`h` `STATUS`	
≒	`h` `x²`	
≠	`h` `XOR`	
&	`h` `AND`	[α] Appends the corresponding character to *alpha*.
\	`h` `/`	
¦	`h` `OR`	
¬	`h` `NOT`	
ᛒ	`f` `↑`	In a *catalog*, enters ᛒ for fast access to the print functions (see p. 280).

(right margin of first row: See pp. 123ff for examples.)

There are more characters you can enter in alpha mode – see p. 259f for an overview of all the letters and symbols provided in alpha *catalogs* and pp. 321ff for the complete character sets.

Nonprogrammable Control, Clearing and Information Commands

The commands CLALL, CLPALL, LOAD, LOADP, PSTO, RESET, SAVE, all *catalog*, *browser*, or application calls cannot be programmed. The same applies for the following keystrokes in the modes (indicated by the respective annunciators) or under the conditions stated below:

Key(s)	Conditions, modes	Remarks
[8]	Asking for confirmation	Answers the question $ure? with **N** for 'no'. Any other response except [R/S] = **Y**, [EXIT] or ⬅ for 'no' will be ignored.
	In CAT, SHOW, STATUS	Will be honored as described in the corresponding sections.
[ENTER↑] [127]	In CAT, SHOW, STOPW	Will be honored as described in the corresponding sections.
	÷	Selects the current item like [XEQ] below.
	INPUT, α'	Leaves alpha group mode (see p. 226).
	INPUT	Leaves alpha mode.
	Else	Calls the programmable command ENTER.

---

[127] The mode conditions specified here will be checked top down for this command at execution time:

If CAT, SHOW, or STOPW is open, [ENTER↑] will be served as described there;
  else if there is an open *catalog*, the current item will be selected;
    else if alpha group mode is set, it will be left;
      else if alpha mode is set, it will be left;
        else the programmable command ENTER will be executed or inserted.

This method holds for all commands listed here using this triangular symbolic.

Key(s)	Conditions, modes	Remarks
(EXIT)	¬RPN	Clears the *temporary message* displayed (see p. 76) returning to the calculator state as was before that message was thrown.
	Asking for confirmation	Answers the question $\mathtt{Sure?}$ with **N** for 'no'. Any other response except (R/S) = **Y** , (8) or ← for 'no' will be ignored.
	In STOPW	Leaves the application (see pp. 282ff).
	Command input pending	Cancels the execution of the pending operation, returning to the *WP 34S* status as it was before.
	In a *catalog* or *browser*	Leaves the current *catalog* or *browser* without executing anything, returning to the *WP 34S* status as it was before.
	RCL	Stops the running routine like (R/S) below.
	STO	Leaves programming mode like (P/R) below.
	INPUT	Leaves alpha mode like (ENTER↑) above.
	Else	Does nothing.
(h) (GTO) (.) (A), (B), (C), or (D)	¬INPUT	Puts the program pointer to the respective label. Compare p. 196.
(h) (GTO) (.) *n*	¬INPUT	Puts the program pointer to step *n* .[128]
(h) (GTO) (.) (▲)	¬INPUT	Puts the program pointer to the top of *current program* (i.e. to the step immediately after previous END statement).
(h) (GTO) (.) (▼)	¬INPUT	Puts the program pointer to the top of next program (i.e. to the step immediately after next END statement).

---

[128] GTO. will execute as soon as the address specified becomes unambiguous within the program memory used. Assume the memory is filled up to step 123, then e.g. GTO.**45** will immediately jump to step 45 without letting you enter a third digit, GTO.**13** to step 13, and GTO.**129** to the last step filled (i.e. to the one containing the final END statement).

WP 34S v3.3d

Key(s)	Conditions, modes	Remarks
h GTO . .	¬INPUT	Puts the program pointer on the very last step in program memory (i.e. to the final END statement).
(R/S)	Asking for confirmation	Answers the question Sure? with **Y** for 'yes'. Any other response except 8 or (EXIT) or ⟵ for 'no' will be ignored.
	In CAT, STOPW	Will be honored as described in the corresponding sections.
	RCL	Stops program execution immediately. Stopped will be displayed until the next keystroke.
	¬STO & ¬INPUT	Runs the *current program* or resumes its execution starting with the *current program step* (cf. p. 156).
	INPUT	Appends a Y or y to *alpha*.
	STO	Enters the programmable command STOP described in the *IOP* on pp. 214ff.
(XEQ)	In CAT	Will be honored as described in the corresponding sections. See the note below this list.
	÷	Selects the item currently displayed and exits after executing the respective command.
	Else	Calls the programmable command XEQ described in the *IOP* on p. 223.
(XEQ) .	¬INPUT	Calls GTO . (see above).

Key(s)	Conditions, modes	Remarks
	¬RPN	Clears the *temporary message* displayed (see p. 76) returning to the calculator state as was before that message was thrown.
	Asking for confirmation	Answers the question Sure? with **N** for 'no'. Any other response except R/S = **Y** , 8 or EXIT for 'no' will be ignored.
	In STOPW	Resets the timer (see p. 282).
←	Command input pending	Deletes the last digit or character put in. If there is none yet, cancels the pending command like EXIT above.
	In a *catalog* or *browser*	Leaves the *catalog* or *browser* like EXIT above.
	INPUT	Deletes the rightmost character in *alpha*.
	STO	Deletes the *current program step* (cf. p. 156).
	Else	Calls the programmable <u>command</u> CLx described in the *IOP* on pp. 185f.
→ f 2		
→ 8	DECM	Shows x as an integer to base 2, 8, 10, or 16, respectively. Returns to floating point notation set with the next keystroke. Prefix g may be omitted here.
→ f 10		
→ 16		
	÷	Calls the character ☐.
f t	INPUT	Toggles upper and lower case (the latter is indicated by ↓).
	Else	Calls the programmable command ☐r X (see there).

Key(s)	Conditions, modes	Remarks
▲ / ▼	In a *browser* or in STOPW	Will be honored as described in the corresponding sections. See the note below this list.
	± / ∓	Goes to previous / next item in the current *catalog*.
	INPUT	Scrolls the display window six characters to the left/right in *alpha* if possible. If fewer than six characters are beyond the limits of the display window on this side, the window will be positioned to the beginning/end of string. Useful for longer strings.
	Else	Acts like BST / SST in the *HP-42S*. I.e. browses routines in programming mode, where ▲ / ▼ will repeat with 5*Hz* when held down for longer than 0.5*s* on the calculator. Out of programming mode, the keys will not repeat, but SST will also execute the *current program step* (cf. p. 156).

See the following section to learn more about *catalogs*, *browsers*, and the stopwatch.

SECTION 6: CATALOGS, BROWSERS, AND AN APPLICATION

Due to the large set of items your *WP 34S* features, most of them are stored in *catalogs* as was discussed from p. 52 on.

Opening a *catalog* on your *WP 34S* will set alpha mode to allow for typing the first character(s) of the item wanted for rapidly accessing it. A subset of the full alpha virtual keyboard (shown on p. 151) is sufficient for *catalog* browsing:

There are three deviations, however:

1. ⬛ B (= 1/x) is employed in <u>CONV</u> for reverting conversions easily (see pp. 270f).

2. ⬛ → just calls the right arrow →, and

3. ⬛ EXIT calls the print character ⧈ in *catalog* browsing (since case switching is not needed here).

Beyond that,

- ▲ and ▼ will browse the open *catalog*.

- (ENTER↑) or (XEQ) select the item displayed, recall or execute it, and exit the *catalog*.

- (EXIT) or ⬅ leave the *catalog* without executing anything, i.e. they cancel the *catalog* call.

You may switch *catalogs* easily by just calling a new one accessible in current mode directly from the *catalog* you are browsing – no need to (EXIT) first.

When the last *catalog* called is reopened, the last item viewed therein is immediately displayed for easy repetitive use. A single function may be contained in more than one *catalog*.

There are also three *browsers* featured for checking memory, flags, program labels and registers (i.e. (CAT), (SHOW), and (STATUS)). They may be called in all modes except alpha. Therein, (EXIT) and ⬅ work as in *catalogs*. (SHOW) and (STATUS) operate in α_T mode, however (see p. 62). And some special keys and special rules may apply in *browsers* as explained in the table below.

Browser	Contents and special remarks
h (CAT)	Displays the alphanumeric (i.e. global) labels defined. The first item displayed is the top global label of the *current program* (cf. p. 156) – if there is no such label, the end of this program is shown. If there is no program at all in this memory section, the end of this section is displayed, e.g.
	<div align="center">**END** ᴮᴱᴳ ₃₆₀ ᵣ𝘈𝘙𝘔</div>
	▲ and ▼ browse global labels and END statements, while the location of the label or statement displayed is indicated in the lower line (ᵣ𝘈𝘙𝘔 for RAM, Lıb for the *FM* library, or bᵤP for the backup region in *FM*). See the following display example:
	<div align="center">**LBL'G→C'** ᴮᴱᴳ ₃₆₀ Lıb</div>
	Note the program pointer is moved in browsing.

Browser	Contents and special remarks
h CAT (continued)	Duplicate labels also show their primary address, e.g. `CALLS 012` when found a second time in RAM, or e.g. `CALLS Lib` when found a second time elsewhere.

f ▲ and **f** ▼ browse programs, i.e. they show the first label in previous or next program (cf. p. 156).

0, 1, and 2 allow for quick jumps to the top of `rAM`, `Lib`, or `buP`, respectively. Note the program pointer is moved accordingly.

ENTER↑ goes to the alpha label displayed, while XEQ executes it. Both keystrokes will perform a label search as described on p. 159.
In programming mode (**STO**), ENTER↑ will insert a GTO and XEQ an XEQ with said label trailing.

R/S starts the *current program* without performing a label search first.

RCL and STO execute PRCL or PSTO for the *current program*, respectively. The latter makes sense if called in `rAM` or `buP` only.

P/R enters programming mode (**STO**), allowing for browsing or editing the *current program*. The latter will work in `rAM` only. Note that ← will delete a program step, while EXIT or another P/R will leave CAT immediately.

CLP will delete the *current program*, be it in `rAM` or *FM* `Lib`. You will be asked for confirmation. Think about it before confirming – else there may well be some extra work for you! |

Browser	Contents and special remarks
g SHOW	Browses all allocated *stack* and general purpose registers showing their contents, starting with **X**. So the first screen you see is (the numeric value may deviate) $$\text{Reg} \quad X \qquad \overset{\text{\tiny ...}}{6.022}{}^{23}$$ ▲ goes up the *stack*, continuing with the other lettered registers, then with **R00**, **R01**, etc. ▼ browses the registers going down from the highest allocated numbered register (**R99** in startup default) to **R00** if applicable, then continuing with **K, J**, etc. . turns to local registers if applicable, starting with **R.00**. Then, ▲ and ▼ browse local registers up and down until another . returns to **X**. Local register addresses may exceed **.15** here! Input of any legal letter or two-digit number jumps to the corresponding register (see p. 63). ENTER↑ or RCL recall the register displayed. In programming mode, they enter a corresponding step RCL … (In your *WP 34S*, the keys ◀ and ▶ do what SHOW did in vintage calculators – see p. 80.)
h STATUS	Displays the memory status and browses all user flags (inspired by STATUS on the *HP-16C*). It shows the amount of free memory *words* in *RAM* and *FM* first, e.g.: $$\text{Free:} \qquad \overset{\text{\tiny ...}}{} \\ 516 \, , \, FL. \ 9999$$ Press ▼ and read if there are summation registers used, plus the number of global numbered registers and local registers allocated: $$\text{Regs:} \qquad \overset{\text{\tiny ...}}{} \\ 96 \, , \, Loc. \ 7 \qquad \text{or} \qquad \begin{array}{l}\text{Regs: } \Sigma + \\ 96 \, , \, Loc. \ 7\end{array}$$ Another ▼ presents the status of the first 30 user flags in one very concise display as explained below.

Browser	Contents and special remarks
h (STATUS) (continued)	**Example:** If flags 2, 3, 5, 7, 11, 13, 14, 17, 19, 20, 26, and X are set, and labels B and D are defined in the *current program*, (STATUS) (▼) (▼) will display this:

$$FL\ 00-29$$

Where the mantissa is displayed usually, there are now three rows of horizontal bars. Each row shows the status of 10 flags. If a particular flag is set, the corresponding bar is lit. So here the top row of bars indicates flags 0 and 1 are clear, 2 and 3 set, and 4 clear. Then a ⁞⁞ separates the first five flags from the next. The following top-row bars indicate flag 5 set, 6 clear, 7 set, 8 and 9 clear. The next two rows show the status up to flag 29.

Pressing (▼) once again will increment the start address by ten; so the display will look like:

$$FL\ 10-39$$

Another (▼) will show flags 20 - 49 etc. until 70 - 99, 80 - 99, 90 - 99. A final (▼) will display the last 12 global flags in rows of four – note flag X is shown being set as we expect:

$$XYZT\ A:D\ LIJK$$

The exponent section indicates the status of the four *hotkeys* – if all four labels are defined in the *current program* then ALL will be shown there.

(▲) browses backwards.

Alternatively, pressing a digit (e.g. (5)) will display up to 30 flags starting with 10 times this digit (flags 50 – 79 here). Pressing a legal letter such as (D) will display the top 12 flags.

Finally, see the following list of *catalogs* featured:

Catalog	Applicable modes, contents and special remarks
h CONST	[d & ¬**STO**] Constants like in the *HP-35s*, but more. See them listed on pp. 261ff. While browsing this *catalog*, the values of the constants are displayed. Picking a constant will recall it.
	[n] Calls the command # (see p. 240).
	[d & **STO**] Picking a constant will insert a program step containing the name of the constant selected, preceded by **#** . This step will then recall the value of said constant in program execution.
CPX **h** CONST	[d & ¬**STO**] Opens the same *catalog* of constants as **h** CONST, but picking a constant will execute a complex recall. So, a *stack* looking like $[x, y, ...]$ before will contain $[constant, 0, x, y, ...]$ after picking.
	[d & **STO**] Picking a constant will insert a program step containing the name of the constant selected, preceded by **ᶜ#** . This step will then perform a complex recall of the value of said constant in program execution.
h CONV	[d] Conversions as listed on pp. 270ff. While browsing CONV, the converted content of **X** is displayed. Picking a conversion will return this value.
f CPX	[α] 'Complex' letters mandatory for many languages (see p. 259). Case may be toggled here (see ⇧ above).
h MATRIX	[d] Matrix operations.
h MODE	[¬α] Mode setting functions.
h PROB	[d] Probability distributions beyond the *standard normal* and its inverse.
h P.FCN	[¬α] Extra programming and I/O functions.
h R↑	[α] Superscripts and subscripts (see p. 259).
h STAT	[d] Extra statistical functions.

Catalog	Applicable modes, contents and special remarks
h SUMS	[d] All summation registers. While browsing <u>SUMS</u>, register contents are displayed. Picking a register will recall its contents.
h TEST	[¬α] All tests except the two on the keyboard (see pp. 255ff).
	[α] Comparison symbols and brackets, except ⟮, ⟯, and ≠ (cf. p. 151 and see pp. 259f).
h X.FCN	[d] Extra real functions.
	[n] Extra integer functions. See pp. 255ff. These three *catalogs* are merged in mode **STO** to ease programming.
	[α] Extra alpha functions.
CPX **h** X.FCN	[d] Extra complex functions (see pp. 255ff).
h .⁄.	[α] Punctuation marks and text symbols (see p. 259).
f →	[α] Arrows and mathematical symbols (see pp. 259f).

See the next pages for full contents of the various *catalogs*. Items are sorted alphabetically within the *catalogs* (see p. 171 for the sorting order). You may access a particular item quickly by typing the first characters of its name – see pp. 280f for examples and constraints.

☞ Neither *catalog* nor *browser* calls can be programmed – but most functions contained in *catalogs* can.

Catalog Contents in Detail

CONST
See p. 261

CONV
See p. 270

MATRIX
DET
LINEQS
MROW+×
MROW×
MROW⇆
M+×
M^{-1}
M-ALL
M-COL
M-DIAG
M-ROW
M×
M.COPY
M.IJ
M.LU
M.REG
nCOL
nROW
TRANSP

MODE	
12h	RDX.
1COMPL	REGS
24h	RM
2COMPL	SEPOFF
BASE	SEPON
BestF	SETCHN
DBLOFF	SETDAT
DBLON	SETEUR
DENANY	SETIND
DENFAC	SETJPN
DENFIX	SETTIM
DENMAX	SETUK
DISP	SETUSA
D.MY	SIGNMT
ExpF	SLOW
FAST	SSIZE4
FRACT	SSIZE8
JG1582	STOM
JG1752	TSOFF
LinF	TSON
LogF	UNSIGN
LZOFF	WSIZE
LZON	YDOFF
M.DY	YDON
PowerF	Y.MD
RCLM	⌂DLAY
RDX,	⌂MODE

PROB	
Binom	Norml
$Binom_p$	…
$Binom_u$	Poiss
$Binom^{-1}$	…
Cauch	Poisλ
…	…
Expon	$t_p(x)$
…	$t_u(x)$
$F_p(x)$	$t(x)$
$F_u(x)$	$t^{-1}(p)$
$F(x)$	Weibl
$F^{-1}(p)$	…
Geom	$\Phi_u(x)$
…	$\varphi(x)$
Lgnrm	χ^2
…	χ^2 INV
Logis	χ^2_p
…	χ^2_u

P.FCN			STAT	SUMS
BACK	LOADΣ	XEQα	COV	nΣ
BASE?	LocR	y⇆	L.R.	Σln²x
CASE	LocR?	z⇆	SEED	Σln²y
CFALL	MEM?	αGTO	SERR	Σlnx
CLALL	MSG	αOFF	SERR$_W$	Σlnxy
CLPALL	NOP	αON	SUM	Σlny
CLREGS	PopLR	αXEQ	s$_W$	Σx
CLSTK	PRCL	⇆	s$_{XY}$	Σx²
CLα	PROMPT	ADV	x̄g	Σx²y
CNST	PSTO	CHR	x̄$_W$	Σxlny
DEC	PUTK	$^C r_{XY}$	x̂	Σxy
DROP	RCLS	PLOT	ε	Σy
DSL	RECV	PROG	ε$_m$	Σy²
DSZ	REGS?	r	ε$_P$	Σylnx
END	RESET	REGS	σ	
ERR	RM?	STK	σ$_W$	
FF	RTN+1	TAB	%Σ	
FLASH?	R-CLR	WIDTH		
f '(x)	R-COPY	α		
f "(x)	R-SORT	α+		
gCLR	R-SWAP	Σ		
gDIM	SAVE	+α		
gDIM?	SENDA	#		
gFLP	SENDP			
gPLOT	SENDR			
gSET	SENDΣ			
GTOα	SKIP			
INC	SMODE?			
ISE	SSIZE?			
ISZ	STOS			
KTP?	TICKS			
LOAD	t⇆			
LOADP	VIEWα			
LOADR	VWα+			
LOADSS	WSIZE?			

WP 34S v3.3d

TEST	... alpha mode:	... integer modes:		
BC?	VERS	$\sqrt[3]{x}$	IDIV	SL
BS?	x→α	ASR	LCM	SR
CNVG?	αDATE	BATT	LJ	sRCL
DBL?	αDAY	CB	MASKL	ULP
ENTRY?	αIP	CEIL	MASKR	VERS
EVEN?	αLENG	DBLR	MAX	WHO
FC?	αMONTH	DBL×	MIN	x^3
FC?C	αRC#	DBL /	MIRROR	XNOR
FC?F	αRL	dRCL	MOD	x→α
FC?S	αRR	DROP	NAND	$^x\sqrt{y}$
FP?	αSL	FB	nBITS	αIP
FS?	αSR	FIB	NEIGHB	αLENG
FS?C	αTIME	FLOOR	NEXTP	αRCL
FS?F	α→x	GCD	NOR	αRC#
FS?S			RJ	αRL
gPIX?			RL	αRR
INTM?			RLC	αSL
INT?			ROUNDI	αSR
KEY?			RR	αSTO
LBL?			RRC	α→x
LEAP?	x < ?		SB	Γ
M.SQR?	x ≤ ?		SEED	$(-1)^X$
NaN?	x = +0?		SIGN	×MOD
ODD?	x = -0?			^MOD
PRIME?	x ≈ ?			
REALM?	x ≥ ?			
SPEC?	x > ?			
TOP?	∞?			
XTAL?	🔒?			

---

[129] In programming mode, these three contents (for alpha, integer, and decimal modes) are merged.

				CPX X.FCN
$^3\sqrt{x}$	LCM	W_m	%T	$^c{}^3\sqrt{x}$
AGM	L_n	W_p	%Σ	^{c}AGM
ANGLE	LN1+x	W^{-1}	%+MG	^{c}CNST
BATT	$L_n\alpha$	x^3		^{c}CONJ
B_n	LNβ	XNOR		^{c}CROSS
$B_n{}^*$	LNΓ	x→α		^{c}DOT
CEIL	MANT	$^x\sqrt{y}$		^{c}DROP
DATE	MAX	YEAR		$^c e^x\!-\!1$
DATE→	MIN	αDATE		^{c}FIB
DAY	MOD	αDAY		$^c g_d$
DAYS+	MONTH	αIP		$^c g_d{}^{-1}$
DECOMP	NAND	αLENG		^{c}IDIV
DEG→	NEIGHB	αMONTH		^{c}LN1+x
dRCL	NEXTP	αRCL		^{c}LNβ
DROP	NOR	αRC#		^{c}LNΓ
D→J	P_n	αRL		^{c}SIGN
erf	RAD→	αRR		^{c}SINC
erfc	RDP	αSL		$^c W_p$
EXPT	ROUNDI	αSR		$^c W^{-1}$
$e^x\!-\!1$	RSD	αSTO		$^c x^3$
FIB	SDL	αTIME		$^c{}^x\sqrt{y}$
FLOOR	SDR	α→x		$^c z\leftrightarrows$
GCD	SIGN	β		$^c\beta$
g_d	SINC	Γ		$^c\Gamma$
$g_d{}^{-1}$	SLVQ	Γ_p		$^c(-1)^x$
GRAD→	sRCL	Γ_n		
H_n	STOPW	γ_{XY}		
H_{np}	TIME	Γ_{XY}		
H.MS+	T_n	ΔDAYS		
H.MS−	ULP	ζ		
IDIV	U_n	$(-1)^x$		
iRCL	VERS	→DATE		
I_x	WDAY	%MG		
J→D	WHO	%MRR		

Below follow the contents of the alpha catalogs. Small font is printed on light grey background. The first catalog is for international letters:

CPX											
À	À	À	à	à	à	Ñ Ň	Ñ	Ñ	ñ ň	ñ	ñ
Á	Á	Á	á	á	á	Ò	Ò	Ò	ò	ò	ò
Â Ã Ā Ă	Â	Â	â ã ā ă	â	â	Ó	Ó	Ó	ó	ó	ó
Ä	Ä	Ä	ä (ă)	ä	ä	Ô Õ Ō Ŏ	Ô	Ô	ô õ ō ŏ	ô	ô
Æ	Æ	Æ	æ	œ	œ	Ö	Ö	Ö	ö (ŏ)	ö	ö
Å	Å	Å	å	å	å	Ø	Ø	Ø	ø	ø	ø
Ć	Ć	Ć	ć	ć	ć	Ř	Ř	Ř	ř	ř	ř
Č	Č	Č	č	č	č	Š	Š	Š	š	š	š
Ç	Ç	Ç	ç	ç	ç		ẞ	ẞ	ß	ẞ	ß
Đ	Đ	Đ	đ	đ	đ	Ù	Ù	Ù	ù	ù	ù
È	È	È	è	è	è	Ú	Ú	Ú	ú	ú	ú
É	É	É	é	é	é	Û Ũ Ū Ŭ	Û	Û	û ũ ū ŭ	Û	Û
Ê Ē Ě	Ê	Ê	ê ē ě	ê	ê	Ü	Ü	Ü	ü (ŭ)	ü	ü
Ë	Ë	Ë	ë (ě)	ë	ë	Ů	Ů	Ů	ů	ů	ů
			ħ	ħ	ħ		x̂	x̂	x̂ / x̄	x̂	x̄
Ì	Ì	Ì	ì	ì	ì	Ý	Ý	Ý	ý	ý	ý
Í	Í	Í	í	í	í		ŷ	ŷ	ŷ / ȳ	ŷ	ŷ
Î Ĩ Ī Ĭ	Î	Î	î ĩ ī ĭ	î	î	Ÿ	Ÿ	Ÿ	ÿ	ÿ	ÿ
Ï	Ï	Ï	ï (ĭ)	ï	ï	Ž	Ž	Ž	ž	ž	ž

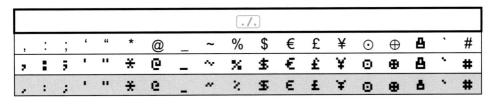

./,																		
,	:	;	'	"	*	@	_	~	%	$	€	£	¥	⊙	⊕	🔒	`	#

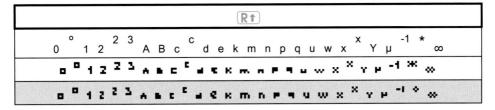

R↑																						
0	°	1	2	2	3	3	A	B	c	C	d	e	k	m	n	p	q	u	w	x	x	Y	µ	-1	*	∞

The letters provided in your *WP 34S* allow for correctly writing the languages of more than $3 \cdot 10^9$ people using Greek or simple variants of Latin alphabets, i.e. the following languages:

Afrikaans, Català, Cebuano, Česky, Cymraeg, Dansk, Deutsch, Eesti, English, Español, Euskara, Français, Gaeilge, Galego, Ελληνικά, Hrvatski, Bahasa Indonesia, Italiano, Basa Jawa, Kiswahili, Kreyòl ayisyen, Magyar, Bahasa Melayu, Nederlands, Norsk, Português, Quechua, Shqip, Slovensky, Slovenščina, Srpski, Basa Sunda, Suomi, Svenska, Tagalog, Winaray, and Zhōng-wén.[130]

This coverage makes the *WP 34S* the most versatile calculator known on this planet. If you know further living languages covered, please tell us. Find the full character set provided in *App. E* on pp. 321ff.

---

[130] Mandarin Chinese (Zhōng-wén) features four tones, usually transcribed like e.g. **mā** (= mother), **má** (= hemp), **mǎ** (= horse), **mà** (= locust), in addition to **ma** (question particle). So we need different letters for **ā** and **ă** here, and for **e, i, o,** and **u** as well. With six pixels total character height, we found no way to display these in both fonts nicely, keeping letters and accents separated for easy reading. For an unambiguous solution, we suggest using a dieresis (else not employed in Hàn-yŭ pīn-yīn) representing the third tone here like this: hän-yü pin-yin. Pīn-yīn writers, we ask for your understanding.

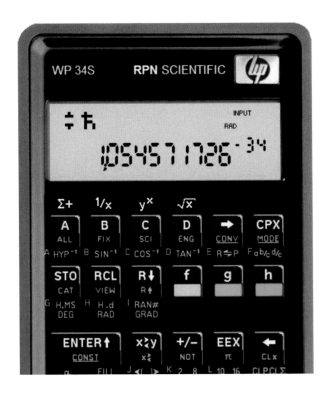

Constants (CONST)

Your *WP 34S* contains a set of 89 physical, astronomical, and mathematical constants. Entering CONST for the first time, you will see:

All constants provided are listed a table below. Names of astronomical and mathematical constants are printed on colored background there. Values of physical constants (including their relative standard deviations – or uncertainties – in *red print* below) are printed on light background if they are exact or almost exact – the darker the background, the less precisely the particular value is known.[131]

---

[131] For the physical constants, the values and their relative standard deviations are from *CODATA 2014*, copied in September 2015. They are the best values known in the scientific community, agreed on by the national standards institutes worldwide.

Relative uncertainties are included in the printed table though not contained in CONST. They are, however, important for determining the precision of results you

For the units, remember *tesla* with $1T = 1\dfrac{Wb}{m^2} = 1\dfrac{V \cdot s}{m^2}$,

joule with $1J = 1N \cdot m = 1\dfrac{kg \cdot m^2}{s^2}$ and on the other hand

$1J = 1W \cdot s = 1V \cdot A \cdot s$. Thus $1\dfrac{J}{T} = 1A \cdot m^2$.

Employ the constants stored here for further useful equivalences, like calculating the wavelength from the frequency of electromagnetic radiation via $\lambda = {c}/{f}$, expressing *joules* in *electron-volts* ($1J = 1A \cdot s \cdot V = 1{eV}/{e} \approx 6.24 \cdot 10^{18} eV$), etc.

Within programs, constants are stored as **#name** – so e.g. the Bohr radius a_0 will be stored and listed as **# ᴀₒ** .

Now please find below the constants contained in <u>CONST</u> (with commas as radix marks for sake of visibility):

	Numeric value	Remarks
1/2	0,5	Trivial but helpful constant for some iterations.
ᴀ	365,242 5 *d* (per definition)	Gregorian year
ᴀₒ	5,291 772 106 7·10⁻¹¹ *m* (2,3·10⁻¹⁰)	Bohr radius[132] $a_0 = \dfrac{\alpha}{4\pi \cdot R_\infty}$

may obtain using the constants given, through the process of 'error propagation' going back to *C. F. Gauß* (1777 – 1855). This procedure is essential if your results are to be trustworthy – not only in science. Please consult suitable reference (e.g. http://physics.nist.gov/cgi-bin/cuu/Info/Constants/definitions.html). There is <u>no way</u> yardstick measurements can yield results accurate to four decimals.

While we are at it, the terms *resolution* and *accuracy* are confused frequently for measuring instruments. In a nutshell, *resolution* is the least significant digit such an instrument indicates. Using this instrument for measuring the same object under identical conditions multiple times, you get an idea of its *repeatability* (or *precision*); this can be no better than its *resolution* but may be significantly worse – a factor of ten or more may be observed easily in real life. *Accuracy* of a measuring instrument, however, can never be better than its *repeatability*.

[132] This is a good estimate for the radius of a hydrogen atom. On the other hand, a typical radius of an atomic nucleus is some $10^{-15} m$. So the nucleus takes far less

	Numeric value	Remarks
a_m	$3{,}844 \cdot 10^{8}\, m$ $(1 \cdot 10^{-3})$	Semi-major axis of the Moon's orbit around the earth.
$a_⊕$	$1{,}495\ 979 \cdot 10^{11}\, m$ $(1 \cdot 10^{-6})$	Semi-major axis of the Earth's orbit around the sun. Within the uncertainty stated here, it equals $1\, AU$.
c (5)	$2{,}997\ 924\ 58 \cdot 10^{8}\, m/_s$ (per definition)	Speed of light in vacuum $\approx 300\ 000\ {km}/_s = 300\ {m}/_{\mu s}$ $= 30\ {cm}/_{ns} = 0{,}3\ {mm}/_{ps}$ etc.
c_1	$3{,}741\ 771\ 79 \cdot 10^{-16}\, m^2 W$ $(1{,}2 \cdot 10^{-8})$	First radiation constant $c_1 = 2\pi \cdot h \cdot c^2$
c_2	$0{,}014\ 387\ 773\ 6\ m \cdot K$ $(5{,}7 \cdot 10^{-7})$	2nd radiation constant $c_2 = \dfrac{hc}{k}$
e	$1{,}602\ 176\ 620\ 8 \cdot 10^{-19}\, A\,s$ $(6{,}1 \cdot 10^{-9})$	Elementary charge $e = \dfrac{2}{K_J R_K} = \Phi_0 G_0$
e_E	$2{,}718\ 281\ 828\ 459\ 045\ 2...$	Euler's e. Note the letter e represents the elementary charge elsewhere in this table.
F (10)	$96\ 485{,}332\ 89\ {A \cdot s}/_{mol}$ $(6{,}2 \cdot 10^{-9})$	Faraday constant $F = e \cdot N_A$
$F\alpha$	$2{,}502\ 907\ 875\ 095\ 892\ 8...$	Feigenbaum's α and δ
$F\delta$	$4{,}669\ 201\ 609\ 102\ 990\ 6...$	
g	$9{,}806\ 65\ {m}/_{s^2}$ (per definition)	Standard earth acceleration

than a billionth of the volume of an atom. Thus an atom is almost completely empty space. Our world as we know and see it every day is built of atoms. Think about it!

By the way, these facts also give some hand-waving arguments why cancer therapy using heavy ion beams works (and significantly better than using x-rays).

	Numeric value	Remarks
G	$6{,}674\,08 \cdot 10^{-11}\ \dfrac{m^3}{kg \cdot s^2}$ $(4{,}7 \cdot 10^{-5})$	Newtonian constant of gravitation. Also called γ by other authors. See **GM** below for a more precise value.
G□ (15)	$7{,}748\,091\,731 \cdot 10^{-5} \ / \ \Omega$ $(2{,}3 \cdot 10^{-10})$	Conductance quantum $G_0 = \dfrac{2e^2}{h} = \dfrac{2}{R_K}$
Gc	$0{,}915\,965\,594\,177\,219\,0\ldots$	Catalan's constant
gₑ	$-2{,}002\,319\,304\,361\,82$ $(2{,}6 \cdot 10^{-13})$	Landé's electron g-factor
GM	$3{,}986\,004\,418 \cdot 10^{14}\ m^3\!\big/\!s^2$ $(2{,}0 \cdot 10^{-9})$	Newtonian constant of gravitation times the Earth's mass with its atmosphere included (according to *WGS84* [133])
h	$6{,}626\,070\,04 \cdot 10^{-34}\ J\,s$ $(1{,}2 \cdot 10^{-8})$	Planck constant
ħ (20)	$1{,}054\,571\,8 \cdot 10^{-34}\ J\,s$ $(1{,}2 \cdot 10^{-8})$	$= h\!\big/\!2\pi$, so called 'Dirac constant'
k	$1{,}380\,648\,52 \cdot 10^{-23}\ J\!\big/\!K$ $(5{,}7 \cdot 10^{-7})$	Boltzmann constant $k = R\!\big/\!N_A$
Kj	$4{,}835\,978\,525 \cdot 10^{14}\ Hz\!\big/\!V$ $(6{,}1 \cdot 10^{-9})$	Josephson constant $K_j = 2e\!\big/\!h$
lₚ	$1{,}616\,229 \cdot 10^{-35}\ m$ $(2{,}3 \cdot 10^{-5})$	Planck length $l_P = \sqrt{\dfrac{\hbar G}{c^3}} = t_p c$
mₑ	$9{,}109\,383\,56 \cdot 10^{-31}\ kg$ $(1{,}2 \cdot 10^{-8})$	Electron mass

---

[133] *WGS84* is a model used to define the Earth's surface for surveying and GPS (see *http://earth-info.nga.mil/GandG/publications/tr8350.2/tr8350_2.html*).

	Numeric value	Remarks
M_m (25)	$7{,}349 \cdot 10^{22}\ kg$ $(5 \cdot 10^{-4})$	Mass of the Moon
m_n	$1{,}674\ 927\ 471 \cdot 10^{-27}\ kg$ $(1{,}2 \cdot 10^{-8})$	Neutron mass
m_p	$1{,}672\ 621\ 898 \cdot 10^{-27}\ kg$ $(1{,}2 \cdot 10^{-8})$	Proton mass
M_P	$2{,}176\ 47 \cdot 10^{-8}\ kg$ $(2{,}3 \cdot 10^{-5})$	Planck mass $M_P = \sqrt{\dfrac{\hbar c}{G}} \approx 22 \mu g$
m_u	$1{,}660\ 539\ 04 \cdot 10^{-27}\ kg$ $(1{,}2 \cdot 10^{-8})$	Atomic mass constant $= 10^{-3}\ kg / N_A$
$m_u c^2$ (30)	$1{,}492\ 418\ 062 \cdot 10^{-10}\ J$ $(1{,}2 \cdot 10^{-8})$	Energy equivalent of atomic mass constant
m_μ	$1{,}883\ 531\ 594 \cdot 10^{-28}\ kg$ $(2{,}5 \cdot 10^{-8})$	Muon mass
$M\odot$	$1{,}989\ 1 \cdot 10^{30}\ kg$ $(5 \cdot 10^{-5})$	Mass of the Sun
$M\oplus$	$5{,}973\ 6 \cdot 10^{24}\ kg$ $(5 \cdot 10^{-5})$	Mass of the Earth. See **GM** above for a more precise value.
N_A	$6{,}022\ 140\ 857 \cdot 10^{23} / mol$ $(1{,}2 \cdot 10^{-8})$	Avogadro's number
NaN (35)	not numeric	'Not a Number', e.g. $\ln(x)$ for $x \le 0$ or $\tan(90°)$ unless in complex domain. So NaN covers poles as well as regions where a function result is not defined at all. Note that infinities, however, are considered numeric (see the end of this table). Non-numeric results will lead to an error message thrown – unless flag **D** is set.
P_0	$101\ 325\ Pa$ *(per definition)*	Standard atmospheric pressure

	Numeric value	Remarks
q_p	1,875 545 9·10^{-18} $A\,s$ $(6{,}0{\cdot}10^{-5})$	Planck charge $$q_p = \sqrt{4\pi\varepsilon_0 \hbar c} \approx 11.7e\,.$$ This constant was in *CODATA 2006*, but did not appear in the data sets thereafter anymore.
R	8,314 459 8 $\dfrac{J}{mol \cdot K}$ $(5{,}7{\cdot}10^{-7})$	Molar gas constant
r_e	2,817 940 322 7·10^{-15} m $(6{,}8{\cdot}10^{-10})$	Classical electron radius $r_e = \alpha^2 a_0$
R_K (40)	25,812 807 455 5 $k\Omega$ $(2{,}3{\cdot}10^{-10})$	von Klitzing constant $R_K = \dfrac{h}{e^2}$
R_m	1,737 530·10^6 m $(5{\cdot}10^{-7})$	Mean radius of the Moon
R_∞	10 973 731,568 508 $/m$ $(5{,}9{\cdot}10^{-12})$	Rydberg constant $R_\infty = \dfrac{\alpha^2 m_e c}{2h}$
$R_\odot$	6,96·10^8 m $(5{\cdot}10^{-3})$	Mean radius of the sun
$R_\oplus$	6,371 010·10^6 m $(5{\cdot}10^{-7})$	Mean radius of the Earth
Sa (45)	6,378 137 0·10^6 m *(per definition)*	Semi-major axis	
Sb	6,356 752 314 2·10^6 m $(1{,}6{\cdot}10^{-11})$	Semi-minor axis	of the Earth model *WGS84* (see the footnote on p. 264)
Se^2	6,694 379 990 14·10^{-3} $(1{,}5{\cdot}10^{-12})$	1st eccentricity squared	
Se'^2	6,739 496 742 28·10^{-3} $(1{,}5{\cdot}10^{-12})$	2nd eccentricity squared	
Sf^{-1}	298,257 223 563 *(per definition)*	Flattening parameter	

	Numeric value	Remarks
T_0 (50)	273,15 K (per definition)	= 0°C, standard temperature
t_P	5,391 16·10^{-44} s $(2,3·10^{-5})$	Planck time $t_P = \sqrt{\dfrac{\hbar G}{c^5}} = \dfrac{l_p}{c}$
T_P	1,416 808·10^{32} K $(2,3·10^{-5})$	Planck temperature $T_P = \dfrac{c^2}{k}\sqrt{\dfrac{\hbar c}{G}} = \dfrac{M_p c^2}{k} = \dfrac{E_p}{k}$
V_m	0,022 413 962 $m^3\!/mol$ $(5,7·10^{-7})$	Molar volume of an ideal gas at standard conditions $V_m = \dfrac{RT_0}{p_0} \approx 22.4 \dfrac{l}{mol}$
Z_0	376,730 313 461 770 6... Ω	Characteristic impedance of vacuum $Z_0 = \mu_0 c$
α (55)	7,297 352 566 4·10^{-3} $(2,3·10^{-10})$	Fine-structure constant $\alpha = \dfrac{e^2}{2\varepsilon_0 hc} \approx \dfrac{1}{137}$
γEM	0,577 215 664 901 532 9...	Euler-Mascheroni constant
γ_p	2,675 221 9·10^8 $\dfrac{1}{s \cdot T}$ $(6,9·10^{-9})$	Proton gyromagnetic ratio $\gamma_P = 4\pi \dfrac{\mu_P}{h}$
ε_0	8,854 187 817 620 389 8... ·10^{-12} $\dfrac{A\,s}{V\,m}$	Electric constant or vacuum permittivity $\varepsilon_0 = \dfrac{1}{\mu_0 c^2}$
λ_C	2,426 310 236 7·10^{-12} m $(4,5·10^{-10})$	Compton wavelengths of the electron $\lambda_C = h\!/m_e c$,
λ_{Cn} (60)	1,319 590 904 81·10^{-15} m $(6,7·10^{-10})$	neutron $\lambda_{Cn} = h\!/m_n c$, and
λ_{Cp}	1,321 409 853 96·10^{-15} m $(4,6·10^{-10})$	proton $\lambda_{Cp} = h\!/m_p c$, respectively

	Numeric value	Remarks
μ_0	1,256 637 061 435 917 2... $\cdot 10^{-6} \dfrac{V\,s}{A\,m}$ *(per definition)*	Magnetic constant or vacuum permeability $\mu_0 := 4\pi \cdot 10^{-7} \frac{V\,s}{A\,m}$
μ_B	9,274 009 994$\cdot 10^{-24}\;{}^{J}\!\!\big/_{T}$ $(6{,}2\cdot10^{-9})$	Bohr magneton $\mu_B = \dfrac{e\hbar}{2m_e}$
μ_e	-9,284 764 62$\cdot 10^{-24}\;{}^{J}\!\!\big/_{T}$ $(6{,}2\cdot10^{-9})$	Electron magnetic moment
μ_n (65)	-9,662 365$\cdot 10^{-27}\;{}^{J}\!\!\big/_{T}$ $(2{,}4\cdot10^{-7})$	Neutron magnetic moment
μ_p	1,410 606 787 3$\cdot 10^{-26}\;{}^{J}\!\!\big/_{T}$ $(6{,}9\cdot10^{-9})$	Proton magnetic moment
μ_u	5,050 783 699$\cdot 10^{-27}\;{}^{J}\!\!\big/_{T}$ $(6{,}2\cdot10^{-9})$	Nuclear magneton $\mu_u = \dfrac{e\hbar}{2m_p}$
μ_μ	-4,490 448 26$\cdot 10^{-26}\;{}^{J}\!\!\big/_{T}$ $(2{,}3\cdot10^{-8})$	Muon magnetic moment
σ_B	5,670 367$\cdot 10^{-8}\;\dfrac{W}{m^2 K^4}$ $(2{,}3\cdot10^{-6})$	Stefan-Boltzmann constant $\sigma_B = \dfrac{2\pi^5 k^4}{15 h^3 c^2}$
Φ (70)	1,618 033 988 749 894 8...	Golden ratio $\Phi = \dfrac{1+\sqrt{5}}{2}$
Φ_0	2,067 833 831$\cdot 10^{-15}\;V\,s$ $(6{,}1\cdot10^{-9})$	Magnetic flux quantum $\Phi_0 = \dfrac{h}{2e}$
ω	7,292 115$\cdot 10^{-5}\;{}^{rad}\!\!\big/_{s}$ $(2\cdot10^{-8})$	Angular velocity of the Earth according to *WGS84* (see the footnote on p. 264)

	Numeric value	Remarks
$-\infty$	-I nFI nI tY	May the Lord of Mathematics forgive us calling these 'constants'. Note both are counted as numeric values in your WP 34S.
∞	I nFI nI tY	
#		See the description of this command on p. 240.
(76)	1	Auxiliary numeric constants[134]
(77)	0,367 879 441 171 ...	$1/e$ (high half)
(78)	$8{,}674\ 458\ 111\ 31\ldots \cdot 10^{-34}$	$1/e$ (low half)
(79)	0,447 213 595 5...	$1/\sqrt{5}$
(80)	0,564 189 583 548 ...	$1/\sqrt{\pi}$
(81)	0,221 4	
(82)	0,434 294 481 903 ...	$1/\ln(10)$
(83)	0,693 147 180 56...	$\ln(2)$
(84)	1,442 695 040 89...	$1/\ln(2)$
(85)	3,141 592 653 59...	π
(86)	1,570 796 326 79...	$\pi/2$
(87)	2,506 628 274 63...	$\sqrt{2\pi}$
(88)	122,134	

---

[134] Constants #76 up to #88 are callable via CNST only. Constants #81 and #88 are employed internally and may change without notice.

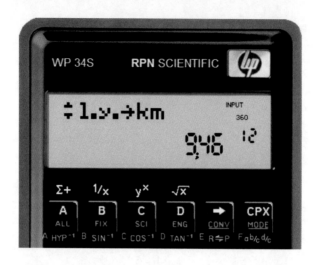

Unit Conversions (<u>CONV</u>)

Your *WP 34S* features 88 unit conversions accessible via ⌈CONV⌉. This *catalog* mainly provides the means to convert local to common units and vice versa. [135] Assuming $x = 21$, startup default format, and pressing ⌈CONV⌉ for the first time, you will see:

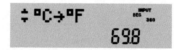

The display looks like the corresponding conversion was executed but that is a temporary indication only and will change when you proceed in <u>CONV</u>; the conversion will be executed (leaving <u>CONV</u>) not earlier than ⌈ENTER↑⌉ is pressed.

Navigation works as in the other *catalogs*. There is one specialty, however: ⌈f⌉ ⌈B⌉ (i.e. ⌈1/x⌉) will execute the inverse of the conversion displayed and leave <u>CONV</u>.

---

[135] The *SI* system of units is agreed on internationally. For many decades, it is adopted by all countries on this planet except three. Thus, for the overwhelming majority of readers, most of the units appearing in <u>CONV</u> may look obsolete at least. They bear witness to dark times but die hard in some corners of this world (English is spoken in all of those). For plain symmetry reasons, we think about adding some traditional Indian and Chinese units to <u>CONV</u>.

The contents of <u>CONV</u> may also give you a slight idea of the mess we had in the world of measurement before going metric some 200 years ago. Without *British Imperial* units, <u>CONV</u> would contain 16 entries only.

Example:

Assume the display set to FIX **3**. Then keying in

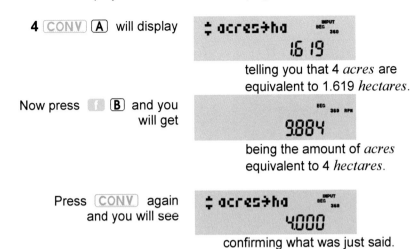

4 CONV A will display

≑ acres→ha

l.6 l9

telling you that 4 *acres* are equivalent to 1.619 *hectares*.

Now press f B and you will get

9.884

being the amount of *acres* equivalent to 4 *hectares*.

Press CONV again and you will see

≑ acres→ha

4.000

confirming what was just said.

Leave CONV via EXIT and the display will return to *9.884*.

All conversions provided are listed alphabetically below:

Conversion	Remarks	Class
°C→°F		Temperature
°F→°C		
°→G	Converts to *gon*, also known as *grads* or *gradians*	Angle
°→rad	Equals D→R, converting to *radians*	Angle
acres→ha	1 *ha* = 10 000 m^2	Area
acreUS→ha	Based on the *U.S. survey foot*, see feetUS below	
ar.→dB	Amplitude ratio	Ratio
atm→Pa	1 *Pa* = 1 N/m^2	Pressure
AU→km	*Astronomic units*	Length
bar→Pa	1 *mbar* = 1 *hPa*	Pressure
Btu→J	*British thermal units*	Energy
cal→J		

Conversion	Remarks	Class
`cft→l`	*Cubic feet*	Volume
`cm→inches`		Length
`cwt→kg`	*(Long) hundredweight* := 112 *lbs*	Mass
`dB→ar.`		Ratio
`dB→pr.`	Power ratio	
`fathom→m`		Length
`feetUS→m`	1 *U.S. survey foot* := $^{1200}/_{3937}$ *m* exactly	
`feet→m`	The so-called 'international feet' as of 1959 – 1 *foot* := $^1/_3$ *yard*	
`flozUK→mL`	1 *ml* = 1 cm^3	Volume
`flozUS→mL`		
`galUK→l`	1 *l* = 10^{-3} m^3	Volume
`galUS→l`		
`G→°`		Angle
`g→oz`	*Ounces*	Mass
`G→rad`		Angle
`g→tr.oz`	*Troy ounces*	Mass
`ha→acres`	1 *ha* = 10 000 m^2	Area
`ha→acreUS`		
`hp(E)→W`	*Electric horsepower.* 1 *hp(E)* = 746 *W*	Power
`hp(I)→W`	*Mechanical (Imperial) hp.* 1 *hp(I)* ≈ 745.7 *W*.	
`hp(M)→W`	*'Metric' hp*[136]. 1 *hp(M)* = 1 *PS* ≈ 735.5 *W*	
`inches→cm`	1 *inch* := $^1/_{12}$ *foot*	Length
`inHg→Pa`		Pressure

---

[136] Translator's note: This *hp* equals *ch* in French and *PS* in German, for example.

Conversion	Remarks	Class
J→Btu		Energy
J→cal		
J→kWh		Energy
kg→cwt		Mass
kg→lb		
kg→stone		
kg→s.cwt	*Short hundredweight* := 100 *lbs*	
km→AU		Length
km→l.y.	*Light years*	Length
km→miles		Length
km→nmi	*Nautical miles*	
km→pc	*Parsec*	Length
kWh→J		Energy
lbf→N		Force
lb→kg		Mass
l.y.→km		Length
l→cft		Volume
l→galUK		
l→galUS		
miles→km		Length
ml→flozUK		Volume
ml→flozUS		
mmHg→Pa		Pressure

Conversion	Remarks	Class
m→fathom		
m→feet		
m→feetUS		Length
m→yards		
nmi→km		
N→lbf		Force
oz→g		Mass
Pa→atm		Pressure
Pa→bar		Pressure
Pa→inHg		Pressure
Pa→mmHg		
Pa→psi	*Pounds per square inch*	Pressure
Pa→torr	1 *torr* = 1 *mm Hg*	
pc→km		Length
pr.→dB		Ratio
psi→Pa		Pressure
rad→°	Equals R→D, converting to *degrees*	Angle
rad→G	Converts to *gon*, also known as *grads* or *gradians* in English	Angle
stone→kg		
s.cwt→kg		Mass
s.tons→t	*Short tons*	
tons→t	*Imperial tons*	
torr→Pa		Pressure

Conversion	Remarks	Class
tr.oz→9		
t→s.tons	1 t = 1 000 kg	Mass
t→tons		
W→hp(E)		
W→hp(I)		Power
W→hp(M)		
yards→m		Length

The constant T_o may be useful for conversions of temperatures to *kelvin*, too. It is found in <u>CONST</u> above and is not repeated here because it is only added or subtracted.

You may, of course, combine conversions as you like.

Example:

For filling your tires with a maximum pressure of 30 *psi* the following will help you at gas stations in Europe and beyond:

30 [CONV] [P][S]	↕ psi→Pa
[XEQ]	206842,7
[CONV] [P][▼]	↕ Pa→bar
[XEQ]	2,1 *bar.*

Now you can set the filler and will not blow your tires.

Example:

Assume your friend tells you she has 10 cubic feet of debris on her veranda after flooding. What does this mean in real units?

1 [CONV] [F][▼][▼]	↕ feet→m
[XEQ]	0,305
3 [y^x]	0,028
10 [x]	0,283 m^3

OK, some work – but manageable.

Example:

A network switch is specified for 3 320 *Btu/h*. What?
We choose ENG 3 for the solution of this engineering problem:

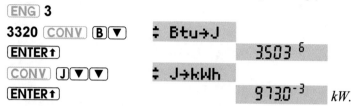

That is almost 1 *kW*. Now you know what will be going on there.

In cases of emergencies of a particular kind,[137] remember *becquerel* equals *hertz*, *gray* is the unit for deposited or absorbed energy (1 *Gy* = 1 *J/kg*), and *sievert* (*Sv*) is *gray* times a radiation dependent dose conversion factor for the damage caused in biological material (alas including human bodies).

In this field, some outdated units may be found in older literature as well: Pour les fidèles amis de Madame *Marie Curie*, $1Ci = 3.7 \cdot 10^{10} Bq = 3.7 \cdot 10^{10} decays/s$. And for those admiring the very first Nobel laureate in physics, Mr. *Wilhelm C. Röntgen*, for discovering the x-rays (ruining his hands in those experiments), the charge generated by radiation in matter was measured by the unit $1R = 2.58 \cdot 10^{-4} As/kg$. A few decades ago, *rem* (i.e. *roentgen equivalent in man*) measured what *sievert* does today: 1 *rem* = 10 *mSv*. And 1 *rad* = 10 *mGy*.

Predefined Global Alpha Labels (CAT)

In addition to the label **δx** reserved for step size definition in calculation of derivatives (see f'(x) in the *IOP* on p. 195), additional labels may be provided for particular tasks already. You will find them listed in CAT when the corresponding library routines are loaded in *FM* (see below). Thus they will not take any steps from user program memory in *RAM*.

All library routines presently available are found on the *WP 34S* website: *http://sourceforge.net/p/wp34s/code/HEAD/tree/library/*. They

---

[137] Our warmest regards go to Belarus, Bikini, Canada, France, Japan, Russia, Ukraine, the United Kingdom, and the USA (in alphabetical order).

are text files with extension `.wp34s` by convention. They include a
suite of basic 3D vector operations, some matrix routines including a
matrix editor, a TVM (time value of money) application, and more. You
may open and browse these text files using e.g. *WordPad*, and you
should find the necessary user information at the beginning of each file
(sometimes, however, they are found at its end). These routines are
written like user programs but with a few extensions of the function set
explained on pp. 355ff.

The **example** below shows the header of `TVM.wp34s` as of
2012-12-12:

```
/*
==================================
* Extended TVM-Solver for WP34s *      Ver. 2.0       Author:
Franz Huber
==================================

Keyboard-Layout:
----------------
    N        I      PV      PMT      FV
[A][A]   [A][B]   [A][C]   [A][D]   [A][->]

    NP           NI
[A][STO]    [A][RCL]

Flags/Registers/Labels:
----------------------
        00      01    02    03    04    05    06    07    08    09    10    11   12
Flag    Entry?  --    2I?   --    --    --    <0?   =0?   --    --    --    --   --
Reg.    Key?    N     I     PV    PMT   FV    NP    NI    i     k     im    I1   I2
Lbl.    Start   N?    I?    PV?   PMT?  FV?   Init  I->i  TVM   TVM'  i->I  --   --

Remarks:
========
- [XEQ]'TVM' to initialize registers and parameters!
- enter values for parameters NP,NI if desired (default=1)
- all financial keys for N,I,PV,PMT,FV and NP,NI work as follows:
  input+key stores the value, key alone calculates the value
  (or just recalls it for NP and NI)
- [R/S] resets the ENTRY? flag (e.g. after own calculations)
- alternative method to use the program:
  [STO/RCL/XEQ]01-05 to store/recall/calculate N,I,PV,PMT,FV
  (result after [XEQ] is not stored automatically!)
  [STO/RCL]06-07 to store/recall NP,NI
- iterative solving for I is limited to ]-1,max(2,I%->i)], i.e.
  from -100% to 200% (or I%->i) interest rate per payment period
  (the upper limit I% can be changed with I [STO]02 or I [A][B])
- if solving for I returns 2 possible solutions ("I1="), then
just
  press [R/S] to switch between I1 and I2 (stored in R11 and R12)
```

- error messages are displayed if invalid values have been
entered:
    (don't use [R/S] after any error message!)
    NP=0 -> "Invalid parameter"
    both N=0 and I=0 -> "Invalid data"
    calculate FV if N=0 -> "Bad mode"
    no solution found for I -> "No root found"
    other invalid entries -> "Domain error" or "+/- Infinity"

Values:

N = total number of periods (or payments)
    N=0 for perpetual payments (N=infinite)
        (not allowed if I=0! -> Error: "Invalid data")

I = annual interest rate (in % per year, -99.9%..999%)
    I=0 for no compounding
        (not allowed if N=0! -> Error: "Invalid data")

PV = present value (or payment)
PMT = periodical payment
FV = future value (or payment)
        (not defined for N=0! -> Error: "Bad mode")

Parameters:

NP = payment frequency PF (payment periods per year)
     NP>0 postnumerand payments (at END of periods)
     NP<0 prenumerand payments (at BEGin of periods)
     NP=0 not allowed! -> Error: "Invalid parameter"

NI = compounding frequency CF (interest periods per year)
     NI>0 decursive interest (compound at end of periods)
     NI<0 anticipative discount (compound at begin of periods)
     NI=0 continuous (theoretical) compounding (NI=infinite)
     |NI|=1 -> effective interest rate
     |NI|>1 -> nominal interest rate

Used formulas:

        / (1+I/(100*NI))^(NI/abs(NP))-1 for NI!=0
   i = |
        \ e^(I/(100*abs(NP)))-1   for NI=0

        / 1   for NP>0
   k = |
        \ 1+i   for NP<0

              / PV*(1+i)^N + PMT*((i+1)^N-1)*k/i + FV = 0   for I!=0
                                                              & N!=0
   TVM eqn: | PV + PMT*N + FV = 0   for I=0
              \ PV + PMT*k/i = 0   for N=0

```
TVM expr:  ((1+i)^N-1)*(PMT*k/i + PV) + PV + FV    (SLV iteration
                                                     for i)
*/
```

The library files are also included in the distribution *ZIP* file in source form (`*.wp34s`). Most of them are also contained in a precompiled library (`wp34s-lib.dat` – some $3kB$) which is part of the firmware files `calc_full.bin`, `calc_xtal_full.bin`, and `calc_ir_full.bin` – so you get this library when you load one of these firmware files into your *WP 34S* (see in *App. A* on pp. 285ff how to do this).

When you copy `wp34s-lib.dat` into the directory your *WP 34S* emulator runs in, you can access all those routines via CAT from your emulator as well. See pp. 317ff.

See pp. 355ff if you want to write such routines yourself. See `README_ASM` for advice how to build your own personal library.

Accessing Catalog Items the Fast Way

You can browse each and every *catalog* just using the cursors ▼ and ▲ as explained on p. 248. You may reach the requested item significantly faster, however, taking advantage of the alphabetical method demonstrated in the left columns of the table following:

1	User input	CONST, CONV, MATRIX, MODE, PROB, P.FCN, STAT, TEST, SUMS, or X.FCN	CPX or R↑ in alpha mode	→, TEST, or ./. in alpha mode
	Echo	Your *WP 34S* shows the first item in this *catalog*[138]		
		(e.g. BC? in TEST)	(e.g. ä in CPX)	(e.g. ; in ./.)
2	User input	First character of command desired (e.g. F)	Desired basic letter (e.g. U)	
	Echo	It shows the first item starting with this character[139]		
		(e.g. FC?)	(e.g. ü)	
3	User input	Second character (e.g. S)		
	Echo	It shows the first item starting with this sequence[139]		
		(e.g. FS?)		
...		Continue browsing with ▼ until you reach the item desired		
		(e.g. FS?C).	(e.g. ü).	(e.g. €).

---

[138] ... unless you visited the same catalog just before – then it will open showing the last item you looked at.

[139] See the text after the table.

n	User input	(XEQ) or (ENTER↑)	
		Your *WP 34S* leaves the *catalog* returning to the mode set before …	
		… and executes or inserts the command chosen, or recalls the constant selected.	… and appends the selected character to *alpha*.
	Echo	**Result** (e.g. **true**)	**Contents of alpha register** (e.g. **ⁿ Rüben à 0,25€**)

This alphabetic search is independent of case (i.e. specifying **A** will find **a** as well). Like in browsing a dictionary, it may be faster to search the letter following alphabetically instead and then browse backwards.

In our example, (TEST) (F)(S) (▼) finds FS?C, but
(TEST) (G) (▲)(▲)(▲) would do as well.

Remember you can also enter Greek letters in such a search string using prefix ⑨, e.g. ⑨ + (A) for α (compare p. 151).

If a character or sequence you specified is not found in the *catalog* chosen then the first item following alphabetically will be shown – see the sorting order on p. 171. If there is no such item, then the last item in this *catalog* is displayed.

You may key in even more than two characters – after 3 seconds, however, or after (▼) or (▲), the search string will be reset and you start over with a new first character.

The Stopwatch Application

As mentioned in the *IOP*, a stopwatch is provided following the *HP-55* timer. [140] It works on your *WP 34S* with a quartz crystal installed and activated (see pp. 359ff in *App. H*) and the corresponding firmware loaded (see *App. A* on pp. 285ff). It works on the emulator as well.

Name	Keys to press	Remarks
STOPW	**h** X.FCN **STOPW**	Stopwatch. When started, the display looks like this: **STOPWATCH** 360 RPN **00h00' 00" 0** unless the timer was already running.
	CPX R/S	

Within STOPW, the following keys will work:

Pressing	
CLx or ⬅	resets the timer to zero without changing its status (running or stopped).
R/S	starts or stops the timer without changing its value.
EEX	hides or displays tenths of seconds. Startup default is 'display'.

---

[140] There are two deviations: Your *WP 34S* will not take the content of **X** as start time. Start times are supported by RCL here. And your *WP 34S* will display tenths instead of hundredth of seconds.

Pressing	
$\boxed{n}\boxed{n}$	sets the *current register address* (*CRA*, startup default is 00). The *CRA* will be displayed in the exponent section as shown here:[141] 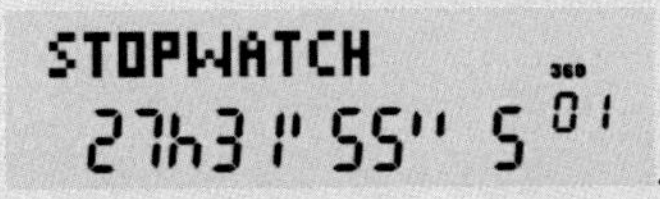 **STOPWATCH** 360 **27h31'55" 5** 01 Attempts to specify a *CRA* beyond the allocated address range will be blocked and may cause '_ _' or the like displayed in the exponent section.
$\boxed{\text{ENTER↑}}$	stores the present timer value in the current register at execution time in format hhh.mmssd without changing the timer status or value. It then increments the *CRA* by one and displays it as shown above.
$\boxed{\rightarrow}$	hides or displays the *CRA*. Startup default is 'hide'.
$\boxed{\blacktriangle}$ or $\boxed{\blacktriangledown}$	increments or decrements the *CRA* by one, respectively.
$\boxed{.}$	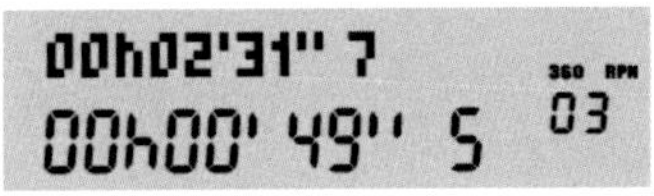 combines $\boxed{\text{ENTER↑}}$ and $\boxed{\text{CLx}}$ in one keystroke, but the total time since the last explicit press of $\boxed{\text{CLx}}$ or ⬅ is shown and updated in the top row like: 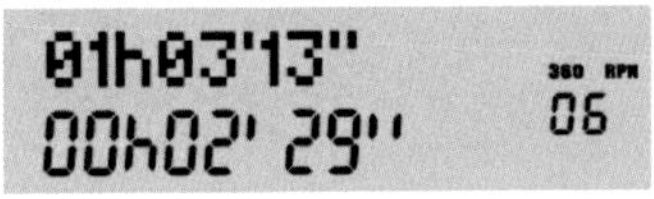 **01h03'13"** 360 RPM **00h02' 29"** 06 or **00h02'31" 7** 360 RPM **00h00' 49" 5** 03 $\boxed{.}$ allows for recording lap times, for example. ☞ The total time in top row is volatile – it will disappear without a trace when $\boxed{\text{CLx}}$ or ⬅ is pressed.
$\boxed{A}$	adds the present timer value to the summation registers like $\boxed{\Sigma+}$ would do. This allows for computing the *arithmetic mean* and *standard deviation* of lap times after leaving STOPW.
$\boxed{+}$	combines $\boxed{A}$ and $\boxed{.}$ in one keystroke. This allows for recording lap times and total time for later offline analysis.

---

[141] On the *HP-55*, input of a single digit was sufficient for storing, since only 10 registers were featured for this purpose there. Furthermore, there was no automatic address increment.

Pressing	
[RCL] *nn*	recalls *rnn* without changing the status of the timer. The value recalled may be used e.g. as start time for further incrementing.
[EXIT]	leaves the application. Unless already stopped, however, the timer continues incrementing in the background (indicated by the small '=' annunciator flashing) until a) stopped explicitly by [R/S] within STOPW or b) your *WP 34S* is turned off by you. [142]

 No other keys will work in STOPW – so e.g. for subtracting split times you have to leave this application. And STOPW is not programmable.

While the stopwatch <u>display</u> is limited to   `99h59' 59'' 9`, internal counting will continue with the display showing the time modulo 100.

---

[142] With the timer running, your *WP 34S* will <u>not</u> turn off automatically with v3.3 of the firmware loaded. That means the tick counter (see TICKS) may overflow while the timer runs. Automatic power-off is set to 1:49 *h* (i.e. 65 536 *ticks*) within STOPW if the timer is <u>not</u> running. – Note that your *WP 34S* will turn off automatically after some 5 *minutes* running earlier builds of the firmware, regardless of the timer status.

APPENDIX A: CREATING AND UPDATING YOUR <u>*WP 34S*</u>

How to Flash Your *HP-20b* or *HP-30b*

Unless you buy a *WP 34S* pre-flashed as explained on p. 5, you must do the flashing yourself. Then you need

1. an *HP-20b* or *HP-30b* calculator,

2. a special interfacing hardware setup,

3. a binary file to load on your computer, and

4. software for the transmission to your calculator.

Let us tackle that list bottom up:

- The transmission software is called *MySamBa*. Go to *http://sourceforge.net/projects/wp34s/files/FlashTool/* , download `MySamBa.zip` and unpack it.

- The binary file you need to transmit to your calculator to make it your *WP 34S* is called `calc.bin` and is included in the zipped release package you can download from *http://sourceforge.net/projects/wp34s/files/* . Or you may download one of the following files directly from *http://sourceforge.net/p/wp34s/code/HEAD/tree/trunk/realbuild/* :

  `calc.bin` offers you maximum space in *FM*, but supports neither the real time clock commands (DATE, TIME, SETDAT, SETTIM) nor STOPW nor the print commands,

  `calc_full.bin` equals `calc.bin` but already includes the *FM* library as well;

  `calc_xtal.bin` requires a quartz crystal installed and includes the real time clock commands and STOPW (costing 1.5kB) but no print commands,

  `calc_xtal_full.bin` includes the *FM* library as well;

  `calc_ir.bin` contains everything also featured in `calc_xtal.bin` plus the print commands (costing another 3.5kB), requiring both the quartz crystal and an *IR* diode built in,

`calc_ir_full.bin` includes the *FM* library as well.

Make your choice! But check the hardware pre-requisites (see pp. 359ff) or your calculator may hang.

- For the interfacing hardware setup, there are three alternatives, presented in order of their appearance:

A. There was a limited production run of special programming cables supplied by *HP*. This item is out of stock. Thus, if you have got one, keep it. Then you will need a computer with a traditional 9-pin serial port.

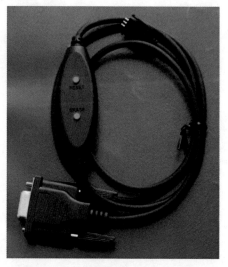

☞ If your computer does not feature such a hardware serial interface (many modern computers do not), you will need a *USB*-to-serial converter to connect this programming cable to your computer. Following our experience, converters containing *FTDI* chips work – others may not. Such an FTDI-based converter is offered e.g. at *http://commerce.hpcalc.org/usbserial.php*

WARNING: As long as this cable is connected to your calculator, it may draw a considerable current from its batteries. If your calculator happens to hang in the flashing procedure described overleaf, its processor may be left running at full speed, draining your coin cells while you are trying to find out what is going wrong. Thus, disconnect your cable from your calculator when you will not need it for the next minutes.

For frequent flashing, an external 3V DC power supply may quickly pay for itself. Take care to connect '+' to the outer and '–' to the inner battery contact properly. Flashing will work best with a stable 3V supply – but as long as the supplied voltage stays between 2.5V and 3.6V it is ok. **Supplied voltages >3.6V may damage your calculator permanently! Supply interruptions during flashing may drive it in a coma – see step A9 below!**

B. You may use an ordinary micro *USB* cable for the connection to your *PC* if you installed a small custom board developed by *Harald Pott*, hosting a *USB* port. With the board pictured here, your calculator will be powered through that port while connected. Thus you neither need the special programming cable nor a hardware serial  port; and you avoid the battery drain observed. If you have got one, keeping it in your calculator is the best you can do. In 2017, however, Harald re-initiated manufacturing this board (cf. http://www.hpmuseum.org/forum/thread-8077.html) so there is an opportunity getting such a board furtheron – find the instructions for its installation on pp. 360ff in *App. H*.

C. You can make your own connector cable and even a suitable serial socket on the calculator board as well. There are several ways – see e.g. *http://www.hpmuseum.org/forum/thread-2378-post-33016.html#pid33016* by *Michael Kathke*, employing another one of *Harald's* custom boards for serial to USB conversion in the cable; or check *http://www.thereminworld.com/Forums/T/29229/diy-calculator-hp30b-to-wp34s?Page=0* for a possible alternative – it includes another flashing procedure as well; we will describe an easy connection using a headphone jack in more detail below (see pp. 367ff in *App. H*).

Having prepared your calculator, computer, software, file, and cable,[143] follow procedure A, B, or C below (depending on your cable) for transforming an *HP-20b* or *HP-30b* into a *WP 34S* for you.

WARNING: Flashing your *HP-20b* or *HP-30b* will erase the firmware present on your calculator (your *HP* business calculator and its contents will then be gone); it will be replaced by the file you downloaded. Thereafter you will have a *WP 34S RPN Scientific* – i.e. your calculator will react as documented in this manual.[144]

---

[143] All three options work. Based on my own experience, *Harald's* board (B) works most conveniently and reliably, though its installation needs some skills – see *App. H* and decide yourself.

[144] If – for any reason whatsoever – you want to return to the original *HP* business calculator firmware, you can do so by sending the respective binary file instead of `calc.bin` or its siblings. An *HP-30b* file is hosted on our website for example – note it represents the firmware status as known to us today and will not be maintained.

This also means your calculator will not do anything useful for you after step 6 and before step 9 is completed successfully in the procedures A, B, or C described below. Your calculator may even look dead – it is not, be assured.

If the following procedures are interrupted at any time (or you pressed a wrong button), don't worry as long as you supplied correct power all the time: Remember the **RESET** button will always turn your calculator off, then (**ON**) shall turn it on (even if you do not see anything on the *LCD*) – simply start over at step 1.

A1. Remove the black battery door of your calculator. Connect the <u>programming cable</u> to its programming port and to your computer.

A2. Start *MySamBa*. Pick the port used for your cable and select the file you want to transmit. The window may look like:

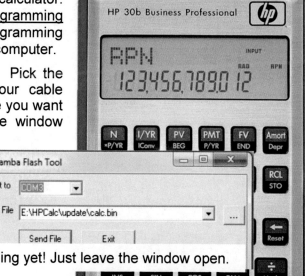

Do **not** start sending yet! Just leave the window open.

A3. Press (**ON/CE**) to turn the calculator on.

A4. Hold down the **ERASE** button on the cable (do not release it until step A7).

A5. Press the **RESET** button on the cable; it will turn the calculator off.

A6. Press (**ON/CE**) to turn the calculator on again.

A7. Release **ERASE** now; press **RESET** to turn the calculator off again.

A8. Press (**ON/CE**) to turn the calculator on again. It will look dead. Do not worry – see the red note above.

A9. Ensure a constant (3 ±0.4) V DC power supply.

WARNING: Even short supply interruptions <2.5 V during this step may drive your calculator in a coma!

Then click "Send File" in the *MySamBa* window and wait for it to finish transmission (it will take some 23 s at 115 200 bits/s). If you have the *FTDI USB / serial adapter* mention-  ed above, you will see the blue TX light blinking. If *MySamBa* should fail,[145] return to A3.

A10. Press **RESET** to turn the calculator off once more.

A11. Press ON/CE. Your calculator should turn on as a *WP 34S* now, displaying a screen as shown on p. 18. Check the firmware version by pressing RCL 3 3 ▲ on the old keys (calling VERS).

A12. Exit *MySamBa*. Disconnect the cable. Check BATT. Close the battery door.

If you have installed the custom *USB* board mentioned above <u>before</u> transforming your *HP-20b* or *HP-30b* into a *WP 34S*, your calculator will be powered through this port while connected to your computer. Standard *USB* cables, however, do not feature the buttons **ERASE** and **RESET** of the programming cable. Thus, the flashing procedure B will work as follows:

B1. Remove the battery door. Connect said <u>micro *USB* cable</u> to the *USB* port of the calculator and to your computer.

B2. Start *MySamBa*. Enter the proper port and file information as explained in step A2 on previous page (see also p. 367). Do <u>not</u>

---

[145] If *MySamBa* fails, it throws either (a) "Error, could not connect to calculator" or (b) "Unable to connect". Then typically:

(a) A wrong COM port was specified (do not type a trailing colon!) or no proper driver for that port was applied,

(b) There is no proper contact through the port specified or your calculator is not turned on.

Anyway, this dead looking calculator is a most annoying state since you do not get the slightest feedback from your system while you keep looping through the steps above. And with the programming cable connected, your battery will be drained in this time ... so press RESET, disconnect, think, and check before reconnecting and retrying. If *MySamBa* fails repeatedly, turn to the *Troubleshooting Guide* (*App. G*).

start sending yet – just leave the window open.

B3. Press (ON/CE) to turn the calculator on.

B4. Shorten the top right and the bottom left of the six pads below the **RESET** hole by a removable link (a paper clip works well).

B5. Use a suitable pin to press the **RESET** button behind the hole. It will turn your calculator off.

B6. Ensure the shorting link makes good contact to both pads. Then press (ON/CE) to turn the calculator on again. It will erase the old firmware.

B7. Remove the shorting link. Press **RESET** to turn your calculator off again.

B8. Press (ON/CE) on the calculator. It will look dead like on the picture. Do not worry – see the red note above.

B9. Click "Send File" in the *MySamBa* window and wait for it to finish transmission (as in step A9 above). If it fails[145], return to B3.

B10. Press **RESET** to turn the calculator off once more.

B11. Press (ON/CE). Your calculator should turn on as a *WP 34S* now, displaying a screen as shown on p. 18. Check the firmware version by pressing (RCL) (3) (3) (▲) on the old keys.

B12. Exit *MySamBa*. Close the battery door. Feel free to leave the cable connected if you want to use it for data transfer from your emulator (see pp. 317ff).

Should you have chosen an alternate solution for connecting, you might need a different flashing procedure C. Unless a dedicated procedure is specified for your solution, the following may guide you:

Step C1 will depend on where your cable will connect, but an open battery door will be required in any way.

C2 will equal step A2 above.

C3 through C11 will most probably equal steps B3 through B11.

Step C12 can be copied from A12 again.

Overlays – Where to Get Them and How to Make Them Yourself if Required

After flashing successfully, a keyboard overlay is very helpful for further work since most labels on your *WP 34S* deviate from those on the *HP-20b/30b*. You get fine adhesive vinyl overlays from *Eric Rechlin* at *http://commerce.hpcalc.org/overlay.php*.

You can choose if you want to apply white labels on the prefix keys (the original design, shown on p. 315) or **f**, **g**, and **h** in their respective colours (see overleaf). Supporters of the 'Great American Divide' can use ÷ instead of / as well; / is far better differentiable from + – but people got used to ÷ apparently. See also the picture at bottom of

this page for the looks of such overlays applied on an *HP-20b* (left) and an *HP-30b*. Remember the keyboard of the *HP-30b* is superior by far.

Eric's vinyls come pre-stamped as you have seen on previous page (note there is a video available demonstrating their proper application – see p. 365 for the link). Detach the key plate part of it from the carrier paper first. Adjust it carefully over your *WP 34S* and attach it starting with the section between ENTER and STO, then proceeding towards the top and bottom. The vinyl shall not contact the keys.

After covering the key plate, detach the individual key labels and apply

them to the corresponding keys. If you need to lift a label once attached – e.g. for readjusting it – a sharp knife will serve you best: put it between key and label and lift a corner of the label, then take it with a pair of tweezers and peel it off.

If *Eric's* vinyls are not available for any reason whatsoever, you can make preliminary paper overlays most easily using the picture shown on p. 409. Cut it out (it shall be 68*mm* wide), span it over your *WP 34S* using transparent adhesive tape, and you are done – the flexibility of this setup allows actuating the keys though there are no holes in your overlay.

If you want adding some extra durability to your paper overlay, you can laminate it. By folding and closing it as shown below, you can create a 'sleeve' for your former financial calculator (see the two pictures below).

It will be considerably stiffer than pure paper but may serve you well until the vinyls will arrive, even if that shall take a little longer.

Updating Your *WP 34S*

Whether you bought your *WP 34S* pre-flashed or did the first flashing yourself, you may want to keep it up-to-date when a new release is published or after you modified its hardware. **We recommend you SAVE your work each time before updating** (your *WP 34S* will show `Saved` when successful). Starting the new firmware, this backup will be restored automatically – if you didn't accidently press the ERASE button on the programming cable.

With the proper binary downloaded as described on p. 285, updating works as follows, depending on the connection available:

1. Remove the battery door of your *WP 34S* by sliding it open.

2. Connect the programming cable to the programming port of your *WP 34S* and to your computer. **Do not touch the ERASE button at any time!**[146] | Connect the micro *USB* cable to the *USB* port of your *WP 34S* and to your computer.

3. Start *MySamBa*. Enter proper port and file information (see pp. 285ff). Do not start sending yet! Just leave this window open.

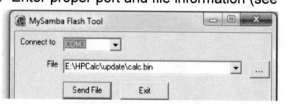

4. Press [ON] to turn your *WP 34S* on. Then press [ON] + [D] simultaneously to set *debug mode*. It is echoed `Debug ON`, and the small **=** annunciator is lit. Release both keys.

5. Press [ON] + [S] simultaneously. [147] It is echoed `SAM-BA? boot`. [148] Release only [S] and press it a second time, then release both keys. This resets the *SamBa* boot bit and turns your *WP 34S* off.

6. Press [ON]. Your *WP 34S* will look dead. Do not worry – it is not.

---

[146] If anything went wrong, however, then a complete 'ab initio' flash will do. Turn to p. 231 in this case.

[147] I.e. [ON] + [6].

[148] This will only work in *debug mode*. See *App. H*.

7. Click "Send File" in the *MySamBa* window as shown in point 3 and wait for it to finish transmission (it will take some 23 *s*). [149]

8. Press the RESET button on the programming cable. Your *WP 34S* will turn off.	Use a suitable pin to trigger the **RESET** button behind the hole on the back of your *WP 34S*. It will turn off.

9. Press (ON). Your *WP 34S* should turn on now with the last backup Restored and the new firmware loaded. Check using VERS. [146]

10. Exit *MySamBa*. Disconnect programming cable. Check BATT. Close battery door.	Exit *MySamBa*. Close battery door.

---

[149] If *MySamBa* fails for any reason, press RESET and disconnect the programming cable. Then take your time and check footnote 145. Return to step 6 when you want to retry.

I/O Overview

Looking at I/O from the point of view of your *WP 34S* <u>calculator</u>, this matter appears as follows schematically:

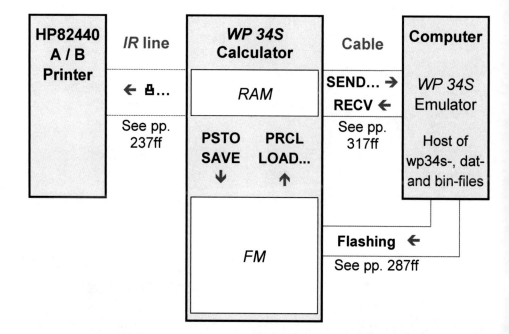

SAVE is for battery-fail-safe internal backup of your work as explained on pp. 168 and 294. The different flavors of LOAD are for recovering from backup. Alternatively to SAVE and LOAD, you may hold down `ON` (i.e. `EXIT`) and press one of the following keys <u>twice</u>:

`STO` for backup: Creates a copy of the *RAM* in *FM* like SAVE does.

`RCL` for restore: Restores the most recent backup like LOAD does.

PRCL recalls an individual program from the *FM* library into *RAM*. PSTO stores a copy of an individual program from *RAM* into the *FM* library.

☞ By recalling a library program from *FM* via PRCL, editing it, and storing it back via PSTO you may modify this part of the *FM* library. See pp. 207ff in the *IOP* for these commands and *App. B* (on pp. 298ff) for details about the *RAM* and *FM* sections of your *WP 34S*.

☞ If you want to get rid of a particular program (e.g. labeled **A1**) already stored in *FM*, proceed as follows:

1) If said program is also in *RAM*, delete it there first. Make sure you are in *RAM* and out of programming mode; enter `GTO`'**A1**', then press `CLP`. It remains in *FM* only.

2) Enter `GTO`'**A1**', and then press `P/R` `CLP`. You are done now!

The different flavors of SEND are for sending your work from *WP 34S RAM* to your computer, where you will enjoy more editing comfort.

Print orders will be sent via the *IR* line if applicable.

Replacing Batteries

Look for fresh batteries (CR2032) when the annunciator ▄ lights up (see p. 73). When you have got two of them, SAVE your data (your *WP 34S* will show **Saved** when successful). Then turn your *WP 34S* off – slide the black battery door open – remove the old batteries – insert the new ones (see the picture on p. 343) – close the battery door and turn your WP 34S on again. It shall display **Restored** at startup, indicating all your data were automatically recalled – so you can just resume your work where you stopped it.

APPENDIX B: MEMORY MANAGEMENT

Your *WP 34S* features 6*kB* of *RAM* (of which 4*kB* are volatile and not usable for you) and 128*kB* of *FM*. The firmware takes some 90% of *FM*, depending on the file you loaded in flashing. The remaining, user accessible part of *FM* may be almost 14*kB*. Of these, 2*kB* are reserved for the backup region corresponding to the 2*kB* of non-volatile *RAM* featured; the remainder may be filled by a collection (a.k.a. *library*) of different programs.

The remaining part of this appendix covers *RAM* only. It discusses how the available memory is divided in program area, local and global data. The 2*kB* (= 1024 *words*) of non-volatile *RAM* are shared by four sectors: [150]

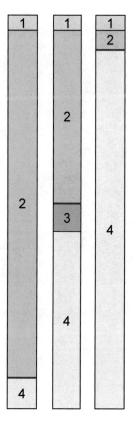

1. Status and configuration data

2. Global registers, i.e. general purpose registers and *stack*

3. Registers used for cumulative statistics (optional)

4. Program memory including the *SRS* (i.e. the *subroutine return stack*, including local registers if applicable).

These sectors are arranged top down as pictured at right to scale. The center bar shows the *RAM* configuration in startup default (but with summation registers allocated). The left bar shows it for maximum register space allowed (but without statistics), the right for maximum program space. This appendix covers the variable boundaries between these sectors.

---

[150] A complete copy of the *RAM* as you configured and loaded it can be written to *FM* using SAVE. It will remain safely preserved not only when your *WP 34S* turns off but also even when its batteries fail. See *App. A* for more information about flashing and handling of *FM* in general.

Status and Configuration Data

This sector of 84 *bytes* is fixed at the top of available memory and is completely user transparent. It contains status and modes data, the 30 *byte* alpha register, and 14 *bytes* holding the 112 global user flags.

Global Registers

Global registers are placed near the end of available memory. In startup default memory layout, the numbered registers **R00** to **R99** precede the twelve *stack* and special registers **X, Y, Z, T, A, B, C, D, L, I, J,** and **K** as shown on pp. 55f. This totals to 112 global registers, which is the maximum available. Their number can be reduced down to the 12 lettered registers using REGS (see p. 211). The command REGS? will return an integer between 0 and 100 corresponding to the number of global numbered registers currently allocated.

REGS controls the lower boundary of the global register sector (the red line on previous page, abbreviated *LBG* in the following). Reducing the number of registers will pull up *LBG* to higher absolute addresses; increasing their number will push it down. The memory contents are moved accordingly, thus preserving the data in the surviving registers. Contents of de-allocated registers are lost; newly added registers are cleared. The lettered registers do not move.

In indirect addressing, zero in the index register points to **R00** always. Index values exceeding the maximum set by REGS will throw an 'out of range' error, unless they fall between 100 and 111 – where the lettered registers live.

Example:

See the global register sector at startup default in the following memory table. The two rightmost columns show what happens after subsequent execution of REGS **96** and REGS **98**. The registers are loaded with arbitrary values here so they can be traced easily. *LBG* is indicated by a red line again.

Absolute address	Default startup memory allocation		After executing REGS 96		Then after executing REGS 98	
	Contents	Relative register address	Contents	Relative register address	Contents	Relative register address
X+ 11	40.7	K = R111	40.7	R111	40.7	R111
...	...	...	...	...	...	...
...	...	...	...	...	...	...
X+2	4.5	Z = R102	4.5	R102	4.5	R102
X+1	-33.8	Y = R101	-33.8	R101	-33.8	R101
X	123.0	X = R100	123.0	R100	123.0	R100
X-1	-13.6	R99	23.1	R95	0.0	R97
X-2	67.9	R98	6.4	R94	0.0	R96
X-3	-45.2	R97	4.8	R93	23.1	R95
X-4	9.7	R96	...	R92	6.4	R94
X-5	23.1	R95		R91	4.8	R93
X-6	6.4	R94		R90	...	R92
X-7	4.8	R93		R89		R91
...	...	...	...		...	
...	...	...	...	...	...	...
X-94	62.4	R06	5.7	R02	29.4	R04
X-95	-0.6	R05	-2.4	R01	81.3	R03
X-96	29.4	R04	1.1	R00	5.7	R02
X-97	81.3	R03			-2.4	R01
X-98	5.7	R02			1.1	R00
X-99	-2.4	R01				
X-100	1.1	R00				
...						

☞ After calling REGS *n* , the absolute addresses of **R00** up to **R*n-1***
change whenever *n* is changed, while their contents are copied. The
lettered registers stay at fixed absolute addresses.

The two sectors following in lower memory (summation registers and
SRS) are tied to *LBG* – their contents will be copied whenever *LBG*
moves. This allows executing REGS in the middle of a subroutine
without disrupting the routine.

Summation Registers

The memory needed for cumulative statistics is allocated separately – these data are no longer held in global general purpose registers. This allows for higher internal precision and prevents destroying these data inadvertently. The only way to update statistical data is via Σ+ and Σ–. The accumulated data are evaluated and recalled by dedicated commands; they are not accessible by STO or RCL (as they were in previous calculators).

The first invocation of Σ+ allocates 70 *words* for the 14 summation registers.[151] They are inserted between *LBG* and *SRS*, pushing the latter down in memory. Depending on the competing requirements for program and data space, it may be necessary to make room first (see overleaf).

After CLΣ, CLALL, or RESET, the memory allocated for the summation registers is released. All pointers are automatically adjusted, so the memory allocation or release will not disrupt a running routine. Recall commands such as e.g. Σxy or SUM will return zero if no data are allocated; other statistical operations will throw an error if not enough data are present.

 The summation data may be cleared automatically when a long program is loaded (from *FM* or via the serial interface) if the registers would no longer fit in *RAM* after that load. You can avoid this by reducing the amount of numbered registers using REGS before the load attempt. This should move the summation data out of the way.

Subroutine Return Stack (*SRS*) and Program Memory

Both share the remaining space at lowest memory addresses.

The **SRS** is used for return addresses and local data. Its upper boundary is given by *LBG* or the lowest summation register if applicable. There is no command to set the size of the *SRS* – it fills all the space down to the top program step currently stored. When new program steps are entered, the *SRS* is reset, not only to make room but because any stored address may become invalid by changing the program.

---

[151] Herein, 2 *words* are employed for Σn, 4 × 8 *words* for Σx^2, Σy^2, Σxy, and $\Sigma x^2 y$, and 9 × 4 *words* for the other sums. If memory allocation for these 70 *words* fails, an error will be thrown.

Local data are pushed on the *SRS*. Thus they cannot overwrite global data; this greatly increases the flexibility of programs. LOCR **n** allocates **n** local registers and a fixed amount of 16 local flags. It does so by pushing a frame on the *SRS* containing a marker, a flag word, and the registers requested (0 to 144). The marker contains the frame size in *words*, depending on the precision mode set (see pp. 351ff). A pointer to this frame in memory is initialized. If the pointer is zero, no local registers exist. Newly allocated registers are cleared.

Calling LOCR again in the same subroutine will adjust the number of local registers. This requires data copying since these registers are allocated from low to high addresses and the *SRS* grows in the opposite direction. LOCR? will return the number of local registers currently allocated in the routine you are in.

See p. 303 for addressing local data, and for an example of recursive programming. The *SRS* must be large enough to hold these data, however, so you may have to make room first – see next paragraph.

Below the *SRS*, **program memory** holds the stored program steps. A typical program step takes just one *word*. Multi-byte labels and multi-character alpha strings take two *words* each. The total size of program memory depends on the number of global and local registers allocated, as explained in the following.

Making Room for Your Needs

The 12 special (lettered) registers are always allocated. The *SRS* has a minimum size of six *words* or levels. Everything else is user distributable within the 982 *words* left for sections 2 to 4, so:

$982 = r + s + p$ with

r = number of *words* allocated for global registers. These are 4 per standard register (and stay the same in integer modes and DECM). There are at least 12 and at most 112 registers. So r varies between 48 and 896 (this maximum is explained on pp. 351ff); startup default is 448.

s = number of *words* allocated for summation registers (70 if they are used; startup default is 0).

p = number of *words* available for program steps and *SRS*. One step is already taken by the inevitable final END statement; 6 *words* is the minimum size of the *SRS*. So

STATUS will show you a maximum of 933 free *words* in *RAM*, meaning up to 927 free program steps. Startup default is 533 steps. Subroutine nesting and local registers expand the *SRS*, thus reducing the program space available.

If, for instance, you need to do statistics and also use 20 global numbered registers, there will be space for 777 program steps maximum in *RAM*.

You have several options for increasing the free space where you need it (see the picture on p. 298):

1. Reduce the number of global numbered registers allocated. One register less typically allows for four additional program steps.

2. Move programs to *FM* and clear the corresponding steps in *RAM*. Four cleared program steps typically allow for one additional register.

3. Release the summation registers when you do not need them anymore. This space may be distributed to up to 70 additional program steps, up to 17 additional registers, or a mix.

Which solution will serve you best depends on your application. You may of course combine options. Use STATUS to monitor the free space available and the amount of global and local numbered registers allocated.

Local Data and Subroutines

Global data take relative addresses from 0 to 111 as described on p. 299. So, relative addresses of local data begin with 112 and may go up to 255 if 144 local registers are allocated. The first 16 local registers and all local flags may also be <u>directly</u> addressed using a dot heading the number – the arguments go from .00 to .15, corresponding to relative addresses from 112 to 127.[152] Any registers beyond 127 are only indirectly addressable. This scheme allows for indirectly addressing …

---

[152] Only arguments up to 127 are storable in an op-code, hence the limit.

- a global register via a global index register
    (e.g. STO→**23** with $r23$ < 112),
- a global register via a local index register
    (e.g. STO→**.15** with $r.15$ < 112),
- a local register via a global index register
    (e.g. STO→**47** with $r47$ ≥ 112), and
- a local register via a local index register
    (e.g. STO→**.06** with $r.06$ ≥ 112).

Subroutine calls: XEQ – executed in a routine – just pushes the return address on the *SRS* before it branches to the target. The subroutine called will keep having access to the caller's local data as long as it does not execute LOCR itself. As soon as it does, the pointer to the local data is newly set, and the subroutine called cannot access the caller's local data anymore.

RTN or POPLR – executed in a routine – check if the current *SRS* pointer points to a local frame (as explained on p. 301). If true then the pointer is moved above that frame, and the *SRS* is searched from this point upwards for another local frame. If such a frame is found then its pointer is stored; otherwise the pointer to the active local frame is cleared. RTN will branch to the return address found, while POPLR will just continue execution. So the current local frame is dropped and the next higher (or older) frame is reactivated if one exists.

On the other hand,

- <u>manually</u> executing RTN,
- starting a new routine by pressing a *hotkey*, XEQ, SLV, etc., or
- program editing

will clear the *SRS* and remove all local registers and flags by clearing the pointer. All such data are lost then!

Recursive programming: Using local registers allows for creating a subroutine that calls itself recursively. Each invocation deals with its local data only. Of course, the *RPN stack* is global so be careful not to corrupt it.

Below is a recursive implementation of the factorial. It is an example for demonstration purposes only, since this routine will neither set the *stack* correctly nor will it work for input greater than some hundred:

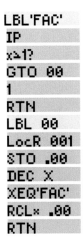

```
LBL'FAC'
IP
x≥1?
GTO 00
1
RTN
LBL 00
LocR 001
STO .00
DEC X
XEQ'FAC'
RCL× .00
RTN
```

Assume $x = 4$ when you call FAC. Then it will allocate one local register (**R.00**) and store **4** therein. After decrementing x, FAC will call itself.

Then FAC_2 will allocate a local register (**R.00$_2$**) and store **3** therein. After decrementing x, FAC will call itself again.

Then FAC_3 will allocate a local register (**R.00$_3$**) and store **2** therein. After decrementing x, FAC will call itself once more.

Then FAC_4 will return to FAC_3 with $x = 1$. This x will be multiplied by $r.00_3$ there, returning to FAC_2 with $x = 2$. This x will be multiplied by $r.00_2$ there, returning to FAC with $x = 6$, where it will be multiplied by $r.00$ and will finally become 24.

Switching Between Standard Real (*SP*) and Integer Modes

Your *WP 34S* starts in standard real mode (DECM) when you get it new. You may use it for integer computations as well, as shown above many times. Going from DECM to any integer mode, register size stays constant but the current *stack* contents will be truncated to integers. Returning from integer mode to DECM, the current *stack* contents (being all integers) will be converted to decimal. All other memory contents will stay as they were!

Note there are no *data types* in your *WP 34S* like they were on the *HP-42S* – it largely depends on you how the data stored are interpreted (see e.g. the commands sRCL and iRCL).

Watch the fate of some register contents undergoing mode switches in the following examples, where *j*, *k*, *r00*, and *r01* <u>will be checked by recalling</u> them:

	X	Y	J	K	R00	R01
Contents at start e.g.	1.1	20.2	300.3	4000.4	50000.5	600000.6
2COMP, WSIZE 32, BASE 10, RCL ...	1 ^{d}	20 ^{d}	3,075 ^{d}	40,964 ^{d}	512,005 ^{d}	6,291,462 ^{d}
sRCL ...			300 ^{d}	4000 ^{d}	50000 ^{d}	600000 ^{d}
567 STO J, -9 STO 00, RCL ...	-9 ^{d}	567 ^{d}	567 ^{d}	40,964 ^{d}	-9 ^{d}	6,291,462 ^{d}
DECM, RCL ...	-9.0	567.0	5.7 $^{-396}$	4000.4	3.0 $^{-389}$	600000.6
iRCL ...			567.0	409640	-9.0	6,291,4620

Note that identical register contents are interpreted quite differently in DECM and integer modes. Even very small integers may lead to very big surprises:

	R00	R01	R02
Contents at start e.g.	0	2	10
WSIZE 64, BASE 16, RCL ...	0 ^{h}	2238000000000002 ^{h}	223C00000000001 ^{h}
sRCL ...	0 ^{h}	2 ^{h}	A ^{h}
2 STO 01, A STO 02, RCL...	0 ^{h}	2 ^{h}	A ^{h}
DECM, RCL ...	0	2 $^{-398}$	1 $^{-397}$
iRCL ...	0	2	10

Thus take care with indirect addressing!

Example:

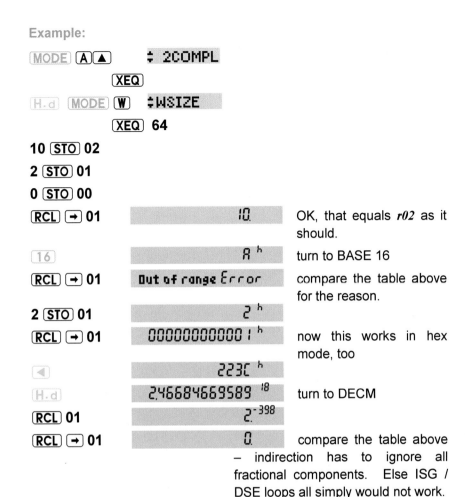

All these effects are caused by the **internal representation of real numbers**: While *integers* are simply stored as such[153] (allowing for $n \leq 1.84 \cdot 10^{19}$ in UNSIGN or $|n| \leq 9.22 \cdot 10^{18}$ in the other modes using 64 bits), *standard floating point numbers* are stored in eight bytes using an internal format as follows:

- Real zero is stored as integer zero, i.e. all bits cleared.

- The mantissa of a real number (also known as *significand* in this context) is encoded in five groups of three digits. Each such group is packed into 10 bits <u>straight forward</u>, meaning e.g. $555_{10} = 10\ 0010\ 1100_2$ or $999_{10} = 11\ 1110\ 0111_2 = 3E7_{16}$. So the 15 rightmost decimal digits of the *significand* take the least

---

[153] Thus we recommend you set an integer mode to deal with individual bits or pixels.

significant 50 bits. Trailing zeroes are omitted, so the *significand* will be right adjusted.

- The most significant (64th) bit takes the sign of the mantissa.
- The remaining 13 bits are used for the exponent and the leftmost digit of the mantissa. Of those 13, the lowest 8 are reserved for the exponent. For the top 5 bits it becomes complicated.[154] If they read ...

  o `00ttt`, `01ttt`, or `10ttt` then `ttt` takes the leftmost digit of the *significand* ($0 - 7_{10}$), and the top two bits will be the most significant bits of the exponent;

  o `11uut` then `t` will be added to 1000_2 and the result (8_{10} or 9_{10}) will become the leftmost digit of the *significand*. If `uu` reads `00`, `01`, or `10` then these two will be the most significant bits of the exponent. If `uu` reads `11` instead, there are codes left for encoding special numbers (e.g. infinities).

In total, we get 16 digits for the mantissa and a bit less than 10 bits for the exponent: its maximum is $10\ 1111\ 1111_2$ (i.e. 767_{10}). For reasons becoming obvious below, 398 must be subtracted from the value in this field to get the true exponent of the number represented. The 16 digits of the *significand* allow for a range from 1 to almost 10^{16}.

Rewarding your patience so far, we will show you some illustrative examples of the encoding in your *WP 34S* instead of telling you more theory:

Floating point number	Hexadecimal value stored	Bottom bits in groups of 10	Top 14 bits in binary representation	Stored exponent
1.	22 38 00 00 00 00 00 01		0010 0010 0011 10	398
-1.	A2 38 00 00 00 00 00 01		1010 0010 0011 10	398
111.	22 38 00 00 00 00 00 6F	06F	0010 0010 0011 10	398
111.111	22 2C 00 00 00 01 bC 6F	06F 06F	0010 0010 0010 11	395

---

[154] Don't blame us – this part follows the standard IEEE 754.

Floating point number	Hexadecimal value stored	Bottom bits in groups of 10	Top 14 bits	Stored exp.
-123.000123	A2 20 00 00 07 b0 00 7b	07b 000 07b	1010 0010 0010 00	392
$9.99 \cdot 10^{99}$	23 bC 00 00 00 00 03 E7	3E7	0010 0011 1011 11	495
$1 \cdot 10^{-99}$	20 AC 00 00 00 00 00 01		0010 0000 1010 11	299
$1 \cdot 10^{-383}$	00 3C 00 00 00 00 00 01		0000 0000 0011 11	15
$0.000\ 000\ 000\ 01 \cdot 10^{-383}$	00 04 00 00 00 00 00 01		0000 0000 0001 00	4

The last number is the smallest that can be entered directly from the keyboard. Dividing it by 10^4 results in $1 \cdot 10^{-398}$, being stored as hexadecimal 1. Divide this by 1.999 999 999 99 and the result will remain $1 \cdot 10^{-398}$ in default rounding mode (and in RM 1, 2, 3, and 5, see the command RM). Divide it by 2 instead and the result will become zero.

Let us look at the high end of our numeric range now:

Floating point number	Hexadecimal value stored	Bottom bits in groups of 10	Top 14 bits	Stored exp.
$9.999\ 999\ 999\ 99 \cdot 10^{384}$	77 FF E7 F9 FE 7F 78 00	9 3E7 3E7 3E7 3dE 000	0111 0111 1111 11	767

This number (featuring the digit 9 twelve times) is the greatest that can be entered directly. Adding $9.999 \cdot 10^{372}$ to it will display $1 \cdot 10^{385}$

...

Floating point number	Hexadecimal value stored	Bottom bits in groups of 10	Top 14 bits	Stored exp.
$1 \cdot 10^{385}$	77 FF E7 F9 FE 7F 9F E7	9 3E7 3E7 3E7 3E7 3E7	0111 0111 1111 11	767

... which is stored as $9.999\ 999\ 999\ 999\ 999 \cdot 10^{384}$. This is the greatest number representable in this format.

All this follows *decimal64* floating point format, though not exactly. Additionally, your *WP 34S* features three special numbers:

Floating point number	Hexadecimal value stored	Top byte in binary representation
Infinity	78 00 00 00 00 00 00 00	0111 1000
-Infinity	F8 00 00 00 00 00 00 00	1111 1000
not numEric	7C 00 00 00 00 00 00 00	0111 1100

An exponent is not applicable here. These special numbers are legal results of your *WP 34S* if flag **D** is set.

APPENDIX C: MESSAGES AND ERROR CODES

There are some commands generating messages, be they in the numeric or in the dot matrix section of the display. Of these, DAY, DAYS+, ERR, STATUS, VERS, and WDAY were introduced above in the section about display (see pp. 71ff). Others are PROMPT, VIEWα and more alpha commands, and the test commands (see p. 160). Also two constants will return a special message when called (see pp. 261ff).

Furthermore, there are a number of error messages. Depending on error conditions, the following messages will be displayed in the mode(s) listed (the messages are sorted alphabetically, EC stands for *error code*).

Each error message is *temporary* (see p. 76), so ◄ or (EXIT) will erase it and allow continuation. Any other key pressed will erase it as well, but will also execute with the *stack* contents present. Thus, another easy and safe return to the display shown before the error occurred is pressing (h) twice.

Message	EC	Explanation and examples
Bad time ▪▪▪ **or dAtE**	2	[d] Invalid date format or incorrect date or time in input, e.g. month >12, day >31 .
Bad digit ▪▪▪ **Error**	9	[n] Invalid digit in integer input, e.g. 2 in binary or 9 in octal mode. Will be displayed as long as the invalid key is pressed.
Bad mode ▪▪▪ **Error**	13	Caused by calling an operation in a mode where it is not defined, e.g. calling a constant in a routine written in DECM but executed in an integer mode.
Domain ▪▪▪ **Error**	1	[¬α] An argument exceeds the domain of the mathematical function called. May be caused by roots or logs of $x < 0$ (both if not preceded by (CPX)), by $0 / 0$, $\Gamma(0)$, $\tan(90°)$ and equivalents, by $\operatorname{artanh}(x)$ for $\left|\operatorname{Re}(x)\right| \geq 1$, by $\operatorname{arcosh}(x)$ for $\operatorname{Re}(x) < 1$, by AGM of a negative input, etc. Though note that e.g. $\tan(90°)$ and logs of 0 are legal results if flag **D** is set.

Message	EC	Explanation and examples
Flash is **FuLL**	23	No more space in *FM*. Delete a program from *FM* to regain space.
Illegal **OPErAti on**	7	May appear in an attempt running an old routine containing a command which turned nonprogrammable after said routine was written.
Invalid **dAtA**	18	Set when there is a checksum error either in *FM* or as part of a serial download. It is also set if a *FM* segment is otherwise not usable.
Invalid **PArAMEtEr**	16	Similar to error 1 but a statistics parameter specified in **J** or **K** is out of valid range for the function called. May appear e.g. if LgNrm is called with $j < 0$.
I/O **Error**	17	See pp. 317ff.
Matrix **MiSMAtCH**	21	• A matrix isn't square when it should be. • Matrix sizes aren't miscible.
No crystal **InStALLEd**	24	May be thrown by DATE, TIME, SETDAT, or SETTIM. See pp. 359ff for curing.
No root **Found**	20	The solver did not converge.
No such **LAbEL**	6	Attempt to address an undefined label.

Message	EC	Explanation and examples
Out of range **···** **Error**	8	• A number exceeds the valid range. This can be caused by specifying decimals >11, word size >64, negative flag numbers, integers $\geq 2^{64}$, *hours* or *degrees* >9000, denominators ≥9999, invalid times, etc. • A matrix *descriptor* (see p. 67) would go beyond the registers available or a row or column index is too large. • A register or flag address exceeds the valid range of currently allocated registers. May also happen in indirect addressing or calling nonexistent local addresses. • An R-operation (e.g. R-COPY) attempts accessing invalid register addresses.
RAM is **···** **Full**	11	No more space in *RAM*. May be caused by attempts to write too large routines, allocate too many registers, and the like. May happen also in program execution due to too many local data dynamically allocated (see pp. 301f).
Singular **···** **Error**	22	• Attempt to use a LU decomposed matrix for solving a system of equations. • Attempt to invert a matrix when it isn't of full rank.
Stack **···** **CLASH**	12	STOS or RCLS attempt using registers that would overlap the *stack*. Will happen with e.g. SSIZE8 and STOS **94** (if REGS **100** is set).
Too few **···** **dAtA Points**	15	A statistical calculation was started based on too few data points, e.g. regression or *standard deviation* for < 2 points.
Too long **···** **Error**	10	Keyboard input is too long for the buffer. Will happen e.g. if you try to enter more than 12 digits.

Message	EC	Explanation and examples
Undefined **OP-COdE**	3	An instruction with an undefined operation code occurred. Should never happen – but who knows?
Word size **too SMALL**	14	Register content is too big for the word size set.
Write **ProtEctEd**	19	Attempt to a) delete or edit program steps in *FM*, b) delete the final END in *RAM*.
+∞ **Error**	4	• Division of a number > 0 by zero. • Divergent sum or product or integral. • Positive overflow in DECM (see p. 80).
−∞ **Error**	5	• Division of a number < 0 by zero. • Divergent sum or product or integral. • Negative overflow in DECM (see p. 80). • Also thrown for a logarithm of (+) 0, while a logarithm of -0 returns NaN.
∫ ⁓ **ί30**	25	This is not an error but just a message. It will be returned by MSG **25** and works exclusively in routines – may be useful while integrating.

APPENDIX D: THE *WP 34S* EMULATOR ON YOUR COMPUTER

On *http://sourceforge.net/projects/wp34s/files/emulator/* , you will find *WP 34S* emulators for Windows, MacOS, Linux, and Linux64. Download and run the application suiting your environment. Starting it the very first time, you will see the message displayed. Just click [Reset] and you are done.

If you own a Windows PC, you may as well run Marcus' traditional true emulator (my favorite) stored at *http://sourceforge.net/p/wp34s/code/HEAD/tree/trunk/windows/bin/* (you will need the two files `wp34Sgui.exe` and `emulator.dll`) – it was the first application used for presenting and testing the software and function set of the *WP 34S* calculator and is still going along with its development. What works with this emulator shall run on your calculator as well. It is described below in more detail – the others work similarly.

While tactile feedback, boot speed, pocketability, and battery life suffer, some things become easier with an emulator, e.g. printing (see below) and execution speed. Typically, the emulator is operated by the computer mouse and the numeric keypad or through a touch screen. You access the corresponding areas of the image instead of pressing keys.

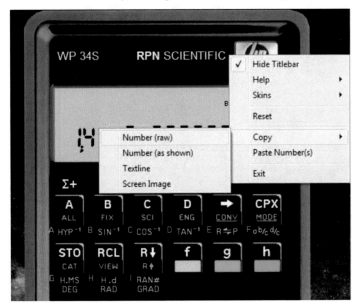

Right clicking on a key area is a shortcut to its **h** -shifted label.

There is one important extra: a right click on the WP logo top right opens a menu as pictured here. It contains links to the project website and the manual (under <Help>) as well as to three different skins for the emulator. The 'medium' skin is shown above; the other two are smaller and are printed below in the same scale.

The automatic link to the manual will only work after you copied the manual in the directory where `wp34sgui.exe` lives on your computer.

Furthermore, this menu allows you to import numbers (e.g. from *Excel* sheets – if you select and copy more than one cell at a time, their contents will be pushed on the *stack* successively with the last one stored in **X**). Vice versa, you can export numbers (as they are shown on the emulator screen or in full 'raw' precision[155]), export *alpha* as text or the complete '*LCD*' screen as a picture to the clipboard for use in other computer applications.

If your computer has a numeric keypad, the digits and arithmetic operation keys there are shortcuts to the corresponding virtual 'keys' of the emulator. The up and down cursor keys are connected to ▲ and ▼, **Backspace** and **Del** to ←, and **Enter** and **CR** to (ENTER↑).

---

[155] So you can copy e.g. the square root of 2 from your emulator with up to 34 digits precision: 1.414 213 562 373 095 048 801 688 724 209 698 (blanks were inserted manually here to ease reading).

Data Transfer between Your *WP 34S* and Your Computer

The emulator on your computer and your calculator can talk to each other over the cable used for flashing (cf. p. 296). Either one of the two cables mentioned on p. 285 will work, or you need a modified calculator as described here (plus a special cable): *http://www.hpmuseum.org/cgi-sys/cgiwrap/hpmuseum/archv020.cgi?read=186826* .

 Remember the 'old' programming cable draws current from the batteries of your *WP 34S*, so disconnect it from your *WP 34S* as soon as it is no longer needed.

In the emulator directory, a plain ASCII text file `wp34s.ini` must be placed that contains just a single line (terminated by CR/LF) stating the name of the computer port used for serial communication with your *WP 34S*, such as e.g. COM2:

The following commands (all stored in P.FCN) allow for sending programs, registers or all *RAM* from your *WP 34S* to your computer or vice versa. With a suitable cable it would be even possible to transfer data directly between two *WP 34S*.

On the receiving device, enter RECV. It will display Wait... .

On the sender you have three alternatives:

1. SENDP will send the *current program* from *RAM* of the sender. It will display Wait... as well. After successful transmission, the sender will show OK and the receiver will display Program .

2. SENDR will send all the global numbered registers allocated, displaying Wait... . After successful transmission, the sender will show OK and the receiver will display Register .

3. SENDA will send the complete two *kilobytes* of non-volatile *RAM*, displaying Wait... . After successful transmission, the sender will show OK and the receiver will display All RAM .

The little = annunciator is lit while the serial port is in use. Take (EXIT) to abort the communication if necessary.

Each of the four commands RECV, SENDP, SENDR, and SENDA features a fixed timeout of some $10s$ for setting up the connection. After an interval of inactivity of said length, an I/O Error is thrown indicating no communication has occurred. If such an error appears in the middle of a transmission, try again.

If your *WP 34S* receives data from the emulator, these data will be stored in the corresponding *RAM* section directly (cf. pp. 298ff). If the emulator receives data from your *WP 34S*, these data may be used immediately as well, and will become part of the file `wp34s.dat` which is written when exiting the emulator (see p. 320).

Using a *WP 34S* <u>without</u> the crystal installed, you may also get an I/O error because of its baud rate setting being a bit too far off. To determine the speed, use the loop

```
CLx
INC X
BACK 001
```

and let it run for 30s while connected to the computer. The expected result at nominal speed is around 123 000 for v3.1. On a crystal-less *WP 34S*, the I/O commands accept a correction factor in percent in X. Divide the counts you measured by 1 230 and leave it in X for RECV or SEND... Already some 2% may make a significant difference. Integer values between 80 and 120 are accepted – all other are ignored. On the emulator or on a *WP 34S* with the crystal installed and initialized, x will be ignored in those commands.

With your data transmitted successfully from your *WP 34S* to your computer, see also *Section 4* of the user guide at *http://sourceforge.net/p/wp34s/code/HEAD/tree/doc/WP34s_Assembler _Tool_Suite.pdf* for the way to extract `.wp34s`-files from the emulator *RAM* state file `wp34s.dat`. These `.wp34s`-files may then be opened and edited by a suitable text file editor on your computer, e.g. *WordPad*. You can create your own `.wp34s`-files from scratch as well.

After completion of editing, you may compile the file with the library tools in the **wp34s/trunk/tools** directory. The following tells in more detail what to do (assuming the file you edited is called `xyz.wp34s` and it contains a statement LBL'ZYX', for example – feel free to replace these two names by whatever applies in your case):

1. Create an empty `wp34s.dat` file by running the emulator and executing

    (P.FCN) END

    (P.FCN) CLALL

    (R/S)

Exit the emulator, and save the emulator's freshly emptied wp34s.dat to the **wp34s/trunk./tools** directory.

2. Make sure that the **wp34s/trunk/tools** directory is listed in your executable PATH environment variable, and from that directory type: **wp34s_lib.pl xyz.wp34s -ilib wp34s.dat -f -state**

3. Then put the compiler updated wp34s.dat file back into the directory where your emulator expects to find it. Start the emulator and – using CAT – you will find the newly compiled **ZYX** program in the program area of *RAM*.

Now, you can test and debug your program on the emulator. After successful completing this, you may want to copy this program to your *WP 34S*. Thus, issue ...

(P.FCN) **RECV**   on your *WP 34S* and use ...

(P.FCN) **SENDP**   on your emulator to send the *current program* from your computer to your *WP 34S*.

What works on the emulator shall work on your *WP 34S* as well (provided the necessary hardware is installed) – both share the same set of functions. Your *WP 34S* is one of the smallest calculators in a commercial package allowing such a bidirectional data exchange and backup.

The newer Qt-based emulators for Windows, MacOS, and Linux contain a setup option for the serial interface. They shortcut calling a **h**-shifted command by clicking on the corresponding green label area. They may show the contents of all registers simultaneously in debugging mode. And they react differently on right clicks. Just try them.

Mapping of Memory Regions to Emulator State Files

Region		State file	Remarks
Backup	bu͏P	`wp34s-backup.dat`	This file is created by SAVE.
Flash library	L͏ b	`wp34s-lib.dat`	This file is written whenever a flash command is executed.
RAM	r͏ΑΠΠ	`wp34s.dat`	Backup of the emulator *RAM* area (registers, state, and programs) – this file is written only when exiting the emulator.

All these files are only read into memory at emulator startup.

Simulating an *HP* Printer on Your Computer

For simulated printing, use *Christoph Gießelink's HP82240B Printer Simulator*, available at *http://hp.giesselink.com/hp82240b.htm* .

It works fine with the traditional emulator described above. Installation and use are self-explanatory. It is an autonomous application, so you have to start and exit it independently. There is another HP82240B simulator accompanying the Qt-based emulators – requiring good eyesight since it lacks the button <Graphic Scale> *Christoph* included.

The 'print' shown here was generated by ▣STK and ▣REGS. Guess what *stack* size was set?

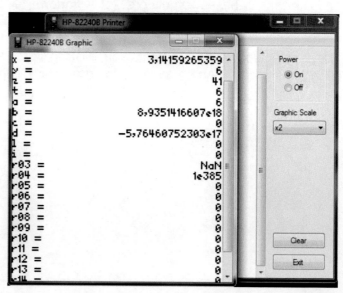

APPENDIX E: CHARACTER SETS

The following table shows the complete dot matrix character set as implemented in big and small font sorted according to the hexadecimal character codes (Unicode). Characters with codes $< 20_{16}$ are for control purposes – some of them (4, 10_{10}, 27_{10}) may be useful for *HP82240B* control. Characters printed on darker grey show identical patterns in both fonts. Characters from 00F0 to 00FF (printed on yellow here) cannot be the last ones in a group of three (see LBL etc.).

	0	1	2	3	4	5	6	7	8	9	A	B	C	D	E	F
017x								ÿ	ÿ						z̄	z̄
023x			ȳ													
039x	Α	Β	Γ	Δ	Ε	Ζ	Η	Θ	Ι	Κ	Λ	Μ	Ν	Ξ	Ο	
03Ax	Π	Ρ	Σ	Τ	Υ	Φ	Χ	Ψ	Ω							
03Bx	α	β	γ	δ	ε	ζ	η	ϑ	ι	κ	λ	μ	ν	ξ	ο	
03Cx	π	ρ	σ	τ	υ	φ	χ	ψ	ω							
1D6x	×			ᵤ			Υ									
1E8x	x̄													x̂		
201x							'	'	'		"	"	"			
207x					-1	✳										
208x	□	1	2				∞									
209x	A	e		×			K		m	n	P	q				
20Ax															€	
219x	←	↑	→	↓	÷											
21Cx				⇄												
221x					⌐						∞					
222x							∫									
223x																
224x							≈									
225x																
226x	≠				≤	≥										
239x							⌂									
249x									b	c	d					
24Ax																
24Bx	w											G				
24Cx																
24Dx				f	g	h										
260x							☉									
264x	⊕															

For the numeric seven-segment display and the annunciators top right, there is another character set and font provided:

	0	1	2	3	4	5	6	7	8	9	A	B	C	D	E	F	Remarks
002x			"					'	[	]			,		-	.	ʳ	
003x	0	1	2	3	4	5	6	7	8	9			ʟ		:	⌐		
004x	O	A	b	C	d	E	F	G	H	i	J		L	r	n	Ō	Note M
005x	P	q	r	S	t	U		u		y		C		]		_	Note W
006x		A	b	c	d	E	F	G	h	ı	J		L	ⁿ	n	o	Note m
007x	P	q	r	S	t	u		J		y							Note w
008x																	
009x																	
00Ax	⁻	-	⁼	_	⁻_	:	⁼	ll									For STATUS
00Bx								.	O	ı							For high bits in BASE 2
00Cx																	
00Dx																	
00Ex	ı	INPUT	=	■▶	BEG	STO	RCL	RAD	360	RPN							Annunciators
00Fx		ı	_	ı	'	-	'	⁻	.	.						8.	Segments

All these fonts are available at
http://sourceforge.net/p/wp34s/code/HEAD/tree/trunk/windows/winfont/

ATTENTION: The commands x→α and α→x use the <u>internal</u> character codes of the *WP 34S*. These codes match Unicode unless framed yellow in the table overleaf. Character 06 is a narrow space.

	0	1	2	3	4	5	6	7	8	9	A	B	C	D	E	F
0		x̄	ȳ	√	∫	°		G	±	≤	≥	≠	€	→	←	↓
1	↑	f	ℎ	ℏ	ᶜ	Ø	ø	≒	ß	∡	∇	ₘ	×	≈	£	¥
2		!	"	#	$	%	&	'	(	)	*	+	,	-	.	/
3	0	1	2	3	4	5	6	7	8	9	:	;	≤	=	≥	?
4	@	A	B	C	D	E	F	G	H	I	J	K	L	M	N	O
5	P	Q	R	S	T	U	V	W	X	Y	Z	[	\	]	^	_
6	`	a	b	c	d	e	f	g	h	i	j	k	l	m	n	o
7	p	q	r	s	t	u	v	w	x	y	z	{	|	}	~	÷
8	¹	∿	Γ	Δ	Đ	♂	♀	Θ	Æ	œ	Λ	×	ᵧ	Ξ	☉	Π
9	✳	Σ	■	▪	Φ	¬	Ψ	Ω	■	↦	²	∞	ˣ	⁻¹	ℏ	∞
A	α	β	γ	δ	ε	ζ	η	θ	ι	κ	λ	μ	ν	ξ	⊕	π
B	ρ	σ	τ	υ	φ	χ	ψ	ω	▫	₁	₂	ₓ	∈	ₙ	ₚ	ᵤ
C	À	Á	Ã	Ä	Å	Ć	Ĉ	Ç	È	É	Ê	Ë	Ì	Í	Î	Ï
D	Ñ	Ò	Ó	Õ	Ö	Ř	Š	▴	Ù	Ú	Û	Ü	Ů	♀	♡	Ž
E	à	á	ã	ä	å	ć	ĉ	ç	è	é	ê	ë	ì	í	î	ï
F	ñ	ò	ó	õ	ö	ř	š	ĸ	ù	ú	û	ü	ů	ý	ÿ	ž

In the font files provided, the characters are repeated in this internal order at codes greater than E000. Do <u>not</u> use these high codes in writing texts, however, since some programs (e.g. *Preview*) may not read them correctly.

WP 34S v3.3d

APPENDIX F: CORRESPONDING OPERATIONS TO THE *HP-42S, HP-16C,* AND *HP-21S* FUNCTION SETS

In the *IOP*, the corresponding functions of vintage *HP* calculators were mentioned under the respective entry of your *WP 34S*. The tables below revert this in a way: the first table shows the functions of the *HP-42S* and the corresponding ones of your *WP 34S* unless they carry identical names and are either both keyboard accessible or both stored in a *catalog* or menu. There is an analog table for the *HP-16C* functions on p. 334 below.

Functional differences of homonymous commands are covered in the *IOP* on pp. 171ff.

HP-42S

Remarks printed on light grey indicate commands being either default settings or keyboard accessible on your *WP 34S* while you must use a menu on the *HP-42S*.

HP-42S	*WP 34S*	Remarks for the *WP 34S*
ABS		Press |x|.
ACOSH		Press HYP⁻¹ COS.
ADV	⊟ADV	
AGRAPH	n/a	The *LCD* of the *HP-20b* and *HP-30b* features only a very small dot matrix section (see p. 71). Striving for full-fledged graphics therein would be futile.
AIP	αIP	
ALENG	αLENG	
ALL		Press ALL.
ALLΣ	Superfluous	Your WP 34S runs in ALLΣ mode always.
▓ ALPHA	α	See the description of *alpha mode* on p. 148.
AND		Press AND.
AOFF	αOFF	

HP-42S	WP 34S	Remarks for the WP 34S
AON	αON	
ARCL	αRCL or αRC#	
AROT	αRL or αRR	
ASHF	αSL or αSR	
ASINH		Press HYP⁻¹ SIN .
ASSIGN	n/a	Not supported since no CUSTOM menu can be featured. Cf. CUSTOM.
ASTO	αSTO	Press f STO in *alpha mode*.
ATANH		Press HYP⁻¹ TAN .
ATOX	α→x	
AVIEW	VIEWα	
BASE	Superfluous	HEXM, DECM, OCTM, BINM, as well as the LOGIC operations AND, OR, XOR, and NOT of *HP-42S* are provided on the keyboard of your *WP 34S* in all modes but *alpha*. The digits A...F are provided in integer modes if applicable. The functions corresponding to BIT? and ROTXY are then in X.FCN.
BASE+, BASE-, etc.	Superfluous	Your *WP 34S* executes these arithmetic commands in integer modes automatically.
BEEP	n/a	The *HP-20b* and *HP-30b* do not contain the necessary hardware.
BINM	BASE 2	Press 2 .
BIT?	BS?	
CATALOG	Replaced	This is split in various *catalogs* on your *WP 34S*.
CF		Press CF .
CLA	CLα	Press CLx in alpha mode.
CLD	Superfluous	Any keystroke will clear a *temporary message*.
CLEAR	P.FCN	CLΣ, CLP, CLST, CLα, and CLx are on the keyboard.
CLKEYS	n/a	Not needed since no CUSTOM menu can be featured. Cf. CUSTOM.

HP-42S	WP 34S	Remarks for the WP 34S
CLLCD	n/a	Use ⍺ CLx to clear the dot matrix section. See AGRAPH.
CLMENU	n/a	Not needed since no CUSTOM menu can be featured. Cf. CUSTOM.
CLP		Press CLP.
CLRG	CLREGS	
CLST	CLSTK	Press 0 FILL.
CLV	n/a	The hardware of the *HP-20b* and *HP-30b* does not provide space for variables. Thus, variable-based commands (e.g. many matrix commands) cannot be featured on your *WP 34S*.
CLx		Press CLx.
CLΣ		Press CLΣ.
COMB		Press Cy,x.
COMPLEX	n/a	The hardware of the *HP-20b* and *HP-30b* does not provide space for different data types. Thus, complex numbers have to be put in two registers each as described on pp. 123ff.
CONVERT	CONV	
CORR		Press r.
COSH		Press HYP COS.
CPXRES, CPX?	n/a	See COMPLEX.
CUSTOM	n/a	The *LCD* of the *HP-20b* and *HP-30b* does not allow for softkeys. This prohibits a CUSTOM menu.
DECM		Press H.d.
DEG		Press DEG.
DEL	n/a	Not featured. Too dangerous, in our opinion.
DELAY	▤DLAY	
DELR, DIM, DIM?	n/a	Matrix commands: see CLV.

HP-42S	WP 34S	Remarks for the WP 34S
▓ DISP	Superfluous	FIX, SCI, ENG, ALL, RDX., and RDX, are provided on the keyboard.
DSE		Press DSE .
E	EEX	
EDIT, EDITN	n/a	Matrix commands: see CLV.
ENG		Press ENG .
EXITALL	n/a	Not needed since no CUSTOM menu can be featured. Cf. CUSTOM.
FCSTX	x̂	
FCSTY	ŷ	Press ŷ .
FIX		Press FIX .
▓ FLAGS	TEST	SF and CF are on the keyboard.
FNRM	n/a	Matrix command: see CLV.
FP		Press FP .
GAMMA	Γ	
GETKEY	KEY?	
GETM	n/a	Matrix command: see CLV.
GRAD		Press GRAD .
GROW	n/a	Matrix command: see CLV.
HEXM	BASE 16	Press 16 .
I+, I-, INDEX	n/a	Matrix commands: see CLV.
INPUT	PROMPT	
INSR	n/a	Matrix command: see CLV.
INTEG	∫	Press ∫ .
INVRT	M^{-1}	
IP		Press IP .
ISG		Press ISG .
J+ and J-	n/a	Matrix commands: see CLV.
KEYASN, KEYG, KEYX	n/a	Not supported since no CUSTOM menu can be featured. Cf. CUSTOM.

HP-42S	WP 34S	Remarks for the WP 34S
▆ LASTx	RCL L	
LBL		Press LBL.
LCLBL	n/a	The *LCD* of the *HP-20b* and *HP-30b* does not allow for soft keys. This prohibits a CUSTOM menu. Nevertheless, your *WP 34S* provides local labels as described on p. 157.
LINΣ	Superfluous	Your *WP 34S* runs in ALLΣ mode always.
LIST	n/a	Use ▆PROG instead.
LOG	LOG₁₀	Press LG.
MAN	CF T	This print mode is startup default on your *WP 34S*.
▆ MATRIX , MAT?	n/a	Matrix commands: see CLV.
MEAN	x̄	Press x̄.
MENU, MVAR	n/a	Not supported since no CUSTOM menu can be featured. Cf. CUSTOM.
▆ MODES	MODE	
N!	x!	Press !.
NEWMAT	n/a	Matrix command: see CLV.
NORM	n/a	Not featured.
NOT		Press NOT.
OCTM	BASE 8	Press 8.
OLD	n/a	Matrix command: see CLV.
ON	n/a	Not featured.
OR		Press OR.
PERM		Press Py,x.
▆ PGM.FCN	P.FCN	LBL, RTN, VIEW, PSE, ISG, and DSE are provided on the keyboard.
PGMINT	Contained in ∫	
PGMSLV	Contained in SLV	
PI	π	

HP-42S	WP 34S	Remarks for the WP 34S
PIXEL	gSET	See AGRAPH.
POLAR	n/a	See COMPLEX.
POSA	n/a	The alpha register contains 30 characters maximum. Automatic searching would be overkill, in our opinion.
PRA	▣α	
PRLCD	▣PLOT	See AGRAPH.
▤ PRGM	P/R	
▤ PRINT	P.FCN	PRX is on the keyboard.
▤ PROB	Replaced	COMB, PERM, N!, and RAN are provided on the keyboard. SEED is in <u>STAT</u>; GAM(MA) is in <u>X.FCN</u>.
PROFF	CF T	Press CF T.
PRON	SF T	Press SF T.
PRP	▣PROG	
PRSTK	▣STK	
PRUSR, PRV	n/a	See CLV.
PRX	▣r X	Press ↑ except in alpha mode.
PRΣ	▣Σ	
PSE		Press PSE.
PUTM	n/a	Matrix command: see CLV.
QUIET	n/a	See BEEP.
RAD		Press RAD.
RAN	RAN#	Press RAN#.
RCLEL, RCLIJ	n/a	Matrix commands: see CLV.
RDX, RDX.		Press ./. except in *alpha mode*.
REALRES REAL?	n/a	See COMPLEX.
RECT	Superfluous	This mode is permanent on your *WP 34S*. See COMPLEX.

HP-42S	WP 34S	Remarks for the WP 34S
RND	ROUND	Press RND.
RNRM	n/a	Matrix command: see CLV.
ROTXY	RL, RLC, RR, and RRC	
RSUM, R<>R	n/a	Matrix commands: see CLV.
SDEV	s	Press s.
SF		Press SF
SHOW	◄	
SINH		Press HYP SIN.
SIZE	REGS	
SLOPE	L.R.	
SOLVE	SLV	Press SLV.
SOLVER	Contained in SLV	
SQRT	√	
STAT	STAT	MEAN, SDEV, FCSTY, and CORR are on the keyboard; the MODL setting commands are in MODE.
STOEL, STOIJ	n/a	Matrix commands: see CLV.
STR?	n/a	See CLV.
TANH		Press HYP TAN.
TONE	n/a	See BEEP.
TOP.FCN	n/a	Not needed since no CUSTOM menu can be featured. Cf. CUSTOM.
TRACE	SF T	Press SF T.
TRANS	TRANSP	
UVEC	^{C}SIGN	
VARMENU	n/a	See CLV.
VIEW		Press VIEW.
WMEAN	$\overline{x}_w$	
WRAP	n/a	Matrix command: see CLV.

HP-42S	WP 34S	Remarks for the WP 34S
X<>		Press [x≷].
X<0?, X<Y?	x< ?	
X≤0?, X≤Y?	x≤ ?	
X=0?, X=Y?	x= ?	Press [x= ?].
X≠0?, X≠Y?	x≠ ?	Press [x≠ ?].
X≥0?, X≥Y?	x≥ ?	
X>0?, X>Y?	x> ?	
XOR		Press [XOR].
XTOA	x→α	
YINT	L.R.	Alternatively, press [0] [ŷ].
∫f(x)	Contained in ∫	
ΣREG, ΣREG?	Superfluous	See p. 301.
→DEC	Superfluous	Conversions are done automatically in integer modes.
→DEG	rad→°	Press [CONV] [R] [XEQ].
→H.MS		Press [→] [H.MS].
→HR		Press [→] [H.d].
→OCT	Superfluous	Conversions are done automatically in integer modes.
→POL		Press [P←].
→RAD	°→rad	Press [CONV] [A][▲] [XEQ].
→REC		Press [→R].
%CH	Δ%	Press [Δ%].

HP-16C

The table for the functions of the *HP-16C* is sorted following their appearance on its keyboard, starting top left. As for the *HP-42S*, only functions carrying different names on both calculators are listed. *HP-16C* functions neither mentioned here nor printed on the keyboard of your *WP 34S* are all found in X.FCN in integer modes.

HP-16C	WP 34S	Remarks for the WP 34S
RL , RLn	RL	In X.FCN.
RR , RRn	RR	
RMD	RMDR	
RLC , RLCn	RLC	
RRC , RRCn	RRC	In X.FCN.
#B	nBITS	
ABS	|x|	
DBL÷	DBL /	In X.FCN.
x≷(i)	Superfluous	Each and every register may be used for indirection.
x≷I		
SHOW HEX	→ 16	
SHOW DEC	→ 10	
SHOW OCT	→ 8	
SHOW BIN	→ 2	
B?	BS?	In TEST.
GSB	XEQ	
HEX	16	
DEC	10	
OCT	8	
BIN	2	
SF 3 , CF 3	LZON, LZOFF	In MODE. Control display of leading zeroes.
SF 4 , CF 4	SF C , CF C	Carry.
SF 5 , CF 5	SF B , CF B	Overflow.

HP-16C	WP 34S	Remarks for the WP 34S
F?	FS?	In TEST.
(i)	Superfluous	Each and every register may be used for indirection.
I		
CLEAR PRGM	CLP	Note there is also CLPALL.
CLEAR REG	CLREGS	In P.FCN.
CLEAR PREFIX	Superfluous	See p. 71.
WINDOW	n/a	
SET COMPL 1'S	1COMP	
SET COMPL 2'S	2COMP	In MODE. Note there is also SIGNMT.
SET COMPL UNSGN	UNSIGN	
SST	▼	
BSP	⬅	
BST	▲	
x≤y	x≤ ?	
x<0	x< ?	In TEST. Note there are more tests covered therein.
x>y	x> ?	
x>0		
FLOAT	FIX	
MEM	STATUS	
STATUS .		
CHS	+/−	
◄	◄(	
►	)►	
LSTX	RCL L	
x≠y	x≠ ?	
x≠0		
x=y	x= ?	
x=0		

HP-21S

The table for the functions of the *HP-21S* follows the same rules as the one for the *HP-16C*. The *HP-21S*, however, is an algebraic calculator, hence its keys [INPUT], ([), (]), and [=] have no direct equivalent on your *WP 34S*.

Feel free to consult the *HP-21S Owner's Manual* for additional information about the four most important continuous statistical distributions and their applications.

HP-21S	WP 34S	Remarks
x̄ᵥᵥ	x̄ᵥᵥ	in STAT
x̄,ȳ	x̄	
Sₓ,Sᵧ	s	
m,b	L.R.	
σₓ,σᵧ	σ	in STAT
x̂,r	r, x̂	
ŷ,r	r, ŷ	
PRGM	P/R	
SWAP	x≷y	
CLPRGM	CLP	
E	EEX	
LOAD	n/a	Loads predefined programs in the *HP-21S*.
ABS	|x|	
FRAC	FP	
SEED	SEED	in STAT
%CHG	Δ%	

HP-21S	WP 34S	Remarks
Q(z)	$\Phi_u(x)$	in <u>PROB</u>
zp	Φ^{-1}	Note the remark below for inverse distribution functions.
Q(t)	$t_u(x)$	
tp	$t^{-1}(p)$	in <u>PROB</u>. Note the implementation of <u>inverse</u> distribution functions deviates on both calculators: your *WP 34S* calculates with the probability P (cf. p. 99ff) while the *HP-21S* calculates with the error probability $Q = 1 - P$ as input. Labeling these functions on the *HP-21S* using the letter p may add some confusion.
Q(F)	$F_u(x)$	
Fp	$F^{-1}(p)$	
Q(χ^2)	χ^2_u	
X^2_p	χ^2INV	
Cn,r	Cy,x	
SHOW	◀	
Pn,r	Py,x	
LAST	RCL L	
n!	!	
CLRG	CLREGS	in <u>P.FCN</u>

Other Vintage Calculators Referenced

As mentioned above several times, some advanced functionality of your *WP 34S* is taken over from other previous *HP* calculators beyond the *HP-42S*, *HP-16C*, and *HP-21S*. The following vintage *HP* material is recommended as source of in depth information (as far as calculating and applications are concerned) about the topics listed. It is completely contained in the museum media mentioned above (see p. 16).

Topic	Recommended literature
Root finding and numeric integration	*HP-34C Owner's Handbook and Programming Guide*
	HP-15C Owner's Handbook
	HP-15C Advanced Functions Handbook
Financial calculations	*HP-17BII+ User's Guide*

APPENDIX G: TROUBLESHOOTING GUIDE

This guide has two parts, concerning calculator operation and flashing. If you experience troubles during flashing, please turn to p. 343.

Overcoming Troubles in Calculator Operation

Usually, your *WP 34S* will throw an error message (taking both lines of the display) when it cannot fulfill your request. On such a message, please check *App. C* on pp. 311ff for hints.

Furthermore, we assume you know the annunciators as explained on p. 72 and the commands RM?, SSIZE?, XTAL?, 🔋? as well as their outputs. Other (possibly confusing) situations are covered here:

Symptoms observed	Diagnosis	Recommended therapy
After entering a decimal number such as 32.4567, the display shows **2c 64** ... **324567** d or similar.	Inadvertently entered an integer mode.	Press ■ H.d to return to default floating point mode.
After entering a decimal number such as 32.4567, the display shows **32 1520/3333** Gt or similar.	Inadvertently entered a fraction mode.	Press ■ H.d to return to default floating point mode.
You are working in binary integer mode and the display shows **un 64** ... **0 100.10110110** b or alike with such strange quotes top right.	Long integer number displayed	See on pp. 137ff how to deal with such numbers.

Symptoms observed	Diagnosis	Recommended therapy
After entering a decimal number such as 32.4567, the display shows  `7` `StEP 013` STO `444` or similar.	Inadvertently entered programming mode.	
Display looks like `RCL X` `Lib 0015` STO `527` or similar. Calculation commands are not executed.		Press (EXIT) or (h)(R/S) to return to run mode.
All input goes to the top line.	Inadvertently entered alpha mode.	Press (EXIT) to return to previous mode.
Display looks strange, but not like the patterns shown above so far.	Inadvertently entered a *browser* or a *catalog*.	Press (EXIT) to return to previous mode and display.
After entering (1)(.)(2)(3) or alike, ... 1. an unsolicited comma is displayed instead of a decimal point;	Wrong radix mark set.	
2. an unsolicited point is displayed instead of a decimal comma.		Press (h)(./,) or choose a suitable regional setting from the table on p. 77.
After entering a decimal number such as 3.4567, the display just shows 3. or 3.4 (there is a radix mark, but decimals are missing).	Wrong output format set.	Set (h)(ALL) 0 to see all the decimals you entered.

Symptoms observed	Diagnosis	Recommended therapy
Your *WP 34S* does not understand the dates or times you enter (anymore).	Wrong date or time format set.	Choose a suitable regional setting from the table on p. 77.
After entering *hours*, *minutes*, and *seconds*, only *hours* and *minutes* are displayed.	Wrong output format set.	Set **h** FIX **4** to see the *seconds* as well.
After entering a date such as 3.021951, 3.0220 is displayed instead.	Wrong output format set.	
After entering a date such as 11.112011, the year is truncated.		Press **h** FIX **6** to see all digits of the year.
On a *WP 34S* with the crystal and capacitors installed, after setting the time, the real time clock deviates significantly from true time.	The crystal is not activated yet.	See p. 349.
In long numbers, there are unwanted points or commas every four, three, or two digits.	TSON or SEPON is set.	If an integer mode is set, press **h** MODE **S** **XEQ** for SEPOFF; if a floating point mode is set, enter **h** MODE **T** **XEQ** for TSOFF.
Converting a number like e.g. 64 ⅟ₓ into a fraction, the result deviates from 1/64.	DENFAC or DENFIX is set.	Press **h** MODE **D** **E** **XEQ** to return to DENANY. If that does not help, turn to next row.

Symptoms observed	Diagnosis	Recommended therapy
After converting a number such as e.g. 0.46875 into a fraction, you get `I/2` `Gt` or a similarly imprecise result.	DENMAX is too low.	Press **0** [h] (MODE) (D)(I) (▲) (XEQ) to get the maximum precision in fraction mode.

Printing a set of data (e.g. a bunch of registers) you see a message like this:
 	
`Reset`
`49 164589`
 	
(the numeric value may differ).
	Processor failed due to low power (showing up in printing since the IR diode draws some current).	Short term workaround:
		Press
		[h] (MODE) [f] (EXIT) (XEQ) **5**
		(or a similar value) to increase print delay, giving the batteries a little time to recover.
		For curing the root cause, insert fresh batteries.

Your *WP 34S* does not start after you flashed a firmware `calc_ir.bin` or alike.	Insufficient hardware.	Make sure the crystal is installed (cf. pp. 359ff) and activated (see p. 349).
Printing does not work although the proper firmware is loaded (cf. pp. 285f).	IR interfacing disturbed.	Make sure that a) the crystal is installed (cf. pp. 359ff) and activated (see p. 349), b) the printer self-test works correctly, [156] c) the printer can 'see' the diode, d) distance between printer and your *WP 34S* is closer than 20*cm*.

---

[156] Turn the printer off. Hold down the paper advance button and turn the printer on again. It should print out its full character set (several lines of text) followed by its battery level (a number from 1 to 5).

Symptoms observed	Diagnosis	Recommended therapy
Turning on your *WP 34S*, you find memory is lost (indicated by `Erased` as shown on p. 18) or you see `Restored`, although you did neither flash nor reset it recently.	Intermittent voltage supply.	Ensure good voltage supply (there may be various causes for insufficiencies sensed). [157]

---

[157] Voltage may have dropped for different reasons, maybe even loose batteries. My first *HP-20b* (frame ID HSTNJ-IN05) featured a little safety bolt for each – they held down the batteries reliably. These two bolts apparently became victims of cost cutting – you can see their traces still in the plastic mold of the new frame HSTNJ-IN07 though the threaded holes are gone. The circular recession south of each battery space is where the head of the safety bolt went in. I guess *HP* believed the (unchanged) battery door BTDR-MJ920 being sufficient to hold the batteries down permanently.

Coin cells of lesser quality may be another reason for occasional voltage drops under load (if you have installed *Harald's* board you can power your *WP 34S* through the USB line and check if the phenomenon disappears). Voltage may also drop at low temperatures or returning from such conditions (when humidity condenses on cold calculator parts). It may be even just a matter of parts specifications. Note the actual root cause is unknown to us so far – we are just condemned to bear the consequences. The following recommendations will help by excluding or at least reducing some unwelcome effects:

1. **If you see `Restored` more than once, use SAVE on a regular basis** (e.g. before turning your calculator off) **since your *WP 34S* will automatically restore the last backup whenever voltage returns from zero to regular level.** `Erased` will only appear if there is no backup available.

2. Increase contact pressure: Remove both batteries. Carefully bend the three legs of both center battery contacts approximately 1*mm* upwards (see the picture overleaf). Then insert batteries again.

3. Overcome battery contact problems permanently: The following alternate ways are <u>strictly at your own risk</u>:

   a) Get an old HP-20b – it may be electronically defective. Check the presence of the safety bolts. Disassemble that calculator and yours (see *App. H – Tuning the Hardware of Your WP 34S* – steps **a** and **b**) and swap their frames. Then turn to step **i** for reassembly.

   b) Get two safety bolts. They look like M1.7×3.5, but feature a flat cylindrical head 0.5*mm* high and 5*mm* in diameter. If you got such bolts, you may proceed according to *App. H – Tuning the Hardware of Your WP 34S* – steps **a**, **b**, **h**, and **i**. See the result pictured overleaf.

With the safety bolts installed, batteries are secured properly at least. To my personal experience, this alone is not sufficient to cure the intermittent voltage problem entirely.

If you experience any strange situation not mentioned here, we recommend you check your display for annunciators as they are shown on p. 72. If it cannot be explained by the calculator settings, SAVE your data, call RESET, and try again. If the problem persists, we will appreciate when you report your observations to us, either before or after you solved the problem – maybe you found a bug hidden so far. Thanks in advance.

Overcoming Flashing Troubles

Sometimes it seems the calculator just does not <u>want</u> to be flashed. You may have tried the procedure described pp. 287ff repeatedly, but the display stubbornly stays blank. Do not despair[158] – the following procedure will help:

1. If there is still a cable linking calculator and computer, remove it a.s.a.p.

2. Check the batteries.

   a. Open the battery door and remove both batteries.

   b. Carefully bend the three legs of both center battery contacts approx. 1mm upwards.[157]

   c. Check battery voltage. Each shall produce 2.8 ... 3.2 V (the higher the better). If it is less or the difference exceeds 0.1 V, replace both batteries with fresh quality coin cells type *CR 2032*.

   d. Insert the batteries properly – with their positive poles up – like pictured here. Now your calculator is well prepared. Leave the battery door open.

---

[158] No such calculator ended as a paperweight just by flashing yet, following the procedures written above – but many batteries were drained for sure by programming cables staying connected for too long and / or by calculators quietly running at full speed for an extended time period.

3. Check your computer interface and connecting cable.

   a. You have either (i) a programming cable (or something similar) or (ii) a micro USB cable (or something similar). The latter requires either *Harald's* custom board or the headphone jack installed in your calculator − if this installation was done and verified according to *App. H* you can be confident it is ok.

   b. Check both sides of your cable: are there any bent or dirty pins? If not and the cable also shows no signs of being cut or torn, it should be ok. If dubious, use another cable of same kind.

   c. Connect your chosen cable to your computer. For case (i), use a suitable converter if required (see p. 285). Using such a converter with a PC, you shall see it listed now in <System Control> <Device Manager> as a "*USB Serial Converter*" (remember its port) − else there is a problem with this converter.

   d. Check the contacts at your calculator being dirt-free. Connect the cable to your calculator. For case (ii) with one of Harald's boards and using a PC, you shall see it listed now in <System Control> <Device Manager> as a "*FT230X USB Half UART*" (remember its port) − else there is a problem with the cable or the custom board (see p. 367).

   e. Make sure all lines of the cable stays firmly connected to your computer and your calculator. E.g. power interruptions during flashing interruptions during flashing may drive your calculator in a coma as mentioned above!

4. Now all the hardware is well prepared. Start *MySamBa* on your computer; enter the port (as determined in 3.c or 3.d, without a colon!) and the file information (see p. 285). Do not start sending yet, just leave the window open!

5. Focus on your calculator again − it is connected to your computer. Press ⟨ON⟩ firmly for two seconds.[159]

   Does the calculator display react now? Fine − continue with <u>step 4</u> on …

    • p. 288 for <u>first flashing</u>, case (i), or on p. 289 for case (ii), or on

    • p. 294 for <u>updating</u> your *WP 34S*.

---

[159] If you employ an external $3V$ power supply as described in *App. A*, you can measure the input current − if it is about $5mA$, the calculator is on, with $0mA$ it is off.

If the display stays blank, however, press **RESET** and continue below.

6. Restart your computer. Verify the chosen port is known to your operating system. On a PC, open the start window and enter CMD – this will open the good old *DOS* command window; therein type MODE COM*x*: with *x* being the port number as determined in step 3.c or 3.d above. The *DOS* command MODE should return data like shown at right or the equivalent in your language. Do not care for particular values

since those parameters will be controlled by *MySamBa* anyway.

If you get a similar message, continue with <u>step 3</u> on …

- p. 288 for <u>first flashing</u>, case (i), or on p. 289 for case (ii), or on

- p. 294 for <u>updating</u> your *WP 34S*.

If the port is unknown to your operating system, however, return to step 3.c above and try another port.[160]

---

[160] There may be three reasons for flashing being no longer possible:

a) the serial I/O or the entire chip became defective for whatever cause,

b) a "Latch Up" occurred, or

c) the *boot loader* firmware has overwritten itself or at least the interrupt vector table or the reset vector. This is the most common *boot loader* software mistake. There is a very short window when the reset vector will be written, some 10 *ms*, and if the transmission is interrupted at that moment, the *boot loader* cannot start up next time. So your calculator lapses into a coma and becomes unusable. This is one of two ways to 'kill' this calculator – see the warnings in *App. A*. All other calculators which dropped out 'just by flashing' could be reanimated.

In case a) nothing can be done but replacing the calculator. Though if case b) or c) happened, there are still some ways to overcome this (thanks to *Barry Mead*):

b1) Most modern *CMOS* and *NMOS* devices have so-called *Input Protection Diodes* to prevent electrostatic shock from damaging the circuitry. These diode pairs provide a low impedance path (diode on) when the voltage at an input goes above *VCC* or below *GND*. The configuration of these diode pairs is very much like that of an *Silicon Controlled Rectifier* and can "Latch Up" into a high current state if the battery voltage ever falls below 2.3 V (when a 3 V input exceeds *VCC* by 0.6 to 0.7 V). Anyway, if the calculator ever gets into this "Latch Up" state the only way to get it out of this state is to remove the batteries and short the *VCC* and *GND* pins of the battery together for a few seconds to bleed off any residual charge held in

APPENDIX H: ADDITIONAL INFORMATION FOR ADVANCED USERS

The information provided here may ease your work when you are going to do advanced computations, especially programming. This section also covers optional hardware modifications (see pp. 359ff). All the topics collected here require special care and / or a deeper under-standing of the corresponding 'mechanics' of the *WP 34S* – else you might be surprised by the consequences. **Use the information provided in this appendix at your own risk!**

---

capacitors. If the current draw returns to a few μA then you may yet be able to salvage your calculator.

c1) Crosscheck: The current draw of the calculator should go way down to a few μA when you press the RESET button, and not go into the mA range until after you press the ON button. Else the odds are high that the *boot loader* portion of the firmware is corrupted, and that the only way you will be able to resurrect your calculator is to use a hardware flashing device known as a *JTAG programmer*.

(Background: The *boot loader* on this device is not located in a <u>protected</u> area of *FM* as it is with many other flash-programmable devices. Unfortunately, it is merely a section of the normal *FM* instead. Each time you flash the *HP-30B* (*WP 34S*), you are overwriting the *boot loader* as well as the rest of the *FM* that define the behavior of the calculator. This is why <u>each attempt</u> to update the firmware has a risk of bricking the device, and why it is so critical that the battery be new, and the cables be wiggle-free and solid. If you attempt to program the *FM* and the process is interrupted, you will end up with a bricked calculator. So the only thing special about the *JTAG* method of programming *FM* is that it can be achieved even without the cooperation of *boot loader* firmware which reads the serial port interface. This is all a moot point if your calculator has a high-current lockup hardware problem, as even a *JTAG programmer* will probably not be able to fix the issue.)

Please note that using a *JTAG programmer* requires a considerable learning curve and skill level that may not be easy for most users of the calculator. If you go this way, you do it <u>strictly on your own risk</u>.

A company named *OLIMEX* makes an open-source software version of the *ARM JTAG programmer* that can be ordered for 39.95 € (about 43 US$) from <u>https://www.olimex.com/Products/ARM/JTAG/ARM-USB-TINY/</u> (see the picture at left). You may also need the *ARM-JTAG-20-10 Accessory* to adapt the *JTAG* pin count to that of the calculator (see at right, costs 4.95 €).

Changing Word Size in Integer Modes

Increasing or reducing the word size in integer modes will affect the current *stack* contents only (see the description of WSIZE in the *IOP* on pp. 222f). All other memory content of your *WP 34S* will stay as is. This differs from the implementation as known from the *HP-16C*, where <u>all</u> registers were remapped on word size changes.

Example starting with your *WP 34S* in BASE **16**, WSIZE **16**, SSIZE4, and with the *stack* (and **I**) filled with F12E:

I	F12E	F12E	F12E	F12E	F12E	F12E	F12E
L	old stuff	old stuff	E61	61	61	61	2E

T	F12E	F12E	F12E	2E	2E	2E	2E
Z	F12E	F12E	F12E	2E	2E	2E	2E
Y	F12E	F12E	F12E	2E	8F	8F	2E
X	F 12E	E61	FF8F	8F	2E	2E	19b2

Input	STO I	E61	+	WSIZE 8	RCL I	WSIZE 16	×

ATTENTION: Increasing the word size will just add empty bits to the significant side. Thus, a negative integer will immediately become positive then. There is no automatic sign extension! If you want it, you will have to take care of it yourself.

Mode Storing and Recalling

STOM stores mode data in a register. The following table shows more details. Types are coded G for general, F for fractions, D for decimal, and I for integer. At startup default and with fresh batteries, all bits are clear in this 64-bit word except the lowest three.

Bits	Type	Contents
0 ... 3	G	*LCD* contrast setting (0 ... 7)
4, 5	F	Fractions denominator mode (DENANY =0, DENFAC =1, DENFIX =2)
6 ... 19	F	DENMAX (14 bits for 0 ... 9998; 9999 is stored as 0)

Bits	Type	Contents
20	F	Clear for PROFRC, set for IMPFRC
21	F	Clear if fraction mode is off
22, 23	D	Decimal display mode (ALL =0, FIX =1, SCI =2, ENG =3)
24 … 27	D	Number of decimals (4 bits for 0 … 11)
28	D	Clear for SCIOVR, set for ENGOVR
29	D	Clear for RDX. – set for RDX,
30	D	Clear if TSON
31	I	Clear if SEPON
32	I	Set if an integer mode is on
33	I	Clear if LZOFF
34, 35	I	Integer sign mode (2COMPL =0, 1COMPL =1, UNSIGN =2, SIGNMT =3)
36 … 39	I	Integer base (4 bits for 2 … 16 coded as 1 … 15)
40 … 45	I	WSIZE (6 bits for 1 … 64 coded as 1 … 63, 0)
46	D	Clear if DBLOFF
47	D	Time format (24h =0, 12h =1)
48, 49	G	Print mode (0 … 3, see ☐MODE)
50		Not used yet
51	G	*Stack* size (SSIZE4 =0, SSIZE8 =1)
52, 53	D	Date format (D.MY =0, Y.MD =1, M.DY =2)
54, 55	D	Angular mode (DEG =0 ,RAD =1, GRAD =2)
56 … 58	D	Curve fit model (LINF =0, EXPF =1, POWERF =2, LOGF =3, BESTF =4)
59	G	Clear for FAST, set for SLOW (always clear on the emulator)
60 … 62	D	Rounding mode (0 … 7, see RM)
63	D	Clear for JG1782, set for JG1582

Commands for Advanced Users

There are several combinations with the (EXIT) (or (ON)) key used on your *WP 34S*: (+) and (−) for display contrast setting, (STO) and (RCL) for saving and loading from FM. Three combinations were not yet documented above:

(ON) + (C) tells the system a quartz <u>c</u>rystal is installed for an accurate real time clock. Find more about this **hardware modification** on pp. 359ff. The quartz crystal is an inevitable prerequisite for the clock being useful in medium to long range (see DATE, TIME, STOPW, SETDAT, SETTIM), and it is required for print operations as well. After pressing (ON) + (C), your *WP 34S* asks `Crystal? InStALLEd` – keep (ON) held down and press (C) a second time to activate the crystal. (ON) + (C) will work only with the crystal not activated yet.

(ON) + (C) should be only necessary if you have loaded the file `calc.bin` or `calc_full.bin`, while the other files enable the crystal automatically.

> **WARNING:** If the crystal is <u>not</u> installed, the system will hang if (ON) + (C) + (C) is entered or if a firmware is booted requiring the crystal, and a hard reset (actuating the **RESET** button) or a battery pull will be required! Both will erase all your data in *RAM*.
>
> Lack of the *IR* diode required for printing cannot cause a system hang since it cannot be checked automatically.
>
> See pp. 359ff for installation instructions for the quartz crystal and / or the *IR* diode.

(ON) + (D) toggles <u>d</u>ebugging mode, echoed by `Debug ON` or `Debug OFF`. The small = annunciator is also lit for debug mode set.

> ☞ Your *WP 34S* will not shut down automatically in this mode. (ON) + (D) is used in the updating procedure on p. 294 (followed by (ON) + (S)) but was not explained there.

(ON) + (S) stands for *My<u>S</u>amBa*: the system asks `SAM−BA? boot` – keep (ON) held down and press (S) a second time to clear the GPNVM1 bit and turn the calculator off. This will work in debugging mode only (see above) to prevent accidental access to this potentially dangerous feature.   It is used in the updating procedure on p. 294 but was not explained there.

WARNING: After issuing ⟨ON⟩ + ⟨S⟩, you can only boot in *MySamBa* boot mode! Without the *MySamBa* software and a proper cable (as mentioned on p. 285ff), you are lost!

Double Precision (*DP*) Calculations and Mode Switching

Your *WP 34S* starts in *SP* mode per default, wherein 16 digit precision is reached in all calculations. Switching between *SP* and integer modes was discussed on pp. 305ff. Additionally, you may use your *WP 34S* in *DP* mode. Each *DP* register will contain sixteen *bytes* instead of eight, allowing for 34 digits instead of 16 (see below).

 Matrix commands will not work in *DP*.

 DP <u>allows for</u> more precise calculations. While some computations will reach high accuracy, **we do not warrant 34 digit precision in all calculations in *DP* mode.** [161]

The following figure illustrates what happens in memory in transitions between *SP* and *DP* modes, assuming startup in *SP* mode with REGS **16**. *RRA* stands for *'relative register address'*.

---

[161] Not all functions are expanded to *DP*, some stay in *SP* or merely a little bit more.

The *WP 34S* software is based on the decNumber library supporting arbitrary precision *BCD* numbers. As mentioned at some places in the *IOP*, internal computations are carried out with 39 digits. Actually this is the minimum, some modulo calculations are performed with a few hundreds of digits to avoid cancellation (e.g. 2π features 451 digits for proper reduction to the standard range for trigonometric functions).

More elaborate algorithms are coded as *DP* keystroke programs to save flash space (for the cost of execution speed and the loss of a few digits of accuracy in *DP* mode). The internal formats used for storing numbers in your *WP 34S* (as shown on pp. 274ff for *SP* and below for *DP*) need to be converted back and forth from and to the decNumber format. This is a lot of overhead and doesn't come for free in terms of execution speed.

There is a quasi standard to find out about processors and test accuracy of calculators to some extent – compute $arcsin\{arccos[arctan(tan\{cos[sin(9°)]\})]\}$. An ideal calculator would return exactly 9 without cheating. Real calculators (all computing with a finite number of digits) differ. Your *WP 34s* returns

- 9.000 000 000 029 361 = $9 + 3 \cdot 10^{-11}$ in *SP* and
- 8.999 999 999 999 999 999 999 999 937 535 = $9 - 6 \cdot 10^{-29}$ in *DP*.

If you are interested in the results of other calculators in that test, too, look at *http://www.rskey.org/~mwsebastian/miscprj/results.htm*.
Another simple test discussed recently in the internet: Enter 1.000 000 1 and then execute x^2 just 27 times. Your *WP 34s* returns

- 674 530.470 539 687 4 in *SP* and
- 674 530.470 741 084 559 382 689 *184 727 772 2* in *DP*.

The latter is the most precise result known of a pocket calculator so far. Nevertheless, its last 9 digits deviate from the truth here. Take these results into account when assessing small systematic deviations or many decimals.

Absolute address	Startup memory allocation Contents	RRA	After executing DBLON Contents	RRA	Then after DBLOFF Contents	RRA
X+11	k = 1.4	R111	1.4	K = R111	1.4	R111
X+10	...	R110			...	R110
...			...	...		
...	...	...	...	...	...	...
X+1	y = -33.8	R101		C = R106	-33.8	R101
X	x = 123.0	R100	...		123.0	R100
X-1	r15 = -43.6	R15		B = R105	0.0	R15
X-2	r14 = 167.9	R14	...		0.0	R14
X-3	...	R13		A = R104	0.0	R13
X-4	...	R12	...		0.0	R12
X-5	...	R11		T = R103	0.0	R11
X-6	...	R10	...		0.0	R10
X-7	...	R09		Z = R102	0.0	R09
X-8	...	R08	...		0.0	R08
X-9	...	R07	-33.8	Y = R101	0.0	R07
X-10	...	R06			0.0	R06
X-11	...	R05	123.0	X = R100	0.0	R05
X-12	r04 = -2.9	R04			0.0	R04
X-13	r03 = -1234.89	R03	-1.95E184	R01	-1234.89	R03
X-14	r02 = 5.43E-396	R02			5.43E-396	R02
X-15	r01 = 6.6	R01	1.03E182	R00	6.6	R01
X-16	r00 = 0.54	R00			0.54	R00
X-17						

Going from *SP* to *DP* mode via DBLON, the contents of the twelve special registers **X ... K** are copied, cutting 48 *bytes* into the former *SP* numbered register sector. So the top twelve numbered *SP* registers will be <u>lost</u> in such a transition. All other memory contents stay where and as they were – just each *DP RRA* covers what two *SP* registers were before. The space allocated for summation registers will not change in such transitions (cf. footnote 151 on p. 301).

Starting with the default memory configuration and executing DBLON then will leave you with 44 *DP* registers. Executing REGS with an argument >44 in *DP* is legal, but the sector of global numbered registers will then cut into the former program sector.

Returning from *DP* to *SP* mode, the lettered registers are copied again. Everything else stays where and as it was, if you used ≤ 44 *DP* registers – just each *SP RRA* points to only one half of a former *DP* register; and the memory released by the shrinking special registers allows for adding (or returning) twelve numbered registers on top, each now containing zero. With >44 *DP* registers, the correspondence becomes more complicated – the number of global registers will never, however, exceed 112.

For the following table, assume startup in BASE **10**, WSIZE **32**, REGS **16**. Now see the contents of **J**, **K**, and the lowest numbered registers, <u>checked by recalling</u> them to **X**:

	J	K	R00	R01	R02	R03
Starts with e.g.	3.504 ^{d}	14 ^{d}	54 ^{d}	66 ^{d}	543 ^{d}	$126,441$ ^{d}
DECM	3.43^{-395}	1.40^{-397}	5.40^{-397}	6.60^{-397}	5.43^{-396}	1.23^{-393}
DBLON 162	3.43^{-395}	1.40^{-397}	1.03^{-HIG}	1.95^{-HIG}	n/a	n/a

---

[162] *DP* mode reals are stored coarsely following *decimal128* packed coding, though with some exceptions. The lowest 110 bits take the rightmost 33 digits of the *significand*. Going left, a 12 bit exponent field follows, then 5 bits used and coded exactly as in *SP*, and finally the sign bit. The greatest value of the stored exponent is $10\ 1111\ 1111\ 1111_2 = 12287_{10}$. For reasons like the ones explained for *SP*, 6176 must be subtracted from this value to get the true exponent of the floating point number represented. Thus, *DP* supports 34-digit numbers within $10^{-6143} \le |x| < 10^{+6145}$. Coding works in full analogy to the way described for *SP* in *App. B*.

Even smaller numbers may be entered using a decimal mantissa, but you will lose one digit per factor of 10. The same happens if you divide 10^{-6143} by 10 several times. At 10^{-6176}, only one digit will be left, stored as hexadecimal 1. Divide it by 1.999 999 999 99 and the result will remain 10^{-6176}. Divide it by 2 instead and the result will become zero.

Numbers beyond the interval $10^{-999} \le |x| < 10^{+1000}$ will be displayed with $-HIG$ or HIG in their exponent, respectively. Only ◀ will show you the true exponent of them. This way *r00* = 1.032 000 000 000 000 054 E-6155 and *r01* = 1.951 656 000 000 000 000 000 543 E-6152 are found here.

Returning to *SP* with numbers in lettered registers exceeding the *SP* number range will cause 0 or $Infinity$ being displayed instead.

	J	K	R00	R01	R02	R03
sRCL ...	140^{-397}	128^{-23}	540^{-397}	660^{-397}	543^{-396}	123^{-393}
iRCL ...	1400	0.00	5400	6600	543.00	$126.44\ 1.00$
DBLOFF	343^{-395}	140^{-397}	540^{-397}	660^{-397}	543^{-396}	123^{-393}
dRCL ...	Out of range Error	Out of range Error	0.00	0.00	n/a	n/a
DBLON	343^{-395}	140^{-397}	103^{-HIG}	195^{-HIG}	n/a	n/a
RCL **J**, STO **J**, **123E456** STO **0**, sRCL ...	140^{-397}	128^{-23}	123^{-396}	512^{-30}	543^{-396}	123^{-393}
iRCL ...	1400	0.00	123.00	0.00	543.00	$126.44\ 1.00$
DBLOFF	343^{-395}	140^{-397}	123^{-396}	512^{-30}	543^{-396}	123^{-393}
dRCL ...	Out of range Error	Out of range Error	$+\infty$ Error	0.00	n/a	n/a

Note iRCL and sRCL keep working as explained on p. 305.

In *DP* mode, ◀ shows the first (most significant) 16 digits of the 34-digit mantissa of *x* and its <u>four</u> digit exponent, and ▶ displays the 18 trailing digits, both as *temporary messages* (compare p. 80 for *SP*).

For example, π ◀ returns here

> 3.141,592
> ,653,589,793 0 BEG 360 000

, and ▶ returns

> ...238,462
> 643,383,279,503 BEG 360

.

Remember not every return may be as precise as this one. And errors accumulate as explained in the footnote on p. 261.

As mentioned above, some calculations are executed in "*internal high precision*" even if *SP* is set. "*Internal high precision*" means even more digits than *DP* – it may go up to some hundred digits in special cases.

 Rounding mode settings (see RM) may affect the results of such calculations!

Further Commands Used in Library and *XROM Routines*

The operations listed below are used by the programmers of *XROM routines*. They ease their work by allowing some more comfort in writing programs than the original function set.

These commands and pseudo-commands are explained here to foster understanding of those routines, but they are not accessible through any *catalog*. The assembler (often already its preprocessor) will translate most of them into proper program steps employing the commands documented above. See the *User Guide* (at *http://sourceforge.net/p/wp34s/code/HEAD/tree/doc/WP34s Assembler Tool Suite.pdf*) for additional information.

(Pseudo-) Command	*XROM* or *LIB*	Function
A..D→	*XROM*	saves a, b, c, and d in a volatile temporary storage. Volatile means it will vanish some 500*ms* after last keystroke.
GSB *longlabel*	Both	allows for calling long alphabetic labels. [163] The assembler translates GSB into BSRB or BSRF (see p. 358) – or into XEQ (via a jump table in *XROM* or via a label in *LIB*) if the distance is too far.

---

[163] Long alphabetic labels (looking like *longlabel*::) may exceed six characters. They may show up anywhere in code written for the assembler but will be resolved at assembly time.

ATTENTION: Note that STOP and PROMPT will not work in *XROM* on your *WP 34S*. And there are no LBL nor END statements in *XROM* code.

(Pseudo-) Command	*XROM* or *LIB*	Function
JMP ***longlabel***	Both	allows for branching to long alphabetic labels. The assembler translates JMP into BACK or SKIP – or GTO (via a jump table in *XROM* or via a label in *LIB*) if the distance is too far.
Num ***sn***	*XROM*	with ***sn*** = 0, π, √2π, ... inserts the corresponding number. Compare _INT.
POPUSR	*XROM*	must follow immediately after XEQUSR to restore the *XROM* execution state (registers, flags, and return addresses) correctly.
XEQ ***label***	*XROM*	calls the <u>user</u> routine carrying the global label specified (there are no LBL statements in *XROM*). See also xIN.
XEQUSR	*XROM*	fills the *stack* with x and calls the user routine containing the function to be solved, integrated, summed, multiplied, or derived, respectively. The label of this function is transmitted as a parameter of the corresponding user command (i.e. SLV, ∫, Σ, Π, f', or f"). See POPUSR.
xIN ***type***	*XROM*	with ***type*** = NILADIC, MONADIC, DYADIC, TRIADIC, or ..._COMPLEX defines how many *stack* levels are used for parameter input to the function under consideration. Furthermore it does some initialization work (e.g. SSIZE8 and DBLON). xIN is the recommended way to start an *XROM* *routine*. Thereafter, SSIZE4 is legal but DBLOFF is not. **Note xIN cannot nest** and *XROM* *routines* using xIN cannot call user code.
XLBL"***label***"	*XROM*	defines the eXternal LaBeL of this routine. XLBL doesn't generate any code, it provides an entry point that the *C* function tables can take advantage of. Typically, ***label*** equals the corresponding command name – it may exceed six characters, however.

(Pseudo-) Command	*XROM* or *LIB*	Function
xOUT *way*	*XROM*	cleans and reverts the settings of xIN, taking care of a proper return including the correct setting of *I* and the *stack*. Typically, *way* = xOUT_NORMAL. Generally, xOUT shall be the last command of an *XROM routine*.
_INT *n*	*XROM*	inserts the corresponding integer like the command # does (see p. 240). Allows also for numbers calculated at assembly time, however. Compare NUM.
"*text*"	Both	The double quotes allow for convenient entry of text strings. The assembler translates the string into the amount of α-statements required.
→A..D	*XROM*	recalls *a*, *b*, *c*, and *d* from their temporary storage (very short range, see A..D→ above).
# *name*	*LIB*	with *name* = ɑ ... inserts the constant carrying that name like recalling it from <u>CONST</u> would do. Extends the command # (see p. 240).
#define *name* *value*	*XROM*	allow for using named variables in such a routine for easier reading. The *name* may exceed six characters. Each #define must be closed by a matching #undef.
#undef *name*	*XROM*	

Furthermore, there are several 'alias' spellings to ease input of some commands or even of individual nonstandard characters on an English computer keyboard. E.g. the Greek letter 'ɑ' is often replaced by a Latin 'a', the print character ᗺ by 'P.' etc. Again, the assembler will take care of translating the aliases.

See the file 8queens_alias.wp34s (or other files of type ...alias.wp34s in 'library' directory) for examples. Command-Aliases.pdf in 'doc' contains a list of all aliases used (some 50 pages).

Assembler Output

The Assembler takes your .wp34s text file as input and generates optimized code for your *WP 34S*. It does <u>not</u> generate optimized code for your further editing nor maintaining your routines. "Optimized" means it will use as little of the limited resources of your *WP 34S* in the programs as possible, less labels in particular. Thus expect heavy use of BACK and SKIP instead of GTO in assembled programs since all required information for this conversion is available at assembly time.

Furthermore, there are two special commands frequently replacing GSB / XEQ in assembled code:

1. BSRB **n** calls a subroutine starting **n** steps backwards with $0 \le n \le 255$. It pushes the program counter on the *SRS* and executes BACK **n** then.

2. BSRF **n** calls a subroutine starting **n** steps forwards. It pushes the program counter on the *SRS* and executes SKIP **n** then.

The subroutines called this way do not require a starting label. So, BSRB and BSRF are useful if you are short on local labels – as BACK, SKIP, and CASE are. On the other hand, if you edit a section of your routine that is crossed by one or more BSRB, BSRF, BACK, SKIP, or CASE jumps, this may well result in a need to manually maintain all those statements individually. We recommend editing unassembled code and leaving the generation of label-less branches to the assembler for sake of readability, maintainability, and reliability of your routines.

Basic Electrical Hardware Specifications of the *HP-20b* and *-30b*

Power supply: $3V$ (2 *CR2032* coin cells)

Processor: *Atmel AT91SAM7L128*
- *ARM 7* core with thumb mode ($32kHz$ to $40MHz$)
- *RAM*: $2kB$ with backup, $4kB$ volatile (see p. 298)
- *ROM*: $128kB$ flash, *SAM-BA* boot loader
- *I/O*: parallel ports, serial port for flashing (see the picture below for pinout)
- *LCD* controller (see *LCD* specifications below)

- Elaborate power management
- Multiple clock sources (RC, quartz, PLL), real time clock

Liquid crystal display with 400 segments (cf. p. 71):
- 12 x 9 segments (mantissa), 3 x 7 segments (exponent), 2 signs,
- 6 x 43 pixels in a dot matrix,
- 10 annunciators and 1 additional fixed symbol.

Keyboard with 37 keys in 5 to 6 columns by 7 rows

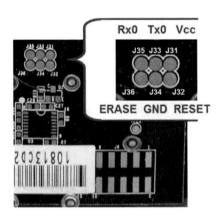

The six-pad serial port of the calculator is located under the battery door. For those who want to connect to it directly, its pitch is $2mm$, and this picture shows the pinout. It is identical in both calculator models (*HP-20b* and *HP-30b*). Voltage level is $0...3V$. The picture is of the printed circuit board uncovered, the RESET button is north of the six pads (pressing this button is equivalent to shorting the RESET and GND pads).

There is an additional *JTAG* connector at the southern end of the main board (not accessible from outside), partially covered by a tag here.

Tuning the Hardware of Your *WP 34S*

As mentioned at the very beginning of this manual, there are three optional hardware modifications you may benefit from. For the connecting cable, only modification C as outlined on p. 287 will work nowadays generally, modification B will only work if you get the board.

Please read the following descriptions and decide what you are interested in. Then read the complete instructions for these cases before actually starting the modification – this is to prevent you will end with your *WP 34S* half usable. These are the opportunities:

1. Create an accurate **real-time clock** by adding a quartz crystal and two capacitors on the main board of your *WP 34S*. This modification

requires some fine soldering skills due to the size of the capacitors – they are *SMD* components and significantly smaller than a grain of rice! Beyond fixing these two properly at the correct location, this modification is an easy job.

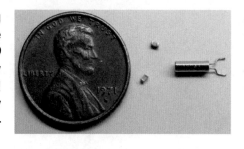

2. Establish an *IR* **line for printing** on an HP-82240A/B by adding an *IR* diode and a resistor to the package after modification 1. Electrically, this part is significantly easier than the job above. There is some additional mechanical work: drilling a little hole in the plastic case, requiring a slow hand and a correct drilling bit. The complete job is also described in the file mentioned above.

3. For the connecting hardware required for **flashing and data exchange**, there are several opportunities as outlined in *App. A*. You will need some soldering skills here as well (not as fine as for modification 1 above, but close). And mechanical skills are required, too, since an extra gap in the calculator case for the jack is needed.

Modification B:

With the necessary material available, start:

a. **Open your calculator (the easy part).**
   Tools needed: Small Phillips screwdriver, wooden toothpick.

   Procedure:

   - Remove the battery cover by sliding it open.
   - Remove the two coin cells using the toothpick.
   - Remove the three screws you see. Two more are hidden under each end of the bottom rubber foot – remove these screws, too.

b. **Open your calculator (the harder part).**
   Tool needed: Swiss Army knife, old credit card, or similar.

   Helpful information: The shiny silver front part of the *HP-30b* is clipped into the grey frame. There are three clips at each side, two at the top, and one at the bottom. See the picture of an opened frame:

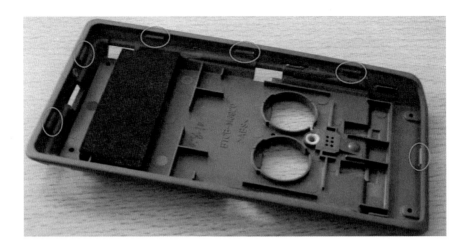

Procedure:

- Carefully insert the big blade of the knife between front part and frame near the center of one side. Force the shiny part up.

- Repeat on the opposite side.

- Move the blade toward the calculator top. Gently force the shiny part up on both sides. Think of the *LCD*, so be careful here!

- Insert the blade between front part and frame at calculator top. Gently force the shiny part up. The top of the shiny part should be loose now.

- Finally, get the bottom part loose the same way.

- Turn the shiny part over (printed circuit board up) and lay it on your desk. Put the grey frame aside.

c. **Prepare the mount for the *USB* board.**
Tool needed: Swiss Army knife or another small knife with a sharp thin blade.

Procedure:

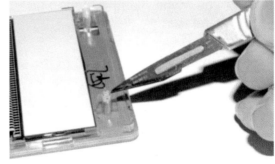

Cut away the plastic supports of the top right screw post and of the *LCD* frame in that area.

The picture overleaf shows how it

shall look when you are done – this post is cylindrical now.

d. Mount the *USB* board.

Material needed: Arbitrary plastic glue, e.g. *UHU*.

Procedure:

Fix the board around said post, left to "h.pott", and below the terminal end. Then lay the assembly aside for drying.

e. Make the opening for the *USB* plug.

Tool needed: Small square file.

Procedure:

- Take the grey frame and lay it on the desk bottom up, rubber foot pointing to you. Then you need to extend the opening top right.

- Take measures looking at the mounted USB board. The pictures show how the frame shall look when you are done. Remember the battery door will cover the lower part of the frame (i.e. the upper part on these pictures here).

f. Connect the *USB* board to the *IR* diode.

Tool needed: Soldering iron (its tip shall not significantly exceed the size of the smallest terminal you want to solder, power < 30W recommended).

Material needed: Solder.

Procedure:

- Heat up the soldering iron.

- Look for a decent place where the diode may peek through the grey frame. Stay away from the clips.

- Turn the diode so its longer leg will be at right. Bend that leg so it will reach terminal 1 (see the picture). Bend the shorter leg so it will reach terminal 2. Cut the legs at proper length. Both legs must not contact each other.

- Apply a tiny bit of solder on terminal 1. Do the same for terminal 2 and for the ends of both legs of the diode.

- Solder the formerly longer diode leg to terminal 1. Solder the other one to terminal 2.

g. Connect the *USB* board to the main board.

Tool needed: Soldering iron as for step f.

Material needed: Isolated wire (diameter about $0.3mm$ to be easily laid out), solder.

Procedure:

As pictured overleaf, there are six connections between both boards and one more on the main board.

- First, however, two components must be removed from the main board:

  1. Remove LB1. Since you are going to discard it anyway, put the tip of the heated soldering iron with a bit of solder on both terminals of component LB1 and heat it up. After a while, the solder below LB1 shall melt, so LB1 can be moved easily. It may even stick to the tip of the soldering iron and may be lifted this way.

  2. Remove LB2 the same way.

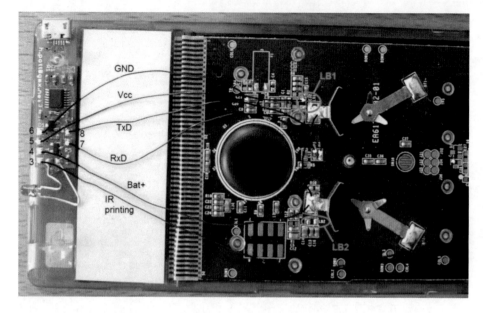

- Connect the terminals as listed in the picture, i.e. number
    - **3** (IR printing) to upper terminal of R18,
    - **4** (Bat+) to the big upper battery terminal,
    - **5** (Vcc) to the right terminal of LB1,
    - **6** (GND) to the top end of C21,
    - **7** (RxD) to either end of jumper JP5,
    - **8** (TxD) to either end of jumper JP6,
    - and connect both big upper battery terminals.

  For each connection, cut a piece of wire (some $150mm$). Skin its first $2mm$, put some solder on it, put some solder on the respective terminals on either board, and solder one end to the terminal on the *USB* board. Then determine the necessary length for an easy connection, cut the wire to proper length, skin its last $2mm$, and put some solder on it. Solder this end to the terminal on the main board. Finally, check the proper connection using an Ohmmeter (test voltage = some $1.5V$).[164]

---

[164] Since the electronic components are small and densely packed on these boards, there is a fair chance of producing solder bridges – thoroughly check and remove where you produced them. Also take care that you do not heat any mounted component to an extent where it will start moving away. Soldering on the main board requires a slow hand, good eyesight, and a bit of experience.

h. If not in place yet: Install the additional components for an accurate real-time clock.

Tools needed: Soldering iron as for step f, wooden toothpick for holding components.

Material needed: Two $18pF$ 0603 capacitors, one $32.768kHz$ quartz crystal, solder.

Procedure:

Check top right of the main board. If the quartz crystal Y1 and the two capacitors C3 and C4 next to it are not installed yet, you can do that now. This is not mandatory for operating your WP 34S, but will help in communication (cf. p. 317). Installation is inevitably required, however, for using the full set of print, time, and date commands including the stopwatch.

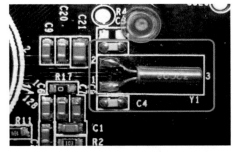

See the picture here for comparison and the file mentioned at point 1 above (on p. 359) for parts specifications and work instructions. There is also a video available (at *http://youtu.be/diJA2cCQenl*) showing *Eric Rechlin* doing this modification and installing the overlay mentioned on pp. 291ff – all in admirable speed and precision.

Soldering these tiny SMD capacitors is a challenge for the common man. Alternatively, you may use wired capacitors: the result may not look half as professional but it is far easier achieved and does the job as well. For precision timing, a trimming capacitor may replace one of the two fixed ones (here, a $6pF$ fixed ceramic and a 2.8-$20pF$ variable capacitor were put in).

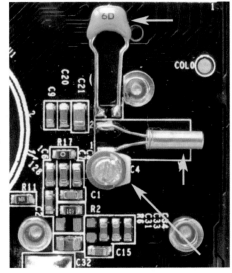

Remember to activate the crystal when the tuning is completed (see p. 349).

i. Drill the hole for the *IR* diode.

Tool needed: Drill bit matching the size of the diode (but also any other tool making decent round holes of suitable size may do as long as you proceed slowly).

Procedure:

Hold the grey frame over the mounted diode to learn the location where to drill the hole. Its center shall be about 5mm away from the edge of the frame. Drill the hole there.

j. Optional: Drill the holes for the battery safety bolts.

Tools and material needed: Two safety bolts like M1.7x3.5, featuring flat cylindrical heads 0.5mm high and 5mm in diameter (cf. the picture on p. 343). Significantly higher heads will collide with the battery door. If (and only if) you manage getting similar bolts, the following procedure will make sense. You will need a 1mm drill bit precisely centered in a light drilling machine then.

Procedure:

Turn the grey frame upside down. Point the tip of the small drill bit to the center of the circular recession south of the battery hole – 1.5mm from its edge. Drill carefully so the bit survives. Repeat for the second hole. Then turn in the safety bolts under adequate pressure so they cut their threads themselves.

k. Reassemble.

Tool needed: Small Phillips screwdriver.

Procedure:

- Check your shiny setup will properly fit. Then insert it in the grey frame with the diode pointing in its hole. Press to click into place (best do top and bottom first – do not press on the *LCD* window nor apply exaggerated force!).

- Turn in the five screws.

- Return the coin cells.

- Close the battery door – the calculator is done!

l. Connect your calculator to a *USB* port of your computer.

Material needed: Micro *USB* cable.

Procedure:

- Plug in the cable in your calculator. Depending on the shape of the plug, a little cutting may be required on the plastic part of the plug to allow for proper insertion.

- Turn on your calculator.

- Connect it to your computer. If you did everything right, the operating system of your PC will automatically start searching for a driver on connection. Most probably it will not find any. Get the newest drivers for your operating system from FTDI for free – look here: *http://www.ftdichip.com/Drivers/VCP.htm* . After driver installation, your calculator will show up in the Device Manager as a '*FT230X USB Half UART*' when connected, and a COM port will be allocated. You will need this COM port for flashing.

- Now you are prepared for easy flashing and updating as described in *App. A* on pp. 287ff.

Modification C:

If you like audio devices, here is a way to connect with a 2.5mm headphone jack for serial communication. The description starting overleaf includes also modifications 1 and 2. It is based on material supplied by *Alexander Oestert*, *Barry Mead*, and *Marcus*. Here is *Barry's* bill of materials as of 1/31/2015 for building a new *WP 34S*:

Part	#	Cost / US$	Part ID	Source
18 pF Ceramic Capacitor	2	0.20	311-1415-1-ND	[165]
32768 Hz Crystal SMT	1	0.69	695-CMR200TB-327K-U	[166]
2.5 mm Audio Headphone Jack SMT	1	1.26	CP-2523SJCT-ND	[167]
HP-30B Calculator	1	12.95	HP-30B	[168]
Vinyl Overlay (Stickers)	1	6.00	Vinyl Overlay	[169]
USB to 3.5mm Serial Cable	1	20.00	768-1098-ND	[170]
2.5mm to 3.5mm Male to Female Adapter	1	1.89	121361322364	[171]
Total Parts Cost		**42.99**		

Note this is excl. modification 2 and excl. shipping from the different sources employed. It may be wise to order two more SMT capacitors, because they tend getting lost easily. For comparison, see *Alexander's* bill of materials as of 17.6.2012 for executing modifications 1 and 2 on an already existing *WP 34S* (also excl. shipping):

Part	#	Cost / €	Part ID (Bestellnr.[172])
KERKO Chip 0603 NP0 18pF 5% 50V	2	0,20	445644
Quarz MH32768C	1	0,79	156007
IR-LED 3mm Typ L-934F3C	1	0,37	154394
Widerstand Kohle 0,25W 5% 390R BF 0207	1	0,10	403202

With the necessary material available, start:

---

[165] *http://www.digikey.com/product-detail/en/CC0402JRNPO9BN180/311-1415-1-ND/2833721*

[166] *http://www.mouser.com/Search/ProductDetail.aspx?R=CMR200T-32.768KDZF-UTvirtualkey69500000virtualkey695-CMR200TB-327K-U*

[167] *http://www.digikey.com/product-detail/en/SJ-2523-SMT-TR/CP-2523SJCT-ND/669702*

[168] *http://www.ebay.com/itm/like/221617390125?lpid=82&chn=ps*

[169] *http://commerce.hpcalc.org/overlay.php*

[170] *http://www.digikey.com/product-search/en?KeyWords=TTL-232R-3V3-AJ&WT.z_header=search_go*

[171] *http://www.ebay.com/itm/2-5mm-Male-to-3-5mm-Female-Headset-Headphone-Stereo-Adapter-Converter-/121361322364*

[172] All parts purchased at *www.conrad.de* .

a. **Open your calculator (the easy part).** See p. 360. See p. 360.

b. **Open your calculator (the harder part).** See p. 360.

c. **Prepare the seat for the headphone jack.**

Tool needed: Swiss Army knife or another small knife with a sharp thin blade.

Procedure:

- Decide where the jack shall be mounted. Mind that you must make a hole in the grey frame of your calculator there. There is space for it at the top of your calculator.
- If you want to put it top left or right, you may have to cut away one clear plastic mounting strut of the calculator to make room for the jack (cf. the picture overleaf). Alternatively, you can mount the jack in the center of the calculator along the top edge – no cutting required then. Compare also the pictures at step **e** on next page.

d. **Connect the jack to the main board.**

Tool needed: Soldering iron (its tip shall not significantly exceed the size of the smallest terminal you want to solder, power $< 30W$ recommended).

Material needed: Isolated wire (diameter about $0.3mm$ to be easily laid out), solder.

Procedure:

As pictured overleaf, there are three connections between the jack and the main board.

1. Tip (cable TX) goes to either end of JP5 (calculator RX). [173]
2. Ring (cable RX) goes to either end of JP6 (calculator TX).
3. Sleeve (ground) goes to battery minus (calculator ground).

For each connection, cut a piece of wire (some $150mm$). Skin its first $2mm$, put some solder on it, put some solder on the respective terminals of the jack, and solder one end to said terminal. Then determine the necessary length for an easy

---

[173] JP5 and JP6 are jumpers, i.e. 0Ω resistors.

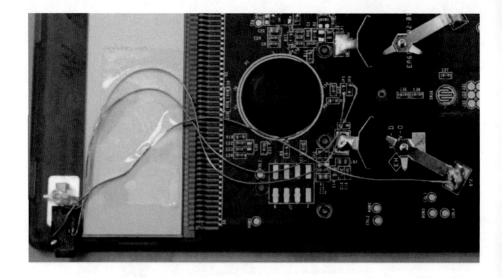

connection, cut the wire to proper length, skin its last $2mm$, and put some solder on it. Solder this end to the terminal on the main board. Finally, check the proper connection using an Ohmmeter (test voltage = some $1.5V$). See also the footnote on p. 364.

e. Make an opening for the headphone plug and mount the jack.

Tool needed: Small square or round file.

Material needed: Arbitrary plastic glue, e.g. *UHU*.

Procedure:

- Take the grey frame and lay it on the desk bottom up, rubber foot pointing to you.

- Take measures looking at the mounted jack. Take into account there must be sufficient clearance for the plug. The pictures here and overleaf show the look of two assemblies when you are almost done with step **e** (though you may be a  better precision mechanic). Remember the battery door will cover the lower part of the frame (i.e. the upper part on these pictures here).

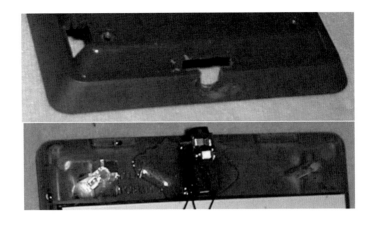

f. If not in place yet: Install the additional components for an accurate real-time clock (cf. mod. 1 above). See p. 365.

g. If not in place yet: Install the additional components required for IR communication to the printer (cf. mod. 2 above).

Tools needed: Soldering iron as for step **d**. Drill bit matching the diameter of the diode (but also any other tool making decent round holes of suitable size may do if you act carefully).

Materials needed: Isolated wire (e.g. as for step **d**), *IR* diode, 390Ω resistor, solder.

Procedure:

- Heat up the soldering iron.

- Look for a decent place where the diode shall peek through the grey frame. Its center shall be about 5mm away from the edge of the frame and min. 10mm from the headphone jack. Stay away from the clips. Drill the hole there.

- Turn the diode so its longer leg (anode) will be at right. You may cut the legs but remember the orientation. Solder the resistor to the anode.

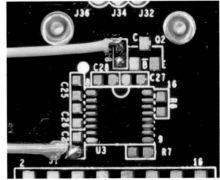

- Apply a tiny bit of solder on pads R18 and C29 (see picture). Do the same for the free ends of both the resistor and the cathode leg of the diode.

- Connect the free end of the resistor to R18 and the cathode leg to C29. You will need the wire for that – proceed as outlined in step **d**.

h. **Optional: Drill holes for the battery safety bolts.** See p. 366.

i. **Reassemble.** See p. 367.

j. **Get or make a custom cable.**

   Material needed: USB cable with male headphone output. Compare step **d** for the connections if you make it yourself.

k. **Connect your calculator to a USB port of your computer.**

   Material needed: Custom cable.

   Procedure: See p. 367.

There is one advantage to this headphone connector over the USB connector (alternative B above): If you have two or more calculators built this way, you can use a 2.5mm crossover cable to transfer programs and data directly from one calculator to the other without a computer.

Loading Previous Software Versions

As mentioned in *App. A* on pp. 285ff, you may download binary calculator files individually. Usually, the most recent build of such a file will be optimum since it represents the state of the art – all the bells and whistles are included and all known bugs are erased.

Sometimes, however, choosing an older build may fill your needs better – e.g. if you got your *WP 34S* early and have the edition v2 of the keyboard overlay attached to it. That overlay looks as shown on p. 244 (look below the EXIT key, for example). It works up to version 2.2 of the firmware. If you wish to update your *WP 34S* to the very latest edition available for version v2.2, download *http://sourceforge.net/p/wp34s/code/3000/tree/branches/V2.2/realbuild/calc.bin* .

If, on the other hand, you have got v3.x already running on your *WP 34S* and want to flash another build of version 3 (but not the latest one) for any reason whatsoever – let us assume build 3333 – then download *http://sourceforge.net/p/wp34s/code/3333/tree/trunk/realbuild/calc.bin*. You will see this directory containing all binary files `cal....bin` you learned about on pp. 285f above, having a build number ≤ 3333.

After downloading, the remaining flashing procedure runs exactly as described in *App. A* on pp. 287ff.

If you want to run a particular build on your emulator, download *http://sourceforge.net/p/wp34s/code/3333/tree/trunk/windows/bin/wp34sgui.exe* instead.

 Note you shall replace 3333 in the address field of your web browser with the build number you are interested in. Check the *Release Notes* (on pp. 400ff) to learn about the features you will get when you load a particular firmware version.

APPENDIX I: ADVANCED MATHEMATICAL FUNCTIONS IMPLEMENTED

Your *WP 34S* contains several operations covering advanced mathematics implemented for the first time on an *RPN* calculator. All of them work in DECM. Find those functions collected here and described in more detail than in the *IOP*, together with a few traditional pocket calculator functions matching the topic.

As mentioned in *Section 1* of this manual, we assume you are able to read and understand mathematical formulas for real domain functions. Wherever complex numbers may be valid input or output, be sure you understand the respective basic mathematical concepts (at minimum as outlined on pp. 123ff); else leave these functions aside. By experience, it is only beneficial to use something you overview and know the background of – otherwise it may even become dangerous for you and your fellow men. [174]

Numbers

The following are all *monadic* functions unless specified otherwise.

Name	Remarks (see pp. 171ff for general information)
B_n	B_n returns the Bernoulli number for an integer $n > 0$ given in **X**: $$B_n = (-1)^{n+1} n \cdot \zeta(1-n)$$
$B_n{}^*$	$B_n{}^*$ works with the old definition instead: $B_n^* = \dfrac{2 \cdot (2n)!}{(2\pi)^{2n}} \cdot \zeta(2n)$. See pp. 389ff for $\zeta(x)$.

---

[174] As mentioned in the main text, we sincerely recommend you look deeply into textbooks to ensure you fully understand what you are going to do with the functions provided in your *WP 34S*. The real world is full of sad examples where people full of good will caused extensive damage by applying tools they did not know sufficiently. "*Wenn Dumme fleißig werden, wird's gefährlich!*" (i.e. "*It's getting dangerous with dumb folks becoming busy!*"), a former boss of mine used to say.

Name	Remarks (see pp. 171ff for general information)
COMB, PERM	For $y \geq x \geq 0$ in real domain, the number of *permutations* is $P_{y,x} = \dfrac{y!}{(y-x)!} = \dfrac{\Gamma(y+1)}{\Gamma(y-x+1)}$, while the number of *combinations* is $C_{y,x} = \dbinom{y}{x} = \dfrac{P_{y,x}}{x!} = \dfrac{P_{y,x}}{\Gamma(x+1)}$. The formulas containing the *gamma function* work also for non-integer numbers as well as for complex arguments. For $y \in \mathbb{N}$, note $C_{y,0} = 1$, $C_{y,1} = y$, and $C_{y,2} = \dfrac{1}{2}y(y-1)$. $C_{y,x}$ applies to the *binomial distribution* (see p. 376): In a *Galton box*[175] (a.k.a. *bean machine*) featuring y rows of pins and fed with 2^y balls, $C_{y,x}$ is the number of balls expected in column x of that box (start column counting with zero).
FIB	For integers, FIB returns the Fibonacci number f_n with $n = x$. These numbers are defined as $f_0 = 0$, $f_1 = 1$, and $f_n = f_{n-1} + f_{n-2}$ for $n \geq 2$. With UNSIGN, f_{93} is the maximum before an overflow occurs. Else FIB returns the extended Fibonacci number $$F_x = \frac{1}{\sqrt{5}}\left[\left(\frac{1+\sqrt{5}}{2}\right)^x - \left(\frac{2}{1+\sqrt{5}}\right)^x \cos(x\pi)\right] = \frac{1}{\sqrt{5}}\left[\Phi^x - \frac{\cos(x\pi)}{\Phi^x}\right] \text{ for}$$ an arbitrary real or complex number x, with Φ denoting the golden ratio.

Statistical Distributions

Stack-wise, the following are all *monadic* functions, stored in <u>PROB</u>. They have more parameters though. In the table below, typical plots are shown for the *PMF*s or *PDF*s.

---

[175] Translator's note: This is called «Planche de Galton» in French, "Galtonbrett" in German, and "macchina di Galton" in Italian. Note the subtle differences in naming. Galton invented his box in 1889.

Binom: *Binomial distribution* with the *number of successes g* in **X**, the *gross probability of a success p_0* in **J** and the *sample size n* in **K**.

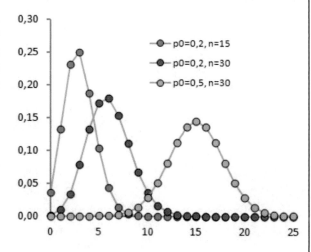

Binom$_P$ returns $p_B(g; n; p_0) = \binom{n}{g} \cdot p_0^g \cdot (1 - p_0)^{n-g} = C_{n,g} \cdot p_0^g \cdot (1 - p_0)^{n-g}$

(see COMB on p. 375).

Binom returns $F_B(m; n; p_0) = \sum_{g=0}^{m} p_B(g; n; p_0)$ with the maximum number of successes *m* in **X**.

The *binomial distribution* is fundamental for error statistics in industrial sampling, e.g. for designing test plans.

Example:
If you want to know the probability for finding <u>no</u> faulty items in a representative sample of 15 items drawn from a batch of 300 wherein you expect 3% defective items overall, this will tell you:

0.03 (STO)(J) **15** (STO)(K) **0** (h) (PROB) Binom (XEQ)

It returns 0.633 – so the odds are almost 2 out of 3 that you will not detect any defect in your sample! [176]

Read here for more information:
http://www.itl.nist.gov/div898/handbook/eda/section3/eda366i.htm .

---

[176] The exact result for said probability is 0.626, calculated using a mathematically more elaborated model of such a test. These results show nicely that two significant digits are a typical accuracy of theoretical statistical statements – frequently the (simplified) statistical model used matches reality no better than that.

Name and remarks (see pp. 171ff for general information)

Cauch: *Cauchy-Lorentz distribution* (also known as *Lorentz* or *Breit-Wigner distribution*) with the *location* x_0 specified in **J** and the *shape* γ in **K** :

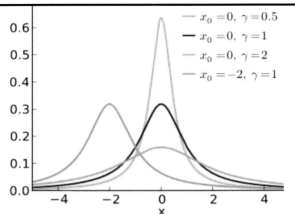

Cauch$_p$ returns $\qquad f_{Ca}(x) = \left\{ \pi\gamma \cdot \left[1 + \left(\dfrac{x - x_0}{\gamma} \right)^2 \right] \right\}^{-1}$,

Cauch returns $\qquad F_{Ca}(x) = \dfrac{1}{2} + \dfrac{1}{\pi} \arctan\left(\dfrac{x - x_0}{\gamma} \right)$,

Cauch^{-1} returns $\quad F_{Ca}^{-1}(p) = x_0 + \gamma \tan\left[\pi \cdot \left(p - \dfrac{1}{2} \right) \right]$.

This distribution is quite popular in physics. It is a special case of *Student's t* distribution. Start reading here for more:
http://en.wikipedia.org/wiki/Cauchy_distribution .

Expon: *Exponential distribution* with the *rate* λ in **J**.

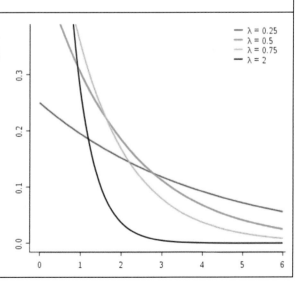

Name and remarks (see pp. 171ff for general information)

Expon$_P$ returns $f_{Ex}(x) = \lambda \cdot e^{-\lambda x}$. See some curves plotted above.

Expon returns $F_{Ex}(x) = 1 - e^{-\lambda x}$.

Read here for more information:
http://www.itl.nist.gov/div898/handbook/eda/section3/eda3667.htm .

F(x): *Fisher's F distribution* with the *degrees of freedom* in **J** and **K**. It is used e.g. for the analysis of variance (ANOVA).

The picture shows the *PDF* plotted for different *degrees of freedom **m** and **n*** corresponding to *j* and *k*.

Read here for more information:
http://www.itl.nist.gov/div 898/handbook/eda/secti on3/eda3665.htm .

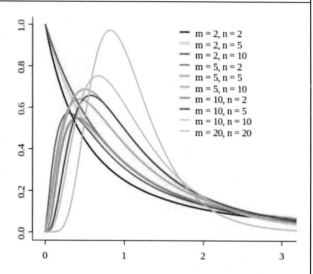

- m = 2, n = 2
- m = 2, n = 5
- m = 2, n = 10
- m = 5, n = 2
- m = 5, n = 5
- m = 5, n = 10
- m = 10, n = 2
- m = 10, n = 5
- m = 10, n = 10
- m = 20, n = 20

Geom: *Geometric distribution.*

Geom$_P$ returns

$$p_{Ge}(n) = p_0(1 - p_0)^n$$

Geom returns

$F_{Ge}(m) = 1 - (1 - p_0)^{m+1}$, being the probability for a first success after **m** = *x* Bernoulli experiments. The probability **p$_0$** for a success in each such experiment must be specified in **J**.

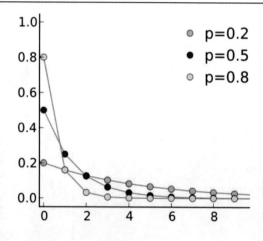

- ○ p=0.2
- ● p=0.5
- ○ p=0.8

Start reading here for more: *http://en.wikipedia.org/wiki/Geometric_distribution*

LgNrm: *Log-normal distribution with the parameters* $\mu = \ln \bar{x}_g$ *in* **J** *and* $\sigma = \ln \varepsilon$ *in* **K** *(see the picture for some PDF plots).*

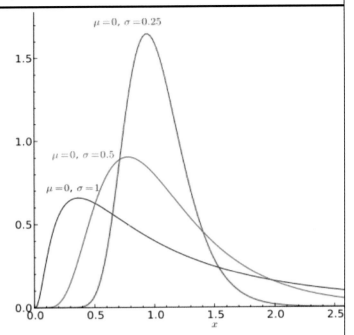

LgNrm$_p$ returns $f_{Ln}(x) = \dfrac{1}{x\sigma\sqrt{2\pi}} e^{-\frac{[\ln(x)-\mu]^2}{2\sigma^2}}$.

LgNrm returns $F_{Ln}(x) = \Phi\left(\dfrac{\ln(x)-\mu}{\sigma}\right)$ with $\Phi(z)$ denoting the *standard normal CDF* as presented on p. 383.

Read here for more information:
http://www.itl.nist.gov/div898/handbook/eda/section3/eda3669.htm .

Name and remarks (see pp. 171ff for general information)

Logis: *Logistic distribution* with an arbitrary *mean* μ given in **J** and a *scale parameter s* in **K**.

Substituting

$$\xi = \frac{x-\mu}{s},$$

Logis$_p$ returns

$$f_{Lg}(x) = \frac{e^{-\xi}}{s \cdot \left(1+e^{-\xi}\right)^2}$$

and **Logis** returns

$$F_{Lg}(x) = \frac{1}{1+e^{-\xi}}.$$

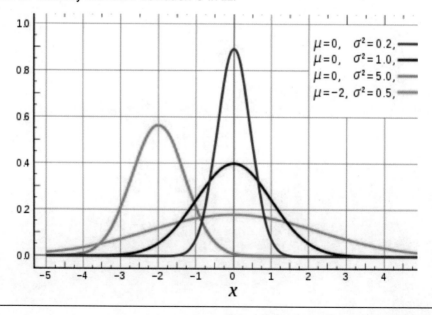

Logis^{-1} returns $F_{Lg}^{-1}(p) = \mu + s \cdot \ln\left(\frac{p}{1-p}\right).$

Start reading here for more: *http://en.wikipedia.org/wiki/Logistic_distribution* .

Norml: *Normal* (or *Gaussian*) *distribution* with an arbitrary *mean* μ given in **J** and an arbitrary *standard deviation* σ in **K**.

Name and remarks (see pp. 171ff for general information)

Norml$_p$ returns $\quad f_N(x) = \dfrac{1}{\sigma\sqrt{2\pi}}\, e^{-\frac{(x-\mu)^2}{2\sigma^2}}$ and

Norml returns $\quad F_N(x) = \Phi\!\left(\dfrac{x-\mu}{\sigma}\right)$ with $\Phi(z)$ denoting the *standard normal*

CDF (i.e. the integral of the red curve plotted above, cf. p. 101). Generally, you will get *standard normal* function results when you store **0** in **J** and **1** in **K** and call the corresponding label of Norml.

Read here for more information:
http://www.itl.nist.gov/div898/handbook/eda/section3/eda3661.htm .

Poiss, Poisλ: *Poisson distribution* with the *number of successes* **g** in **X**, and either the *Poisson parameter* λ in **J** (for Poisλ) or the *gross probability of a success* p_0 in **J** and the *sample size* **n** in **K** (for Poiss). In the latter case, your *WP 43S* calculates the *Poisson parameter* λ with $\lambda = n \cdot p_0$ automatically.

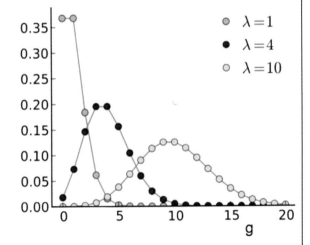

Poisλ$_p$ computes

$$p_P(g;\lambda) = \frac{\lambda^g}{g!}\, e^{-\lambda} \,, \text{ and}$$

Poisλ returns the *CDF* for the maximum number of successes **m** in **X**.

The *Poisson distribution* provides the mathematically simplest model for industrial sampling tests. For the example introduced with Binom above, we get 0.638 here.

Read here for more information:
http://www.itl.nist.gov/div898/handbook/eda/section3/eda366j.htm .

Name and remarks (see pp. 171ff for general information)

t(x): Standardized *Student's t distribution* with its *degrees of freedom* in **J** as used for hypothesis testing and calculating confidence intervals e.g. for means. The picture shows the *PDF* plotted for different *degrees of freedom*. For $df \to \infty$, the shoulders of the function shrink and the *PDF* approaches the one of the *standard normal distribution* (compare the red curve at NORML above).

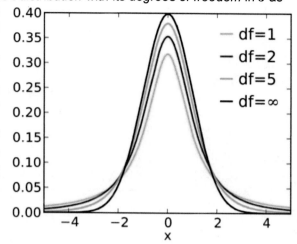

Read here for more information:

http://www.itl.nist.gov/div898/handbook/eda/section3/eda3664.htm.

Weibl: *Weibull distribution* with its *shape parameter b* in **J** and its *characteristic lifetime T* in **K**. It is widely used e.g. for analyzing tool and product lifetimes.

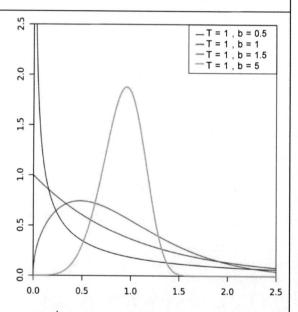

Weibl$_p$ returns $f_W(t) = \dfrac{b}{T}\left(\dfrac{t}{T}\right)^{b-1} e^{-\left(\frac{t}{T}\right)^b}$ for $t \geq 0$ (else it returns 0). This is a very flexible function – see the curves plotted above.

Weibl returns $F_W(t) = 1 - e^{-\left(\frac{t}{T}\right)^b}$.

Name and remarks (see pp. 171ff for general information)

Read here for more information: *http://www.itl.nist.gov/div898/handbook/eda/ section3/eda3668.htm* . Also see *http://en.wikipedia.org/wiki/Weibull_distribu tion#Uses* for some more application fields.

φ(x), Φ(x): $\varphi(x) = \dfrac{1}{\sqrt{2\pi}} e^{-x^2/2}$ is the *standard normal PDF* (the famous

Gaussian bell curve, see the red curve on p. 380), while $\Phi(x) = \displaystyle\int_{-\infty}^{x} \varphi(\tau)d\tau$ is

the corresponding *CDF* (compare the *error function* on p. 389). See the link at NORML above for more information.

χ²: The χ^2 (= *chi-square*) *distribution* is used for calculating confidence intervals for *standard deviations, variances, process and machine capabilities* and the like. The picture shows the *PDF* plotted for different *degrees of freedom*.

Read here for more information: http://www.itl.nist.gov/div 898/handbook/eda/section3/eda3666.htm .

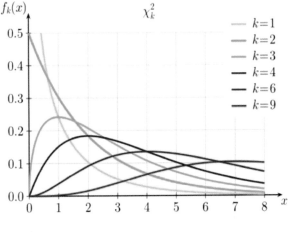

More Statistical Formulas

The following equations are for data measured at samples of n specimens (i.e. n is the *sample size*). Note that in such cases complete measurement results must include information about the expected value as well as about its uncertainty always – there is no way around that commandment.

- For samples drawn out of a *Gaussian* (additive) process, the best guess for the expected value is the *arithmetic mean* (or *average*) and its uncertainty is given by its *standard error* (see x̄ and SERR).

- For samples drawn out of a *log-normal* (multiplicative) process, the best guess for the expected value is the *geometric mean* and its uncertainty is given by its *scattering factor* (see $\bar{x}_g$ and ε_m).

- For samples drawn out of other processes other measures may apply.

Be assured not everything is *Gaussian* in the real world! Process features can be detected (and should be checked well in advance of calculating statistical standard values) using suitable statistical tests – please turn to applicable statistical reference literature. [177]

The following functions as named in the left column are all found in <u>STAT</u>.

Name	Remarks (see pp. 171ff for general information)
CORR	If $R(x)$ is an arbitrary fit model, $r^2 = 1 - \dfrac{\sum[R(x_i) - y_i]^2}{\sum(\bar{y} - y_i)^2}$ is its *coefficient of determination*; it indicates the fraction of the variation of the dependent data y determined by the variation of the independent data x. For $r^2 = 1$, y is fully determined by x; for e.g. $r^2 = 0.9$, 90% of the variation of y is due to x; and for $r^2 = 0$, y is completely independent of x. For a linear fit model, the *coefficient of correlation* is $r = \dfrac{s_{xy}}{s_x \cdot s_y}$. See s_{XY} and s below. A regression is said to be (statistically) *significant* if

---

[177] Generally, the statistical model should be chosen that matches observations best. In real life cases, however, dramatic deviations from the model distribution are frequently found – then you cannot expect the calculated consequences matching reality any better.

By the way: Since the *PDF* of the *Gaussian* distribution will never reach zero, this statistical model tells you to expect individual items far away from the mean value when your sample becomes large enough. This, however, does not match reality. So we must conclude nothing at all is really *Gaussian* in real world. Nevertheless, the *Gaussian* distribution is a very successful model describing a lot of real world observations very well. Just never forget the limits of such models.

WP 34S v3.3d

Name	Remarks (see pp. 171ff for general information)
	$\sqrt{r^2 \dfrac{n-2}{1-r^2}} > t_{n-2}^{-1}(0.99)$, with the right side being the inverse of the *t-distribution* for the *degrees of freedom* $n-2$ and the *confidence level* 99% (see p. 382).
COV, s_{XY}	For a linear fit model, the *population covariance* is $$COV_{xy} = \frac{n\sum x_i y_i - \sum x_i \cdot \sum y_i}{n^2}.$$ On the other hand, the *sample covariance* is $$s_{xy} = \frac{n \cdot \sum x_i y_i - \sum x_i \cdot \sum y_i}{n \cdot (n-1)}.$$
L.R.	For a linear fit model, the line parameters are $a_0 = \dfrac{\sum x_i^2 \cdot \sum y_i - \sum x_i \cdot \sum x_i y_i}{n \cdot (n-1) \cdot s_x^2}$ and $a_1 = \dfrac{s_{xy}}{s_x^2} = r \cdot \dfrac{s_y}{s_x}$ (see CORR above, s_{XY} and s below). Their *standard errors* can be calculated using $s_E(a_1) = \dfrac{s_y}{s_x} \sqrt{\dfrac{1-r^2}{n-2}}$ and $$s_E(a_0) = s_E(a_1) \cdot \sqrt{\frac{n-1}{n} s_x^2 + \overline{x}^2}.$$ Generally, a regression parameter is (statistically) *significant* if $\left. |a_i| \middle/ s_E(a_i) \right. > t_{n-2}^{-1}(0.995)$, with the right side being the inverse of the *t-distribution* for the *degrees of freedom* $n-2$ and 99% *confidence level* (see p. 382).
s, SERR	The *sample standard deviation (SD)* is the positive square root of the *sample variance* $s_x^2 = \dfrac{n \cdot \sum x_i^2 - \left(\sum x_i\right)^2}{n \cdot (n-1)} = \dfrac{\sum x_i^2 - n \cdot \overline{x}^2}{n-1}$. And the *standard error* (i.e. the *SD* of the *mean* $\overline{x}$) is $s_{Ex} = \left. s_x \middle/ \sqrt{n} \right.$.

Name	Remarks (see pp. 171ff for general information)
s_W, $SERR_W$	The *sample SD* for <u>weighted</u> data (where the weight y_i of each data point x_i was entered via $\boxed{\Sigma+}$) is $$s_w = +\sqrt{\frac{\sum y_i \cdot \sum(y_i \cdot x_i^2) - \left[\sum(y_i \cdot x_i)\right]^2}{\left(\sum y_i - 1\right) \cdot \sum y_i}} \; .$$ And the corresponding *standard error* (the *SD* of $\overline{x}_w$) is $$s_{Ew} = +\frac{1}{\sum y_i} \cdot \sqrt{\frac{\sum y_i \cdot \sum(y_i \cdot x_i^2) - \left[\sum(y_i \cdot x_i)\right]^2}{\sum y_i - 1}} \; .$$
$\overline{x}$	The *arithmetic mean* is calculated as $\overline{x} = \dfrac{1}{n}\sum x_i$.
$\overline{x}_g$	The *geometric mean* is calculated as $\overline{x}_g = \sqrt[n]{\prod x} = e^{\frac{1}{n}\sum \ln x}$.
$\overline{x}_w$	The *arithmetic mean* for <u>weighted</u> data (see s_w) is calculated as $\overline{x}_w = \dfrac{\sum x_i y_i}{\sum y_i}$.
ε	The *scattering factor* ε_x for a sample of *log-normally* distributed data is calculated via: $$\ln(\varepsilon_x) = \sqrt{\frac{\sum \ln^2(x_i) - 2n \cdot \ln(\overline{x}_g)}{n-1}} \; .$$ Compare s.
ε_m	The *scattering factor* of the *geometric mean* is $\varepsilon_m = \varepsilon^{1/\sqrt{n}}$ (compare SERR).

Name	Remarks (see pp. 171ff for general information)
ε_p	The *scattering factor* ε_p for a population of *log-normally* distributed data is calculated via: $$\ln(\varepsilon_p) = \sqrt{\frac{n-1}{n}} \cdot \ln(\varepsilon_x).$$ Compare σ.
σ	The *SD* of a population of *normally* distributed data is calculated via: $$\sigma_x = +\frac{1}{n} \cdot \sqrt{\sum(x_i - \bar{x})^2} = \sqrt{\frac{n-1}{n}} \cdot s_x.$$ Compare ε_p.
σ_w	(1) The *SD* of the population for <u>weighted</u> data (where the weight y_i of each data point x_i was entered via $\boxed{\Sigma+}$) is $$\sigma_w = +\sqrt{\frac{\sum y_i \cdot (x_i - \bar{x}_w)^2}{\sum y_i}}.$$

Orthogonal Polynomials

These polynomials are all found in <u>X.FCN</u>.

Name	Remarks (see pp. 171ff for general information)
H_n	*Hermite polynomials* for probability: $H_n(x) = (-1)^n \cdot e^{x^2/2} \cdot \dfrac{d^n}{dx^n}\left(e^{-x^2/2}\right)$ with **n** in **Y**, solving the differential equation $$f''(x) - 2x \cdot f'(x) + 2n \cdot f(x) = 0.$$
H_{np}	*Hermite polynomials* for physics: $H_{np}(x) = (-1)^n \cdot e^{x^2} \cdot \dfrac{d^n}{dx^n}\left(e^{-x^2}\right)$ with **n** in **Y**, solving the same differential equation.

Name	Remarks (see pp. 171ff for general information)
L_n	Laguerre polynomials (compare $L_n\alpha$ below): $$L_n(x) = \frac{e^x}{n!} \cdot \frac{d^n}{dx^n}(x^n e^{-x}) = L_n^{(0)}(x)$$ with n in **Y**, solving the differential equation $$x \cdot f''(x) + (1-x) \cdot f'(x) + n \cdot f(x) = 0$$
$L_n\alpha$	Laguerre's generalized polynomials (compare L_n above): $$L_n^{(\alpha)}(x) = \frac{x^{-\alpha} e^x}{n!} \cdot \frac{d^n}{dx^n}(x^{n+\alpha} e^{-x})$$ with n in **Y** and α in **Z**.
P_n	Legendre polynomials: $P_n(x) = \dfrac{1}{2^n n!} \cdot \dfrac{d^n}{dx^n}\left[(x^2-1)^n\right]$ with n in **Y**, solving the differential equation $$\frac{d}{dx}\left[(1-x^2) \cdot \frac{d}{dx} f(x)\right] + n(n+1)f(x) = 0.$$
T_n	Chebyshev (a.k.a. Čebyšev, Tschebyscheff) polynomials of first kind $T_n(x)$ with n in **Y**, solving the differential equation $$f''(x) - \frac{x}{1-x^2} f'(x) + \frac{n^2}{1-x^2} f(x) = 0$$
U_n	Chebyshev polynomials of second kind $U_n(x)$ with n in **Y**, solving the differential equation $$f''(x) - \frac{3x}{1-x^2} f'(x) + \frac{n(n+2)}{1-x^2} f(x) = 0$$

Even More Mathematical Functions

All the following functions are found in X.FCN. Some of them are for pure mathematics only but were useful at some stage of the *WP 34S* project, so we made them accessible for the public.

Name	Remarks (see pp. 171ff for general information)
AGM	(2) Returns the *arithmetic-geometric mean*. Find more about it here: *http://mathworld.wolfram.com/Arithmetic-GeometricMean.html* .
erf	(1) Returns the *error function* $erf(x) = \dfrac{2}{\sqrt{\pi}} \int_0^x e^{-\tau^2} d\tau$. Note that $erf\left(\dfrac{x}{\sqrt{2}}\right) = 2 \cdot \Phi(x) - 1$ with $\Phi(x)$ representing the *standard normal CDF* as described on p. 383.
erfc	(1) Returns the *complementary error function* $erfc(x) = 1 - erf(x) = \dfrac{2}{\sqrt{\pi}} \int_x^\infty e^{-\tau^2} d\tau$. This function is related to the *error probability* of the *standard normal distribution*.

Name	Remarks (see pp. 171ff for general information)

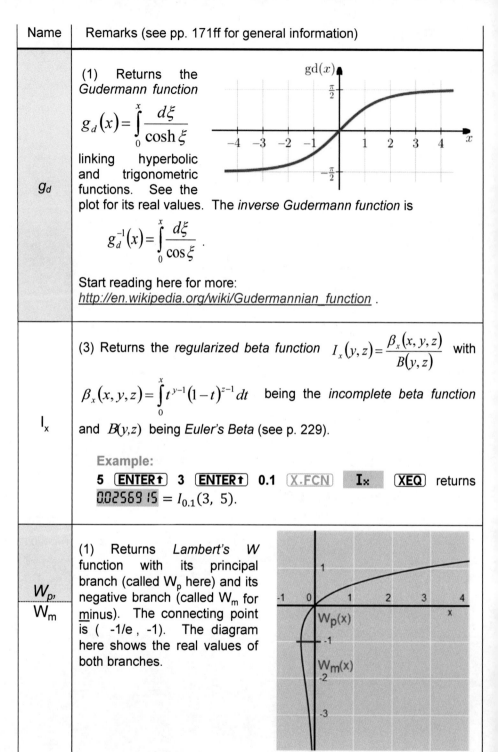

g_d — (1) Returns the *Gudermann function*

$$g_d(x)=\int_0^x \frac{d\xi}{\cosh \xi}$$

linking hyperbolic and trigonometric functions. See the plot for its real values. The *inverse Gudermann function* is

$$g_d^{-1}(x)=\int_0^x \frac{d\xi}{\cos \xi}.$$

Start reading here for more:
http://en.wikipedia.org/wiki/Gudermannian_function .

I_x — (3) Returns the *regularized beta function* $I_x(y,z)=\dfrac{B_x(x,y,z)}{B(y,z)}$ with

$$B_x(x,y,z)=\int_0^x t^{y-1}(1-t)^{z-1}\,dt \quad \text{being the } \textit{incomplete beta function}$$

and $B(y,z)$ being *Euler's Beta* (see p. 229).

Example:
5 [ENTER↑] 3 [ENTER↑] 0.1 [X.FCN] [Ix] [XEQ] returns
$0.0256915 = I_{0.1}(3, 5)$.

W_p, W_m — (1) Returns *Lambert's W function* with its principal branch (called W_p here) and its negative branch (called W_m for minus). The connecting point is (-1/e , -1). The diagram here shows the real values of both branches.

Name	Remarks (see pp. 171ff for general information)
	Start reading here for more information: *http://en.wikipedia.org/wiki/Lambert_W_function* . Learn more here: *http://mathworld.wolfram.com/LambertW-Function.html*
β	(2) Returns *Euler's Beta function* $B(x,y) = \dfrac{\Gamma(x) \cdot \Gamma(y)}{\Gamma(x+y)}$ with $\mathrm{Re}(x) > 0$, $\mathrm{Re}(y) > 0$. Called β here to avoid ambiguity.
Γ_p	(2) Returns the *regularized gamma function* $P(x,y) = \dfrac{\gamma(x,y)}{\Gamma(x)}$. See γ_{XY} below for $\gamma(x,y)$ and p. 229 for $\Gamma(x)$.
Γ_q	(2) Returns the *regularized gamma function* $Q(x,y) = \dfrac{\Gamma_u(x,y)}{\Gamma(x)}$. See Γ_{XY} below for $\Gamma_u(x,y)$ and p. 229 for $\Gamma(x)$.
γ_{XY}	(2) Returns the *lower incomplete gamma function* $\gamma(x,y) = \displaystyle\int_0^y t^{x-1} e^{-t}\,dt$. Required for Γ_p above.
Γ_{XY}	(2) Returns the *upper incomplete gamma function* $\Gamma_u(x,y) = \displaystyle\int_y^\infty t^{x-1} e^{-t}\,dt$. Required for Γ_q above.

Name	Remarks (see pp. 171ff for general information)
ζ(x)	(1) Returns *Riemann's Zeta* function for real arguments, with $$\zeta(x)=\sum_{n=1}^{\infty}\frac{1}{n^{x}} \quad \text{for} \quad x>1,$$ and its analytical continuation for $x<1$: $\zeta(x)=2^{x}\pi^{x-1}\sin\left(\frac{\pi}{2}x\right)\cdot\Gamma(1-x)\cdot\zeta(1-x)$. Note the different vertical scales for negative and positive x. Look here for more: *http://mathworld.wolfram.com/RiemannZetaFunction.html* .

You will find lots of information about the special functions implemented in your *WP 34S* in the internet in addition. Generally, *Wikipedia* is a good starter – check the articles in different languages since they may well contain different material and use different approaches. *Mathworld* may contain more details than you ever want to know. And for applied statistics, the *NIST Sematech* online handbook quoted above is a competent source. Further references are found at these sites.

APPENDIX J: CONCISE HISTORY OF RPN SCIENTIFIC POCKET COMPUTING

There are seven calculator models pictured in this manual which are rated as landmarks in four decades of scientific pocket computing. The picture at right and the one on p. 395 show the *HP-35*, the world's first pocket calculator allowing for transcendental functions, making slide rules obsolete in 1972. See below the world's first <u>programmable</u> pocket calculator, the *HP-65*, launched in 1974.

The other models are the *HP-25C* of 1975 (first with *CMOS* memory, see p. 406), the *HP-34C* (first allowing for solving and integration, see pp. 51 and 70) and *HP-41C* of 1979 (see below and p.

70), the *HP-15C* of 1982 (the first supporting matrices, see →), and the *HP-42S* of 1988 (see pp. 70 and 325). Production of the

HP-42S ceased in 1995.

Below and on next page, two *HP* advertisements for the first electronic scientific pocket calculator are displayed. Remember even lunar landings were a slide rule business still – as is well reflected in the movie *Apollo 13*. The first electronic pocket calculator taken into near space was an *HP-65* in 1975 (see also p. 155).

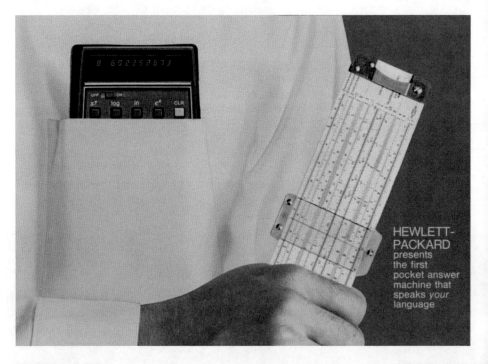

HEWLETT-PACKARD presents the first pocket answer machine that speaks *your* language

Careful human engineering assures convenient, reliable operation

The HP-35 features a bright, easy-to-read light-emitting diode display specially developed for this application by Hewlett-Packard's own opto-electronic design group. Since the displays are made from semi-conductor materials, they—like the large-scale integrated circuits used inside the HP-35—do not wear out with time.

The unique HP-35 keyboard has been carefully laid out for convenient fingertip operation. Because the keys are small and widely separated, there is less chance of misentering data by striking two keys simultaneously. Moreover, each key has a "breakaway" or "overcenter" touch similar to the key action for a high-quality electric typewriter to give a positive indication that contact has been made.

Finally, the compact, contoured HP-35 case represents a break-through in modern packaging techniques. Small enough to fit in a shirt pocket, rugged enough to withstand substantial punishment in field use, the case gives the HP-35 a comfortable "feel" and makes the calculator even more convenient to use.

HP-35 The first pocket calculator designed to fit the needs of today's engineering/scientific world.

Easy-to-read LED display gives answers with accuracy of up to 10 significant digits. Decimal point is automatically positioned. Numbers smaller than 10^{-2} and larger than 10^{10} are displayed in scientific notation, with the exponent of 10 (plus or minus) shown at the extreme right.

Pre-programmed functions let you perform log, trig and exponential calculations 10 times faster than with a slide rule.

Operates on battery or AC-line power.
The HP-35 comes with a rechargeable nickel-cadmium battery pack which provides enough power for three to five hours of continuous operation. Impending battery depletion is indicated by the lighting of all decimal points in the display.

AC-line operation (115 or 230 volts) and simultaneous battery charging are accomplished by simply plugging in the battery charger supplied with the HP-35.

Compact, rugged case fits easily into shirt pocket or briefcase.

Four-register, operational memory-stack automatically stores and retrieves intermediate solutions during complex calculations, eliminates need for scratch notes and re-entry of data. Data manipulation keys allow contents of any register to be displayed for review. A separate, addressable memory register is also provided for storage and retrieval of constants.

Try it for 15 days
Shirt-pocket test the powerful HP-35 scientific pocket calculator for 15 days to see how much time and money it can save you. To take advantage of this offer, or obtain information on the complete line of HP pocket and desktop calculators, contact your local HP sales office. Or, write us at the address shown on the back page of this brochure.

See overleaf the timeline of all the *RPN* scientifics manufactured by *HP* and for *HP* so far. The figures within the colored bars indicate the price in US$ at market entry. Vertical lines separate the product lines: *Classics*, *Woodstocks*, *Spices*, *Nuts*, *Voyagers*, and *Pioneers*.

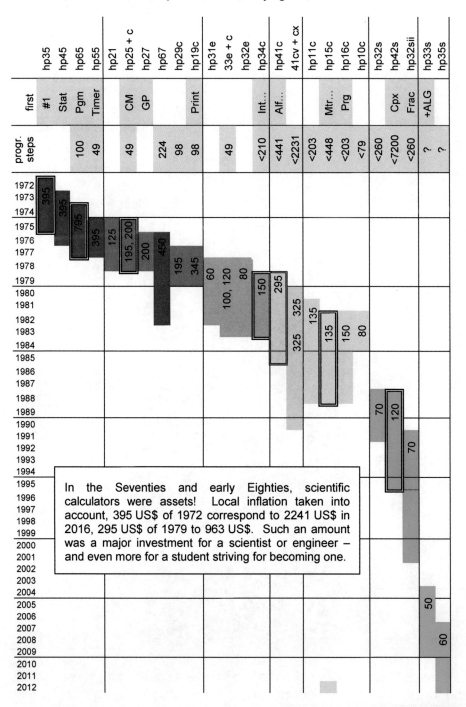

In the Seventies and early Eighties, scientific calculators were assets! Local inflation taken into account, 395 US$ of 1972 correspond to 2241 US$ in 2016, 295 US$ of 1979 to 963 US$. Such an amount was a major investment for a scientist or engineer – and even more for a student striving for becoming one.

The diagram below shows the number of different *RPN* scientific pocket calculator models made by and for *HP* in the years since 1972. The line is just to guide the eye.[178]

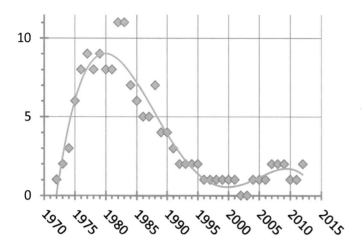

In the Seventies and early Eighties, also a few other companies produced some *RPN* pocket calculator models (e.g. *Commodore, Novus, Omron,* and *Sinclair*).

Why Do the *Stack* and ENTER↑ Work the Way They Do?

HP's first (desktop) electronic calculator, the model *9100A* of 1968, featured only a 3-level *stack* – but all three levels were always displayed on the screen of a small cathode ray tube: the *keyboard (entry) register* **X**, the *accumulator* **Y**, and the *temporary register* **Z**.

Previous mechanical calculators worked with a *keyboard register* and an *accumulator* only. The third register became necessary to enable the calculator to deal with slightly more advanced mathematical expressions.

To solve something like $123/(45 + 67)$, the following steps had to be executed (beginning with a cleared *stack*) leading to displays as shown in separate columns here:

Z	0	0	0	123	123	123	123	123
Y	0	123	123	45	45	<u>112</u>	123	<u>1.0982...</u>
X	123	123	45	45	67	67	112	112
Input	**123**	↑[179]	**45**	↑	**67**	+	↓[180]	÷

---

[178] *HP* launched *RPL* calculators in 1987. From then until today, they are significantly larger than all *RPN* models, thus straining the term 'pocket calculators'. They are not included in this diagram.

But an early pocket calculator like the *HP-35* could display just one register for space and power reasons – and that register had to be X to give feedback during keyboard entry. In consequence, to show the calculation <u>result</u> supplied in the accumulator Y, its content y must be shifted into X. Thus both ⊕ and ⊡ have to be executed immediately after each other, preferably in a single operation (the same applies to the other *dyadic* operations as well).

On the other hand, such an intermediate result in X has to be shifted into the accumulator Y (again) before entering the next number. Thus, ⬆ is executed automatically then. But this is not required, of course, when ⬆ has just been pressed. This is why *automatic stack lift* is disabled after ENTER⬆.

T	0	0	0	0	0	0	0
Z	0	0	0	123	123	0	0
Y	0	123	123	45	45	123	0
X	*123*	*123*	*45*	*45*	*67*	*112*	*1.0982...*
Input	**123**	ENTER⬆	**45**	ENTER⬆	**67**	⊞	⊡

Automatic stack lift is also disabled after CLx since the new number entered shall simply replace the one just deleted then. And Σ+ as well as Σ− are dedicated commands for entry of statistical data points – they are not meant to be used in stack calculations.

The picture overleaf shows US-American astronaut Sally Ride in the shuttle in orbit (1983-6-21) with three customized HP-41CVs floating to her right.

---

[179] This key worked like ENTER⬆ did on subsequent calculators.

[180] In fact, ⊡ did exactly what DROP does on your *WP 34S*. This function disappeared on *HP*'s pocket calculators for keyboard space reasons. R↓ survived – it does <u>almost</u> the same.

APPENDIX K: RELEASE NOTES

This picture is the first recorded draft of a layout for what later became the *WP 34S*, dated 5.12.2008. In fact, it was named *34S* already due to its three prefix keys – a feature only the *HP-65*, *HP-67*, and *HP-34C* had until then. In that early stage, the function set of the new calculator was far smaller than today, the layout did not show a single *catalog* nor *hotkey*, and the device was thought working in both algebraic and *RPN* modes. In course of development some features changed and also the labels on the keyplate became a bit larger – compare the pictures on pp. 407f.

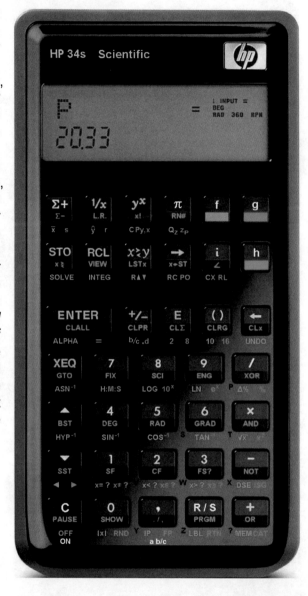

	Date	Release notes
1	9.12.08	**Project start**
1.1	15.12.08	Added the table of indicators; added NAND, NOR, XNOR, RCLWS, STOWS, //, N, SERR, SIGMA, < and >; deleted HR, INPUT, 2 flag commands, and 2 conversions; extended explanations for addressing and COMPLEX & ...; put XOR on the keyboard.
1.2	4.1.09	Added ASRN, CBC?, CBS?, CCB, SCB, FLOAT, MIRROR, SLN, SRN, →BIN, →DEC, →HEX, →OCT, BETA, D→R, DATE, DDAYS, D.MY, M.DY, Y.MD, CEIL, FLOOR, DSZ, ISZ, R→D, EMGAM, GSB, LNBETA, LNGAMMA, MAX, MIN, NOP, REAL, RJ, W and WINV, ZETA, %+ and %-; renamed the top left keys B, C, and D, and bottom left EXIT.
1.3	17.1.09	Added AIP, ALENG, ARCL, AROT, ASHF, ASTO, ATOX, XTOA, AVIEW, CLA, PROMPT (all taken from 42S), CAPP, FC?C, FS?C, SGMNT, and the ...# commands; renamed NBITS to BITS and STOWS to WSIZE; specified the bit commands closer; deleted the 4 carry bit operations.
1.4	10.2.09	Added <u>CONST</u> and a table of constants provided, D→J and J→D, LEAP?, %T, RCL and STO▲ and ▼, and 2 forgotten statistics registers; deleted CHS, EMGAM, GSB, REAL and ZETA; purged and renamed the bit operations; renamed many commands.
1.5	5.3.09	Added RNDINT, <u>CONV</u> and its table, a memory table, the description of XEQ B, C, D to the operation index, and a and g_e to the table of constants; put CLSTK on a key, moved CLΣ and FILL, changed the % and log labels on the keyboard, put CLALL in <u>X.FCN</u>; checked and cleaned alpha mode keyboard and added a temporary alpha keyboard; rearranged the alphabet to put Greek after Latin, symbols after Greek consistently; separated the input and non-programmable commands; cleaned the addressing tables.
1.6	12.8.09	Added BASE, DAYS+, DROP, DROPY, E3OFF, E3ON, FC?F, FC?S, FIB, FS?F, FS?S, GCD, LCM, SETDAT, SETTIM, SET24, SINC, TIME, VERS, αDAY, αMONTH, αRC#, %Σ, as well as F-, t-, and χ^2-distributions and their inverses; reassigned DATE, modified DENMAX, FLOAT, αROT, and αSHIFT; deleted BASE arithmetic, BIN, DEC, HEX, and OCT; updated the alpha keyboards; added flags in the memory table; included indirect addressing for comparisons; added a paragraph about the display; updated the table of indicators; corrected errors.
1.7	9.9.09	Added <u>P.FCN</u> and <u>STAT</u> catalogs, 4 more conversions, 3 more flags, Greek character access, CLFLAG, DECOMP, DENANY, DENFAC, DENFIX, Iβ, IΓ, αDATE, αRL, αRR, αSL, αSR, αTIME, 12h, 24h, fraction mode limits, normal distribution and its inverse for arbitrary μ and σ, and Boolean operations working within FLOAT; deleted αROT, αSHIFT, the timer, and forced radians after inverse hyperbolics; renamed WINV to W^{-1}, and beta and gamma commands to Greek; added tables of catalog contents; modified label addressing; relabeled PRGM to P/R and PAUSE to PSE; swapped SHOW and PSE as well as Δ% and % on the keyboard; relabeled Q; corrected

	Date	Release notes
		CEIL and FLOOR; updated X.FCN and alpha commands; updated the virtual alpha keyboard.
1.8	29.10.09	Added R-CLR, R-COPY, R-SORT, R-SWAP, RCLM, STOM, alpha catalogs, 1 more constant and some more conversions, a table of error messages, as well as the binomial, Poisson, geometric, Weibull and exponential distributions and their inverses; renamed some commands; put $\sqrt{}$ instead of π on hotkey D.
1.9	14.12.09	Added two complex comparisons; swapped and changed labels in the top three rows of keys, dropped CLST; completed function descriptions in the index.
1.10	19.1.10	Added IMPFRC, PROFRC, ^{C}ENTER, αBEG, αEND, and an addressing table for items in catalogs; updated temporary alpha mode, display and indicators, RCLM and STOM, alpha-commands and the message table; renamed the exponential distribution; wrote the introduction.
1.11	21.9.10	Changed keyboard layout to bring Π and Σ to the front, relabeled binary log, swapped the locations of π, CLPR, and STATUS, as well as SF and FS?; created a menu TEST for the comparisons removed and the other programmable tests from P.FCN; added %MG, %+MG, %MRR, RESET, SSIZE4, SSIZE8, SSIZE?, ^{C}DROP, ^{C}FILL, ^{C}R↓, ^{C}R↑, registers J and K, a table of contents and tables for *stack* mechanics and addressing in complex operations; updated memory and real number addressing tables, DECOMP, αOFF, αON, Π, and Σ; renamed ROUNDI, WSIZE?, β(x,y), Γ(x) and the constant p_0 ; deleted DROPY (use x↔y, DROP instead), αAPP, αBEG, αEND, and the "too long error" message; deleted Josephson and von Klitzing constants (they are just the inverses of other constants already included in CONST); brought more symbols on the alpha keyboard.
1.12	22.12.10	Modified keyboard layout; added catalogs MODE and PROB; changed mode word, catalog contents and handling (XEQ instead of ENTER), as well as some non-programmable info commands; expanded IMPFRC and PROFRC; added a paragraph about the fonts provided and explained alpha catalogs in detail; added PRIME? and some conversions; deleted FRACT, OFF and ON.
1.13	3.2.11	Modified keyboard layout; modified αTIME, radix setting, H.MS+ and H.MS-; added EVEN?, FP?, INT?, LZOFF, LZON, ODD?, RCLS, STOS, returned FRACT; added and renamed some conversions; updated the paragraph about display; added appendices A and B; baptized the device *WP 34S*.
1.14	18.3.11	**Started the Windows emulator.** Added DEC and INC, renamed FLOAT to DECM; redefined αTIME and H.MS mode; updated *Appendix A*; documented the annunciators BEG and = as well as underflows and overflows in H.MS; corrected some errors showing up with the emulator.
1.15	21.3.11	Modified FIX, removed ALL from MODE, updated CONV.

	Date	Release notes
1.16	27.3.11	Added LBL?, f(x), and f'(x); modified PSE; upgraded catalog searching.
1.17	9.5.11	Modified keyboard layout for adding a fourth hotkey; added AGM, BATT, B_n, B_n^*, Cauch, Lgnrm, Logis and their inverses, all the *PDFs*, COV, CUBE, CUBERT, DEG→, ENGOVR, ENTRY?, erfc, GRAD→, GTO . *hotkey*, KEY?, RAD→, SCIOVR, SERRw, SLVQ, sw, sxy, TICKS, TVM, xg, ε, ε_m, ε_p, ζ, σw, $(-1)^x$, the polynomials, four angular conversions, four Planck constants, the regional settings, global alpha labels, and three messages; renamed most *CDFs*; changed →DEG, →RAD, →GRAD to leaving angular mode as set; altered PSE for early termination by keystroke; made D.MY default instead of Y.MD; moved degrees to radians conversions to <u>CONV</u>; removed ^{C}CLx, H.MS mode, %+ and %-; corrected errors.
1.18	5.6.11	Expanded program memory; modified label addressing (A ≠ 'A') and fraction mode limits, changed ANGLE to work in real and complex domains, renamed MOD to RMDR, changed the keyboard layout; put BACK, ERR, SKIP, and SPEC? to the main index; added CAT and the I/O commands for flash memory, expanded R-COPY; corrected x→α.
2.0	21.7.11	**Entered beta test phase.** Added DAY, MONTH, YEAR, FAST, SLOW, S.L, S.R, VWα+, flag A, ON + and −, some constants, and a paragraph about I/O; renamed old DAY to WDAY, RRCL to RCFRG, SRCL to RCFST; added an inverse conversion shortcut, stones⇆kg, and changed Pa⇆mbar to Pa⇆bar; modified the VIEW commands, ALL, DISP, <u>MODE</u>, RCLM, STOM, and <u>X.FCN</u>; repaired hyperlinks; corrected some errors; included flash.txt; updated the first chapters, explained *stack* mechanics in more detail.
2.1	3.10.11	Added serial I/O commands, DELP, DSL, EXPT, IBASE?, INTM?, ISE, KTY?, MANT, NEXTP, PUTK, REALM?, RM, RM?, SMODE?, TOP?, $^x\sqrt{y}$, signed tests for zero, some constants, and the paragraph about interactive programming; updated the values in <u>CONST</u> to CODATA 2010, also updated SLVQ, SHOW, Σ, Π, and the paragraphs about statistics, predefined alpha labels and memory; corrected some errors; deleted complex ANGLE, →BIN, →DEC, →HEX, and →OCT; redistributed the contents of <u>X.FCN</u> and <u>P.FCN</u>; renamed S.L and S.R to SDL and SDR; put '?' on the alpha keyboard and moved £ to P to make room for π; expanded *Appendix A*; reorganized the structure of the document; added first aid to the front page; rewrote the keyboard chapter.
2.2	1.11.11	Added MSG, y↔, z↔, and matrix operations, a paragraph about them and two new error messages for them, plus a footnote for DELP; updated the introduction to statistics. **This version is the last one working with the old keyboard overlays**. It was maintained for a while to incorporate common bug fixes – last v2.2 build available is 2739 of 29.3.12. Note that build runs keystroke programs at least 55% <u>faster</u> than v3.1

	Date	Release notes
		– the difference is even significantly greater for some advanced (e.g. statistical) commands, which were moved into *XROM* later. On the other hand, v2.2 offers 'only' some 2500 *words* in *FM*, compared to some 6000 in v3.1. See the release notes below for more differences.
3.0	21.4.12	Added CLPALL, CROSS, DOT, iRCL, sRCL, END, FLASH?, g_d, g_d^{-1}, GTO.▲ and ▼, LOAD…, LocR, LocR?, MEM?, NEIGHB, PopLR, RDP, REGS, REGS?, RSD, SEPOFF, SEPON, SETJPN, STOPW, t↔, ULP, ↔, #, as well as <u>SUMS</u> and <u>MATRIX</u> catalogs and four conversions; renamed CLFLAG to CFALL, CUBE to x^3 and CUBERT to $\sqrt[3]{x}$, KTY? to KTP?, and αVIEW to VIEWα; split Lambert's W into W_p and W_m; returned →BIN, →HEX, and →OCT; made PSTO and SAVE nonprogrammable; redefined SHOW, corrected CLREG, deleted DEL$_P$; changed keyboard layout to bring <u>MATRIX</u>, CLP, SF, and CF to the front and to swap OFF and SHOW, removed x↔α from the key plate and π from <u>CONST</u>; modified the virtual alpha keyboard, some characters and the respective catalogs; redistributed commands in the catalogs; updated and rearranged large parts of the text; added information about complex calculations, bitwise integer operations, browsers, local data, memory management, and the character sets; implemented five new ttf-fonts.
3.1	30.11.12	Added the print commands ⎙…, graphic commands g…, error probabilities, ½, IDIV, IΓ_q, MOD, XTAL?, y_{XY}, Γ_{XY}, ×MOD, ^MOD, four conversions, two messages, an optional back label, and some references to external documents; modified GCD and LCM, DATE, SETDAT, SETTIM, and TIME; expanded STOPW; renamed IBASE? to BASE? and IΓ to IΓ_p; purged <u>TEST</u> moving non-binary tests into P.FCN; abandoned the internal expert's catalog; updated and rearranged large parts of the introductory text and the appendices, also explaining the floating point formats, carry and overflow conditions in integer modes, the emulator, troubleshooting, corresponding operations of *HP-42S and HP-16C*, and some hardware modifications; moved most mathematical explanations into *Appendix I*; modified many internal page number references to ease working with a printed manual.
		The corresponding *pdf* manual is downloadable for free from the project website – as were the previous ones. Thus, there are copies in the web. It is even hosted by *HP* on its own Support Forum – see here: *http://h30434.www3.hp.com/psg/attachments/psg/Calulators-Handhelds/2636/3/Manual_wp_34s_3_1.pdf* . The *"Beginner's Guide"* mentioned above dates from the summer of 2012 and is based on v3.1 build 2932.
3.2	22.2.13	Changed output of complex results and the descriptions of complex calculations, COMB, DENMAX, PERM, RDP, and RSD; added ^{C}VIEW, some cases to the troubleshooting guide, imprint information, and some examples; moved the chapters to odd pages, inserted pictures where space arose, refined some keyboard pictures and cross references, added the information about previous software versions, an appendix about *RPN* pocket calculator history, and the quick reference sheet.

	Date	Release notes
		See the project website for a printed manual of this version.
3.3	22.6.14	Added YDOFF and YDON; extended stopwatch run time; renamed E3ON/OFF to TSON/OFF, Iβ to I_x, $I\Gamma_p$ to Γ_p , $I\Gamma_q$ to Γ_q, and renamed three power conversions; changed fraction entry display as well as the output of →REC and →POL (introduced for the *WP 31S*); corrected errors and updated many parts of the manual; reformatted the print edition (had to remove the history appendix in that course for page size reasons).
	29.9.14	Refined explanation of addressing special registers. Corrected the descriptions of BEG, RTN, RTN+1, an error in the start example, and a wrong display; added XEQ., a remark to ⊟DLAY, and one case to the *Troubleshooting Guide*; refined page formatting; made the hotkey descriptions equal and unambiguous; refined the beginning of *Section 3*; returned the history appendix by public demand – good eyesight required.
	10.2.15	Update following changed fraction input; updated LEAP? and prefix handling. Minor copyediting. Changed page size and released for individual print on demand.
	27.3.15	Corrected and expanded the description of αIP.
a	6.6.16 28.1.17, 5.6.17	Added the *Key Response Table, Loops and Counters,* and *Why Do the Stack and ENTER↑ Work the Way They Do,* the section about *Advanced Problem Solving,* and many examples. Switched the hardware tuning instructions in *App. H.* Rearranged & renamed some chapters. Refined & expanded descriptions of addressing, matrix handling, *error probability,* labels, direct keyboard access, AGM, DROP, f(x), f'(x), LINEQS, SAVE, SLV, ΔDAYS, Π, Σ, & ∫, the *I/O Overview,* the chapter about overlays, *Appendices A, B, D, F, G, H, I,* & *J,* and the *QRS.* Updated ^{C}X.FCN, and CONST following *CODATA 2014.* Documented changed displays following ◀ & ▶; corrected contents of P.FCN & X.FCN, the description of CASE, a mode error for FS? , and a naming error in χ^2. Some copyediting in addition. – Made CONV more precise.
b	8.12.17	Expanded App. G.
c	26.3.18	Added two hyperlinks about the random number generator, explanations for BATT and a new integration method.
d	15.10.18	Returned installation instructions for Harald's USB board.

← Some people did strange stuff with our software: This is an advertising picture found on *cncalc.org* for a port of *WP 34S* on a *Texas Instruments Inspire* graphic calculator – a device exceeding the size of your *WP 34S* by far.

ABOUT THE AUTHOR

Walter studied Physics at *Technische Universität Darmstadt* (*TUD*) in the Seventies – the era of the so-called 'calculator wars'. Educated on slide rules, he started electronic pocket computing using a *Texas Instruments TI SR-50* in 1975 (spent 615 DM for it), turned to a refurbished *HP-25C* in 1977 (for > 250 DM), and became an *RPN* aficionado from then on.

He advanced to a Ph.D. in Nuclear Physics at *TUD*, doing also a lot of programming for real time nuclear spectroscopy data acquisition and online analysis (on a 64$\underline{k}B$ *pdp11*). Computer work continued after moving in the weighing industry. Walter held R&D positions with increasing responsibilities there and at a large manufacturer of electrical household appliances. In the Nineties, he turned to quality management and became Head of Corporate QM of a company employing some 7 000 people worldwide – a textbook example of a German 'hidden champion' in its technical field. In 2013, he became responsible for quality of a 1.6 billion € accelerator project at a renowned Nuclear Physics research institute.

In all those years, Walter replaced his *HP-25C* by an *HP-11C*, then an *HP-32S*, and eventually an *HP-42S* supported by an *HP-21S*. In 2003, he started collecting *HP* calculators, discovered the forum at *http://hpmuseum.org* and soon became an active member. The 'forumers' know him for many colorful calculator design drafts, some of which eventually materialized in the designs of the *WP 34S* and *WP 31S*. Currently, he works for the *WP 43S* project in his spare time.

This is his second book – his first was about bicycle gearing, written in German and published in 1995. Walter is married with two adult children and seven small grandchildren who he and his wife enjoy spending time with.

TEMPORARY KEYBOARD OVERLAYS

You can use the pictures below for making a do-it-yourself keyboard overlay as described on pp. 293f. The upper picture is for v3.3, the lower for v2.2.

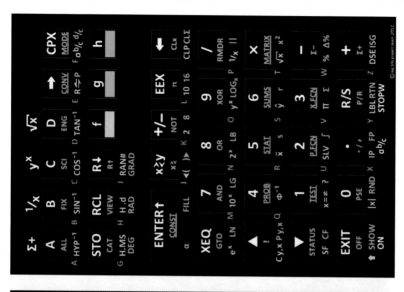

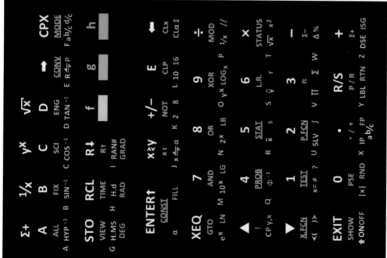

Note that SHOW in v2.2 works like in vintage *HP* calculators, i.e. it displays the full mantissa, while SHOW in v3.x works as explained on p. 251. See the *Release Notes* (on pp. 400ff) for more information about functional differences between different versions of the firmware. Turn to p. 372 to learn how to load an arbitrary firmware version into your calculator.

The following v3.3 keyboard overlay works even better than the one shown above in the large part of the world employing decimal commas instead of points. Note you get rid of the multiplication × in that course, too (and you learn why the English acronym PEMDAS is simply "Punkt vor Strich" in German):

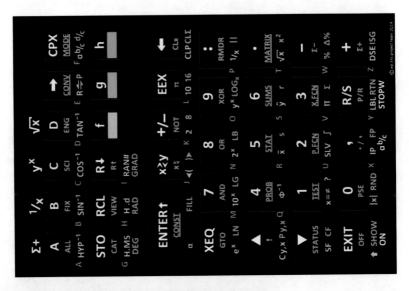

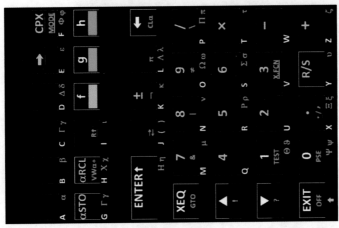

Cut out the picture at left representing the virtual alpha keyboard and attach it to the back of your calculator for learning the respective assignments valid therein (see p. 151 for further explanations).

QUICK REFERENCE SHEET

WP 34S generally works like an *HP-42S* <u>but</u>:

In general:
- `STATUS` is for checking memory available and viewing all flags. Memory segmentation is determined by you.
- Display mode switching keys are:

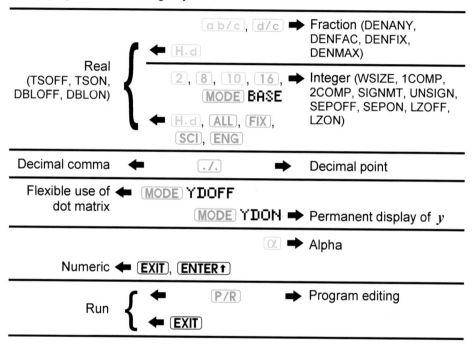

	`a b/c`, `d/c` ➡	Fraction (DENANY, DENFAC, DENFIX, DENMAX)
Real (TSOFF, TSON, DBLOFF, DBLON)	⬅ `H.d`	
	`2`, `8`, `10`, `16`, `MODE` BASE ➡	Integer (WSIZE, 1COMP, 2COMP, SIGNMT, UNSIGN, SEPOFF, SEPON, LZOFF, LZON)
	⬅ `H.d`, `ALL`, `FIX`, `SCI`, `ENG`	

Decimal comma ⬅	`./,`	➡ Decimal point

Flexible use of dot matrix ⬅	`MODE` YDOFF	
	`MODE` YDON ➡	Permanent display of *y*

	`α` ➡ Alpha
Numeric ⬅ `EXIT`, `ENTER↑`	

Run	⬅ `P/R`	➡ Program editing
	⬅ `EXIT`	

In numeric modes:
- Set *stack* size via SSIZE4 or SSIZE8. Levels are **X, Y, Z, T, A, B, C, D** maximum. `FILL` fills all *stack* levels with *x*.
- `RCL` `L` recalls LAST*x* .
- Up to 100 general purpose global numbered registers (00 … 99), no variables, no data types. *Stack* and further lettered registers start at register #100.
- Address indirectly via e.g. `STO` `➡` …

In numeric modes (continued):

- [◀] shows the full 16-digit mantissa and the exponent of x.
- [SHOW] is for viewing all register contents.
- [CONV] is for unit conversions.
- [PROB] is for probability distributions.
- [SUMS] is for accessing the summation registers.
- Matrices are arrays of registers on the *WP 34S*. Thus, matrix handling differs significantly from the *HP-42S*.
- [CPX] + [function] calls a complex function. Each complex number takes 2 registers.

In alpha mode:

- Alpha register features 30 bytes (*alpha*).
- Primary function of most keys is appending the corresponding grey Latin letter to *alpha*.
- [g] + [letter] appends a Greek letter, if applicable.
- Use [f] + [CPX] for more letters.
- Toggle upper and lower case using [↑].
- [f] + [digit] appends a digit to *alpha*, if applicable.

In programming mode:

- [CAT] : view all global labels in *RAM* and flash memory.
- Global labels may be 3 characters maximum.
- [STATUS] : view all global flags.
- There are no program specific step numbers.
- Up to 144 local registers and 16 local flags may be allocated for each routine via LOCR (depending on memory setup). Address local objects via e.g. [STO][.]...

In I/O:

- Use SAVE for battery-fail-safe backup. Recall using LOADP, LOADR, LOADSS, LOADΣ, or simply LOAD
- Send data from your *WP 34S* to the emulator on your computer using SEND...;
  get data from the emulator using RECV.
- Print commands are contained in [P.FCN].

Made in the USA
Las Vegas, NV
10 November 2024

11532149R00245